9th International Workshop on Tree Adjoining Grammars and Related Formalisms 2008 (TAG+9)

Tubingen, Germany
6 – 8 June 2008

ISBN: 978-1-5108-2680-9

TAG+9

the ninth international workshop
on tree adjoining grammars
and related formalisms

Tübingen, Germany
June 6–8, 2008

Proceedings

The Ninth International Workshop
on Tree Adjoining Grammars
and Related Formalisms

PROCEEDINGS

Program co-Chairs

Claire Gardent (CNRS/LORIA)
Anoop Sarkar (Simon Fraser University)

Local Organization

Laura Kallmeyer (University of Tübingen)
Timm Lichte (University of Tübingen)
Wolfgang Maier (University of Tübingen)

Tübingen, Germany

June 6-8, 2008

Preface

It is with great pleasure that we present the current volume of papers accepted for presentation at the Ninth International Workshop on Tree Adjoining Grammar and Related Formalisms (TAG+9). We would like to acknowledge the authors who submitted to TAG+9 and the members of the program commitee who reviewed the submissions; this meeting would not be possible without their hard work. We would like to thank our invited speakers, Uwe Mönnich and Stuart Shieber, for their participation and offering support to this meeting.

A valuable addition to the TAG+9 meeting is the tutorial program on various aspects of TAG, which was organized by Laura Kallmeyer. The tutorial features Eric de la Clergerie, Denys Duchier, Robert Frank and Maribel Romero. We would like to acknowledge their effort in fostering new interest in TAG and more generally in formal research into natural language.

Funding for TAG+9 was provided by the German Research Foundation (DFG). Laura Kallmeyer was not only responsible for securing this funding, but also was in charge of hosting TAG+9 at the University of Tübingen. Together with Timm Lichte and Wolfgang Maier, Laura Kallmeyer handled the local organisation of the meeting and the preparation of the proceedings. Their contributions to TAG+9 have been invaluable.

As at previous TAG+ workshops, the topics addressed by the presentations belong to diverse areas of research: mathematics of grammar formalisms and parsing, the syntax and semantics of natural languages, compact grammar representations and grammar engineering, and the relation between TAG and other grammar formalisms. By bringing together these different topics under the common theme of Tree Adjoining Grammars, the workshop promises to be a venue for interesting discussion of the latest research in this area.

TAG+9 received submissions from all over the world. We were able to accept 22 out of the 29 abstract submissions to the workshop. This volume contains the 22 research papers that will be presented at TAG+9. They are divided into two parts; the first part covering the 11 papers that are to be deliverd in oral presentations and the second part covering the 11 papers that are to be presented as posters.

Claire Gardent and Anoop Sarkar
Program co-Chairs for TAG+9

Program Committee

Claire Gardent, CNRS/LORIA Nancy, (France). Program Co-Chair.
Anoop Sarkar, Simon Fraser University, (Canada). Program Co-Chair.
Srinivas Bangalore, AT&T Research (USA)
Tilman Becker, DFKI Saarbruecken (Germany)
Pierre Boullier, INRIA Rocquencourt, Paris (France)
John Chen, Columbia University (USA)
Joan Chen-Main, University of Pennsylvania (USA)
David Chiang, USC Information Sciences Institute (USA)
Eric de la Clergerie, INRIA (France)
Robert Frank, Johns Hopkins University (USA)
Chung-hye Han, Simon Fraser University (Canada)
Karin Harbusch, University of Koblenz (Germany)
Julia Hockenmaier, University of Illinois at Urbana-Champaign (USA)
Aravind Joshi, University of Pennsylvania (USA)
Laura Kallmeyer, University of Tübingen (Germany)
Marco Kuhlmann, University of the Saarland (Germany)
Alessandro Mazzei, University of Torino (Italy)
David McDonald, BBN Technologies (USA)
Martha Palmer, University of Colorado (USA)
Owen Rambow, Columbia University (USA)
Frank Richter, University of Tübingen (Germany)
James Rogers, Earlham College (USA)
Maribel Romero, University of Konstanz (Germany)
Tatjana Scheffler, University of Pennsylvania (USA)
Sylvain Schmitz, INRIA Nancy Grand Est (France)
Vijay K. Shanker, University of Delaware (USA)
Mark Steedman, University of Edinburgh (UK)
Matthew Stone, Rutgers University (USA)
Bonnie Webber, University of Edinburgh (UK)
Naoki Yoshinaga, University of Tokyo (Japan)

Table of Contents

Binding Theory in LTAG

Lucas Champollion
Department of Linguistics
619 Williams Hall
University of Pennsylvania
Philadelphia, PA 19104-6305
champoll@ling.upenn.edu

Abstract

This paper provides a unification-based implementation of Binding Theory (BT) for the English language in the framework of feature-based lexicalized tree-adjoining grammar (LTAG). The grammar presented here does not actually coindex any noun phrases, it merely outputs a set of constraints on co- and contraindexation that may later be processed by a separate anaphora resolution module. It improves on previous work by implementing the full BT rather than just Condition A. The main technical innovation consists in allowing lists to appear as values of semantic features.

1 Introduction

BT (see Büring (2005) for a recent overview) accounts for the distribution of reflexives, pronouns, and full noun phrases.[1]

The focus of this paper is on implementing all binding conditions in the classical formulation by Chomsky (1981) in a toy LTAG grammar of English. At first sight, this poses a problem for LTAG since at least Condition C makes reference to potential antecedents that may lie outside LTAG's local domain (the verbal elementary tree, see Frank (2002)). Even in the case of Conditions A and B, the local domains of BT and of LTAG do not always correspond: a local domain for the purposes of BT may encompass more than just a verbal elementary tree, as shown by binding into adjuncts and binding of ECM subjects.

In all these cases, information on potential antecedents has to be transmitted across several elementary tree boundaries. This is analogous to the "missing link" problem well known in LTAG semantics. The analysis advocated here adopts the solution to the missing link problem introduced in Gardent and Kallmeyer (2003), in that information is transmitted across tree boundaries by repeated use of feature unification, as opposed to e.g. multicomponent sets.[2] Features also provide the expressive power required to encode cases in which the structural configuration does not correspond to classically defined c-command at the surface level (the only syntactic level available in LTAG), such as binding into PPs that adjoin at VP (*John saved Mary$_i$ from herself$_i$*) (Pesetsky, 1995) or topicalization (*Himself$_i$, he$_i$ likes.*).

2 Previous Work

There are two previous attempts at implementing BT in LTAG syntax: Ryant and Scheffler (2006) and Kallmeyer and Romero (2007). Both restrict themselves to Condition A.[3]

Ryant and Scheffler (2006) propose a multicomponent lexical entry for reflexives and reciprocals. One of the components is the reflexive and

---

[1] This paper uses the term *reflexive* to denote a word like *himself* subject to Condition A (excluding reciprocals, which are not treated in this paper). The term *pronoun* is used for words like *him* that are subject to Condition B.

[2] (Kallmeyer and Romero, 2004; Kallmeyer and Romero, 2008) analyze a wide variety of semantic phenomena in English, using a notational variant of Gardent and Kallmeyer (2003). Once list-valued features are adopted (see below), the present analysis is compatible with all incarnations of their framework.

[3] See also Steedman (2000) for an early account that mixes LTAG and CCG and introduces a level of logical form to handle both binding and semantics.

the other one is a degenerate NP tree which has no phonological content and which adjoins into its antecedent. Tree-local MCTAG (Weir, 1988) together with flexible composition (Joshi et al., 2007) and a number of specialized constraints concerning subject interveners and c-command ensure that the structural configuration in which the two components stand corresponds exactly to the local domain of standard BT.

Kallmeyer and Romero (2007) use almost the same approach but allow the degenerate tree to tree-locally adjoin directly into the *host tree* (i.e. the tree into which the reflexive and its antecedent substitute). This is achieved by changing the label of the degenerate tree from "NP" to "VP" and making sure that the host tree will always contain a VP node for each potential antecedent. Features on the relevant places of the host tree propagate the individual variable from the antecedent to the reflexive via the degenerate tree. This move is an attempt to avoid flexible composition and to show that "tree-local MCTAG display exactly the extended domain of locality needed to account for the locality of anaphora binding in a natural way" (Kallmeyer and Romero, 2007).

3 This Proposal

This analysis uses the standard framework of feature-based LTAG (Vijay-Shanker, 1987), that is: Each node n has (possibly empty) top and bottom feature structures. If n is a substitution slot, then its bottom feature structure must be empty. Substituting a tree with root r into n will trigger unification of the top feature structures on n and r. If n is an adjunction site, then adjoining a tree with root r and foot node f into n will unify the top features on n and r, and separately, the bottom features on n and f. Finally, for any node n on which neither substitution nor adjunction takes place throughout the derivation, the top and bottom feature structures on n are unified.

The only way in which this analysis extends the standard framework consists in using lists as values of features (as in HPSG, Pollard and Sag (1994)), as well as simple list operations such as creating a list from one ($\langle \cdot \rangle$) or two ($\langle \cdot , \cdot \rangle$) elements, adding elements (::), and appending a list to another one ($\cup$). All these operations can be given computationally tractable implementations. Allowing lists (or sets) as values of features may

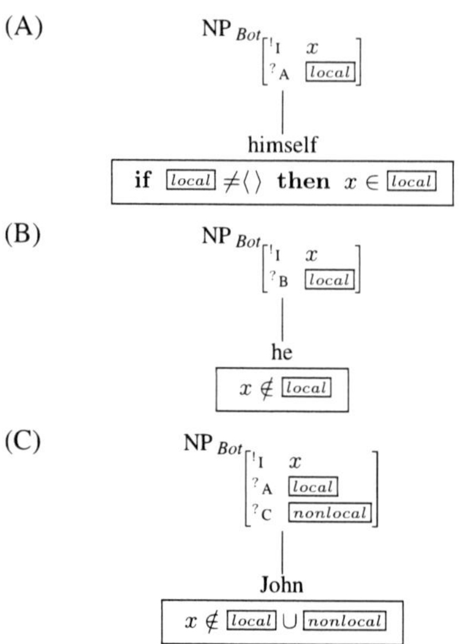

Figure 1: Noun phrases

perhaps look like a theoretically undesirable step. But this move seems unavoidable if potential antecedents of a noun phrase are to be encoded compactly in the output of the grammar. This in turn is necessary in order to avoid a combinatorial explosion of indexations (see Section 7).

Through the features on its root node, every noun phrase receives several items from the tree it attaches to (Branco, 2002): a list A of potential local antecedents for the purpose of condition A, a list B of potential local antecedents for the purpose of condition B, and a list C of potential nonlocal antecedents. (Keeping two separate lists A and B is necessary since there exist environments in which reflexives and pronouns are not in complementary distribution, as will be discussed later.)[4]

As is independently needed for semantic purposes (Gardent and Kallmeyer, 2003; Kallmeyer and Romero, 2008), every noun phrase provides a different I(NDIVIDUAL VARIABLE) to its envi-

---

[4]A fourth BT constraint, Condition Z, has been proposed for long-distance reflexives (LDRs): "a LDR must be (locally or nonlocally) bound" (Xue et al., 1994). A reviewer remarks that unlike condition C items, LDRs may sometimes accept only subject antecedents, or only within the domain of subjunctive tense. To the extent that such restrictions cannot be locally checked on the antecedent, a fourth list may need to be introduced. See Section 6.

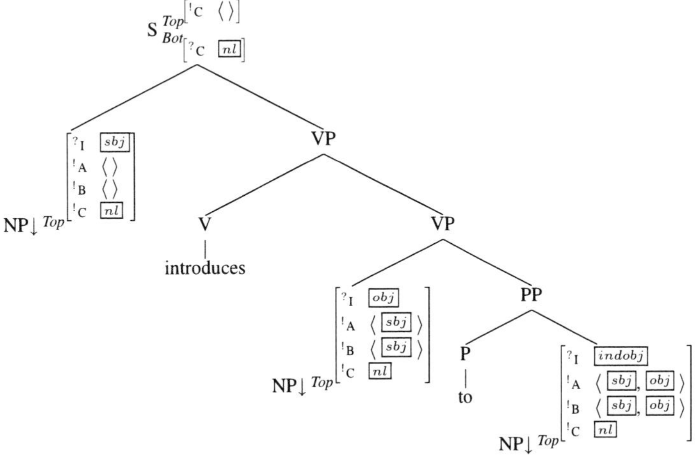

Figure 2: Finite ditransitive verb

ronment. Note that these variables do not correspond to BT indices, as each of them is assumed to be unique to its noun phrase even if another noun phrase ends up having the same referent. (This can be achieved by renaming before parsing starts.) They are thus more comparable to the reference markers of DRT (Kamp and Reyle, 1993). Finally, every noun phrase is associated with pseudocode that states the applicable BT condition (Fig. 1).[5] It is assumed that a separate resolution module will interpret this pseudocode in the obvious way. Take for example the statement for reflexives:

$$\textbf{if } \boxed{\textit{local}} \neq \langle\rangle \textbf{ then } x \in \boxed{\textit{local}} \qquad (1)$$

This statement constrains the resolution module to equate the variable x with one of the members of the value of $\boxed{\textit{local}}$, provided that that value is not the empty list.[6] (This analysis does not use the order of the lists, but the grammar could be set up

to use it to rank potential antecedents according to recency or grammatical prominence for the benefit of the resolution module.)

The rest of the grammar is responsible for providing the correct A, B and C lists to the noun phrase substitution slots. The next two sections describe how this is done in the verbal and nominal domains, respectively.

4   The Verbal Domain

In the standard case, the verb tree will collect the variables from its substitution slots and include them into A and B lists at these same substitution slots as appropriate (Fig. 2).

C lists are transmitted across clauses via their root nodes. If a verbal tree is a subordinate clause, then its C list is supplied by the matrix verb via the bottom feature on its S node. If it is a matrix clause, then the top and bottom features on its S node will unify and cause its C list to be empty. If

---

[5]Metavariables in the feature structures have been given names like *sbj*, rather than just numbers as usual. Also, the direction of information flow has been indicated by annotating features that *receive* information from another tree with ? and features that *send* information to another tree with !. These annotations are only there for clarity of exposition and have no formal significance.

[6]This formulation implements the idea of exemption (Pollard and Sag, 1992; Pollard and Sag, 1994): A reflexive has to be bound locally only if its local domain is not empty. Reflexives whose domain is empty are argued there to fall outside of the scope of syntactic BT. Examples are reflexives within picture NPs in subject position. The following example is from Pollard and Sag (1992):

(2)   a. John$_i$ was going to get even with Mary. That picture of himself$_i$ in the paper would really annoy her, as would the other stunts he had planned.
b. Mary was quite taken aback by the publicity John$_i$ was receiving. *That picture of himself$_i$ in the paper had really annoyed her, and there was not much she could do about it.

Besides illustrating that BT-exempt *himself* may find its antecedent across sentences, this example also shows that the licensing conditions on BT-exempt *himself* are subject to nonsyntactic restrictions. For this reason, they have been set aside in this paper.

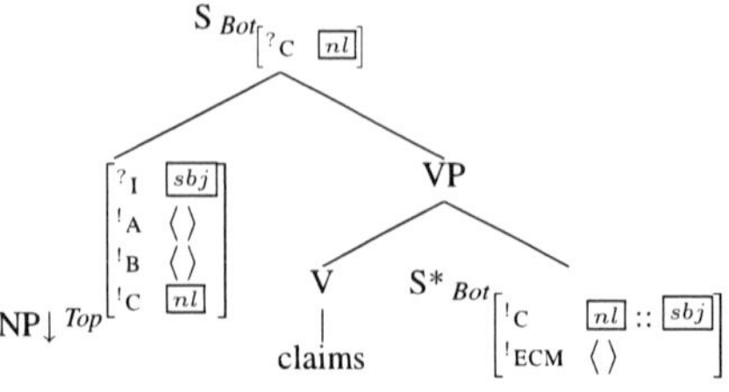

Figure 3: Sentential complement verb

a verbal tree subcategorizes for a sentential complement, then it appends its own argument(s) to its C list and makes the result available to the sentential complement (Fig. 3).

A special case are ECM verbs. The subject of an ECM verb is in the local domain of the subject of the verb's complement clause (*John$_i$ believes himself$_i$ to be the best candidate*). However, due to the LTAG version of the theta criterion (Frank and Kroch, 1995), the subject of the complement clause belongs to the LTAG local domain of the lower clause. ECM verbs therefore make their subject available via a special ECM feature (Fig. 4). In non-ECM verbs, the value of the ECM feature is the empty list (Fig. 3).

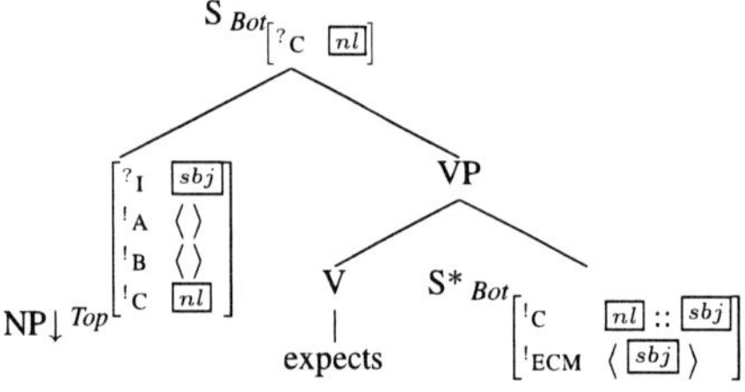

Figure 4: ECM verb

Nonfinite verbs (Fig. 5) function like finite verbs except for their subject position: If the matrix clause is headed by an ECM verb, its subject will be added to their A and B lists via the ECM feature. This gets the desired effect in *John$_i$ expects himself$_i$/*him$_i$ to win the game*.

LTAG's local domain only encompasses the arguments of a verb, not its adjuncts nor any raising verbs, because all recursion is factored away into separate elementary trees (Frank, 2002; Joshi,

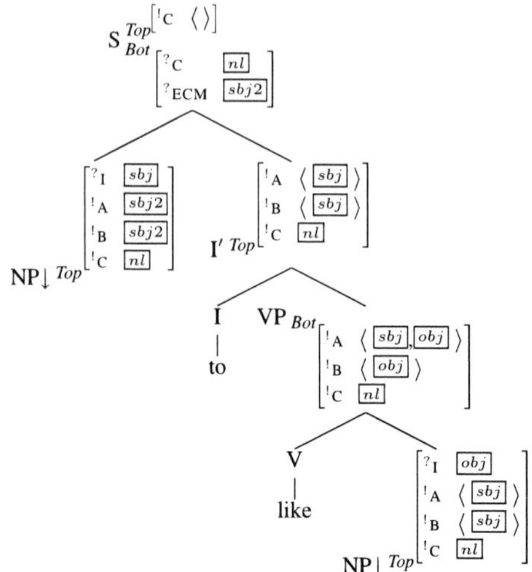

Figure 5: Nonfinite transitive verb

2004). Verbs therefore have to extend their local binding domain by propagating their A, B and C values to trees that adjoin on the VP spine,[7]. This includes raising verbs with PP complements (Fig. 6) in order to derive *John$_i$ seems to himself$_i$/*him$_i$ to be a decent guy*[8], and PP adjuncts (Fig. 7), in order to derive *John$_i$ saved Bill$_j$ from himself$_{i/j}$*.

For those prepositions that take both reflexives and pronouns as locally-referring complements (*John$_i$ wrapped a blanket around himself$_i$/him$_i$*), differing A and B lists are made available. In these PP trees, the value of the B feature on the NP node (the asterisk in Fig. 7) will be $\boxed{b}$, while in those PP trees that do not allow pronouns in this position (*John$_i$ speaks with himself$_i$/*him$_i$*), the value of that feature will be $\boxed{a}$.[9] Finally, the PP adjunct tree carries an additional set of features on its root node that enables local binding from one adjunct to another, as in *Mary spoke to Bill$_i$ about himself$_i$*.

---

[7]For clarity of exposition, the feature structures on the VP spine have been omitted in the figures other than Fig. 5.

[8]See also Storoshenko (2006) for the syntax of this construction in LTAG.

[9]The generalization (Marantz, 1984; Reinhart and Reuland, 1993) is that a locally referring PP complement may be a pronoun only if the PP as a whole, rather than just the complement, is assigned a thematic role. How to implement this syntax-semantics interaction is left for future work.

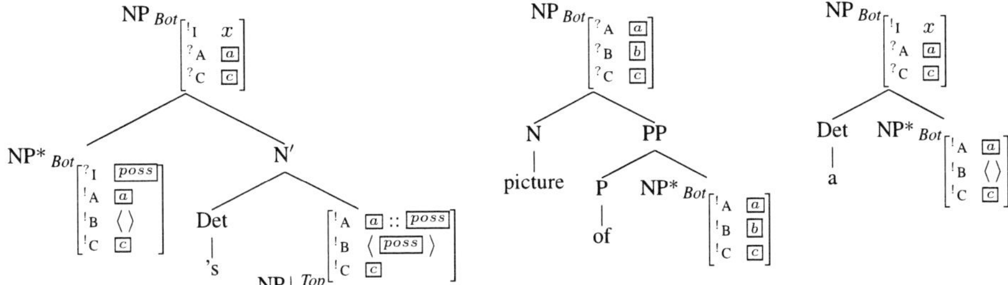

Figure 8: Picture NP components

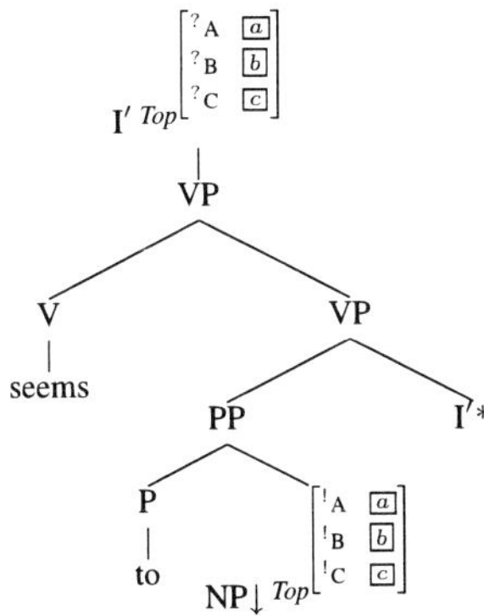

Figure 6: Raising verb with PP complement

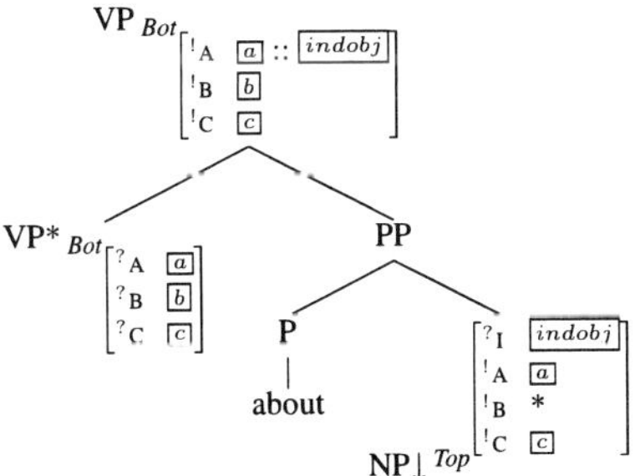

Figure 7: PP adjunct. See text for an explanation of the asterisk.

5 The Nominal Domain and Picture NPs

Complex NPs (Fig. 8) allow possessors (*"John's friend"*). Following the syntactic analysis of (Kallmeyer and Scheffler, 2004; Kallmeyer and Romero, 2007), the "possessed" argument substi-

tutes into a tree anchored in *'s*, which in turn adjoins into the possessor. The possessed argument may, for example, be a simple noun[10], or a constituent that contains an NP complement, such as "picture of X", where X can be any NP. Following the same authors, this constituent is analyzed as an NP tree whose yield is X, and into whose root a *"picture of"* tree is adjoined.

Both possessors and picture NP complements behave nonuniformly with respect to the different binding conditions.[11] Possessors count as locally bound within their clause only for the purpose of condition A, but not B (Huang, 1983):

(3)   a. They$_i$ saw each other$_i$'s friends.
      b. John$_i$ saw his$_i$ friend.

As for picture NP complements, for the purpose of condition A, their local domain includes the c-commanding arguments of the verb (here: the subject) and the possessor:[12]

(4)   a. John$_i$ finally saw Mary's picture of himself$_i$.
      b. Mary finally saw John$_i$'s picture of himself$_i$.

For the purpose of condition B, however, the local domain of a picture NP complement only includes the possessor:

[10]Because the label of the argument slot is NP and not N, this possibility is actually wrongly ruled out. This defect is a part of the syntactic analysis imported here from the literature.

[11]So-called exempt reflexives like *John$_i$ thinks that the pictures of himself$_i$ are horrid* are discussed in fn. 6.

[12]The example sentences in the rest of this section are taken from a series of experiments (Keller and Asudeh, 2001; Runner et al., 2002; Runner, 2003), as discussed in Jaeger (2004). Note that local binding across possessors as in (4a) is incorrectly reported (and predicted) to be ungrammatical in many treatments of BT, including Kallmeyer and Romero (2007).

(5)   a. John$_i$ finally saw Mary's picture of him$_i$.
      b. *Mary finally saw John$_i$'s picture of him$_i$.

These facts are straightforwardly represented by the values of the A and B features on the NP complement node of the "'s" tree.

Of course, picture NPs can also occur without a possessor. Again, the local domain of the picture NP complement includes the c-commanding arguments of the verb for the purpose of condition A, but not condition B.

(6)   John$_i$ found a picture of him$_i$/himself$_i$.

In other words, whether or not a possessor is present, both pronouns and reflexives may be the complement of a picture NP and be bound by the subject.[13] This is modeled by letting the determiner trees pass on only the A but not the B list.

6   Other Constraints on Anaphora

Apart from the Chomskyan binding conditions, there are other syntactic constraints on anaphoric relations, including agreement (7) and accessibility relations when the antecedent is a quantifier (8).

(7)   *John$_i$ likes myself$_i$/themselves$_i$/herself$_i$.

(8)   Every man loves [a woman]$_i$. Her$_i$ name is
     Mary.   ($\exists > \forall$, *$\forall > \exists$)

The implementation of these constraints is outside of the scope of BT and is therefore not treated in this paper. Note, though, that the existence of these constraints does not mean that the number of lists passed around needs to be multiplied, as long as the constraints apply in addition to the binding conditions and can be locally computed and passed on to the anaphora resolution module.[14] For example, it is not necessary to keep separate lists of potential first, second, and third person antecedents since it is possible to check locally on the antecedent whether it has a given person feature. As for accessibility constraints of quantifiers,

these constraints interact with scope, and can be integrated with scope resolution by using underspecified dynamic semantics in the style of Koller and Niehren (2000).

7   Improvements on Previous Work

The present account improves on previous BT implementations in LTAG (Ryant and Scheffler, 2006; Kallmeyer and Romero, 2007) in a number of ways:

1) All conditions are implemented. The previous approaches only implemented Condition A and do not generalize well to the other conditions. For example, consider Condition B: The degenerate tree that picks out the antecedent of a pronoun would have to adjoin nonlocally and be barred from adjoining locally.

2) It is well known (Fong, 1990) that a sentence with n (independent) noun phrases corresponds to an exponential number of referentially distinct indexations. Therefore, it becomes crucial to avoid producing a separate parse tree for every possible indexation. Unlike the previous approaches, a parser that uses the present grammar on unindexed input will return a compact set of constraints on co- and contraindexation, rather than an exhaustive forest of indexed trees. This constraint set can then be sent to an anaphora resolution module. Thus, the present approach integrates well with computational approaches to coreference resolution. This insight has been taken from Branco (2002), who provides an HPSG implementation similar to the present one.

3) Mismatches between BT's and LTAG's local domains are encoded using the feature mechanism. There is no need to resort to nonstandard extensions of the framework such as flexible composition or subject intervention constraints, as Ryant and Scheffler (2006) do. Two examples of such mismatches are ECM verbs and binding into adjuncts. The latter poses a problem for Kallmeyer and Romero (2007), who would have to introduce flexible composition to handle it – the very same operation that their analysis was designed to avoid.

4) Binding from possessors into picture NPs (*John$_i$'s picture of himself$_i$*) is problematic for the analysis in Kallmeyer and Romero (2007), as the host tree for the possessor (in this case, the tree anchored in 's) would have to contain a VP (or S) node so that the antecedent tree for *himself* can

---

[13]It is possible to make the pronoun less acceptable in this position by changing the sentence so that the subject is more likely interpreted as a creator of the picture NP, for example by using a verb of creation: *John$_i$ painted a picture of himself$_i$/#him$_i$*. As (Jaeger, 2004) shows by experiment, this effect also occurs if a possessor is present, and it can even be triggered by merely changing the subject to a salient creator. Thus, it is not (or at least not primarily) syntactic in nature.

[14]Thanks to an anonymous reviewer for raising this point.

adjoin into it. But apart from stipulation, no such node is present in the *'s* tree. For the present analysis, this case raises no particular problem.

5) Each noun phrase introduces only one tree. Previous approaches stipulated that every reflexive introduces a set of two trees, one of which is degenerate and lacks independent syntactic motivation. Cf. an analogous move in the analysis of quantifiers (Gardent and Kallmeyer, 2003).

6) Finally, there is no need to stipulate any lexical ambiguity. Previous approaches required two separate lexical entries for each reflexive in order to handle special cases of ECM (Kallmeyer and Romero, 2007) or extraction (Ryant and Scheffler, 2006). ECM has been discussed above. As for extraction, (*Himself$_i$, he$_i$ likes.*), due to the inverted c-command relation, it could previously (Ryant and Scheffler, 2006) only be handled by an *ad hoc* lexical entry for the reflexive. In contrast, in the present analysis, object slots can simply be made to carry identical features in base (e.g. Fig. 5) and extraposed (Fig. 9) position. More generally, the notion of c-command plays no role in the present implementation. This is actually an advantage, given that c-command as classically defined is not empirically adequate for BT purposes (Pollard and Sag, 1992; Pollard and Sag, 1994), even less so in a system like LTAG which does not make D-Structure or LF available as additional levels on which c-command relationships could be checked.

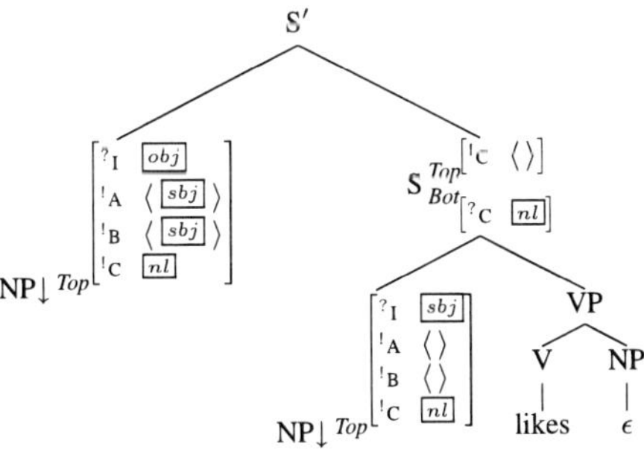

Figure 9: Transitive verb with extraposed object

8 Conclusion

The analysis presented in this paper implements binding conditions A, B, and C in LTAG. The non-local behavior of Condition C, as well as mis-

matches between the LTAG and BT local domains, do not align well with LTAG's notion of locality. The solution adopted here addresses this problem by using feature unification to pass information across boundaries of elementary trees. Following Branco (2002), specification of binding constraints has been kept apart from anaphora resolution.

This solution achieves descriptive adequacy at the cost of stipulating a great number of features. Admittedly, this method does not restrict the range of crosslinguistic options very much. For example, it would be easy to write a nonsensical grammar in which reflexives must c-command (!) their antecedents. Future work might look for concise statements of the possible positions and values of the features used here. The feature lists might also provide the right kind of structure to define a notion analogous to HPSG's o-command (Pollard and Sag, 1994). It appears promising to formulate such statements within a metagrammar framework (Kinyon et al., 2006).

Acknowledgements

I am grateful to the members of the XTAG group at Penn for helpful comments and discussion, and in particular to Josh Tauberer for proofreading. I also thank the anonymous TAG+9 reviewers for extensive feedback.

References

Branco, António. 2002. Binding machines. *Computational Linguistics*, 28:1–18.

Büring, Daniel. 2005. *Binding theory*. Cambridge University Press, Cambridge, UK.

Chomsky, Noam. 1981. *Lectures on Government and Binding*. Dordrecht: Foris.

Fong, Sandiway. 1990. Free indexation: Combinatorial analysis and a compositional algorithm. In *Proceedings of the 28th annual meeting of the Association for Computational Linguistics (ACL'90)*, pages 105–110.

Frank, Robert and Anthony Kroch. 1995. Generalized transformations and the theory of grammar. *Studia linguistica*, 49:103–151.

Frank, Robert. 2002. *Phrase structure composition and syntactic dependencies*. MIT Press, Cambridge, MA.

Gardent, Claire and Laura Kallmeyer. 2003. Semantic construction in feature-based TAG. In *Proceedings of the Tenth conference of the European Chapter of the Association for Computational Linguistics (EACL03)*, pages 123–130, Budapest.

Huang, C.-T. James. 1983. A note on the binding theory. *Linguistic Inquiry*, 14:554–561.

Jaeger, T. Florian. 2004. Binding in picture NPs revisited: Evidence for a semantic principle of extended argument-hood. In Butt, Miriam and Tracy Holloway King, editors, *Proceedings of the Ninth International Conference on Lexical Functional Grammar (LFG04), Christchurch, New Zealand*, pages 268–288, Stanford, CA. CSLI Publications.

Joshi, Aravind K., Laura Kallmeyer, and Maribel Romero. 2007. Flexible composition in LTAG: Quantifier scope and inverse linking. In Bunt, Harry, editor, *Computing Meaning*, volume 3, pages 233–256. Springer.

Joshi, Aravind K. 2004. Starting with complex primitives pays off: Complicate locally, simplify globally. *Cognitive Science*, 28:637–668.

Kallmeyer, Laura and Maribel Romero. 2004. LTAG semantics with semantic unification. In *Proceedings of the Seventh International Workshop on Tree Adjoining Grammar and related formalisms (TAG+7)*, volume 155-162, Vancouver, BC.

Kallmeyer, Laura and Maribel Romero. 2007. Reflexives and reciprocals in LTAG. In Geertzen, Jeroen, Elias Thijsse, Harry Bunt, and Amanda Schiffrin, editors, *Proceedings of the Seventh International Workshop on Computational Semantics (IWCS-7)*, pages 271–282, Tilburg.

Kallmeyer, Laura and Maribel Romero. 2008. Scope and situation binding in LTAG using semantic unification. *Reseach on Language and Computation*, 6(1):3–52.

Kallmeyer, Laura and Tatjana Scheffler. 2004. LTAG analysis for pied-piping and stranding of wh-phrases. In *Proceedings of the Seventh International Workshop on Tree Adjoining Grammar and related formalisms (TAG+7)*, pages 32–39, Vancouver, BC.

Kamp, Hans and Uwe Reyle. 1993. *From discourse to logic*. Kluwer, Dordrecht.

Keller, Frank and Ash Asudeh. 2001. Constraints on linguistic coreference: structural vs. pragmatic factors. In Erlbaum, Lawrence, editor, *Proceedings of the 23rd annual conference of the Cognitive Science Society*, Mahawa.

Kinyon, Alexandra, Owen Rambow, Tatjana Scheffler, Sinwon Yoon, and Aravind K. Joshi. 2006. The metagrammar goes multilingual: A crosslinguistic look at the V2-phenomenon. In *Proceedings of the Eighth International Workshop on Tree Adjoining Grammar and related formalisms (TAG+8)*, Sydney.

Koller, Alexander and Joachim Niehren. 2000. On underspecified processing of dynamic semantics. In *Proceedings of the the 18th International Conference on Computational Linguistics (COLING-2000)*, Saarbrücken.

Marantz, Alec. 1984. *On the nature of grammatical relations*. MIT Press, Cambridge, MA.

Pesetsky, David. 1995. *Zero syntax: Experiencers and cascades*. MIT Press, Cambridge, MA.

Pollard, Carl and Ivan A. Sag. 1992. Anaphors in English and the scope of binding theory. *Linguistic Inquiry*, 23:261–303.

Pollard, Carl and Ivan A. Sag. 1994. *Head-driven Phrase Structure Grammar*. University of Chicago Press.

Reinhart, Tanya and Eric Reuland. 1993. Reflexivity. *Linguistic Inquiry*, 24(4):657–720.

Runner, Jeffrey T., Rachel S. Sussmann, and Michael K.Tanenhaus. 2002. Logophors in possessed picture noun phrases. In *Proceedings of the 21st West Coast Conference on Formal Linguistics (WCCFL 21)*, pages 401–414.

Runner, Jeffrey T. 2003. Insights into binding and ellipsis from head-mounted eye-tracking experiments. In *Proceedings of the Chicago Linguistic Society 39*, Chicago, IL. Chicago Linguistic Society.

Ryant, Neville and Tatjana Scheffler. 2006. Binding of anaphora in LTAG. In *Proceedings of the Eighth International Workshop on Tree Adjoining Grammar and related formalisms (TAG+8)*, Sydney.

Steedman, Mark. 2000. Implications of binding for lexicalized grammars. In Abeillé, Anne and Owen Rambow, editors, *Tree adjoining grammars*. CSLI Publications, Stanford.

Storoshenko, Dennis Ryan. 2006. Reconsidering raising and experiencers in English. In *Proceedings of the Eighth International Workshop on Tree Adjoining Grammar and related formalisms (TAG+8)*, pages 159–164, Sydney. Association for Computational Linguistics.

Vijay-Shanker, K. 1987. *A study of Tree Adjoining Grammars*. Ph.D. thesis, University of Pennsylvania.

Weir, David Jeremy. 1988. *Characterizing mildly context-sensitive grammar formalisms*. Ph.D. thesis, University of Pennsylvania.

Xue, Ping, Carl Pollard, and Ivan A. Sag. 1994. A new perspective on Chinese *ziji*. In *Proceedings of WCCFL '94*, Stanford, CA. CSLI Publications.

Flexible Composition, Multiple Adjoining and Word Order Variation

Joan Chen-Main* and Aravind K. Joshi*[+]
*Institute for Research in Cognitive Science, and
[+]Dept of Computer and Information Science
University of Pennsylvania
Philadelphia, PA 19104-6228
{chenmain,joshi}@seas.upenn.edu

Abstract

Tree-Local Multi-Component TAGs (called hereafter just MC-TAG for short) are known to be weakly equivalent to standard TAGs, however, they can describe structures not derivable in the standard TAG. There are other variants of MC-TAG, such as MC-TAG with (a) flexible composition and (b) multiple adjoining of modifier (non-predicative) auxiliary trees that are also weakly equivalent to TAGs, but can describe structures not derivable with MC-TAG. Our main goal in this paper is to determine the word order patterns that can be generated in these MC-TAG variants while respecting semantic dependencies in the grammar and derivation. We use some word order phenomena such as scrambling and clitic climbing to illustrate our approach. This is not a study of scrambling or clitic climbing per se. We do not claim that the patterns of dependencies that are derivable are all equally acceptable. Other considerations such as processing will also come into play. However, patterns that are not derivable are predicted to be clearly unacceptable.

1 Introduction

This paper examines the different word orders that can be generated while maintaining the same word to word dependencies using several extensions of tree-local Multi-Component TAG (MC-TAG). We find that when the system is enriched to allow *flexible composition*, not all patterns can be derived beyond two levels of embedding. Flexible composition is the mirror operation to adjoining; if tree α adjoins into tree β, the combination can be alternatively viewed as tree β "flexibly" composing with tree α (Joshi et al. 2003, Kallmeyer and Joshi 2003). By enriching MC-TAG with this perspective of adjoining, some derivational steps which appear to permit components from the same MC-set to combine into different trees can be recast as abiding by tree-locality. Tree-local MC-TAGs with flexible composition have been investigated from the point of view of understanding the range of structures they can generate. Some of the phenomena where flexible composition has been useful include scope ambiguity and available readings in nested quantifications (Joshi et al. 2003, Kallmeyer and Joshi 2003), complex noun phrases in pied-piping and stranding of wh-phrases (Kallmeyer and Scheffler 2004), and binding (Ryant and Scheffler 2006). The full range of flexibility that can be allowed without going outside the weak generative capacity of standard LTAG is not known yet. In this paper, the flexible composition we explore is limited to reverse adjoining at the root.

Our investigation also includes a look at the effects of enforcing binary branching. The TAG composition operations, substitution and adjoining are binary, in the sense that each operation involves composing two trees into one, two structures into one. However, there is another dimension for this issue of binarization in TAG which does not arise in other systems, such as CFGs or Categorial Grammars, for example, as these are essentially string rewriting systems. In the case of TAG, we have a choice at the level of the elementary trees. We can require all elemen-

Proceedings of The Ninth International Workshop on Tree Adjoining Grammars and Related Formalisms
Tübingen, Germany. June 6-8, 2008.

tary trees to be binary or we can allow some elementary trees to be non-binary. We find that binarizing the elementary trees results in additional nodes (in comparison to its non-binarized counterpart), allowing additional patterns to be derived in MC-TAG with flexible composition.[1]

Most of this paper is devoted to illustrating our approach using scrambling in German. We assume a single set of linguistic dependencies, and we consider the possible word orders when the dependencies are respected throughout the derivation. Lastly, we take a preliminary look at clitic climbing under the same approach.

2   German Scrambling

In subordinate clauses in Standard German, the canonical order of verbs and their subject arguments is a nested dependency order. However, other orderings are also possible. For example, in the case of a clause-final cluster of three verbs, the canonical order is as given in (1), $NP_1NP_2NP_3V_3V_2V_1$, but all other permutations of the NP arguments are also possible orderings.[2]

(1) NP_1 NP_2 NP_3 V_3 V_2 V_1
        . . . Hans Peter Marie schwimmen lassen sah.
        . . . Hans Peter Marie swim   make saw
      " . . . Hans saw Peter make Marie swim."

However, with an additional level of embedding, i.e. four NPs and four verbs, the situation is less clear both linguistically and formally. Some orderings, such as (2), are consistently taken to be (more) acceptable, while others, such as (3) are consistently dispreferred.

(2) NP_4 NP_1 NP_2 NP_3 V_4 V_3 V_2 V_1

(3) NP_3 NP_1 NP_4 NP_2 V_4 V_3 V_2 V_1

Interestingly, just as natural language appears not to permit all permutations of nouns at this deeper level of embedding, so too does tree-local MC-LTAG allow only certain permutations. (Becker

et al.,1991, Rambow 1994, Joshi et al., 2000). Here, we closely examine the situation involving three levels of embedding. Twenty four orderings result from permuting the four nouns while keeping the verb order fixed.[3] Our focus is on making the formal predictions of a system that allows flexible composition precise. The linguistic dependencies we assume here are (a) that between a verb and its NP argument and (b) that between a verb and its VP argument. The former is respected by the standard TAG approach to verbs and their arguments: the set anchored by V_i includes a substitution node for NP_i. The latter is respected both by having a VP_{i+1} node in the set anchored by V_i as well as requiring the VP argument of V_i to be V_{i+1} throughout the derivation.[4] For example, tree sets for V_1 and V_3 can only combine with one another if one of them has combined with V_2 first. The task at hand is to see which variants of MC-LTAG derive which permutations, setting the stage to compare whether the sequences that require more powerful extensions align with dispreferred sequences.

3   Tree-Local MC-TAG Extensions

We take tree-local MC-LTAG as our starting point: all components belonging to the same MC-set must combine into a single elementary tree. In the linguistic context, there is always a constraint between the two components of an elementary tree set of an MC-TAG. Usually, there is an implied "top" and "bottom" tree, and we require the foot node of the top tree to dominate (but not immediately) the root node of the bottom tree. Using Grammar 1 in Figure 1 as an example, this means that the Ni component must be above the Vi predicative component in the derived phrase structure. The constraint can also be a c-command relation. In any case, the constraint does not permit the immediate domination of the root node of the bottom tree by the foot node of the top tree. There would be no point of having a two component tree if this were to be the case.

An outcome of prohibiting immediate domination between the two components is that each

---

[1] Conversely, when binarization eliminates nodes, e.g. binarizing a grammar that allowed nodes with a single non-terminal daughter, binarization is expected to decrease the possible derivations.

[2] Some permutations sound better with full NPs instead of proper names. Examples can be found in (Rambow 1994). Our purpose here is just to illustrate possible patterns.

[3] There are other patterns of scrambling, for example, $N_1 N_2 N_3 V_1 V_3 V_2$, involving permutations of V's. We do consider these here for now.

[4] I.e. We adopt the strong co-occurrence constraint of Joshi et al (2000).

component must target two distinct nodes for the composition to be valid. If both components were to target the same node, the non-immediate domination constraint would violated. This kind of composition is ill-defined for MC-TAG.

3.1 Permitting Flexible-composition

We first investigate the effect of allowing flexible composition, but only when adjoining would have taken place at a root. We do not consider reverse adjoining at internal nodes. Thus, if tree A flexibly composes into tree B, then it is the reverse of B adjoining into A's root.

Under this extension, we also do not allow flexible-composition at a node that also serves as a target for adjoining. For example, this prohibits the derivational steps in Figure 1: A and B are auxiliary trees with the same root and foot node labels. B adjoins into the root of C, and C flexibly composes at its root with A. If we take the notion of flexible-composition as "reverse adjoining" seriously, then allowing flexible-composition and adjoining at the same node would be multiple adjoining in disguise. In our example, the derivation shown is the same as adjoining both A and B into the root node of C. Some cases of flexible-composition and adjoining at the same node will be permitted under the multiple adjoining extension described below.

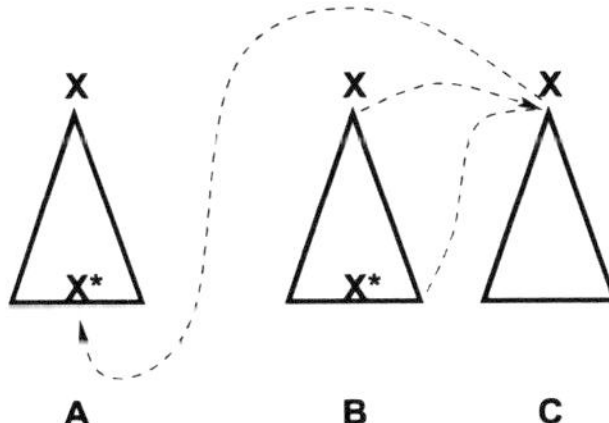

Figure 1: Flexible composition and adjoining at the same node. This is prohibited in TAG extensions without multiple adjoining.

3.2 Permitting Multiple-adjoining

What we mean by *multiple adjoining* is the Schabes and Shieber (1994) style multiple adjoining extended to apply to MC-sets: more than one component tree may adjoin into a host node so long as at most one of those trees is a predicative tree.[5] We follow Schabes and Shieber (1994)

in assuming that although either one of the multiply-adjoined structures may be on top (i.e. one derivation tree may correspond to more than one phrase structure), the order of the elementary trees in the final derived tree is determined by the order of adjoining: if tree A adjoins into a node X before tree B adjoins into the same node X, then tree A will be below tree B in the derived tree.[6] Additionally, we require that trees that target the same node belong to different MC-sets.

4 Non-binarized Phrase Structure

The grammar we first explore is shown in Figure 2. These tree sets are based on the tree-sets for a verb with two arguments given in Becker et al, (1991) which have been assumed for subsequent TAG approaches to German scrambling. A point of departure, however, is that these trees have more than one VP node. While we assume that the VP nodes belonging to the noun components do not carry the indexing information for the verb it is associated with, we do assume that both the root VP node and internal VP nodes, if any, of a predicative elementary tree carry the indexing information associated with the verb. This means that there is an additional potential "host" node for adjoining, and hence, each scrambled sequence may have more than one structural description. For example, consider the singleton sets in Grammar 1 for V_1 and V_2. The V_1 tree may adjoin into either the root node or the internal VP node of the V_2 tree and maintain semantic coherence. In contrast, we also assume that the noun components in Grammar 1 do not have host nodes for predicates. This has the effect of banning adjoining into the noun components in general: an NP_i component cannot combine into an NP_j component without leaving the predicate V_i

---

tiple noun components, or b) any number of noun components and one verb component. Since we have a different notion of modifier and predicate, we diverge from Schabes and Shieber (1994) by assuming predicative trees appear below modifier trees.

[6] Multiple-adjoining is related to tree-local MCTAG with shared nodes (SN-MCTAG) (Kallmeyer, 2005) in that a node which hosts adjoining is not seen as having disappeared in the tree-rewriting process. Rather, the host node and the root node of the tree being adjoined are identified, and the node is considered to belong to both trees. Thus, the targeted node is still available as a host for additional adjoining. SN-MCTAG also considers the foot node to have identified with the host node and to be available as a host for additional adjoining, unlike Schabes and Shieber (1994).

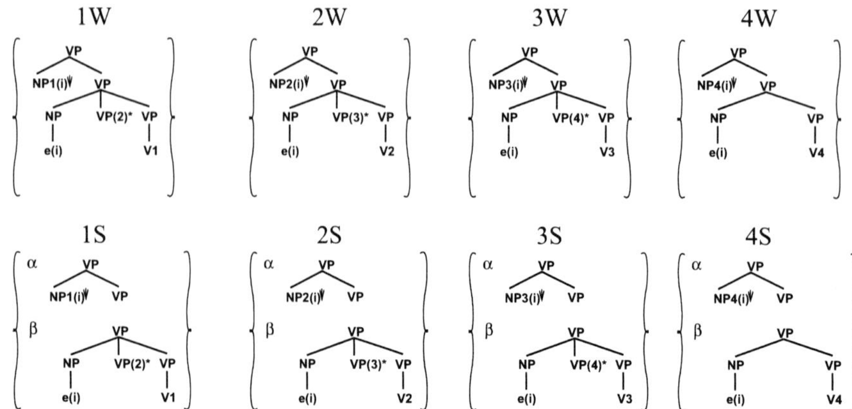

Figure 2: Scrambling Grammar 1. Each verb anchors a singleton set and a set with a two components

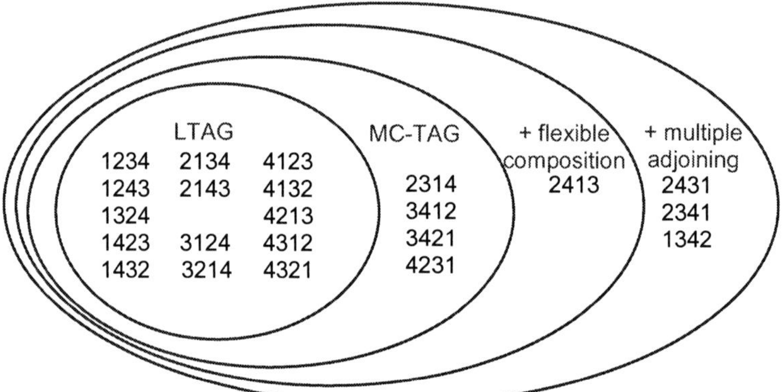

Figure 3: Derivable sequences given Grammar 1. MC-TAG with flexible composition derives structures for 15 permutations. Allowing multiple adjoining as well derives 22 permutations. The remaining 2 permutations require composition that is essentially ternary.

component without a host to combine into. Figure 3 shows which sequences are derivable under which TAG extensions.[7] Since we hold the sequence of verbs fixed, we use a number sequence to refer to the order of the NPs. E.g. We use 1234 as shorthand for $NP_1 NP_2 NP_3 NP_4 V_4 V_3 V_2 V_1$.

Given Grammar 1, fourteen sequences are derivable with LTAG (i.e. using only the singleton sets in Grammar 1), and four additional sequences are derivable with MC-LTAG. Since deriving one of the noun sequences in the case of three noun-verb pairs, 231, already requires MC-TAG, this is no surprise.

For this particular grammar, only one additional sequence is derivable as the result of extending MC-LTAG to include flexible composition. Since each tree has at most three host VPs, there is no tree in Grammar 1 into which two MC-sets can combine. Since a tree from Grammar 1 only hosts at most one MC-set, many derivations involving flexible composition can be recast using classic adjoining. Additionally, because the singleton sets' trees include more than one host VP for a higher verb, more than one semantically coherent derivation are actually available for some sequences, even in LTAG.

When the system allows multiple-adjoining, three more sequences become derivable. Consider the derivation for 2341 in Figure 4. Flexible composition allows the singleton set anchored by

---

[7] Note that not all of the subset relationships in Figure 3 and Figure 6 are obligatory. E.g. It is possible to allow multiple adjoining without allowing multi-component sets.

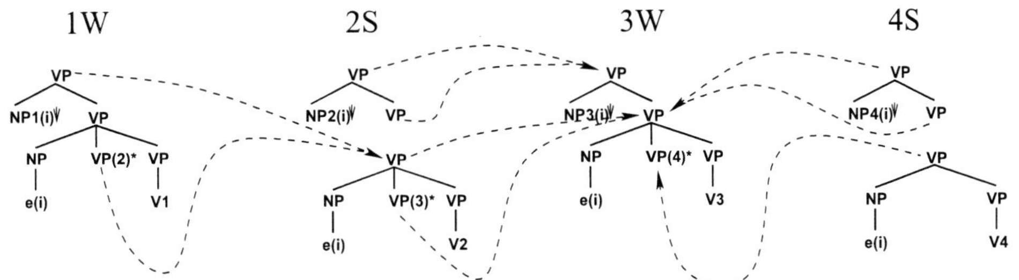

Figure 4: Derivation for 2341. Multiple-adjoining allows the upper components from 4S to target the internal VP node of 3W after 2S has already adjoined into the same node. Flexible composition allows the predicate component of 4S to combine into the foot node of 3W.

V_3 to be the root-tree of the derivation (i.e. the root in the derivation structure) even though it is an auxiliary tree. The MC-set anchored by V_4 and that anchored by V_2 both combine into V_3. One component from each set targets the internal VP node in V_3's tree.

Two sequences remain underivable: 3142 and 3241. We also explore what kind of modification is needed to derive these sequences. We find that a type of adjoining that appears effectively to be a ternary operation is capable of doing so, and we conjecture that deriving these sequences require some sort of ternary composition. We refer to this "ternary" operation as *same-set multiple adjoining*: components belonging to the same MC-set are permitted to adjoin into the same host node. The difference between adjoining a "whole tree" into a single node and adjoining two components of the same set into a single node is that a non-predicative component from a different set is permitted to also adjoin into the same node. E.g. Given Grammar 1, an NP component associated with V_2 can separate the top and bottom components of the set anchored by V_3 when all three components adjoin into the same node. Note, however, that if we abide by the Schabes and Shieber (1994) convention that order of adjoining determines the order of the trees that adjoin into the same node, then the ordering $NP_3NP_2V_3$ requires that the predicate component of the V_3 set adjoin first, the NP_2 component of the V_2 set to adjoin next, and the NP_3 component of the V_3 set to adjoin in last. This application of same-set multiple adjoining needs access to three MC-sets: the host tree, the V_3 set, and the V_2 set.

Note that the need for same-set multiple adjoining to derive structures for these sequences is an observation about a formal system, not an argument that this system is needed to adequately model natural language. It is not clear that these scrambling sequences are actually accepted by German speakers. Thus, unlike flexible composition and the Schabes and Shieber (1994) style multiple adjoining, same-set multiple adjoining has not been linguistically motivated.

5 Binarized Phrase-structure

Though Grammar 1 is empirically motivated, the tree structures lack a characteristic that has been assumed of phrase structures since the mid-eighties: these trees are not binary branching. Binary branching has been assumed for reasons such as linearizability (as in Kayne 1994) and as the result of the generative machinery. In many formalisms (e.g. combinatory categorical grammar (Steedman 1996), minimalist grammar (Stabler 1997), binary composition and binary branching are collapsed. In the TAG formalism, however, binary composition and binary branching can be separated. That is, the derivation is distinct from the derived phrase structure. Though the TAG operations are binary, the trees that they combine are not necessarily binary branching. Note, though, that enforcing binary branching phrase structure can easily be stated in TAG by requiring the kernel trees to be binary branching. Because TAG allows us to separate binary branching from binary composition, we can more clearly see the contribution of each by examining possible derivations in the case where binary branching is enforced vs. the case where binary branching is not enforced. The second grammar we consider is the binarized counterpart to the first grammar. This is shown in Figure 5.

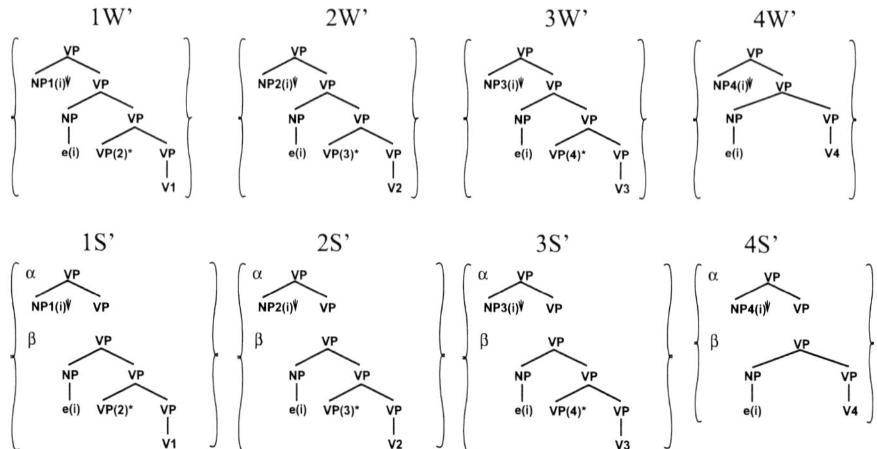

Figure 5: Scrambling Grammar 2. The binarized counterpart to Grammar 1

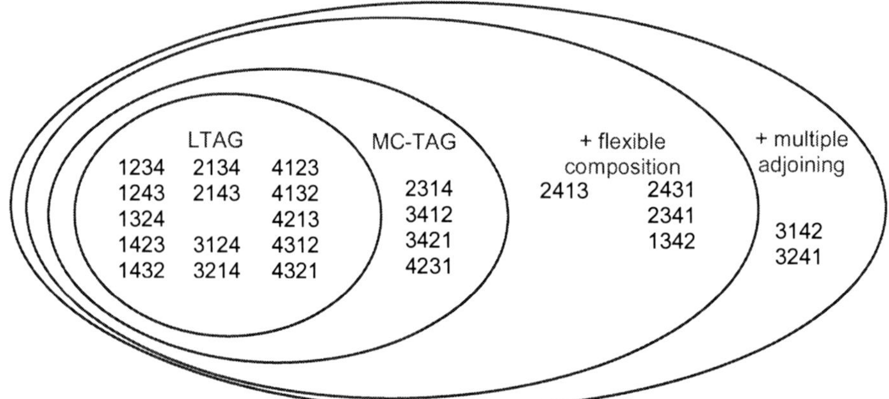

Figure 6: Derivable sequences given Grammar 2. Sequences which required multiple adjoining under Grammar 1 can be derived with MC-TAG with flexible composition. The two sequences requiring ternary composition under Grammar 1 can be derived when multiple adjoining is permitted.

Figure 6 shows which sequences require which TAG extensions given Grammar 2. The same sequences are derivable with LTAG and MC-TAG. However, allowing flexible composition now allows additional sequences to be derived. Because recasting ternary branching structure as binary branching increases the nodes available to adjoin into, adjoining components into the same node is no longer needed in some cases. The three sequences that required multiple adjoining in Figure 3 now only require flexible composition. Similarly, the two sequences that required same-set multiple adjoining under Grammar 1 can now be derived with the Schabes and Shieber (1994) style multiple adjoining.

6   Clitic Climbing and MC-TAG

In Romance languages, pronominal clitics can optionally appear post-verbally, as in (4), or higher in the clause, preceding the tensed verb, as in (5).

(4) V_0 V_1 NP_1 V_2NP_2
     Quiere permitir-**te**   ver-**lo**
     wants to.permit-you to.see-it
     'S/he wants to permit you to see it.'

(5) NP_1 NP_2 V_0 V_1 V_2
     Te **lo**   quiere permitir ver

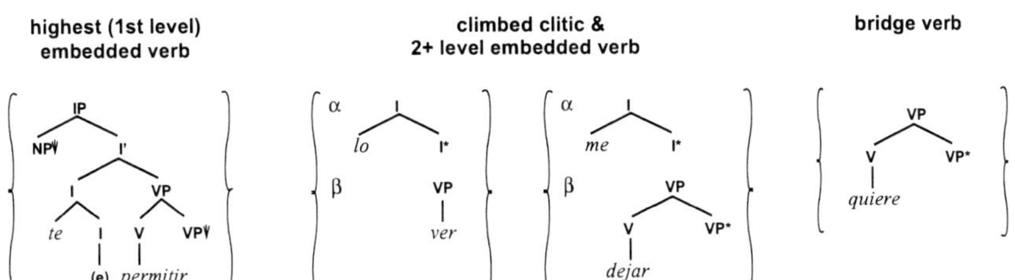

Figure 7: Grammar fragment for clitic climbing patterns. The highest embedded verb anchors a singleton set in which the clitic is climbed. Deeper embedded verbs and their climbed clitics are modeled with an MC-set. Bridge verbs are modeled with an auxiliary tree

As with scrambling, we approach (4) and (5) as different word orders, $V_0V_1NP_1V_2NP_2$ and $NP_1NP_2V_0V_1V_2$, that correspond to the same linguistic dependencies, (a) that between a verb and its clitic argument and (b) that between a verb and its VP argument. Given the grammar fragment in Figure 7, one can see how MC-TAG (without flexible composition or multiple-adjoining) allows the derivation of clitic climbing patterns shown here. Note that the tree for *quiere* in Figure 7 can host additional verbs, allowing clitic climbing across an unbounded number of triggering verbs.

These examples are taken from Bleam (2000), who argues that although sentences involving two climbed clitics and two verbs, such as (6), can be generated with a tree-local MC-TAG, the additional level of embedding in (5), requires the power of set-local MC-TAG.

(6) **Te　lo** permito ver
　　　you it I.permit to.see
　　　'I permit you to see it.'

Interestingly, while (5) and (6) show us that a cluster of two climbed clitics is permissible, our native speaker informants do not accept sentence (7) which involves three levels of embedding and includes a cluster of three climbed clitics, each of which is associated with a different verb. It is not clear whether the absence of clusters of three climbed clitics results from a restriction on clitic climbing per se or whether it is due to other restrictions (e.g. on the clitic cluster template) (Bleam, p.c.) If, however, we assume that this unacceptability is strictly the result of the grammar rather than some other constraints on the output of the grammar, then the need for set-local MC-TAG dissolves.

(7) *Mari **me te　lo** quiere permitir　dejar ver.
　　　Mari me you it　wants to.permit to.let to.see
　　　'Mari wants you to permit me to see it.'

Further, given the MC-TAG discussed above, $V_0V_1NP_1V_2NP_2$ and $NP_1NP_2V_0V_1V_2$ are derivable, but $NP_1NP_2NP_3V_0V_1V_2V_3$ is not. Above, we noted that assuming a grammar comprised of MC-sets of the type in Figure 7 predicts clitics can climb across an unbounded number of trigger verbs. However, this grammar cannot generate an unbounded number of climbed clitics. The tree for *permitir* does not have enough nodes to host a third clitic-verb MC-set. Thus, the unacceptability of (7) is expected.[8]

7　Conclusion

This paper shows that even when we enrich tree-local MC-TAG by allowing flexible composition, not all word order permutations are derivable. Our claim is not that all derivable patters are equally acceptable, but that we expect underivable patterns to be clearly unacceptable.

We note two main observations from our study of scrambling. First, even MC-LTAG with flexible composition cannot derive all twenty four permutations of the NPs at three levels of embedding. Specifically, the extensions required to derive more difficult cases involve allowing different degrees of multiple adjoining. The two most difficult cases require a type of composition that is otherwise unmotivated. This is a desirable outcome, as it makes MC-LTAG with flexible composition a candidate for aligning with the linguistic judgments for scrambling. Second, for

---

[8] Even when MC-TAG in enriched with a flexible composition perspective, Bleam's (2000) set-local MC-TAG analysis cannot be recast as a tree-local account, leading us to posit that (7) will remain underivable.

MC-LTAG with flexible composition, converting a grammar with non-binary branching elementary trees to a grammar in which binary branching is enforced allows additional scrambling patterns to be derived. Enforcing binary branching requires fewer modifications to MC-LTAG to derive all twenty four permutations. The additional derivations are possible because of the increase in the nodes available nodes to adjoin into. In fact, given enough nodes, the need for multiple-adjoining can be completely eliminated. In our case study, we consider the minimal additional branching required to enforce binary branching. This sets a bound on the additional nodes that can be added. We conjecture that with an additional level of embedding (i.e. 5 NPs), binary branching will no longer provide enough nodes for generating all scrambling patterns using tree-local MC-TAG with flexible composition and multiple adjoining.

Our first observation from our preliminary look at clitic climbing is that the patterns at up to two levels of embedding diverge from the patterns at deeper levels of embedding. Tree-local MC-TAG is sufficient for accounting for the patterns up to two levels of embedding, and also makes at least some correct predictions regarding possible patterns at three levels of embedding. This is similar to the scrambling case in that a tree-local MC-TAG generates all patterns for two levels of embedding, but not for three. This is relevant to a study on recursion being carried out by Joshi (2008, in prep).

Acknowledgements

We thank the XTAG group, in particular Lucas Champollion, Tatjana Scheffler, and Joshua Tauberer, for helpful discussion and Tonia Bleam, Laia Mayol, and Irving Rodriguez-Gonzalez for Spanish data.

References

Becker, Tilman, Aravind K. Joshi and Owen Rambow. (1991). Long-distance scrambling and tree adjoining grammars. In: Fifth Conference of the European Chapter of the Association for Computational Linguistics, Berlin, pp. 21-26.

Bleam, Tonia. (2000). Clitic climbing and the power of Tree Adjoining Grammar. In Anne Abeillé and Owen Rambow, eds., Tree Adjoining Grammars: formalisms, linguistic analysis, and processing. CSLI Publications, Stanford, CA, pp. 193-220.

Joshi, Aravind K.. (2008, in preparation) Does recursion in language behave the same way as in formal systems? (preliminary version presented at *Recursion in Human Language*, University of Illinois, April, 2007).

Joshi, Aravind K., Tilman Becker and Owen Rambow. (2000). Complexity of scrambling: a new twist to the competence-performance distinction. In: Anne Abeillé and Owen Rambow (eds.). 2000. *Tree Adjoining Grammars. Formalisms, Linguistic Analysis and Processing.* CSLI Publications, Stanford, CA, pp. 167-181.

Joshi, Aravind K., Laura Kallmeyer and Maribel Romero. (2003). Flexible composition in LTAG: quantifier scope and inverse linking. In H. Bunt and R. Muskens, eds., *Computing Meaning 3.* Kluwer, Dordrecht.

Kallmeyer, Laura. 2005. Tree-local multicomponent tree adjoining grammars with shared nodes. *Computational Linguistics*, 31(2):187–225.

Kallmeyer, Laura and Aravind K. Joshi. (2003). Factoring predicate argument and scope semantics: underspecified semantics with LTAG. *Research on Language and Computation*, 1(1-2):3–58.

Kallmeyer, Laura and Tatjana Scheffler. (2004). LTAG Analysis for Pied-Piping and Stranding of wh-Phrases. *Proceedings of the Seventh International Workshop on Tree Adjoining Grammar and Related Formalisms (TAG+7)* Vancouver, Canada, 32-39.

Kayne, Richard. (1994). The anti-symmetry of syntax. The MIT-Press, Cambridge, MA.

Rambow, Owen. (1994). Formal and Computational Aspects of Natural Language Syntax. PhD thesis, University of Pennsylvania.

Ryant, Neville and Tatjana Scheffler. 2006. Binding of anaphors in LTAG. *Proceedings of the Eighth International Workshop on Tree Adjoining Grammar and Related Formalisms (TAG+8)*, Sydney, Australia, 65-72

Schabes, Yves and Stuart M. Shieber. An alternative conception of tree-adjoining derivation. *Computational Linguistics*, 20(1):91-124, 1994

Stabler, Edward. 1997. Derivational Minimalism. In Retoré (ed.), *Logical Aspects of Computational Linguistics.* Springer. 68-95.

Steedman, Mark. 1996. *Surface Structure and Interpretation.* MIT Press, Cambridge, MA.

Weir, David J. (1988). Characterizing mildly context-sensitive grammar formalisms. PhD thesis, University of Pennsylvania.

Flexible Composition and Delayed Tree-Locality

David Chiang
USC Information Sciences Institute
4676 Admiralty Way, Suite 1001
Marina del Rey, CA 90292 USA
chiang@isi.edu

Tatjana Scheffler
Department of Linguistics
619 Williams Hall
University of Pennsylvania
Philadelphia, PA 19104-6305 USA
tatjana@ling.upenn.edu

Abstract

Flexible composition is an extension of TAG that has been used in a variety of TAG-analyses. In this paper, we present a dedicated study of the formal and linguistic properties of TAGs with flexible composition (TAG-FC). We start by presenting a survey of existing applications of flexible composition. In the main part of the paper, we discuss a formal definition of TAG-FCs and give a proof of equivalence of TAG-FC to tree-local MCTAG, via a formalism called delayed tree-local MCTAG. We then proceed to argue that delayed tree-locality is more intuitive for the analysis of many cases where flexible composition has been employed.

1 Introduction

Flexible composition (FC) is a way of viewing TAG derivations so that the operation of adjoining of a tree β into a tree γ can be alternatively viewed as attachment of γ to β. That is, γ splits at the adjunction site and wraps around β (see Figure 1b). This "flexible" view of the attachment operation does not have much effect on standard TAG, but has been used in multicomponent TAG (MCTAG) analyses of various linguistic phenomena in order to preserve tree-locality of an otherwise non-local derivation.

First, it has been employed in (Joshi et al., 2003) to derive quantifier-scope restrictions in nested quantifications such as:

(1) Two politicians spy on someone from every city. (Joshi et al., 2003, ex. (6))

Other applications of flexible composition include the modelling of complex noun phrases in pied-piping and stranding of wh-phrases (Kallmeyer and Scheffler, 2004), an analysis of anaphor binding (Ryant and Scheffler, 2006), discourse semantics (Forbes-Riley et al., 2006), and scrambling patterns (Chen-Main and Joshi, 2007).

With the proposal of unification-based semantics for TAG, noun phrase quantifiers have been analysed as multi-component sets, where one component is the lexical quantifier and the other is just an S-node carrying the scopal information for the quantifier. But this kind of analysis can be problematic for tree-local MCTAG, since the two components will in general attach to different elementary trees. For example, see Figure 2a for the sentence

(2) Whom does John like a picture of? (Kallmeyer and Scheffler, 2004, ex. (2a))

Flexible composition has been used to avoid this problem (Joshi et al., 2003; Kallmeyer and Scheffler, 2004), as shown in Figure 2b. In this derivation, the edge label "rev" (to be defined more precisely in the following section) indicates that the adjunction of $\beta_{\text{a-2}}$ into β_{picture} is reversed. This turns the nonlocal derivation in Figure 2a into a tree-local derivation..

All the other proposals mentioned share this property as well: in each case, flexible composition is used in order to make a potentially nonlocal MCTAG derivation be possible in a tree-local MCTAG. Here, we present a new variant of TAG, called *delayed tree-local* multicomponent TAG, that relaxes the tree-local constraint. We define both formalisms and show that both are weakly equivalent to standard TAG. We then illustrate how

Proceedings of The Ninth International Workshop on Tree Adjoining Grammars and Related Formalisms
Tübingen, Germany. June 6-8, 2008.

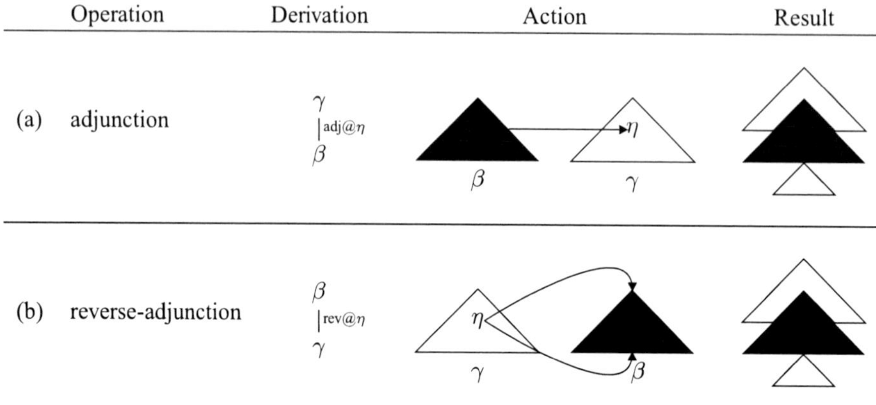

Figure 1: TAG-FC composition operations. (a) Adjunction. (b) Reverse-adjunction.

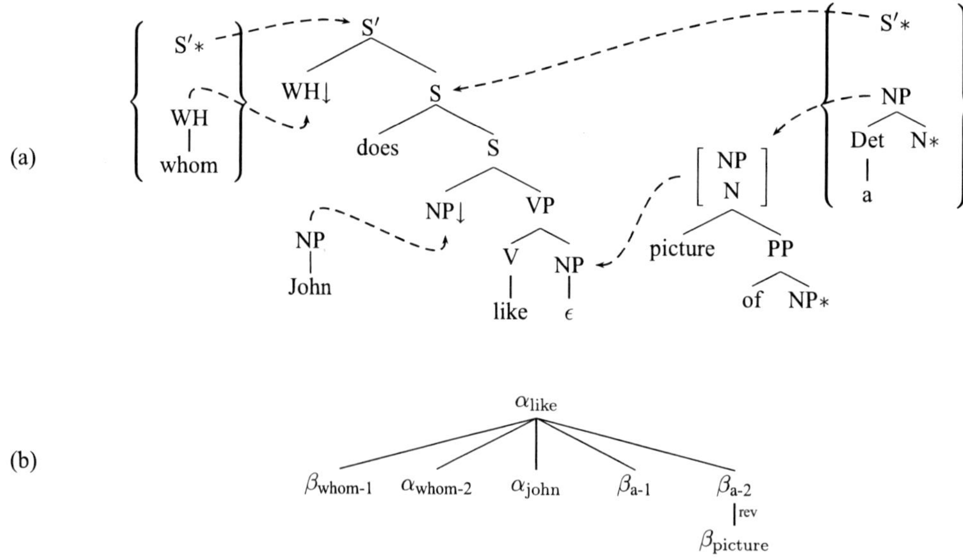

Figure 2: Derivation of "Whom does John like a picture of?" using flexible composition. (a) Syntactic analysis given in (Kallmeyer and Scheffler, 2004, Fig. 4). (b) Derivation tree, according to the notation used in this paper. The derivation is tree-local with flexible composition: The tree for "picture of" β_{picture} wraps around (reverse-adjoins into) the tree for "a" β_{a-2}, which then adjoins into the complement NP node of α_{like}.

linguistic analyses using flexible composition can be instantiated in our new formalism and argue that in many cases this new formulation is better.

2 Flexible composition

We present here a formal definition of TAG-FC, to our knowledge the first such definition.

Definition 1. A *TAG with flexible composition (TAG-FC)* is a TAG with two composition operations: adjunction and reverse-adjunction. A derivation of a TAG-FC is represented by a tree with labeled edges: each edge is labeled with an operation (adj for adjunction or rev for reverse-adjunction) and an adjunction site η. An edge labeled adj@η with γ above and β below, where η is a node of γ (see Figure 1a), represents adjunction at η. An edge labeled rev@η with β above and γ below, where η is again a node of γ (see Figure 1b), represents reverse-adjunction at η, in which γ is split at η and wraps around β.

Ambiguity arises in TAG-FC derivations whenever two elementary trees reverse-adjoin around the same elementary tree, or when an elementary tree both adjoins and is reverse-adjoined around (see Figure 3). In these cases a different derived tree will result depending on the order of operations. Thus, we simply rule out the former case,[1] and in the latter case, we stipulate that the reverse-adjunction occurs first.

Flexible composition generalizes to tree-local multicomponent TAG (Weir, 1988) in the obvious way. Note that there are two ways of defining tree-local MCTAG derivation trees: one in which the derivation nodes are elementary *tree sets* (as in Weir's definition), and the other in which the derivation nodes are elementary *trees*. We use the latter notion.

Definition 2. A *multicomponent TAG (with flexible composition)* is a TAG (with flexible composition) whose elementary trees are partitioned into *elementary tree sets*. In a derivation of a multicomponent TAG, the nodes of the derivation are also partitioned into sets such that each partition is an instance of a complete elementary tree set.

Definition 3. A *tree-local multicomponent TAG (with flexible composition)* is a multicomponent

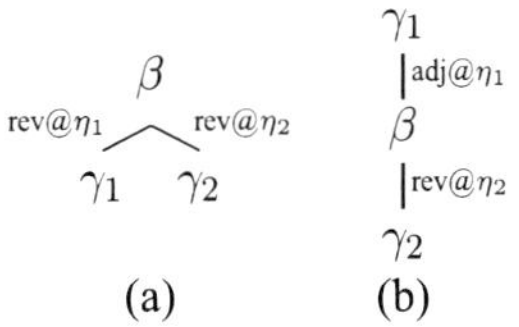

(a)   (b)

Figure 3: Ambiguity in TAG-FC derivations. (a) Multiple reverse-adjunction is disallowed. (b) The reverse-adjunction of γ_2 takes place before the adjunction of β.

TAG (with flexible composition) whose derivations have the following property: for each elementary tree set instance, all the member derivation nodes are sisters.

In other words, all the members of an elementary tree set must adjoin at the same time, and must adjoin into the same elementary tree.

3 Delayed tree-locality

Next, we present another variant of MCTAG that relaxes the tree-locality constraint without losing weak equivalence with standard TAG, but uses only standard adjunction, not reverse adjunction.

Definition 4. A *k-delayed tree-local multicomponent TAG* is a multicomponent TAG whose derivations have the following property. Let the *destination* of an elementary tree set instance S be the lowest derivation node that dominates all the members of S. Let the *delay* of S be the union of the paths from the destination down to each member of S, minus the destination itself. Then no derivation node can be a member of more than k delays.

See Figure 4. Intuitively, this means that the members of an elementary tree set can adjoin into different trees, arriving at the same elementary tree (the destination) after some delay; and there can be at most k delays at any point in the derivation. (Note that this definition also allows one member of an elementary tree set to adjoin into another.) For a more practical example, observe that the derivation in Figure 2a is a 1-delayed tree-local MCTAG derivation.

---

[1] We are not aware of any examples of this case in the literature. If this case should prove to be useful, the definitions and results in this paper would need to be modified. We leave this possibility for future work.

	Action		Derivation

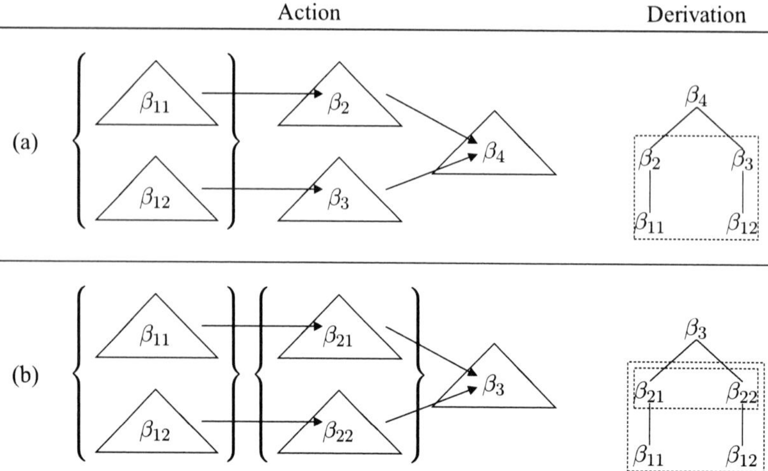

Figure 4: Delayed tree-locality. Nonlocal adjunction of an elementary tree set is allowed as long as the members eventually compose into the same elementary tree. The dashed boxes mark the delays. (a) One simultaneous delay. (b) Two simultaneous delays are allowed in 2-delayed tree-local MCTAG but not 1-delayed tree-local MCTAG.

4   Formal results

In this section, we show the equivalence of both tree-local MCTAG-FC and delayed tree-local MCTAG to standard TAG.

Proposition 1. *Any tree-local MCTAG with flexible composition G can be converted into a 2-delayed tree-local MCTAG G' that is weakly equivalent to G and has exactly the same elementary structures as G.*

The fact that G' has the same elementary structures as G means that if we convert an analysis from tree-local MCTAG-FC to delayed tree-local MCTAG, its domains of locality will be preserved. However, the dependencies between them will in general be different.

Proof. The conversion is trivial: G' has exactly the same elementary structures as G. In order to demonstrate weak equivalence, we show how to convert any TL-MCTAG-FC derivation into a nonlocal MCTAG derivation, and then show that this derivation is a 2-delayed TL-MCTAG derivation.

Given a TL-MCTAG-FC derivation, consider the subgraph formed by erasing all adjunction edges and keeping only the reverse-adjunction edges. Call the components of this subgraph the *reverse chains* (see Figure 5a).

It is easy to see from the definition of TAG-FC that reverse chains are all subpaths; thus, to convert the derivation to a nonlocal MCTAG derivation, we simply invert all the reverse chains. We continue to refer to the inverted reverse chains in the new derivation as reverse chains, even though they are only definable with reference to the original derivation (see Figure 5b).

Now we must show that this derivation is a 2-delayed TL-MCTAG derivation. Actually, we prove a stronger claim, by induction on the height of the derivation tree: (i) no node belongs to more than two delays, and moreover (ii) the nodes in the root's reverse chain belong to no more than one delay. (See Figure 5c for an example.)

Let R be the root's reverse chain, and let C be those nodes which are children of nodes in R but are not themselves in R. Apply the transformation to the subderivations rooted by nodes in C. By the induction hypothesis, the transformation creates (i) no more than two delays for the nodes in those subderivations, and (ii) no more than one delay for the reverse chains of the nodes in C.

Next, reverse R itself. For a node η in R that belongs to an elementary tree set, a new delay is created that comprises η and the reverse chains of all the other members of the elementary tree set.

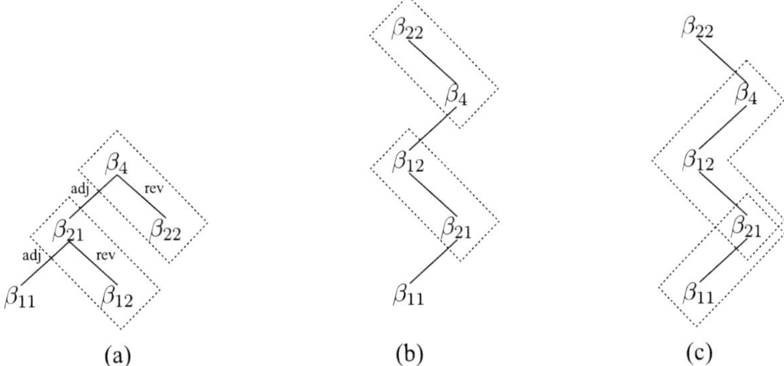

Figure 5: (a) Example tree-local MCTAG-FC derivation tree with reverse chains marked. (b) Result of conversion to delayed tree-local MCTAG derivation tree, again with reverse chains marked. (c) Same derivation tree but with delays marked.

But by (ii), the nodes in those reverse chains belonged to no more than one delay already, so even after creating this new delay, they still belong to no more than two delays.

Thus, (i) holds for all nodes in the derivation. The nodes in R that belong to an elementary tree set belong to only one delay, satisfying (ii), and the other nodes in R do not belong to any delays, also satisfying (ii). □

Next we show that k-delayed tree-local MCTAG is, in turn, weakly equivalent to standard TAG.

Proposition 2. *Any k-delayed tree-local MCTAG can be converted into a weakly equivalent TAG.*

Proof. The construction is a generalization of the conversion of tree-local MCTAG to TAG. We consider 1-delayed tree-local MCTAG first. First, we normalize the grammar so that all adjunction is obligatory and no adjunction is allowed at root/foot nodes, following Lang (1994): for each auxiliary tree, create new null-adjunction root and foot nodes; and for each nonterminal X, create a trivial auxiliary tree with a single null-adjunction X that is both root and foot. Next, create a new feature *tree* whose values are of the form $S^\bullet$ or $S_\bullet$, where S is a multiset of elementary trees. We replace each elementary tree γ with copies of γ that have the *tree* feature set in all possible ways that satisfy the following properties:

- The top of each interior node has *tree* $=$ $S^\bullet$ and the bottom of each interior node has *tree* $=$ $S_\bullet$, where S is a nonempty proper subset (without duplicates) of an elementary tree set.

- If γ is an auxiliary tree, the top/bottom of the root node of γ has *tree* $=$ $S^\bullet$ and the top/bottom of the foot node has *tree* $=$ $S_\bullet$, where S is as above, and is equal to:

    - $\{\gamma\}$,
    - plus the union of the values of the *tree* features of all the interior nodes,
    - minus any complete elementary tree sets.

- If γ is an initial tree, we define S as for auxiliary trees, but require that S be empty.

The effect of the *tree* feature is to keep track of any incomplete elementary tree sets that have been used in a subderivation. Each elementary tree combines the *tree* features of the elementary trees adjoining into it, and discharges any complete elementary tree sets that are formed. If the resulting S contains elementary trees from more than one set, there would be more than one simultaneous delay, so the construction rules out this case. In an initial tree, S is required to be empty because there can be no outstanding delays at the top of the derivation.

To move from 1-delayed tree-locality to k-delayed tree-locality, we simply allow S to be the multiset union of k nonempty proper subsets of elementary tree sets. □

5 Discussion

As noted above, flexible composition has been used in TAG analyses of linguistic phenomena when the description necessitated by the linguistic facts would lead to a non-local (or set-local) derivation. As we have shown, this move is useful because adding flexible composition increases the descriptive power of TL-MCTAG, but not the weak generative power.

In a linguistic analysis, flexible composition can be used to reverse a non-local attachment edge (or path) and thus make the derivation tree-local. However, this process also makes the derivation hard to read and linguistically unintuitive if it creates attachment edges between non-dependent lexical items in the derivation tree. As we have shown above, any derivation that uses flexible composition can alternatively be expressed in a 2-delayed tree-local MCTAG. The advantage of using this alternative formalism directly is that the linguistic dependencies can be retained. In effect, we have shown that non-local MCTAG derivations are benign in many cases that are needed for linguistic analyses of certain phenomena, such as complex noun phrases, binding, and scrambling. This kind of non-locality is handled by a delayed tree-local MCTAG.[2]

It might be objected that 2-delayed tree-local MCTAG imposes an somewhat arbitrary limit on the number of simultaneous delays. We would agree that 1-delayed tree-locality is a more natural constraint, and believe that it is probably sufficient in practice, and that the example of Figure 5, which requires two simultaneous delays, is unusual.

On the other hand, there may be some cases where there is a 1-delayed tree-local analysis, but no analysis using TL-MCTAG with flexible composition. For example, consider the following sentence (3):

(3)   John believes himself to be a decent guy.
          (Ryant and Scheffler, 2006, ex. (10))

In the TAG-FC derivation previously proposed (see Figure 6a), α_{dg} is attached to $\alpha_{\mathrm{himself}}$ by

reverse-substitution, and the result of this is attached to β_{believe} by reverse-adjunction. However, the reverse-adjunction site (S) does not come from $\alpha_{\mathrm{himself}}$, and therefore the reverse-adjunction of $\alpha_{\mathrm{himself}}$ into β_{believe} is not allowed according to our definition of flexible composition (Definition 1), since reverse-adjunction of γ into β at node η requires γ to be split at η, which must be a node in γ.

This operation was not explicitly excluded under previous definitions of flexible composition.[3] But if we tried to modify our definition of TAG-FC to allow such an operation, it is not clear how one would write the derivation trees, or whether the results obtained above would still hold.

In contrast, there is a straightforward 1-delayed TL-MCTAG derivation for the example. This derivation is shown in Figure 6b. In addition to readability, all the intuitive dependencies are retained explicitly in this derivation, for example the dependency between β_{believe} and α_{dg}.

6 Conclusion

This paper takes a closer look at the mechanism of flexible composition, which has been employed in TAGs for linguistic analysis for some time. Based on a survey of existing applications of flexible composition, we provide a formal definition of TAG-FC. We then prove the weak equivalence of tree-local MCTAG-FC to standard TAG via a variant called delayed tree-local MCTAG introduced here. Finally, we argue that delayed tree-local MCTAG is more intuitive than flexible composition for linguistic analyses that need slightly more descriptive power than tree-locality.

It remains for future work to reformulate existing analyses that use TAG-FC to use delayed tree-locality instead, and to compare the resulting analyses against the originals. On the formal side, it is also possible to give a formulation of TAG-FC as a special case of regular-form two-level TAG (Dras, 1999; Dras et al., 2003; Rogers, 2004; Rogers, 2006), a connection that deserves to be explored further.

---

[2]It needs to be tested more thoroughly how well the additional descriptive power of delayed tree-local MCTAG fares for other linguistic analyses, in particular those cases that have been claimed to necessitate non-local analyses in regular MCTAG (Bleam, 2000, for clitic climbing, for example).

[3]The definition in (Joshi et al., 2003) merely requires that the goal of reverse-adjoining is an elementary tree, but the reverse-adjoining tree may be a derived tree resulting from previous attachments.

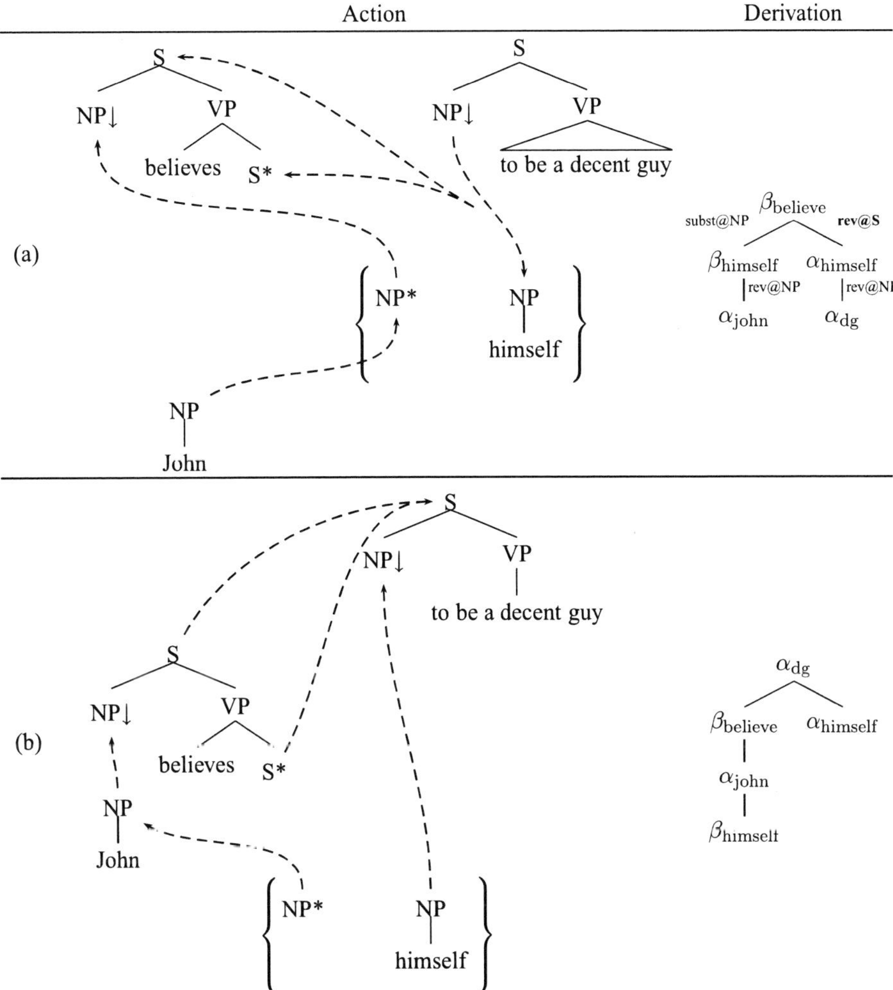

Figure 6: Derivation of "John believes himself to be a decent guy." (a) Illegal use of flexible composition, proposed in (Ryant and Scheffler, 2006): α_{himself} is claimed to reverse-adjoin at the S-node, but there is no S-node in α_{himself} (it originates from α_{dg}). (b) Straightforward analysis using 1-delayed TL-MCTAG.

Acknowledgements

The first author would like to acknowledge the person who first suggested delayed tree-locality. He thought it was Seth Kulick, but Seth thinks it must be somebody else.

The second author would like to thank the members of the XTAG weekly meeting at Penn, in particular Aravind Joshi, Joan Chen-Main, Lucas Champollion, and Joshua Tauberer, for comments and discussion about flexible composition.

References

Bleam, Tonia. 2000. Clitic climbing and the power of tree-adjoining grammar. In Abeillé, A. and O. Rambow, editors, *Tree Adjoining Grammars: Formalisms, Linguistic Analysis and Processing*. CSLI Publications, Stanford.

Chen-Main, Joan and Aravind K. Joshi. 2007. Some observations on a "graphical" model-theoretical approach and generative models. In *Proceedings of the Workshop on Model-Theoretic Syntax*, pages 53–62, Trinity College, Dublin. European Summer School in Logic, Linguistics, and Information.

Dras, Mark, David Chiang, and William Schuler. 2003. On relations of constituency and dependency grammars. *Research on Language and Computation*, 2:281–305.

Dras, Mark. 1999. A meta-level grammar: redefining synchronous TAG for translation and paraphrase. In *Proceedings of ACL 1999*, pages 80–87.

Forbes-Riley, Katherine, Bonnie Webber, and Aravind Joshi. 2006. Computing discourse semantics: The predicate-argument semantics of discourse connectives in D-LTAG. *Journal of Semantics*, 23(1):55–106.

Joshi, Aravind K., Laura Kallmeyer, and Maribel Romero. 2003. Flexible composition in LTAG: Quantifier scope and inverse linking. In Bunt, Harry, Ielka van der Sluis, and Roser Morante, editors, *Proceedings of the Fifth International Workshop on Computational Semantics (IWCS-5)*, pages 179–194, Tilburg, Netherlands.

Kallmeyer, Laura and Tatjana Scheffler. 2004. LTAG analysis for pied-piping and stranding of wh-phrases. In *Proceedings of the Seventh International Workshop on Tree Adjoining Grammar and Related Formalisms (TAG+7)*, pages 32–39, Vancouver, BC, Canada.

Lang, Bernard. 1994. Recognition can be harder than parsing. *Computational Intelligence*, 10(4):484–494. Special Issue on Tree Adjoining Grammars.

Rogers, James. 2004. One more perspective on semantic relations in TAG. In *Proceedings of TAG+6*.

Rogers, James. 2006. On scrambling, another perspective. In *Proceedings of TAG+7*.

Ryant, Neville and Tatjana Scheffler. 2006. Binding of anaphors in LTAG. In *Proceedings of the Eighth International Workshop on Tree Adjoining Grammar and Related Formalisms (TAG+8)*, pages 65–72, Sydney, Australia.

Weir, David J. 1988. *Characterizing Mildly Context-Sensitive Grammar Formalisms*. Ph.D. thesis, University of Pennsylvania.

A Psycholinguistically Motivated Version of TAG

Vera Demberg and **Frank Keller**
School of Informatics, University of Edinburgh
2 Buccleuch Place, Edinburgh EH8 9LW, UK
{v.demberg,frank.keller}@ed.ac.uk

Abstract

We propose a psycholinguistically motivated version of TAG which is designed to model key properties of human sentence processing, viz., incrementality, connectedness, and prediction. We use findings from human experiments to motivate an incremental grammar formalism that makes it possible to build fully connected structures on a word-by-word basis. A key idea of the approach is to explicitly model the prediction of upcoming material and the subsequent verification and integration processes. We also propose a linking theory that links the predictions of our formalism to experimental data such as reading times, and illustrate how it can capture psycholinguistic results on the processing of *either ... or* structures and relative clauses.

1 Introduction

Current evidence from psycholinguistic research suggests that language comprehension is largely *incremental*, i.e., that comprehenders build an interpretation of a sentence on a word-by-word basis. This is a fact that any cognitively motivated model of language understanding should capture. There is also evidence for full *connectivity* (Sturt and Lombardo, 2005), i.e., for the assumption that all words are connected by a single syntactic structure at any point in the incremental processing of a sentence. While this second point of full connectivity is more controversial, the model we are proposing here explores the implications of incrementality in its strict interpretation as full connectivity.

Furthermore, recent work on human sentence comprehension indicates that people make *predictions* of upcoming words and structures as they process language (Frazier et al., 2000; Kamide et al., 2003; Staub and Clifton, 2006). The concepts of

connectedness and prediction are closely related: in order to assure that the syntactic structure of a sentence prefix is connected at every point in time, it can be necessary to include phrases whose yield has not been processed yet. This part of the structure needs to be generated by the parser in order to connect the words that have been seen so far, i.e., to achieve full connectivity (which in turn is required to build an incremental interpretation). This process has been formalized by (Lombardo and Sturt, 2002) using the notion of *connection path*.

In this paper, we explore how these key psycholinguistic concepts (incrementality, connectedness, and prediction) can be realized within a new version of tree-adjoining grammar (TAG), which we call Psycholinguistically Motivated TAG (PLTAG). We argue that TAG is better suited for this modeling task than other formalisms such as CCG or PCFGs and propose a linking theory that derives predictions of processing difficulty from aspects of the PLTAG formalism.

2 Related Work

A number of incremental versions TAG have been proposed over the years (Shen and Joshi, 2005; Kato et al., 2004; Mazzei et al., 2007). The version proposed here differs from these approaches in a number of ways. Spinal LTAG (Shen and Joshi, 2005) does not implement full connectivity, and cannot easily be used to model prediction since it does not encode valencies. The proposals by (Mazzei et al., 2007) and (Kato et al., 2004) are more similar to our work, but are less well-suited for psycholinguistic modeling since they do not implement a verification mechanism, which is required to account for standard complexity results in the spirit of (Gibson, 1998). In addition, (Kato et al., 2004) do not distinguish between modifiers and arguments, since they operate on the Penn Treebank, where this information is not directly available.

Incremental parsers for other grammar formalisms include Roark's (2001) for PCFGs, and Nivre's (2004) for dependency grammars. Neither of these parsers implement strict incrementality, in the sense of always building connected structures. Furthermore, there are principled problems with PCFGs are a model of prediction difficulty, even if fully connected structures are built (see Section 7).

The main contributions in this version of TAG introduced in this paper is that it is incremental and respects full connectivity, whiles also modeling the verification and integration of syntactic material. Our main emphasis is on the modeling of prediction, which has been the subject of much recent research in psycholinguistics, as outlined in the previous section.

3   Incrementality and Prediction

We propose variant of TAG that incorporates two different types of prediction: prediction through substitution nodes in lexicon entries (e.g., if a verb subcategorizes for an object which has not yet been seen), and prediction via connection paths. The first type of prediction models the anticipation of upcoming syntactic structure that is licensed by the current input; the second type models prediction which is required to ensure that fully connected structures are built. We will discuss the mechanism for prediction due to connectivity first.

3.1   Prediction due to Connectivity

TAG elementary trees can not always be connected directly to a previously built syntactic structure. Examples are situations where two dependents precede a head, or where a grandparent and a child have been encountered, but the head of the parent node has not. For instance, in the sentence *the horse seldom fell*, the elementary tree of *the horse* cannot directly be combined with elementary tree of the adverbial modifier *seldom*, see Figure 1(a). The head *fell* which provides the intervening structure, has not been encountered at that point. Therefore, this intervening structure has to be predicted in order to connect *the horse* and *seldom*.[1] We use the substitution symbol $\downarrow$ to mark predicted structure. As a prediction mark, the substitution symbol can therefore also occur tree-internally. We assume

that prediction is conservative, and only includes the structure as far as it is needed, i.e., only as far as it is included in the connection path (see Section 4 and Figure 3). It is important to bear in mind, however, that prediction grain size remains an open research question (for instance, we could predict the full elementary tree down to the lexical item, as proposed by (Mazzei et al., 2007), to even include the remaining subcategorized nodes or likely modifiers of that node).

Our minimal prediction method implies that adjunction must be possible at predicted nodes, as shown in Figure 1(a). When this happens, the head node of the auxiliary tree is marked as seen, while the foot node of the auxiliary tree takes over the prediction mark from the predicted connection structure, because we need to mark that we have not in fact yet seen the node that it adjoined to. If we marked both as non-predicted nodes, then we would not be able to guarantee that we can correctly keep track of what has been encountered in the input and what we have predicted.

We treat those connecting structures as special lexicon entries, where each predicted node is marked. A predicted node differs from the rest of the structure in that it needs to be verified, i.e., it has to be matched (through substitution of internal nodes) with later upcoming structure, as illustrated in Figure 1(b). A derivation of a sentence is only valid if all predicted nodes are matched. Our example shows how the tree structure for *the horse seldom* is connected with the elementary tree of *fell*. Each node of the new elementary tree can either be matched with a predicted node in the prefix tree, or it can be added (the structure for *the horse seldom*. It could therefore just as easily unify with a transitive or ditransitive verb. (Note that by unification we simply mean node matching and we will use these two terms interchangeably in this paper.)

Issues arise in the verification process, e.g., how to unify structures after additional material has been adjoined. In our example, an additional VP node has been introduced by the adverb. The new nodes in the tree cannot unify with a random predicted node of the same category, but have to follow constraints of accessibility and have to have identical dominance relations. For example, consider a situation where we predict the structure between an object relative pronoun like *whom* and its trace (see the top tree in Figure 4). If we encountered a verb next, we could match up the nodes of the verb el-

---

[1] Because of the recursiveness of natural language, it is possible that there are infinitely many ways to connect two trees. Although embedding depth can be infinite in theory, we assume that it is finite and indeed very small due to limitations of human memory.

ementary tree (S, VP, V) with the predicted nodes, and would still predict the subject noun phrase. If we then encountered a noun phrase, and again did not take into account any accessibility constraints (the substitution node is not accessible any more because filling it at this point would violate the linear order), we could substitute that noun into the subject position. That is, we would accept impossible RCs like *whom thanked Peter*, or misanalyze subject relative clauses as object relative clauses.

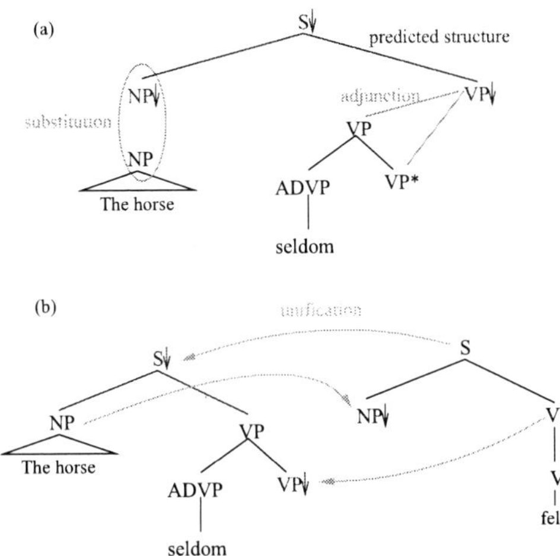

Figure 1: Example for prediction and verification of predictions

3.2 Prediction from Substitution Nodes

Another source for predictions are the lexicon entries themselves. Each substitution node that is to the right of the tree's anchor naturally becomes a prediction during the parsing process. This means that we do not predict modifiers or any other kind of recursive structures, unless we have already seen a word that depends on the modifier (i.e., through connectivity, e.g., for a sentence prefix such as *the horse very*). Whether or not modifiers are predicted syntactically is currently an open research question. Preliminary evidence suggests that modifiers are predicted when they are required by the discourse context.

We also exploit TAG's extended domain of locality in order to construct lexicon entries such that are more appropriate for modeling psycholinguistic findings. An example is the *either ... or* construction. Results by (Staub and Clifton, 2006) show that hearing the word *either* triggers prediction of *or* and the second conjunct: reading times on these

regions were shorter in the *either* condition, and participants also did not misanalyze disjunctions at sentence level as noun disjunctions in the condition where *either* was present.

As (Cristea and Webber, 1997) point out, there are a number of constructions with two parts where the first part can trigger prediction of the second part in, similar to *either ... or*. A related form of prediction is syntactic parallelism; experimental findings by (Frazier et al., 2000) indicate that the second conjunct of a coordinate structure is processed faster if its internal structure is identical to that of the first conjunct. This can be seen as a form of prediction, i.e., the parser predicts the structure of the second conjunct as soon as it has processed the conjunction.

Here, we will discuss in more detail how *either ... or* prediction can be implemented our framework. We assign a lexicon entry to *either* which predicts the occurrence of coordination with two entities of the same category, and requires *or* as a coordinator, see Figure 2(a). Figure 2 shows an example of how the word *either* impacts parsing of the *either ... or* disjunction in PLTAG, as opposed to a simple *or* disjunction. In the no *either* case, a sentence structure like Figure 2(c) can be combined with either of the elementary tree of *or*, as shown in Figure 2(b). Two different analyzes are created, one for the noun disjunction case and one for the sentence disjunction. Later on in processing, one of these is ruled out when disambiguating information is processed. The position of *either* can help disambiguate this ambiguity before it arises, which explains why participants were not misanalyzing sentence disjunctions when *either* was present. Furthermore, changes in the probabilities of the analyses occur at different points in time in the *either* and no *either* cases. Structures that have been predicted and do not add any new nodes incur integration costs but do not cause any changes in probabilities of the analysis.

In this case, *either* and *or* provide overlapping information, in particular, *or* does not give any new information. This means that we either have to have a different lexicon entry for *or* following *either*, or that adjunction works differently for those partly redundant nodes. Because both the foot and the head node of *or* have been predicted by previously by *either*, the head node of the auxiliary tree just verifies the prediction, while the foot node adopts whatever annotation is on the node

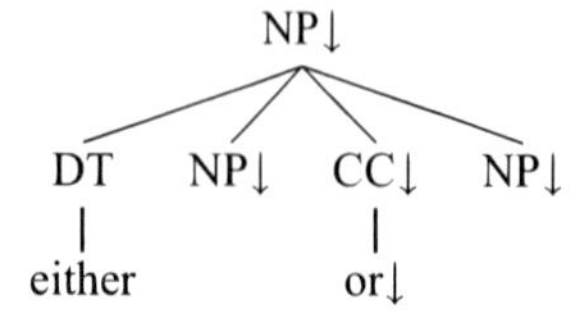

(a) lexicon entry for *either*

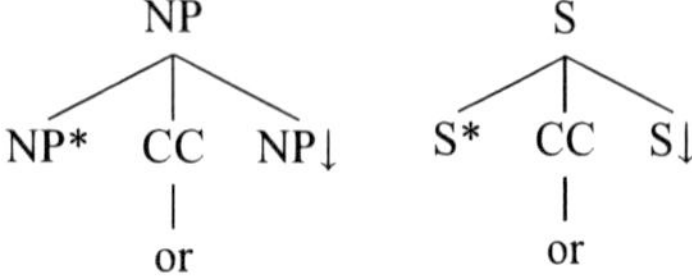

(b) lexicon entries for *or*

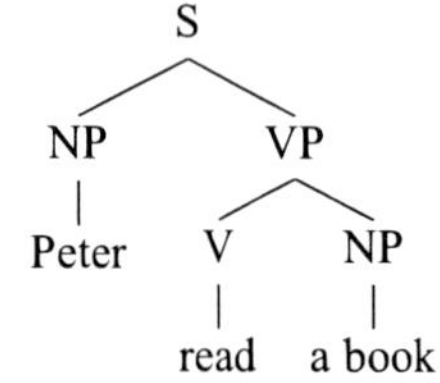

(c) no *either*

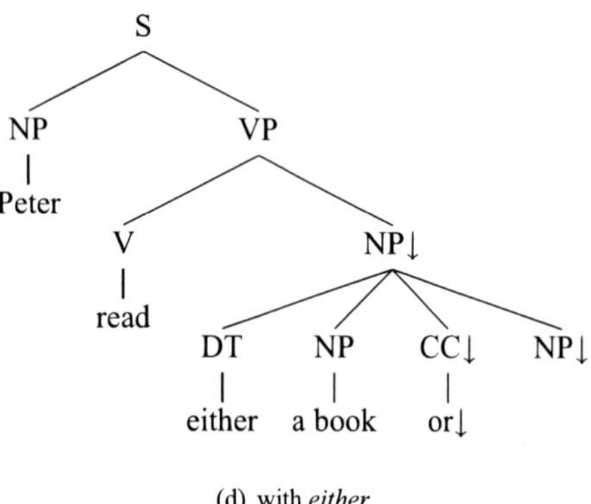

(d) with *either*

Figure 2: Example for the use of TAG's extended domain of locality to model expressions that trigger predictions, such as *either … or*

that it matches. This situation can be automatically recognized because the lexical anchor for the *or*-auxiliary tree was itself predicted. Also note that in this case, the missing second conjunct gets marked twice for substitution (both by the lexicon entry for *either* in Figure 2(a) and 2(b)). This double prediction changes the time stamp on the predicted node, which gets set to the most recent time it was predicted.

This kind of redundancy by eager prediction also

occurs in our analysis of relative clauses. In theory, encountering the object relative pronoun *whom* is sufficient to predict the argument structure of the relative clause (namely that there has to be a head for the relative clause, and that there has to be a subject, and a trace for the object). We will investigate in future work whether there is evidence that humans predict the whole structure given the relative pronoun. For now we assume that a trace is always predicted when its filler is encountered. For an example of how this works, see Figure 4.

4 Treebank-based Lexicon Induction

We induce the lexicon needed for our incremental version of TAG from the Penn Treebank, complemented by Nombank (Vadas and Curran, 2007) and Propbank (Palmer et al., 2003), as well as Magerman's head percolation table (Magerman, 1994). These additional resources help determine the elementary trees and distinguish arguments from modifiers. (Modifiers are not predicted unless they are needed for a connection path.) In Figure 3 each inner node is indexed with the number of the word that is its lexical anchor in order to show which parts of the syntactic tree belong to which lexicon entry.

Once the parsed trees have been segmented into elementary trees (following procedures in Xia et al. 2000), we calculate connection paths for each prefix, as proposed by (Lombardo and Sturt, 2002). A connection path for words $w_1 \ldots w_n$ is the minimal amount of structure that is needed to connect all words $w_1 \ldots w_n$ into the same syntactic tree. The amount of structure needed at each word for the sentence *the Italian people often vote Berlusconi* is indicated in Figure 3 by the structure enclosed in the circles.

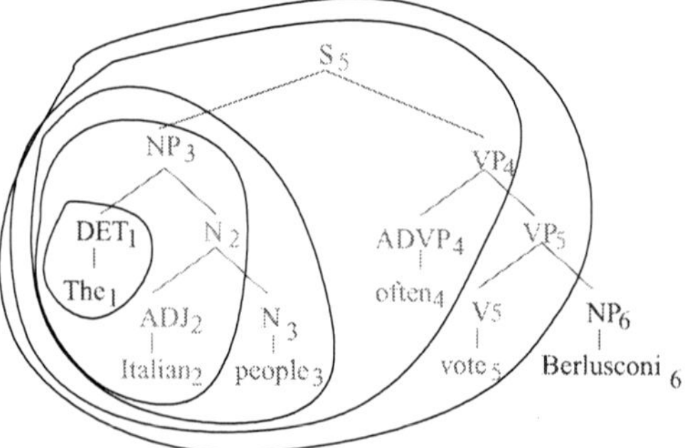

Figure 3: Generating lexicon entries from the Penn Treebank for an example sentence

We then use the connection paths and the canonical elementary trees to determine which parts of the structure that are included in the connection path for words $w_1 \ldots w_n$, but not part of any of the elementary trees with feet $w_1 \ldots w_n$. In Figure 3, this occurs twice: firstly when *Italian* has been read, and the determiner and adjective can only be combined by predicting that they must be part of the same noun phrase, and secondly at *often*, when the VP and S nodes have to be predicted.

By definition, all nodes of these connecting structures are predicted nodes, and therefore annotated as substitution nodes. We store these connecting structures as non-lexicalized lexicon entries. They differ from other lexicon entries in that all their nodes are substitution nodes, and in that they are not lexicalized. The advantage of generating these separate non-lexicalized entries over simply adding a second predicted version of all lexicon entries is that we retain a smaller lexicon, which reduces the sparse data problem for training, and makes parsing more efficient.

The connection structure is non-lexicalized, and therefore creates additional challenges for the parser: the non-lexicalized structures can be triggered at any point in parsing, in particular when simple substitution and adjunction are not successful. They can also in principle be chained, i.e., several of non-lexicalized structures can be applied one after the other, without ever applying any lexicalized rules. As a first approximation, we therefore restrict these prediction rules to instances that we encountered in the corpus, and do not only allow several non-lexicalized rules in a row. This restriction means that there may be sentences which this incremental parser cannot cover, even though a non-incremental parser (or one without this restriction) can find an analysis for them. (CCG has a similar problem with the application of type-raising; in current CCG parsers, the search problem in type-raising is solved by lexicalizing type raising.) Because of recursive rules in natural language, embedding can in principle also be infinitely deep. However, (Lombardo and Sturt, 2002) have shown that for 80% of the word tokens, no connection paths are needed, and that two or more predictions have to be made for about 2% of the tokens.

5 Linking Parsing Complexity to Processing Difficulty

The grammar design proposed here implements a specific set of assumptions about human language processing (strong incrementality with full connectedness, prediction, ranked parallel processing) which can be tested by linking an incremental parser for this formalism with a theory of human sentence comprehension.

The relation between the incremental parsing algorithm and processing difficulty can be formalized as follows: At each word, a set E of syntactic expectations e is generated (they can be easily read off the syntactic structure in the form of substitution nodes). These expectations can be interpreted as denoting the categories needed to build a grammatical sentence from the current input, and are associated with probabilities $P(e)$, estimated by the parser. Each structure also has a timestamp corresponding to when it was first predicted, or last activated. Based on this, decay is calculated, under the assumption that recently-accessed structures are easier to access and integrate (decay is weighted for verification (substitution of inner nodes), regular substitution and, adjunction).

In this model, processing difficulty is incurred either when expectations are incompatible with the current input (algorithmically, this corresponds to the parser trying to substitute, adjoin, or unify a new tree with the currently maintained structure, but failing for all structures), or when successful integration takes place (i.e., unification of predicted nodes and the elementary tree is successful, or a node can be successfully adjoined). Intuitively, integration is costly because the parser has to bring together the meaning of the matched categories.

Processing difficulty is proportional to the inverse probability of all integrated structures (less activated structures are harder to integrate) plus the probability of all deleted structures (more probable structures are harder to discard), where both probabilities weighted by recency:

$$D_w \propto \sum_{e \in E_i} f\left(\frac{1}{P(e)}\right) + \sum_{e \in E_d} f(P(e))$$

Here, D_w is the difficulty at word w, and E_i is the set of expectations that could be integrated, while E_d is the set of expectations that have been discarded at w. A decay is implemented by the function f.

6   Example

The following example aims to show how PLTAG can explain increased processing difficulty at object relative clauses (ORC) as opposed to subject relative clauses (SRC). We chose this example because there is evidence that object relative clauses are more difficult for humans to process from both experimental sources (King and Just, 1991; Gibson, 1998) and broad-coverage corpus data (Demberg and Keller, 2007).

Figure 4 shows two alternative structures for the phrase *grand-parents who* (all probabilities in this example are fictitious and just for illustrative purposes). The two analyses differ by whether they analyze *who* as an object relative pronoun or a subject relative pronoun, and predict traces in different positions. (Whether traces should be predicted when their fillers are encountered is an open question, but we will assume that they are for the time being.) Both of these analyses have a certain probability, which is higher for the SRC (0.0003) than for the ORC (0.00004), since SRCs are more frequent. When the next word is encountered, that word may also be ambiguous, such as the word *time* in our example, whose probability is higher as noun (0.08) than as a verb (0.02). All possible elementary trees for the new word have to be matched up with all prefix trees (analyses whose probability is below a certain threshold are ignored to limit the search problem and simulate memory limitations). In our example, the noun interpretation of *time* is compatible with the object relative clause interpretation, while the verb interpretation can be unified with the SRC analysis. The ORC structure still has lower probability than the SRC structure at this point, because $0.00003 \cdot 0.08 < 0.0004 \cdot 0.02$. If an ORC verb was encountered next, we would correctly predict that this verb should be more difficult to process than the SRC verb, because five nodes have to be matched up instead of four, and the predicted nodes in the ORC analysis are one clock-cycle older than the ones in the SRC at the time of integrating the verb.

On encountering a disambiguating word, the processing difficulty proportional to the probability mass of all incompatible structures would be incurred. This means that higher processing difficulty occurs when the more probable structure (the SRC in our example) has to be discarded.

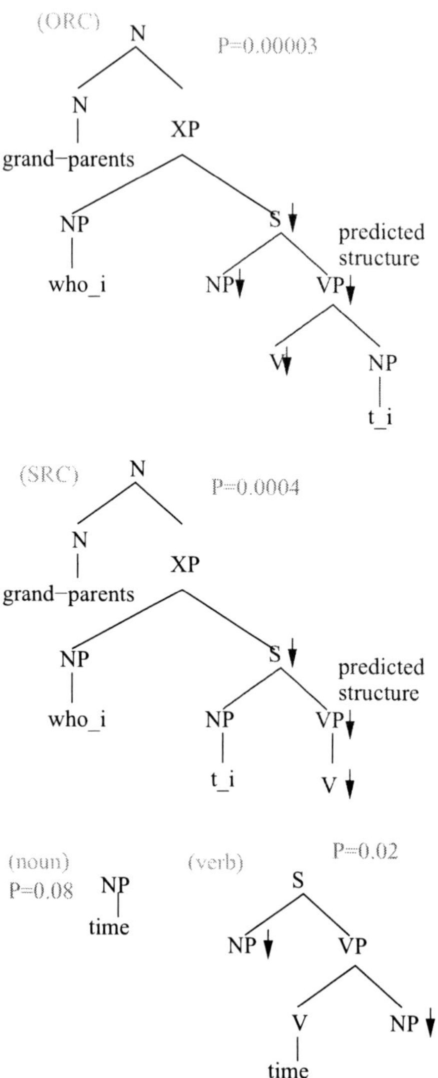

Figure 4: Example of the interaction of lexical probabilities and verification cost in PLTAG

7   Comparison with Other Grammar Formalisms

We decided to use tree-adjoining grammar instead of alternative formalisms like Combinatory Categorial Grammar (CCG) or Probabilistic Context Free Grammar (PCFG) because we felt that TAG best met our requirements of strict incrementality with full connectivity.

In standard CCG with bottom-up parsing (Steedman, 2000), it is not possible to always find an incremental derivation. For example, in object relative clauses, the subject NP of the relative clause cannot be integrated in an incremental fashion because the category of the relative pronoun $((N\backslash N)/(S/NP))$ is too abstract: it does not contain the category for the subject NP explicitly and the subject NP therefore has to connect with the verb first. Another example are coordinated clauses. The second conjunct can only be combined with the first conjunct when they both have the same category. However, (Sturt and Lombardo, 2005) show that human sentence processing is more incremental than the most incremental CCG derivation for a sentence like *the pilot embarrassed John and put himself/herself in an awkward situation*, where the c-command relation between *the pilot* and *himself/herself* is understood at the point of reading the reflexive pronoun, and not only after reading the full second conjunct, as CCG would predict under the assumption that the syntactic relation has to be established first in order to determine c-command relations.

Coordination in tree-adjoining grammar does not have this problem of connecting with the beginning of the sentence only once the second conjunct has been seen, because the elementary tree for *and* is an auxiliary tree and adjoins into the previous structure, and therefore is connected to the preceding context right away, and *himself* can be substituted into the connected structure and is c-commanded by *the pilot* right away and will therefore be available for binding at an early processing stage.

Furthermore, pre- and post-modification is asymmetric for incremental derivations in CCG (and we are not aware of such an asymmetry in human sentence processing). CCG requires either type-raising at a noun that comes before a modifier, or non-connectivity. The reason for the asymmetry is that for pre-modification, e.g., an adjective before noun, there is no type-raising necessary in incremental processing (see Figure 5(b)). On the other hand, for post-modification it is necessary to type-raise the head before the post-modifier is processed (see Figure 5(d)). This would lead to the unintuitive situation of having an ambiguity for a noun when it is post-modified, but not when it is pre-modified. Alternatively, the structure either has to be undone once the modifier is encountered in order to allow for the composition (serial account), or the noun is explicitly ambiguous as to whether it will be modified or not (parallel ac-

count), or we cannot satisfy full connectivity. In both cases, post-modification requires more operations than pre-modification. This is not the case in TAG, because pre- and post-modification are adjoined into the tree in the same fashion (see Figure 5(a) and (c)).

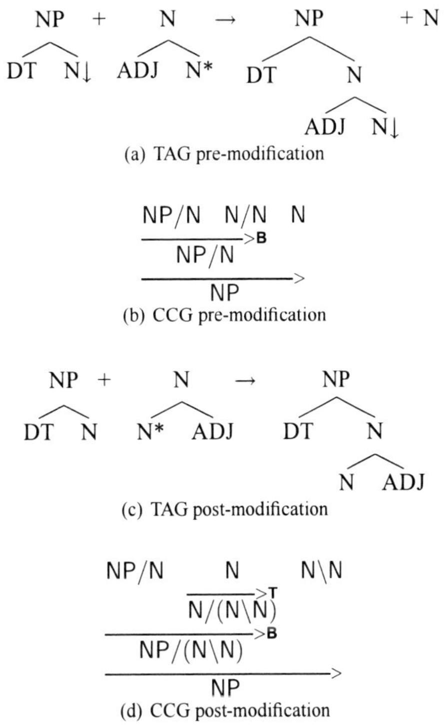

Figure 5: Comparision of pre- and post-modification in TAG and CCG

In order to use PCFGs as a basis for the psycholinguistic model it would be necessary to introduce composition into the parsing process in order to avoid having to predict all the processing difficulty at the end of phrases. Standard arc-eager parsing would for example complete a rule only once all of its children have been seen. For a more in-depth discussion of this question see (Thompson et al., 1991). Composition is also needed to keep track of the predictions. For example, once we have seen the verb, we do not want to expect the verb phrase itself anymore, but only any potential arguments. Furthermore, PCFGs do not provide the extended domain of locality that we exploit in TAG.

8 Summary

We propose a framework for a new version of TAG which supports incremental, fully connected derivations, and makes explicit predictions about upcoming material in the sentence. This version of TAG can be combined with a linking theory to model human processing difficulty, and aims to account for recent findings on prediction and connectivity in human sentence comprehension.

References

Cristea, Dan and Bonnie Webber. 1997. Expectations in incremental discourse processing. In *Proceedings of the 8th. Conference of the European Chapter of the Association for Computational Linguistics (ACL-EACL97)*, pages 88–95, Madrid, Spain, July. Association for Computational Linguistics.

Demberg, Vera and Frank Keller. 2007. Eye-tracking evidence for integration cost effects in corpus data. In *Proceedings of the 29th Annual Conference of the Cognitive Science Society*, Nashville.

Frazier, Lyn, Alan Munn, and Charles Clifton. 2000. Processing coordinate structure. *Journal of Psycholinguistic Research*, 29:343–368.

Gibson, Edward. 1998. Linguistic complexity: locality of syntactic dependencies. *Cognition 68*, pages 1–76.

Kamide, Yuki, Christoph Scheepers, and Gerry T.M. Altmann. 2003. Integration of syntactic and semantic information in predictive processing: Cross-linguistic evidence from German and English. *Psycholinguistic Research*, 32.

Kato, Yoshihide, Shigeki Matsubara, and Yasuyoshi Inagaki. 2004. Stochastically evaluating the validity of partial parse trees in incremental parsing. In Keller, Frank, Stephen Clark, Matthew Crocker, and Mark Steedman, editors, *Proceedings of the ACL Workshop Incremental Parsing: Bringing Engineering and Cognition Together*, pages 9–15, Barcelona, Spain, July. Association for Computational Linguistics.

King, J. and M. A. Just. 1991. Individual differences in syntactic processing: The role of working memory. *Journal of Memory and Language*, 30:580–602.

Lombardo, Vincenzo and Patrick Sturt. 2002. Incrementality and lexicalism. In *Lexical Representations in Sentence Processing, John Benjamins: Computational Psycholinguistics Series*, pages 137–155. S. Stevenson and P. Merlo.

Magerman, David M. 1994. *Natural language parsing as statistical pattern recognition*. Ph.D. thesis, Stanford University.

Mazzei, Alessandro, Vincenzo Lombardo, and Patrick Sturt. 2007. Dynamic tag and lexical dependencies. *Research on Language and Computation, Foundations of Natural Language Grammar*, pages 309–332.

Nivre, Joakim. 2004. Incrementality in deterministic dependency parsing. In *Proceedings of the ACL Workshop on Incremental Parsing: Bringing Engineering and Cognition Together*, pages 50–57, Barcelona.

Palmer, Martha, Dan Gildea, and Paul Kingsbury. 2003. The proposition bank: An annotated corpus of semantic roles. *Computational Linguistics*, 31(1):71–106.

Roark, Brian. 2001. Probabilistic top-down parsing and language modeling. *Computational Linguistics*, 27(2):249–276.

Shen, Libin and Aravind K. Joshi. 2005. Incremental ltag parsing. In *HLT '05: Proceedings of the conference on Human Language Technology and Empirical Methods in Natural Language Processing*, pages 811–818.

Staub, Adrian and Charles Clifton. 2006. Syntactic prediction in language comprehension: Evidence from either...or. *Journal of Experimental Psychology: Learning, Memory, and Cognition*, 32:425–436.

Steedman, Mark. 2000. *The syntactic process*. The MIT press.

Sturt, Patrick and Vincenzo Lombardo. 2005. Processing coordinate structures: Incrementality and connectedness. *Cognitive Science*, 29:291–305.

Thompson, Henry S., Mike Dixon, and John Lamping. 1991. Compose-reduce parsing. In *Proceedings of the 29th annual meeting on Association for Computational Linguistics*, pages 87–97, Morristown, NJ, USA. Association for Computational Linguistics.

Vadas, David and James Curran. 2007. Adding noun phrase structure to the penn treebank. In *Proceedings of the 45th Annual Meeting of the Association of Computational Linguistics*, pages 240–247, Prague, Czech Republic, June. Association for Computational Linguistics.

Xia, Fei, Martha Palmer, and Aravind Joshi. 2000. A uniform method of grammar extraction and its applications. In *Proceedings of the 2000 Joint SIGDAT conference on Empirical methods in natural language processing and very large corpora*, pages 53–62.

Compositional Semantics of Coordination using Synchronous Tree Adjoining Grammar

Chung-hye Han
Department of Linguistics
Simon Fraser University
chunghye@sfu.ca

David Potter
Department of Linguistics
Simon Fraser University
dkp1@sfu.ca

Dennis R. Storoshenko
Department of Linguistics
Simon Fraser University
dstorosh@sfu.ca

Abstract

In this paper, we propose a compositional semantics for DP/VP coordination, using Synchronous Tree Adjoining Grammar (STAG). We first present a new STAG approach to quantification and scope ambiguity, using Generalized Quantifiers (GQ). The proposed GQ analysis is then used in our account of DP/VP coordination.

1 Introduction

In this paper, we propose a compositional semantics for DP coordination and VP coordination, using Synchronous Tree Adjoining Grammar (STAG). We take advantage of STAG's capacity to provide an isomorphic derivation of semantic trees in parallel to syntactic ones, using substitution and adjoining in both syntax and semantics. In addition, we use unreduced λ-expressions in semantic elementary trees, as in Han (2007). This allows us to build the logical forms by applying λ-conversion and other operations defined on λ-expressions to the semantic derived tree.

DP meanings cannot be directly conjoined in an STAG approach that does not make use of unreduced λ-expressions in semantic trees, as in Shieber (1990) and Nesson and Shieber (2006; 2007). In this approach, a quantified DP introduces an argument variable and a formula consisting of a quantifier, restriction and scope. The argument variables cannot be conjoined as conjunction is defined on formulas. Although the formula components can be conjoined in principle, it is not clear how the conjoined formulas can compose with the meaning coming from the rest of the sentence.

In our analysis, we redefine the semantics of DPs as Generalized Quantifiers (GQ) (Barwise and Cooper, 1981), enabling the DP meanings to be directly conjoined. GQs can be conjoined through the application of the Generalized Conjunction Rule, and the conjoined GQs can com-

pose with the meaning coming from the rest of the sentence through λ-conversion.

Our approach is in contrast to previous works on DP coordination (Babko-Malaya, 2004) and VP coordination (Banik, 2004) that use feature-unification-based TAG semantics (Kallmeyer and Romero, 2008). While the two accounts handle DP and VP coordination separately, they cannot together account for sentences with both DP and VP coordination, such as *Every boy and every girl jumped and played*, without adding new features. Furthermore, due to the recursive nature of coordination, an indefinite number of such features would potentially need to be added.

We first present a new STAG approach to quantification and scope ambiguity in section 2, using GQs. We then extend the proposed GQ analysis to DP coordination in section 3 and VP coordination in section 4. It will also be shown how sentences with both DP and VP coordination can be handled under the proposed analysis.

2 Quantification and scope ambiguity

A sentence such as (1) is ambiguous between two readings: for every course there is a student that likes it (1a), and there is a student that likes every course (1b).

(1) A student likes every course. ($\forall > \exists, \exists > \forall$)

    a. $\forall x_2[\text{course}(x_2)][\exists x_1[\text{student}(x_1)][\text{likes}(x_1, x_2)]]$

    b. $\exists x_1[\text{student}(x_1)][\forall x_2[\text{course}(x_2)][\text{likes}(x_1, x_2)]]$

Figure 1 contains the elementary trees to derive (1). For the DP *a student*, we propose that (αa_student) on the syntax side is paired with the multi-component set $\{(\alpha'\text{a\_student}),(\beta'\text{a\_student})\}$ on the semantics side. In the semantic trees, F stands for formula, R for relation and T for term. (αa_student) is a valid elementary tree conforming to Frank's (2002) Condition on Elementary Tree Minimality

Proceedings of The Ninth International Workshop on Tree Adjoining Grammars and Related Formalisms
Tübingen, Germany. June 6-8, 2008.

(CETM), as a noun can form an extended projection with a DP, in line with the DP Hypothesis. (α'a_student) provides an argument variable, and (β'a_student) provides the existential quantifier with the restriction and scope in the form of a GQ. We define the syntax and semantics of the DP *every course* in a similar way. In the $<$(αlikes), (α'likes)$>$ pair, the boxed numerals indicate links between the syntactic and semantic tree pairs and ensure synchronous derivation between the syntax and semantics: an operation carried out at one such node in the syntax side must be matched with a corresponding operation on the linked node(s) in the semantics side. The symbols $\boxed{1}$ and $\boxed{2}$ at the F node in (α'likes) indicate that two elementary trees will adjoin at this node using Multiple Adjunction, as defined in Schabes and Shieber (1994). In the derivation of (1), (β'a_student) and (β'every_course) will multiply-adjoin to it. Figure 2 depicts the isomorphic syntactic and semantic derivation structures for (1).

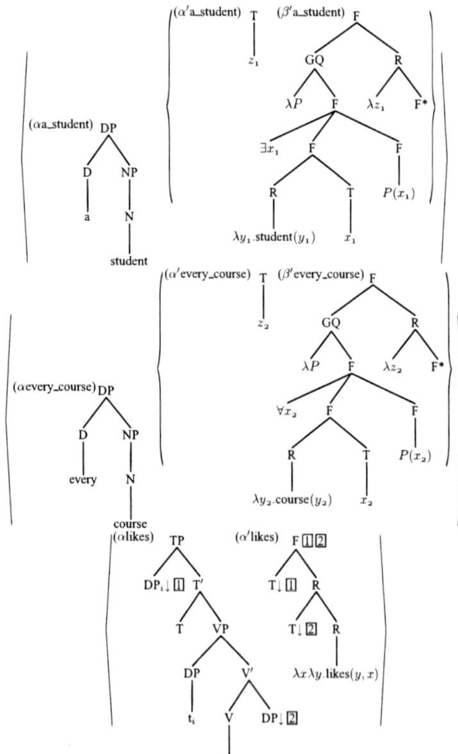

Figure 1: Elementary trees for *A student likes every course*

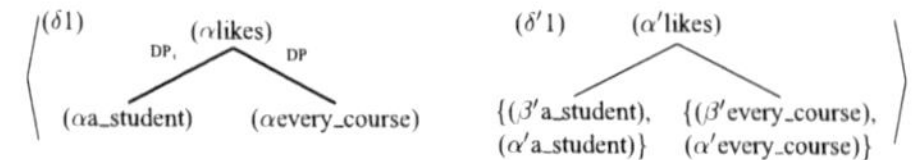

Figure 2: Derivation structures for *A student likes every course*

Note that while the derivation in the syntax produces a single derived tree (γ1) in Figure 3, the derivation in semantics produces two semantic derived trees in Figure 3: (γ'1a) for the $\forall > \exists$ reading, and (γ'1b) for the $\exists > \forall$ reading. This is because the semantic derivation structure provides an underspecified representation for scope ambiguity, as the order in which (β'a_student) and (β'every_course) adjoin to the F node in (α'likes) is unspecified. The application of λ-conversion to the semantic derived trees yields the formulas in (1a) and (1b).

3   DP coordination

We now extend our GQ analysis to DP coordination. Our analysis captures two generalizations of scope in DP coordination, as discussed in Babko-Malaya (2004). First, coordinated quantified DPs must scope under the coordinator (2). Second, scope interaction is possible between a coordinated DP and other quantifiers in a sentence (3).

(2)   Every boy and every girl jumped. ($\wedge > \forall$)

   a. $\forall x_2[\text{boy}(x_2)][\text{jumped}(x_2)] \wedge$
        $\forall x_2[\text{girl}(x_2)][\text{jumped}(x_2)]$

(3)   Every boy and every girl solved a puzzle.
      ($\wedge > \forall > \exists, \exists > \wedge > \forall$)

   a. $\forall x_2[\text{boy}(x_2)][\exists x_1[\text{puzzle}(x_1)][\text{solved}(x_2, x_1)]] \wedge$
        $\forall x_2[\text{girl}(x_2)][\exists x_1[\text{puzzle}(x_1)][\text{solved}(x_2, x_1)]]$

   b. $\exists x_1[\text{puzzle}(x_1)][\forall x_2[\text{boy}(x_2)][\text{solved}(x_2, x_1)] \wedge$
        $\forall x_2[\text{girl}(x_2)][\text{solved}(x_2, x_1)]]$

Figure 4 includes the elementary trees necessary to derive (2). We adopt a DP coordination elementary tree (βand_every_girl) where the lexical anchor projects to a DP that contains a determiner and a coordinator. This is in accordance with CETM as both the determiner and the coordinator are functional heads. We propose that (βand_every_girl) is paired with (β'and_every_girl). In (β'and_every_girl), two GQ nodes are coordinated where one of the conjuncts contributes the meaning of *every girl*.

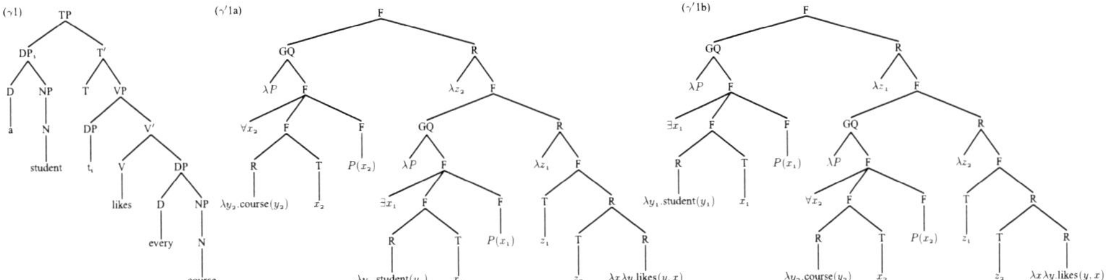

Figure 3: Derived trees for *A student likes every course*

This specification ensures that the coordinator scopes over the conjoined quantified DPs. Further, (β'and_every_girl) does not include an argument component for *every girl*. Instead, the argument variable will be provided when (β'and_every_girl) adjoins to (β'every_boy).

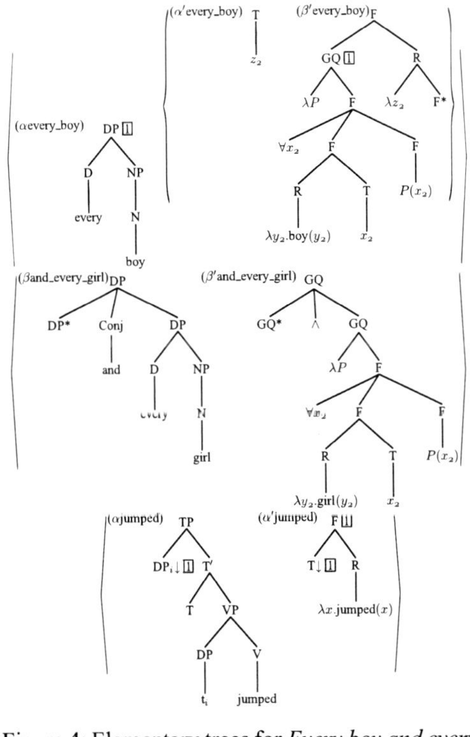

Figure 4: Elementary trees for *Every boy and every girl jumped*

The isomorphic syntactic and semantic derivation structures of (2) are in Figure 5, and the syntactic and semantic derived trees are in Figure 6.

As we are coordinating GQs, we can use the Generalized Conjunction (GC) rule of Barwise and Cooper (1981) to compose them. The GC rule

takes two coordinated GQs and λ-abstracts over them, as in (4). Application of the GC rule and λ-conversion to ($\gamma'2$) yields the formula in (2a).

(4)   Generalized Conjunction (GC) Rule:
$$[GQ1 \wedge GQ2] = \lambda Z[GQ1(Z) \wedge GQ2(Z)]$$

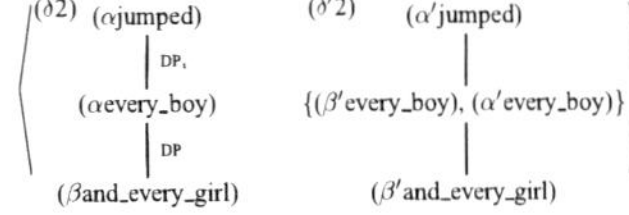

Figure 5: Derivation structures for *Every boy and every girl jumped*

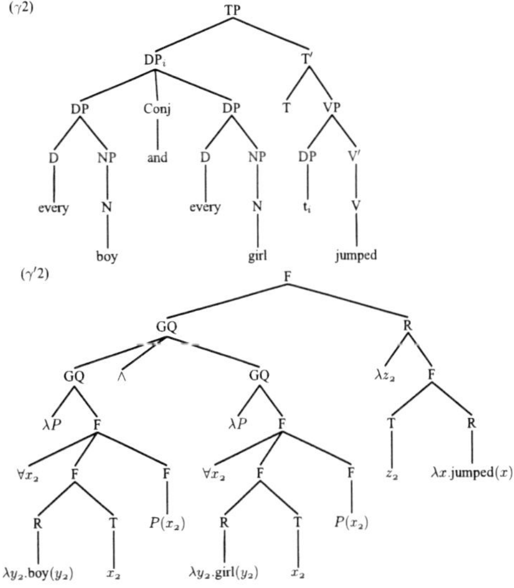

Figure 6: Derived trees for *Every boy and every girl jumped*

The new elementary trees needed for (3) are given in Figure 7. In (α'solved), the F node is specified with two links, ⓵ and ⓶. This means that scope components of two GQs will multiply adjoin to it, providing underspecified derivation structure and thus two separate semantic derived trees, predicting scope ambiguity.

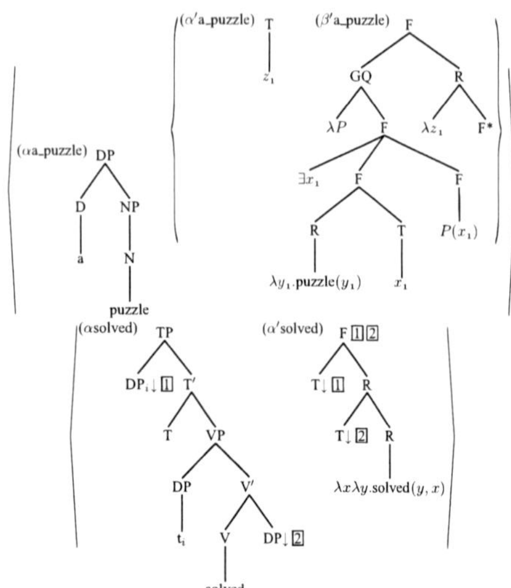

Figure 7: Elementary trees for *Every boy and every girl solved a puzzle*

The derivation structures and semantic derived trees for (3) are in Figures 8 and 9. To save space, we have reduced all the GQ nodes in the semantic derived trees and omitted the syntactic derived tree. The semantic derivation is accomplished with no additional assumptions and proceeds in the same manner as the derivation for (2) with the exception that the scope components, $(\beta'\text{every\_boy})$ and $(\beta'\text{a\_puzzle})$, may adjoin to $(\alpha'\text{solved})$ in two orders in the derived tree: the reading in (3a) is derived if $(\beta'\text{every\_boy})$ is adjoined higher than $(\beta'\text{a\_puzzle})$, as in $(\gamma'3a)$. The opposite ordering as in $(\gamma'3b)$ derives the reading in (3b).

Our analysis also handles coordination of proper names as in (5a), if they are treated as GQs.

(5)   a.   John and Mary jumped.

       b.   jumped(john) $\wedge$ jumped(mary)

The new elementary trees needed for (5a) are given in Figure 10. In syntax, (αJohn) substitutes into

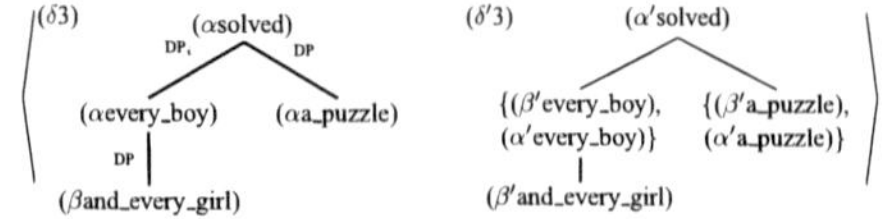

Figure 8: Derivation structures for *Every boy and every girl solved a puzzle*

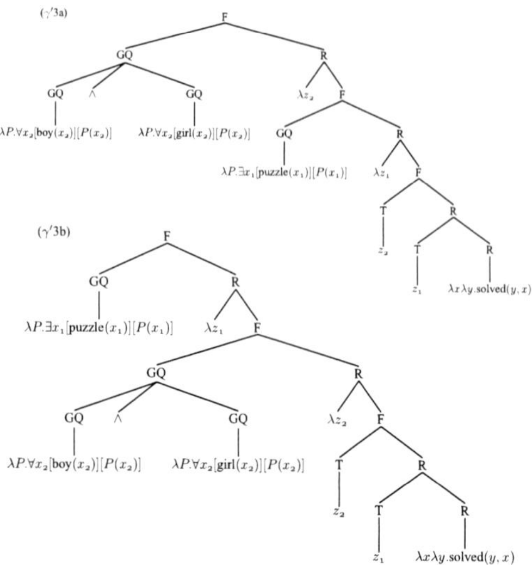

Figure 9: Semantic derived trees for *Every boy and every girl solved a puzzle*

DP_i in (αjumped) in Figure 4, and $(\beta\text{and\_Mary})$ adjoins to DP in (αJohn). In semantics, $(\beta'\text{John})$ adjoins to F in $(\alpha'\text{jumped})$, $(\alpha'\text{John})$ substitutes into T in $(\alpha'\text{jumped})$, and $(\beta'\text{and\_Mary})$ adjoins to GQ in $(\beta'\text{John})$. The application of λ-conversion and GC rule to the resulting semantic derived tree yields the formula in (5b).

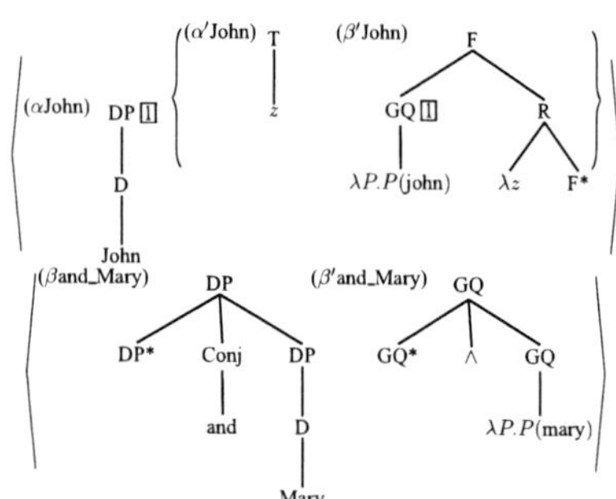

Figure 10: Elementary trees for *John and Mary jumped*

4   VP coordination

In VP coordination, one or more arguments are shared by verbal predicates. In general, shared arguments scope over the coordinator, and non-shared arguments scope under the coordinator (6)-(7). Moreover, VP coordination with multiple shared arguments displays scope ambiguity (8).

(6)   A student read every paper and summarized every book. ($\exists > \wedge > \forall$)

    a. $\exists x_1[\text{student}(x_1)][\forall x_2[\text{paper}(x_2)][\text{read}(x_1, x_2)] \wedge \forall x_2[\text{book}(x_2)][\text{summarized}(x_1, x_2)]]$

(7)   A student takes and a professor teaches every course. ($\forall > \wedge > \exists$)

    a. $\forall x_2[\text{course}(x_2)][\exists x_1[\text{student}(x_1)][\text{takes}(x_1, x_2)] \wedge \exists x_1[\text{professor}(x_1)][\text{teaches}(x_1, x_2)]]$

(8)   A student likes and takes every course. ($\exists > \forall > \wedge, \forall > \exists > \wedge$)

    a. $\exists x_1[\text{student}(x_1)][\forall x_2[\text{course}(x_2)][\text{likes}(x_1, x_2) \wedge \text{takes}(x_1, x_2)]]$

    b. $\forall x_2[\text{course}(x_2)][\exists x_1[\text{student}(x_1)][\text{likes}(x_1, x_2) \wedge \text{takes}(x_1, x_2)]]$

Figure 11 illustrates the elementary trees necessary to derive (6). We follow Sarkar and Joshi (1996) for the syntax of VP coordination: we utilize elementary trees with contraction sets and assume that their Conjoin Operation creates coordinating auxiliary trees such as (βsummarized$_{\{DP_i\}}$). In (αread$_{\{DP_i\}}$), the subject DP$_i$ node is in the contraction set, marked in the tree with a circle, and represents a shared argument. (βsummarized$_{\{DP_i\}}$), also with the subject DP$_i$ node in the contraction set, contains the coordinator. Elementary trees such as (βsummarized$_{\{DP_i\}}$) are in accordance with CETM, as coordinators are functional heads. When (βsummarized$_{\{DP_i\}}$) adjoins to (αread$_{\{DP_i\}}$), the two trees will share the node in the contraction set. As for the semantics, we propose that (αread$_{\{DP_i\}}$) is paired with (α'read$_{\{DP_i\}}$), and (βsummarized$_{\{DP_i\}}$) is paired with (β'summarized$_{\{DP_i\}}$). In (α'read$_{\{DP_i\}}$), the T node linked to the contracted DP$_i$ node is marked as contracted with a circle. Crucially, the link for the scope component of the DP$_i$ is absent on F. Instead, the scope information will be provided by the shared argument coming from the coordinating auxiliary tree. This specification will prove to be crucial for deriving proper scope relations. As usual, the non-contracted node, the object DP, has a link for the argument component on T and a link for the scope component on F. In the coordinating auxiliary tree (β'summarized$_{\{DP_i\}}$), the contracted node DP$_i$ has a link for the argument component on T, which is marked as a contracted node, and a link for the scope component

on the highest F. This ensures that the shared argument scopes over the coordinator. Moreover, the link for the scope component of the non-contracted object DP node is placed on the lower F, ensuring that it scopes below the coordinator.

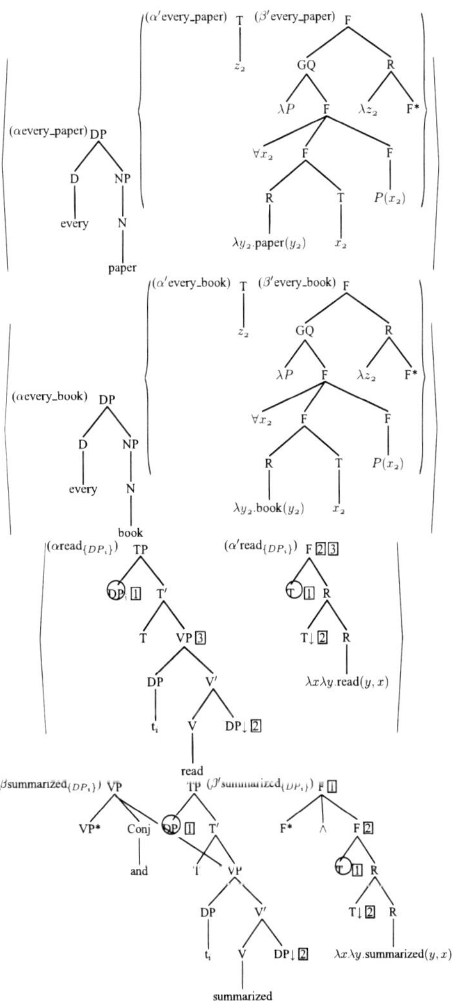

Figure 11: Elementary trees for *A student read every paper and summarized every book*

Figure 12 depicts the derivation structures for (6). These are directed graphs, as a single node is dominated by multiple nodes. In (δ6), (αa_student) substitutes into (αread$_{\{DP_i\}}$) and (βsummarized$_{\{DP_i\}}$) simultaneously at the DP$_i$ node. This produces the syntactic derived tree in (γ6) in Figure 13. In (δ'6) in Figure 12, guided by the links in syntactic and semantic elementary tree pairs, (α'a_student) substitutes into a T node in (α'read$_{\{DP_i\}}$) and (β'summarized$_{\{DP_i\}}$) simultaneously, and (β'a_student) adjoins to the root F node in (β'summarized$_{\{DP_i\}}$). This produces the semantic derived tree in (γ'6) in Figure 13. We define functional application for shared arguments as in (9). Application of λ-conversion to (γ'6) thus yields the formula in (6a).[1]

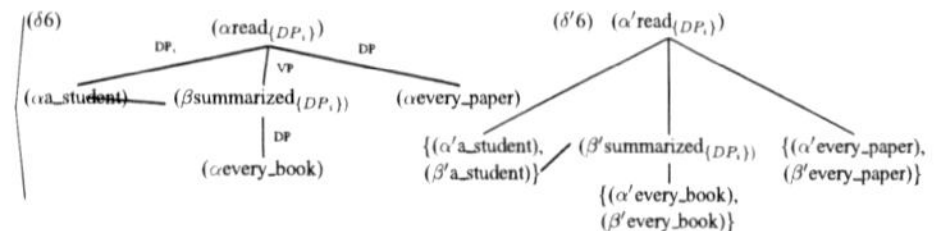

Figure 12: Derivation structures for *A student read every paper and summarized every book*

(9)   Functional application for shared arguments:
If α and β are branching nodes sharing one daughter γ, and α dominates δ and β dominates χ, and γ is in the domain of both δ and χ, $\alpha = \delta(\gamma)$ and $\beta = \chi(\gamma)$.

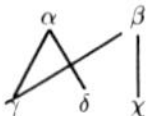

(7) is derived similarly, with the exception that the elementary trees for (7) has the object DP node in the contraction sets. These elementary trees are in Figure 14: in (αtakes$_{\{DP\}}$), the object DP node is contracted, and thus in (α'takes$_{\{DP\}}$), the link for the scope component of the DP is absent on F; in (β'teaches$_{\{DP\}}$), the scope component of the DP is placed on the root F node. In addition to these trees, a pair of elementary trees for the DP *a professor* is required, which is exactly the same as the elementary trees for *a student* in Figure 1. The derivation structures for (7) are in Figure 15.

---

[1] A second semantic derived tree is available for (6), where (β'every_paper) adjoins higher than (β'summarized), as they are multiply adjoined to the F node of (α'read). We thank an anonymous reviewer for pointing this out. We do not currently have a way to block this second derived tree. However, the formula in (i) that results from the application of λ-conversion and the GC rule to the second derived tree has the same meaning as the one in (6a) reduced from the first derived tree in (γ'6) in Figure 13. Similarly, (7) has available a second derived tree that yields the formula in (ii) which is equivalent to (7a) above.

(i) $\exists x_1[\text{student}(x_1)][\forall x_2[\text{paper}(x_2)]$
     $[\text{read}(x_1, x_2) \wedge \forall x_2[\text{book}(x_2)][\text{summarized}(x_1, x_2)]]]$

(ii) $\forall x_2[\text{course}(x_2)][\exists x_1[\text{student}(x_1)]$
     $[\text{takes}(x_1, x_2) \wedge \exists x_1[\text{professor}(x_1)][\text{teaches}(x_1, x_2)]]]$

The application of λ-conversion to (γ'7) yields the formula in (7a).

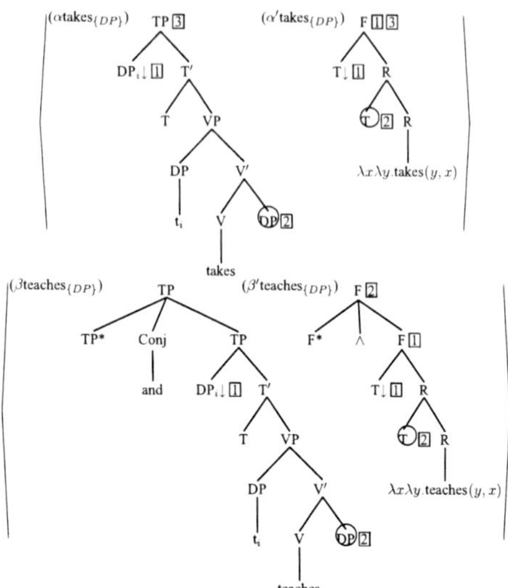

Figure 14: Elementary trees for *A student takes and a professor teaches every course*

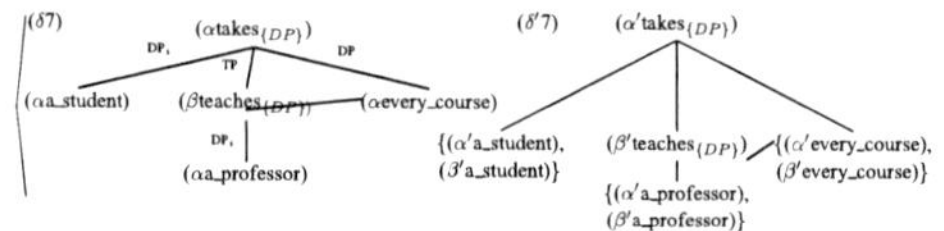

Figure 15: Derivation structures for *A student takes and a professor teaches every course*

The derivation of (8) requires elementary trees with two contracted nodes, as both subject and object are shared. These elementary trees are in Figure 16. Since both the subject DP_i and the object DP are contracted, the links for the scope components of both are absent in F in (α'likes$_{\{DP_i,DP\}}$), and placed on the root F in (β'takes$_{\{DP_i,DP\}}$). This means that the two scope components will multiply-adjoin to the F node, and as the order in which the two components adjoin is not specified, scope ambiguity is predicted. The derivation structures and the derived trees are in Figures 17 and 18. The application of λ-conversion to (γ'8a) and (γ'8b) yields the formulas in (8a) and (8b) respectively.

The derivation of sentences with both DP and VP coordination, such as *Every boy and every girl jumped and played*, follows from our analysis. In addition to the DP elementary trees

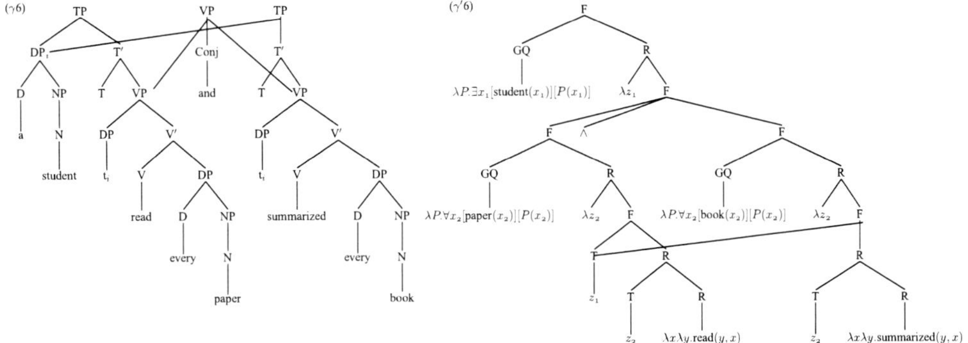

Figure 13: Derived trees for *A student read every paper and summarized every book*

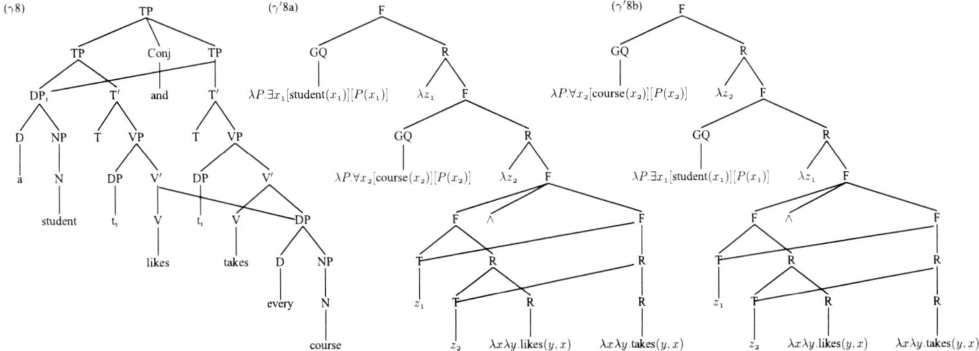

Figure 18: Derived trees for *A student likes and takes every course*

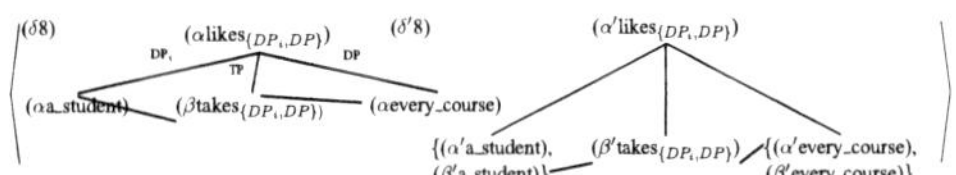

Figure 17: Derivation structures for *A student likes and takes every course*

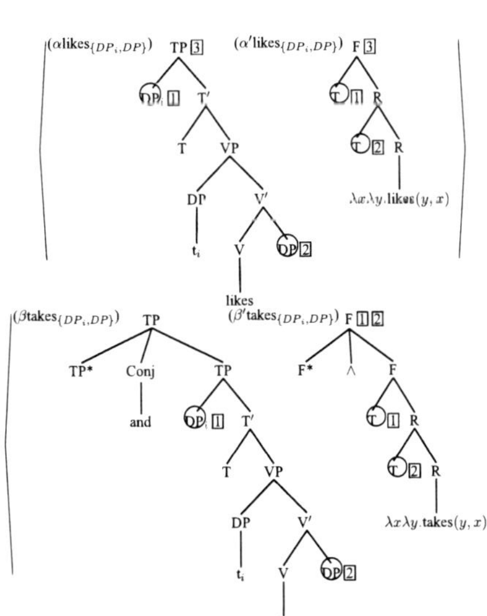

Figure 16: Elementary trees for *A student likes and takes every course*

in Figure 4, (αjumped$_{\{DP_i\}}$), (α'jumped$_{\{DP_i\}}$), (βplayed$_{\{DP_i\}}$), and (β'played$_{\{DP_i\}}$), which are intransitive variants of the verb elementary trees in Figure 11, are necessary. In syntax, (βand_every_girl) adjoins to DP in (αevery_boy), (βplayed$_{\{DP_i\}}$) adjoins to VP in (αjumped$_{\{DP_i\}}$), and (αevery_boy) substitutes simultaneously into (αjumped$_{\{DP_i\}}$) and (βplayed$_{\{DP_i\}}$) at DP$_i$. In semantics, (β'and_every_girl) adjoins to GQ in (β'every_boy), which adjoins to the root F in (β'played$_{\{DP_i\}}$), and (α'every_boy) substitutes simultaneously into T in (α'jumped$_{\{DP_i\}}$) and T in (β'played$_{\{DP_i\}}$), deriving the formula in (10)

(10) $\forall x_2[\text{boy}(x_2)][\text{jumped}(x_2) \wedge \text{played}(x_2)] \wedge$
      $\forall x_2[\text{girl}(x_2)][\text{jumped}(x_2) \wedge \text{played}(x_2)]$

5   Conclusion and future work

We have shown that our STAG analysis of DP/VP coordination accounts for the scope interaction between the coordinator and quantified DPs. Our analysis utilizes GQs, appropriate placement of links between the syntactic and semantic elementary tree pairs, and parallel syntactic and semantic derivations, using substitution and adjoining in both syntax and semantics.

Potential counterexamples to our analysis of VP coordination are those where the coordinator has scope over the shared argument, as in (11). However, world knowledge or discourse context is necessary to achieve such a reading, and we therefore suspect that an additional operation such as ellipsis may be required to properly account for them.

(11)   A woman discovered radium but [a man invented the electric light bulb and developed the theory of relativity]. (Winter, 2000)

Our analysis of DP/VP coordination does not account for all the scope possibilities of phrasal *either...or*, as a reviewer points out: the $\vee > \forall > \exists$ reading in (12a), and the $\vee > \forall$ reading in (12b). One possible analysis is that *either* is interpretable from a displaced position in the beginning of the sentence. If so, then we can adopt the ellipsis analysis of Schwarz (1999) that a displaced *either* marks the left boundary of an ellipsis site.

(12)   a.   Every boy met either a baseball player or a soccer player.

       b.   Every boy will either go to a baseball game or stay at home.

Further, our analysis does not handle the non-distributive reading associated with coordinated DPs as in (13a), as pointed out by a reviewer.

(13)   a.   Every boy and every girl met/gathered.

       b.   The boys met/gathered.

Non-distributivity however is not restricted to coordinated DPs, but occurs with plural DPs in general, as in (13b). We thus speculate that *and* in a non-distributive DP should be defined as a function that turns the coordinated DP to a plural object. All these issues are left for future research.

Acknowledgment

We thank the three anonymous reviewers of TAG+9 for their insightful comments. All remaining errors are ours. This work was supported by NSERC RGPIN/341442 to Han.

References

Babko-Malaya, Olga. 2004. LTAG semantics of focus. In *Proceedings of TAG+7*, pages 1–8, Vancouver, Canada.

Banik, Eva. 2004. Semantics of VP coordination in LTAG. In *Proceedings of TAG+7*, pages 118–125, Vancouver, Canada.

Barwise, Jon and Robin Cooper. 1981. Generalized quantifiers and natural language. *L&P*, 4:159–219.

Frank, Robert. 2002. *Phrase Structure Composition and Syntactic Dependencies*. MIT Press, Cambridge, MA.

Han, Chung-hye. 2007. Pied-piping in relative clauses: Syntax and compositional semantics using Synchronous Tree Adjoining Grammar. *Research on Language and Computation*, 5(4):457–479.

Kallmeyer, Laura and Maribel Romero. 2008. Scope and situation binding in LTAG using semantic unification. *Research on Language and Computation*, 6(1):3–52.

Nesson, Rebecca and Stuart M. Shieber. 2006. Simpler TAG Semantics through Synchronization. In *Proceedings of the 11th Conference on Formal Grammar*, Malaga, Spain. CSLI.

Nesson, Rebecca and Stuart Shieber. 2007. Extraction phenomena in Synchronous TAG syntax and semantics. In Wu, Dekai and David Chiang, editors, *Proceedings of the Workshop on Syntax and Structure in Statistical Translation*, Rochester, New York.

Sarkar, Anoop and Aravind Joshi. 1996. Coordination in Tree Adjoining Grammars: formalization and implementation. In *Proceedings of COLING '96*, pages 610–615, Copenhagen.

Schabes, Yves and Stuart M. Shieber. 1994. An Alternative Conception of Tree-Adjoining Derivation. *Computational Linguistics*, pages 167–176.

Schwarz, Bernhard. 1999. On the syntax of *either...or*. *NLLT*, 17(2):339–370.

Shieber, Stuart and Yves Schabes. 1990. Synchronous Tree Adjoining Grammars. In *Proceedings of COLING '90*, Helsinki, Finland.

Winter, Yoad. 2000. On some scopal asymmetries of coordination. In Bennis et al, editors, *Proceedings of the KNAW conference on Interface Strategies*.

Non-local scrambling: the equivalence of TAG and CCG revisited

Julia Hockenmaier and Peter Young
Department of Computer Science, University of Illinois,
201 N. Goodwin Ave., Urbana-Champaign, 61801 IL, USA
{juliahmr,pyoung2}@cs.uiuc.edu

Abstract

It is well known that standard TAG cannot deal with certain instances of long-distance scrambling in German (Rambow, 1994). That CCG can deal with many instances of non-local scrambling in languages such as Turkish has previously been observed (e.g. by Hoffman (1995a) and Baldridge (2002)). We show here that CCG can derive German scrambling cases which are problematic for TAG, and give CCG analyses for other German constructions that require more expressive power than TAG provides. Such analyses raise the question of the linguistic significance of the TAG-CCG equivalence. We revisit the original equivalence proof, and show that a careful examination of the translation of CCG and TAG into Indexed Grammar reveals that the IG which is strongly equivalent to CCG can generate dependencies which the corresponding IG obtained from an LTAG cannot generate.

1 Introduction

Vijay-Shanker and Weir (1994) proved that Tree-Adjoining Grammar (TAG (Joshi and Schabes, 1997)), Combinatory Categorial Grammar (CCG (Steedman, 2000)) and Linear Indexed Grammars (LIG, (Gazdar, 1988)) are weakly equivalent, i.e. can generate the same sets of strings. All of these grammars can generate the languages $\{a^n b^n c^n d^n\}$ (which does not correspond to any known construction in natural language), and $\{a^n b^n\}$ with cross-serial dependencies (i.e.

$a_1...a_n b_1...b_n$), corresponding to the cross-serial dependencies that arise in Dutch (Bresnan et al., 1982) and Swiss German (Shieber, 1985).

Although this result has important algorithmic consequences (Vijay-Shanker and Weir, 1993), it is easy to overestimate its linguistic relevance. Weak equivalence does, of course, not necessarily imply that two formalisms are capable of recovering the same set of dependencies between the elements of a string. Since the notion of strong equivalence is often hard to define, strong equivalene proofs are rarely found in the literature. But examples of structures that can only be analyzed in one formalism can provide insight into where their strong generative capacities differ.

2 Combinatory Categorial Grammar

In addition to function application ($>$ and $<$), CCG allows the combinatory rules of (generalized) function composition ($\mathbf{B}_n$), which allows a functor $X|Y$ to compose with another functor $Y|Z_1...Z_n$ to form a category $X|Z_1...Z_n$, and type-raising $\mathbf{T}$, which allows a category X to be transformed into a category $T/(T\backslash X)$ or $T\backslash(T/X)$:

$$
\begin{array}{llll}
X/Y & Y & \Rightarrow_> & X \\
Y & X\backslash Y & \Rightarrow_< & X \\
X/Y & Y/Z_1|....Z_n & \Rightarrow_{>\mathbf{B}_n} & X/Z_1...Z_n \\
Y\backslash Z_1...Z_n & X\backslash Y & \Rightarrow_{<\mathbf{B}_n} & X\backslash Z_1....Z_n \\
X/Y & Y\backslash Z_1...Z_n & \Rightarrow_{>\mathbf{B}_{\times n}} & X\backslash Z_1..Z_n \\
Y/Z_1...Z_n & X\backslash Y & \Rightarrow_{<\mathbf{B}_{\times n}} & X/Z_1..Z_n \\
X & & \Rightarrow_{>\mathbf{T}} & T/(T\backslash X) \\
X & & \Rightarrow_{<\mathbf{T}} & T\backslash(T/X)
\end{array}
$$

Steedman (2000) furthermore uses a unary topicalization rule, which is only allowed to be applied to a sentence-initial constituent:

$$
X \quad \Rightarrow_{>\mathbf{T}} \quad T/(T/X)
$$

Proceedings of The Ninth International Workshop on Tree Adjoining Grammars and Related Formalisms
Tübingen, Germany. June 6-8, 2008.

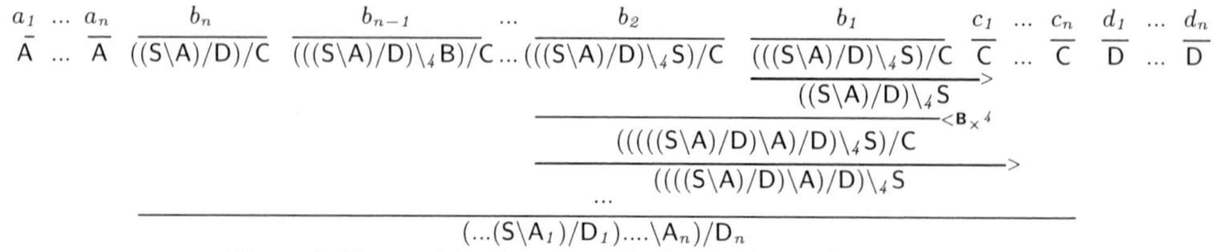

$$\frac{a_1}{\mathsf{A}} \; \dots \; \frac{a_n}{\mathsf{A}} \quad \frac{b_n}{((\mathsf{S}\backslash\mathsf{A})/\mathsf{D})/\mathsf{C}} \quad \frac{b_{n-1}}{(((\mathsf{S}\backslash\mathsf{A})/\mathsf{D})\backslash_4\mathsf{B})/\mathsf{C}} \dots \frac{b_2}{(((\mathsf{S}\backslash\mathsf{A})/\mathsf{D})\backslash_4\mathsf{S})/\mathsf{C}} \quad \cfrac{\cfrac{b_1}{(((\mathsf{S}\backslash\mathsf{A})/\mathsf{D})\backslash_4\mathsf{S})/\mathsf{C}} \quad \frac{c_1}{\mathsf{C}} \; \dots \; \frac{c_n}{\mathsf{C}}}{\dfrac{((\mathsf{S}\backslash\mathsf{A})/\mathsf{D})\backslash_4\mathsf{S}}{} } \qquad \frac{d_1}{\mathsf{D}} \; \dots \; \frac{d_n}{\mathsf{D}}$$

$$\cfrac{(((((\mathsf{S}\backslash\mathsf{A})/\mathsf{D})\backslash\mathsf{A})/\mathsf{D})\backslash_4\mathsf{S})/\mathsf{C}}{\cfrac{((((\mathsf{S}\backslash\mathsf{A})/\mathsf{D})\backslash\mathsf{A})/\mathsf{D})\backslash_4\mathsf{S}}{\dots}}{}^{<\mathbf{B}_\times{}^4}$$

$$(\dots(\mathsf{S}\backslash\mathsf{A}_1)/\mathsf{D}_1)\dots\backslash\mathsf{A}_n)/\mathsf{D}_n$$

Figure 1: Type-raising is not required to derive $a^n b^n c^n d^n$ in CCG.

Both the maximal arity n up to which generalized composition $\mathbf{B}_n$ is allowed and the maximal arity k of the variable T that results from type-raising are assumed to be bounded (typically to the maximal arity of lexical categories required by a language (Steedman, 2000)). These bounds are known to be important: Weir (1988) shows that if there is no bound on generalized composition, CCG can generate $\{a^n a'^m b^n c^n b'^m c'^m d'^m d^n\}$, which cannot be generated by a TAG or LIG, and Hoffman (Hoffman, 1993) shows that a CCG with $\mathbf{B}_\times{}^2$ and no bounds on the arity of type-raised categories can derive $a^n b^n c^n d^n e^n$, which also cannot be generated by a TAG or LIG.

In English, type-raising and composition allow derivations of *wh*-extraction, right node raising and argument cluster coordination in which the verbs involved have the same lexical categories as in standard sentences that do not involve non-local dependencies. In TAG, these constructions either require either additional elementary trees, or non-standard coordination rules (Sarkar and Joshi, 1996) that were not taken into account in the original equivalence proof. On the other hand, the Dutch cross-serial dependencies (without extraction or coordination[1]) and the weakly equivalent $a^n b^n$, can easily by a CCG with bounded generalized composition and without type-raising. In fact, Vijay-Shanker and Weir (1994) show that a TAG can be translated into a CCG that uses only function application and composition, but does not require type-raising.

Deriving $a^n b^n c^n d^n$ The language $a^n b^n c^n d^n$ can be generated by a TAG with one auxiliary tree β_1 with yield a_bc_d (where the _'s indicate where β_1 can be adjoined again), resulting in strings of the form $a^{1..n}\_b^{n..1} c^{1..n}\_d^{n...1}$ (Joshi

and Schabes, 1997). Weir (1988) gives a CCG for this language, but since his grammar assumes that the string contains n empty strings ϵ with lexical categories, we give in Figure 2 a different analysis. This grammar assigns the lexical category $(\mathsf{S}\backslash\mathsf{A})/\mathsf{D})\backslash_4\mathsf{S})/\mathsf{C}$ to any but the leftmost b, where we have used $\backslash_4$ to indicate a modality which requires backward crossed 4-ary composition.[2]

3 CCG for a fragment of German

We follow Steedman (2000) and Hockenmaier (2006) in most of our basic analyses. German has three different word orders that depend on the clause type. Main clauses (3) are verb-second. Imperatives and questions are verb-initial (4). If a modifier or one of the objects is moved to the front, the word order becomes verb-initial (4). Subordinate and relative clauses are verb-final (5):

(3)   a.   *Peter gibt ihm ein Buch.*
          Peter gives him a book.
      b.   *Ein Buch gibt Peter ihm.*
      c.   *dann gibt Peter ihm ein Buch.*
(4)   a.   *Gibt Peter ihm ein Buch?*
      b.   *Gib ihm ein Buch!*
(5)   a.   *dass Peter ihm das Buch gibt.*
      b.   *das Buch, das Peter ihm gibt.*

We assume that the underlying word order in main clauses is always verb-initial, and that the sentetnce-initial subject is in fact topicalized. We use the features S_{v1} and S_{vfin} to distinguish verbs in main and subordinate clauses. Main clauses have the feature S_{dcl}, requiring either a sentential modifier with category $\mathsf{S}_{dcl}/\mathsf{S}_{v1}$, a topicalized subject ($\mathsf{S}_{dcl}/(\mathsf{S}_{v1}/\mathsf{NP}_n)$), or a type-raised argument ($\mathsf{S}_{dcl}/(\mathsf{S}_{v1}\backslash\mathsf{X})$), where X can be any argument category, such as a noun phrase, prepositional phrase, or a non-finite VP.

---

[1] Steedman (2000, p.212) points out that generalized coordination would be required for the coordination of unboundedly long noun or verb clusters, which would require the full generative capacity of Indexed Grammars.

[2] In multimodal versions of CCG (Baldridge, 2002), modalities that are this specific are not typically assumed, but here this is required in order to avoid overgeneration. Weir (1988) gives similar constraints in his grammar.

Proceedings of The Ninth International Workshop on Tree Adjoining Grammars and Related Formalisms
Tübingen, Germany. June 6-8, 2008.

(1) **Case 1: Two verbs with two NP arguments each**

    a. dass der Detektiv dem Klienten **den Verdächtigen des Verbrechens zu überführen** versprochen hat.

    b. dass **des Verbrechens** der Detektiv **den Verdächtigen** dem Klienten **zu überführen** versprochen hat.

(2) **Case 2: N verbs with one NP argument each**

    a. **Dieses Buch₁** hat₂ **den Kindern₃** *niemand₄* **zu geben₅** *versucht₆*.
       this book   has   to-the-children nobody   to give   tried.

       Nobody has tried to give this book to the children.

    b. dass *der Rat*   *dem Pfarrer* die Menschen **der Opfer gedenken**   zu lassen *versprochen* hat.
       that the council the priest   the people   the victims commemorate let   promised   has.

       that the council has promised the priest to let the citizens commemorate the victims.

    c. dass die Menschen **der Opfer** *dem Pfarrer der Rat*   **gedenken**   zu lassen *versprochen* hat.
       that the people   the victims the priest   the council commemorate let   promised   has.

       that the council has promised the priest to let the citizens commemorate the victims.

Figure 2: Non-local scrambling examples (from Rambow (1994) and Becker *et al.* (1991).

The treatment of subjects Unlike Hockenmaier (2006), we treat subjects as arguments of main verb, and assume auxiliaries are categories of the form S/S and $S\backslash S$ (with appropriate features to avoid overgeneration). Evidence for this analysis (which is similar to the standard analysis of subjects in TAG) comes from coordinations that would otherwise not be derivable (see Figure 7).

Local Scrambling In the so-called "Mittelfeld" all orders of arguments and adjuncts are potentially possible. In the following example, all 5! permutations are grammatical (Rambow, 1994):

(6) *dass [eine Firma] [meinem Onkel] [die Möbel] [vor drei Tagen] [ohne Voranmeldung] zugestellt hat.*
that [a company] [to my uncle] [the furniture] [three days ago] [without notice] delivered has.

Such local scrambling cases can easily be derived with generalized composition and type-raising. However, argument-cluster coordinations are possible with all subsets of arguments:

(7) Dir   gibt Maria den Ball und Peter das Buch.
to-you gives Maria the ball and Peter the book.

    To you, Maria gives the ball and Peter the book.
    Dir gibt den Ball Maria und das Buch Peter.

(8) Das Buch gibt Maria dir und Peter mir.
Das Buch gibt dir Maria und mir Peter.

(9) Peter gibt mir das Buch und dir den Ball.
Peter gibt das Buch mir und den Ball dir.

Like in a TAG analysis of local scrambling, we will therefore assume separate lexical categories for each possible permutation[3].

---

[3]To avoid this combinatorial explosion of the lexicon, extensions of CCG have been proposed (Hoffman, 1995b; Baldridge, 2002); albeit, at least in Hoffman's case, these raise its generative capacity beyond that of standard CCG

Partial VP fronting requires an analysis in which the remnant arguments in the Mittelfeld for a constituent, similar to argument cluster coordination (here $TV_{v1} = (S_{v1}\backslash NP_n)\backslash NP_a$):

$$
\frac{\underset{S_{dcl}/TV_{v1}}{\text{Gelesen}}\ \underset{S_{v1}/S_{pt}}{\text{hat}}\ \frac{\frac{\underset{NP_n}{\text{Peter}}}{S/(S\backslash NP_n)}{}^{>T}\ \frac{\underset{NP_a}{\text{das Buch}}}{(S\backslash NP)/((S\backslash NP)\backslash NP_a)}{}^{>T}}{S/((S\backslash NP_n)\backslash NP_a)}{}^{>B}}{(S_{v1}\backslash NP_n)\backslash NP_a}{}^{>B}
$$

Other constructions If verbs like *versprechen (promise)* have lexical categories of the form $((S\backslash NP_n)\backslash NP_d)/(S[zu]\backslash NP_n)$, with a suitable modality on the $S[zu]\backslash NP$ that requires composition, VP extraposition and the so-called Third construction can easily be derived (figure 7).

4 TAG and non-local scrambling

4.1 Non-local scrambling

Non-local scrambling, a construction in which the argument of an (arbitrarily deeply) embedded verb is moved to the matrix clause, occurs commonly in languages such as German. Becker *et al.* and Rambow (1994) show that this can result in dependencies that a standard TAG cannot capture. For instance, in sentence 2a), *das Buch* (the book), the direct object of *geben* (give), appears in the matrix clause headed by *versucht* (tried). This sentence has six segments with dependencies (1,5), (2,6), (3,5) and (4,6). It contains a discontinuous constituent 1-3-5 (*zu geben* and its objects), corresponding to an elementary tree anchored in *(zu) geben*. But in TAG, discontinuous constituents can only be created by wrapping adjunction, resulting in a string consisting of five segments (Figure 3).

Figure 3: The dependencies in example (2a) left, and the dependencies that TAG adjunction can express (right). Blue segments are the yield of the tree that has been adjoined into the red tree.

Becker *et al.* (1991) consider two different cases which they show cannot be captured by a TAG:

1) Two verbs and four NPs TAG cannot generate $\{\sigma(NP_1{}^1, NP^2{}_1, NP^1{}_2, NP^2{}_2)V_1V_2\}$ which consists of any permutation of the two NP arguments of two verbs followed by the verbs themselves. This arises when a control verb such as *versprechen (promise)* takes a ditransitive complement such as *überführen (to prove X guilty of Y)* (see examples (1)).

2) k verbs and k NPs Becker *et al.* (1991) also consider the more general case where N verbs take one NP object each, resulting in the language $\{\sigma(NP_1, ..., NP_n)V_1...V_n\}$, and show that this not a tree-adjoining language (see examples (2)).

Based on a this observation, Becker *et al.* (1992) provide a proof that non-local scrambling of the k arguments of k verbs cannot in general be captured by Linear Context-Free Rewriting Systems, a class of formalisms to which CCG also belongs. It is, however, doubtable that an analysis of the general case is required for natural language. Joshi *et al.* (2000) show that tree-local multicomponent Tree-Adjoining Grammar (Weir, 1988), a variant of TAG that is weakly equivalent to standard TAG (and hence CCG) can deal with a limited range of scrambling cases.

5 CCG analyses for German scrambling

5.1 Non-local scrambling

1) Two verbs and four NPs The two verbs combine to a category of the form $(((S\backslash NP_1)\backslash NP'_1)\backslash NP_2)\backslash NP'_2$, where the two most embedded NP_1s are arguments of the matrix verb and the two NP'_2s are arguments of the embedded verb. With $\mathbf{B}_\times{}^2$ and two lexical categories for the matrix verb (or $\mathbf{B}_\times{}^3$), all permutation orders can be derived.

2) k verbs and k NPs Under an analysis where the verb cluster forms one constituent, a category $(...(S\backslash NP_1)\backslash....)\backslash NP_k$ is obtained. We will consider this general case in more detail below, but as can be seen from Figure 4, which gives a derivation for example 2a that cannot be derived with a standard TAG, CCG can derive more cases than TAG.

6 The equivalence of TAG and CCG revisited

Vijay-Shanker and Weir (1994) show the (weak) equivalence of TAG and CCG via a translation to head grammars and linear indexed grammars (LIG, (Gazdar, 1988)). In an indexed grammar, nonterminals are associated with stacks of indices. In a LIG, the stack associated with the LHS symbol X is copied to one of the RHS nonterminals Y, the top symbol can be popped off the stack of X, or a new symbol can be pushed onto the copy of the stack that is passed down to Y:[4]

$$\begin{aligned} \textbf{copy:} \quad & X[\alpha] \rightarrow ...Y[\alpha]... \\ \textbf{pop:} \quad & X[\alpha c] \rightarrow ...Y[\alpha]... \\ \textbf{push:} \quad & X[\alpha] \rightarrow ...Y[\alpha c]... \end{aligned}$$

We show that translating both LTAG and CCG directly into strongly equivalent indexed grammars which capture all dependencies in the extended domain of locality via nonterminal stacks reveals that CCG requires a LIG with registers which is not strongly equivalent to any LIG that can be obtained from a LTAG.

6.1 TAG as a LIG

We define a function $\mathbf{f}$ which translates a TAG into a strongly equivalent LIG that captures all the dependencies represented within the elementary trees of the TAG via stack features (fig. 3). This function translates every local tree $X \rightarrow Y_1..Y_n$ of an elementary tree into one LIG production rule $\mathbf{f}(X) \rightarrow \mathbf{f}(Y_1)...\mathbf{f}(Y_n)$, and adds one push and one pop rule for each adjunction node. Substitution nodes and root nodes of initial trees labeled with nonterminal X are translated into a nonterminal $\mathbf{f}(X) = X[]$ with an empty stack. In order to avoid overgeneration, every internal (non-root)

---

[4]We will use *push_n* and *pop_n* rules which push or pop n top symbols onto or off the stack as convenient abbreviations of corresponding n operations with appropriately unique nonterminals Y on the RHS.

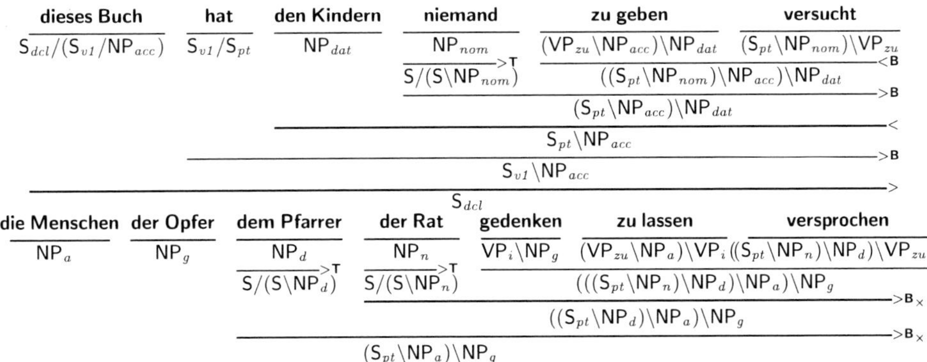

Figure 4: CCG derivations for examples (2a) and (2c) (here, VP=S\NP)

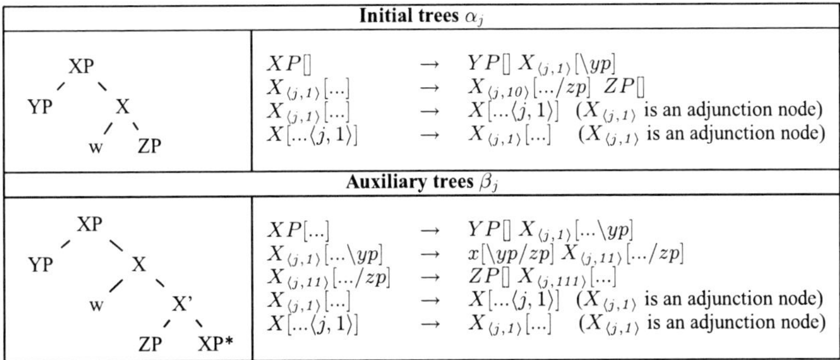

Figure 5: A toy example of how TAG elementary trees are translated to LIG. The directionality of the arguments is indicated here in categorial-grammar-like notation.

node labeled X on the head path of an elementary tree is translated into a unique nonterminal $X_{\langle i,GA \rangle}$, where the index i identifies the original elementary tree and GA is the Gorn address of the corresponding node in this tree.

We assume that all nodes in an initial tree either lie on the head path from root to the single lexical anchor or are immediate descendants of a node on the head path, and that all nodes which are not on the head path are dependents of the lexical anchor. In the resulting LIG, every dependency represented by an initial tree then corresponds to a *push* operation, resulting in the lexical anchor being associated with a preterminal whose stack corresponds to its subcategorization frame:

Generating a dependent Z (initial tree):
$X[...] \rightarrow Z[] \ Y[...c]$
Generating the anchor w of an initial tree:
$X[\alpha] \rightarrow w$

Root nodes of auxiliary trees are translated into nonterminals $X[...]$ with a stack variable. This stack is passed through the productions that correspond to the auxiliary tree until it reaches the corresponding foot node, which is also translated into the same nonterminal $X[...]$ with a stack variable. The dependencies within the auxiliary tree correspond to indices which are pushed onto and popped off this stack. Every auxiliary tree defines n dependencies where the dependents have scope over the lexical anchor and m dependencies where the lexical anchor has scope over the dependents. Every dependent Y_i that has scope over the lexical anchor is generated by a rule which pushes a symbol y_i onto the stack. The anchor is generated by a rule which pops the top n elements off the stack and pushes m new elements onto the stack. These m elements are popped off the stack by the rules which generate the m dependents that have scope below the anchor. Therefore, the stack associated with the translation of the foot node is identical to the stack of the root node. Dependencies represented by auxiliary trees correspond to push operations if the dependent has scope over the lexical anchor and to pop operations if the lexical anchor has scope over the dependent. The lexical anchor of a preterminal with arguments α_n that have scope over it and β_m arguments that have scope below it is associated with a preterminal $t[\alpha_n]$, whereas the arguments β_m that appear below it are pushed onto the stack when the lexical anchor is generated:

> Generating a dependent Y with scope
> *over* the anchor (auxiliary tree):
> $X[...] \quad \rightarrow \quad Z[] \ Y[...c]$
> Generating a dependent Y with scope
> *below* the anchor (auxiliary tree):
> $X[...c] \quad \rightarrow \quad Z[] \ Y[...]$

Every such preterminal $t[\alpha_n]$ associated with the lexical anchor of an auxiliary tree is uniquely generated by a rule (corresponding to $n + m$ LIG *pop* and *push* productions) of the following form:

> Generating the preterminal
> for the anchor of an auxiliary tree
> $X[...\alpha_n] \quad \rightarrow \quad t[\alpha_n] \ Y[...\beta_m]$

where α_n corresponds to all arguments that have been pushed onto the stack by the rules corresponding to the original auxiliary tree. Every adjunction node requires two additional unary rules which push and pop a node identifier:

> **push:** $\quad X_{\langle i, GA\rangle}[...] \quad \rightarrow X[...\langle i, GA\rangle]$
> **pop:** $\quad X[...\langle i, GA\rangle] \quad \rightarrow X_{\langle i, GA\rangle}[...]$

6.2 CCG as a LIG with $pop_{n,m}$

When we describe CCGs as LIGs, *Categories c* consist of a *target t* and a *stack* α: $c = t : [\alpha]$. *Stacks* $[\alpha]$ are lists of categories: $\alpha \in c^i$, with $i \geq 0$ and $|\alpha| = i$. We will write α_i for any α with length $|\alpha| = i$, and $\alpha_0 = \epsilon$. *Target categories t* are drawn from a finite set of atomic categories, $t \in \mathcal{C}_{target} = \{S, NP, PP, ...\}$, with a designated start symbol $S \in \mathcal{C}_{target}$. Ignoring order restrictions, the combinatory rules can then be written as in figure 6. Type-raised categories are not allowed to be type-raised again, and the arity of $t : [\alpha]$, $m = |\alpha|$, is typically limited to

the maximal arity of lexical categories. In analyses of constructions involving non-local dependencies (including scrambling), type-raising and composition are typically applied in lockstep. If the primary category in (generalized) composition $\mathbf{B}_n$ is type-raised (with the arity of T=m), the result can be viewed as a single operation $pop_{n,m}$, which allows the top $n + 1$th symbol of a stack of size $m + 1 + n$ to be popped off the stack (Fig. 6):

Typeraising + composition :
$$X/(X\backslash Y) \quad (X\backslash Y)|Z_1...Z_n$$
$$\overline{\qquad\qquad\qquad\qquad} >\mathbf{B}^n$$
$$X|Z_1...Z_n$$

$\mathbf{pop}_{n,m}$:
$$t:[\alpha_m \ t:[\alpha_m c]] \quad t:[\alpha_m c \beta_n]$$
$$\overline{\qquad\qquad\qquad\qquad} >\mathbf{B}^n$$
$$t:[\alpha_m \beta_n]$$

The effect of $pop_{n,m}$ Bounds n on composition $\mathbf{B}_n$ and m on type-raising in CCG correspond thus to a LIG that allows all $pop_{i,j}$ operations for $i \leq n$ and $j \leq m$. Given a category $t : [c_1...c_{n+m+1}]$, a standard LIG could pop the c_is only in the reverse order $c_{n+m+1}...c_1$, whereas a LIG with $pop_{n,m}$ could also pop off c_{m+1} as the first symbol. In general, if n and m are the assumed bounds on composition and type-raising, any argument c_k with $i \leq k \leq j$ for $i = |\alpha| - n$ and $j = m + 1$ can be popped of a stack α with length $|\alpha| \leq n+m+1$, generating considerably more possible strings.

7   Conclusion

By translating both CCG and LTAG into strongly equivalent Indexed Grammars, we show that CCG's strong generative capacity exceeds that of TAG in a limited way, because the CCG-IG can pop symbols off the inside of the stack when the stack size does not exceed a small finite limit. This allows CCG to handle certain scrambling cases which cannot be analyzed by a TAG. We conjecture that this effect could be captured by a linear indexed grammar with a finite number of registers where stack symbols can be stored. The LIG obtained from LTAG does not allow such operations, and is therefore somewhat less expressive. Similar to Joshi *et al.* (2000), we conjecture furthermore that the limit on the stack size, albeit small, may be close to what is needed for the cases for which reliable grammaticality judgments can be obtained.

Application	Generalized Composition $\mathbf{B}_n$	Type-raising $\mathbf{T}$	Type-raising + Composition
$\dfrac{X/Y \quad Y}{X} >$	$\dfrac{X/Y \quad Y\lvert Z_1\rvert...\lvert Z_n}{X\lvert Z_1\rvert...Z_n} > \mathbf{B}$	$\dfrac{X}{T/(T\backslash X)} > \mathbf{T}$	$\dfrac{X/(X\backslash Y) \quad (X\backslash Y)\lvert Z_1...Z_n}{X\lvert Z_1...Z_n} > \mathbf{B}^n$
$\dfrac{t:[\alpha u:[\gamma]] \quad u:[\gamma]}{t:[\alpha]} >$	$\dfrac{t:[\alpha u:[\gamma]] \quad u:[\gamma\beta_n]}{t:[\alpha\beta_n]} > \mathbf{B}^n$	$\dfrac{c}{t:[\alpha_m t:[\alpha_m c]]} > \mathbf{T}$	$\dfrac{t:[\alpha_m t:[\alpha_m c]] \quad t:[\alpha_m c\beta_n]}{t:[\alpha_m\beta_n]} > \mathbf{B}^n$

Figure 6: CCG's combinatory rules translated to Indexed Grammar. Greek lowercase letters α, β indicate strings of stack variables. Indices β_n and α_m indicate the length of α or β. Both typeraising and composition impose limits on β_n and α_m.

References

Baldridge, Jason. 2002. *Lexically Specified Derivational Control in Combinatory Categorial Grammar*. Ph.D. thesis, School of Informatics, University of Edinburgh.

Becker, Tilman, Aravind K Joshi, and Owen Rambow. 1991. Long-distance scrambling and Tree Adjoining Grammars. In *Proceedings of the Fifth Conference of the European Chapter of the Association for Computational Linguistics*, pages 21–26, Berlin, Germany.

Becker, Tilman, Owen Rambow, and Michael Niv. 1992. The derivational generative power of formal systems or scrambling is beyond LCFRS. Technical report, IRCS, University of Pennsylvania.

Bresnan, Joan W., Ronald M. Kaplan, Stanley Peters, and Annie Zaenen. 1982. Cross-serial dependencies in Dutch. *Linguistic Inquiry*, 13:613–636.

Gazdar, Gerald. 1988. Applicability of indexed grammars to natural languages. In Reyle, Uwe and Christian Rohrer, editors, *Natural Language Parsing and Linguistic Theories*, pages 69–94. Reidel, Dordrecht.

Hockenmaier, Julia. 2006. Creating a CCGbank and a wide-coverage CCG lexicon for German. In *Proceedings of the 21st International Conference on Computational Linguistics and 44th Annual Meeting of the Association for Computational Linguistics*, pages 505–512, Sydney, Australia, July.

Hoffman, Beryl. 1993. The formal consequence of using variables in CCG categories. In *Proceedings of the 31st Annual Meeting of the Association for Computational Linguistics*, pages 298–300, Palo Alto, Calif. Morgan Kaufmann.

Hoffman, Beryl. 1995a. *Computational Analysis of the Syntax and Interpretation of 'Free' Word-order in Turkish*. Ph.D. thesis, University of Pennsylvania. IRCS Report 95-17.

Hoffman, Beryl. 1995b. Integrating free word order syntax and information structure. In *Proceedings of the Seventh Conference of the European Chapter of the Association for Computational Linguistics*, pages 245–252, Dublin, March.

Joshi, Aravind K. and Yves Schabes. 1997. Tree-adjoining grammars. In Rozenberg, G. and A. Salomaa, editors, *Handbook of Formal Languages*, volume 3, pages 69–124. Springer, Berlin, New York.

Joshi, Aravind K., Tilman Becker, and Owen Rambow. 2000. Complexity of scrambling: A new twist to the competence-performance distinction. In Abeillé, Anne and Owen Rambow, editors, *Tree-Adjoining Grammars*, pages 167–181. CSLI.

Rambow, Owen. 1994. *Formal and Computational Aspects of Natural Language Syntax*. Ph.D. thesis, University of Pennsylvania, Philadelphia PA.

Sarkar, Anoop and Aravind Joshi. 1996. Coordination in Tree Adjoining Grammars: Formalization and implementation. In *COLING96: Proceedings of the 16th International Conference on Computational Linguistics*, pages 610–615, Copenhagen, August.

Shieber, Stuart. 1985. Evidence against the context-freeness of natural language. *Linguistics and Philosophy*, 8:333–343.

Steedman, Mark. 2000. *The Syntactic Process*. MIT press, Cambridge, MA.

Vijay-Shanker, K. and David Weir. 1993. Parsing some constrained grammar formalisms. *Computational Linguistics*, 19:591–636.

Vijay-Shanker, K. and David Weir. 1994. The equivalence of four extensions of context-free grammar. *Mathematical Systems Theory*, 27:511–546.

Weir, David. 1988. *Characterising Mildly Context-sensitive Grammar Formalisms*. Ph.D. thesis, University of Pennsylvania. Tech. Report CIS-88-74.

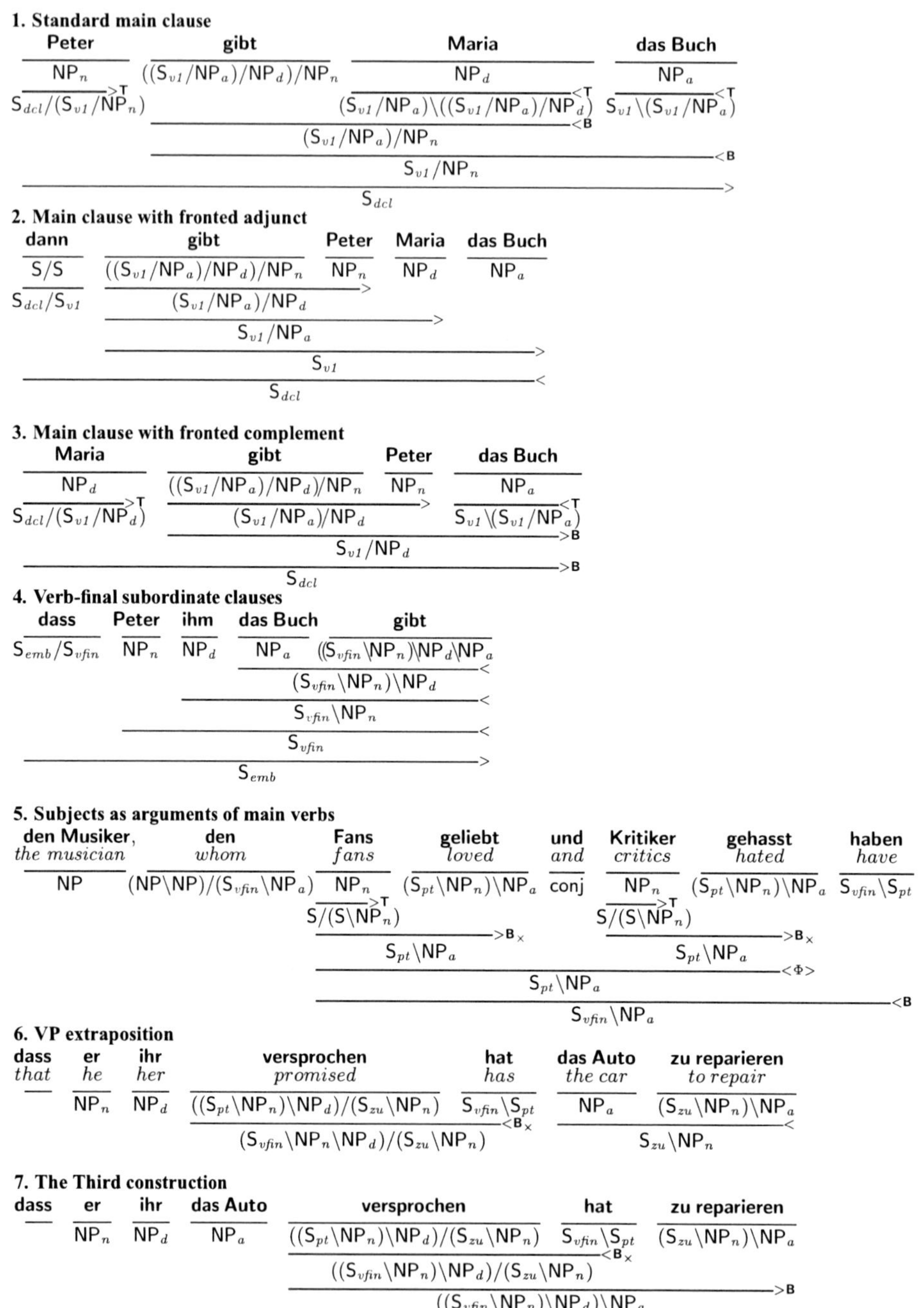

Figure 7: CCG uses topicalization (1.), a type-changing rule (2.), and type-raising (3.) to capture the different variants of German main clause order with the same lexical category for the verb, and assumes a different lexical category for verb-final subordinate clauses (4.)

Acknowledgements We would like to thank Aravind Joshi, Mark Steedman, and David Weir, as well as the anonymous TAG+ reviewers for their valuable comments and feedback.

A Prefix-Correct Earley Recognizer for Multiple Context-Free Grammars

Makoto Kanazawa
National Institute of Informatics
2–1–2 Hitotsubashi, Chiyoda-ku, Tokyo, 101–8430, Japan
`kanazawa@nii.ac.jp`

Abstract

We present a method for deriving an Earley recognizer for multiple context-free grammars with the correct prefix property. This is done by representing an MCFG by a Datalog program and applying generalized supplementary magic-sets rewriting. To secure the correct prefix property, a simple extra rewriting must be performed before the magic-sets rewriting. The correctness of the method is easy to see, and a straightforward application of the method to tree-adjoining grammars yields a recognizer whose running time is $O(n^6)$.

1 Deriving an Earley-style recognizer by magic-sets rewriting

We use the following 2-MCFG generating $\text{RESP}_+ = \{\, a_1^m a_2^m b_1^n b_2^n a_3^m a_4^m b_3^n b_4^n \mid m, n \geq 1 \,\}$ as our running example:[1]

(1) $S(x_1 y_1 x_2 y_2) :\!- P(x_1, x_2),\ Q(y_1, y_2).$
$\quad P(\mathsf{a}_1 \mathsf{a}_2, \mathsf{a}_3 \mathsf{a}_4).$
$\quad P(\mathsf{a}_1 x_1 \mathsf{a}_2, \mathsf{a}_3 x_2 \mathsf{a}_4) :\!- P(x_1, x_2).$
$\quad Q(\mathsf{b}_1 \mathsf{b}_2, \mathsf{b}_3 \mathsf{b}_4).$
$\quad Q(\mathsf{b}_1 y_1 \mathsf{b}_2, \mathsf{b}_3 y_2 \mathsf{b}_4) :\!- Q(y_1, y_2).$

The equivalence between this MCFG and the following *Datalog* program (i.e., function-free Horn clause logic program) is straightforward:

(2) $S(i, m) :\!- P(i, j, k, l),\ Q(j, k, l, m).$
$\quad P(i, k, l, n) :\!- \mathsf{a}_1(i, j),\ \mathsf{a}_2(j, k),\ \mathsf{a}_3(l, m),$
$\qquad\qquad \mathsf{a}_4(m, n).$
$\quad P(i, l, m, p) :\!- \mathsf{a}_1(i, j),\ P(j, k, n, o),\ \mathsf{a}_2(k, l),$
$\qquad\qquad \mathsf{a}_3(m, n),\ \mathsf{a}_4(o, p).$
$\quad Q(i, k, l, n) :\!- \mathsf{b}_1(i, j),\ \mathsf{b}_2(j, k),\ \mathsf{b}_3(l, m),$
$\qquad\qquad \mathsf{b}_4(m, n).$

$\quad Q(i, l, m, p) :\!- \mathsf{b}_1(i, j),\ \mathsf{b}_2(k, l),\ \mathsf{b}_3(m, n),$
$\qquad\qquad Q(j, k, n, o),\ \mathsf{b}_4(o, p).$

Nonterminals and terminals of the grammar become *intensional* and *extensional* predicates of the Datalog program, respectively. The program (2) together with the *extensional database* $\{a_1(0, 1), \ldots, a_n(n-1, n)\}$ derives $S(0, n)$ if and only if $a_1 \ldots a_n$ is in the language of the grammar (1).[2] Programs like (2) may be used as *deduction systems* (Shieber et al., 1995) or *uninstantiated parsing systems* (Sikkel, 1997) for chart parsing.

As demonstrated by Kanazawa (2007), Datalog offers an elegant unifying treatment of parsing for various string and tree grammars as well as tactical generation (surface realization) from logical forms reprensented by lambda terms.[3] Since deduction systems for parsing can be thought of as Datalog programs, we may view various *parsing schemata* (Sikkel, 1997) (i.e., mappings from grammars to deduction systems) as transformations of Datalog programs.

Magic-sets rewriting of Datalog programs is a technique to allow bottom-up evaluation to incorporate top-down prediction. As is well-understood, if we apply *generalized supplementary magic-sets rewriting* (Beeri and Ramakrishnan, 1991) to a Datalog program representing a context-free grammar, the result is essentially the deduction system for Earley's algorithm. Let us see how this technique applies to the program (2) (see Ullman (1989a; 1989b) for exposition).

First, *adornments* are attached to predicates, which indicate the free/bound status of each argu-

---

[1]Note that we are using the notation of *elementary formal systems* (Smullyan, 1961; Arikawa et al., 1992) aka *literal movement grammars* (Groenink, 1997), instead of that of Seki et al. (1991), to represent MCFG rules.

[2]If i is a natural number, we let "i" stand for the constant symbol representing i. We let "0", "1", etc., stand for themselves.

[3]Not only does the Dataog representation imply the existence of a polynomial-time algorithm for recognition, but it also serves to establish the tight complexity bound, namely *LOGCFL*, which presumably is a small subclass of P. See Kanazawa (2007) for details.

Proceedings of The Ninth International Workshop on Tree Adjoining Grammars and Related Formalisms
Tübingen, Germany. June 6-8, 2008.

$$1: S^{bf}(i, m) :- P^{bfff}(i, j, k, l), Q^{bbbf}(j, k, l, m).$$
$$2: P^{bfff}(i, k, l, n) :- \mathsf{a}_1^{bf}(i, j), \mathsf{a}_2^{bf}(j, k), \mathsf{a}_3^{ff}(l, m), \mathsf{a}_4^{bf}(m, n).$$
$$3: P^{bfff}(i, l, m, p) :- \mathsf{a}_1^{bf}(i, j), P^{bfff}(j, k, n, o), \mathsf{a}_2^{bf}(k, l), \mathsf{a}_3^{fb}(m, n), \mathsf{a}_4^{bf}(o, p).$$
$$4: Q^{bbbf}(i, k, l, n) :- \mathsf{b}_1^{bf}(i, j), \mathsf{b}_2^{bb}(j, k), \mathsf{b}_3^{bf}(l, m), \mathsf{b}_4^{bf}(m, n).$$
$$5: Q^{bbbf}(i, l, m, p) :- \mathsf{b}_1^{bf}(i, j), \mathsf{b}_2^{fb}(k, l), \mathsf{b}_3^{bf}(m, n), Q^{bbbf}(j, k, n, o), \mathsf{b}_4^{bf}(o, p).$$

Figure 1: Adorned Datalog program.

ment in top-down evaluation of the program (Figure 1). These adornments determine what arguments newly created predicates take in the new program.

There are two classes of new predicates. For each intensional predicate A, a corresponding *magic predicate m_A* is created, which takes only the bound arguments of A as its arguments. For each rule with n subgoals, *supplementary predicates $sup_{i,j}$* for $j = 1, \ldots, n - 1$ are introduced, where i is the rule number. The set of arguments of $sup_{i,j}$ is the intersection of two sets: the first set consists of the bound variables in the head of the rule and the variables in the first j subgoals, while the second set consists of the variables in the remaining subgoals and the head. The new program is in Figure 2. The rules for the magic predicates express top-down prediction, while the remaining rules serve to binarize the original rules, adding magic predicates as extra subgoals.

The program in Figure 2 can be used as a correct recognizer in combination with the control algorithm in Kanazawa (2007). This algorithm, however, reads the entire input string before accepting or rejecting it, so it cannot satisfy the *correct prefix property* with any program.[4] For this reason, we use the following alternative control algorithm in this paper, which is designed to reject the input as soon as the next input symbol no longer immediately contributes to deriving new facts. Note that the input string $a_1 \ldots a_n$ is represented by an extensional database $\{a_1(0, 1), \ldots, a_n(n - 1, n)\}$.

Chart recognizer control algorithm

1. (INITIALIZE) Initialize the chart to the empty set, the agenda to the singleton $\{m\_S(0)\}$, and i to 0.

2. Repeat the following steps:

(a) Repeat the following steps until the agenda is exhausted:

   i. Remove a fact from the agenda and call it the trigger.

   ii. Add the trigger to the chart.

   iii. (PREDICT/COMPLETE) Generate all facts that are immediate consequences of the trigger together with all facts in the chart, and add to the agenda those generated facts that are neither already in the chart nor in the agenda.

(b) If there is no more fact in the input database, go to step 3.

(c) i. Remove the next fact $a_{i+1}(i, i + 1)$ from the input database and call it the trigger.

   ii. (SCAN) Generate all facts that are immediate consequences of the trigger together with all facts in the chart, and add the generated facts to the agenda.

   iii. If the agenda is empty, reject the input; otherwise increment i.

3. If $S(0, i)$ is in the chart, accept; otherwise reject.

The trace of this recognizer on input $a_1 a_2 a_3 a_4$ is as follows, where the generated facts are listed in the order they enter the agenda (assuming that the agenda is first-in first-out), together with the type of inference, rule, and premises used to derive them:

1.	$m\_S(0)$	INITIALIZE	
2.	$m\_P(0)$	PREDICT, r_1, 1	
3.	$sup_{2.1}(0, 1)$	SCAN, r_6, 2, $\mathsf{a}_1(0, 1)$	
4.	$sup_{3.1}(0, 1)$	SCAN, r_9, 2, $\mathsf{a}_1(0, 1)$	
5.	$m\_P(1)$	PREDICT, r_3, 4	
6.	$sup_{2.2}(0, 2)$	SCAN, r_7, 3, $\mathsf{a}_2(1, 2)$	
7.	$sup_{2.3}(0, 2, 2, 3)$	SCAN, r_8, 6, $\mathsf{a}_3(2, 3)$	!!
8.	$P(0, 2, 2, 4)$	SCAN, r_{21}, 7, $\mathsf{a}_4(3, 4)$	
9.	$sup_{1.1}(0, 2, 2, 4)$	COMPLETE, r_5, 1, 8	
10.	$m\_Q(2, 2, 4)$	PREDICT, r_2, 9	

---

[4]A recognizer is said to have the *correct prefix property* or to be *prefix-correct* if it processes the input string from left to right and rejects as soon as the portion of the input that has been processed so far is not a prefix of any element of the language.

$r_1: m\_P(i) :\!- m\_S(i).$

$r_2: m\_Q(j,k,l) :\!- sup_{1.1}(i,j,k,l).$

$r_3: m\_P(j) :\!- sup_{3.1}(i,j).$

$r_4: m\_Q(j,k,n) :\!- sup_{5.3}(i,j,k,l,m,n).$

$r_5: sup_{1.1}(i,j,k,l) :\!- m\_S(i), P(i,j,k,l).$

$r_6: sup_{2.1}(i,j) :\!- m\_P(i), a_1(i,j).$

$r_7: sup_{2.2}(i,k) :\!- sup_{2.1}(i,j), a_2(j,k).$

$r_8: sup_{2.3}(i,k,l,m) :\!- sup_{2.2}(i,k), a_3(l,m).$

$r_9: sup_{3.1}(i,j) :\!- m\_P(i), a_1(i,j).$

$r_{10}: sup_{3.2}(i,k,n,o) :\!- sup_{3.1}(i,j), P(j,k,n,o).$

$r_{11}: sup_{3.3}(i,l,n,o) :\!- sup_{3.2}(i,k,n,o), a_2(k,l).$

$r_{12}: sup_{3.4}(i,l,m,o) :\!- sup_{3.3}(i,l,n,o), a_3(m,n).$

$r_{13}: sup_{4.1}(i,j,k,l) :\!- m\_Q(i,k,l), b_1(i,j).$

$r_{14}: sup_{4.2}(i,k,l) :\!- sup_{4.1}(i,j,k,l), b_2(j,k).$

$r_{15}: sup_{4.3}(i,k,l,m) :\!- sup_{4.2}(i,k,l), b_3(l,m).$

$r_{16}: sup_{5.1}(i,j,l,m) :\!- m\_Q(i,l,m), b_1(i,j).$

$r_{17}: sup_{5.2}(i,j,k,l,m) :\!- sup_{5.1}(i,j,l,m), b_2(k,l).$

$r_{18}: sup_{5.3}(i,j,k,l,m,n) :\!- sup_{5.2}(i,j,k,l,m), b_3(m,n).$

$r_{19}: sup_{5.4}(i,l,m,o) :\!- sup_{5.3}(i,j,k,l,m,n), Q(j,k,n,o).$

$r_{20}: S(i,m) :\!- sup_{1.1}(i,j,k,l), Q(j,k,l,m).$

$r_{21}: P(i,k,l,n) :\!- sup_{2.3}(i,k,l,m), a_4(m,n).$

$r_{22}: P(i,l,m,p) :\!- sup_{3.4}(i,l,m,o), a_4(o,p).$

$r_{23}: Q(i,k,l,n) :\!- sup_{4.3}(i,k,l,m), b_4(m,n).$

$r_{24}: Q(i,l,m,p) :\!- sup_{5.4}(i,l,m,o), b_4(o,p).$

Figure 2: The result of applying generalized supplementary magic-sets rewriting to the program in Figure 1.

Although the input is correctly rejected, the correct-prefix property is violated at line 7. The problem comes from the fact that in rule r_8 of Figure 2, both arguments of a_3 are free (see the adornment on a_3 in rule 2 of Figure 1). This means that a_3 is predicted somewhere, but not necessarily at the current position in the input string. So after a_3 is scanned at position 2, there is no guarantee that the input that has been processed so far is a correct prefix. In fact, the problem is even worse, as this particular recognizer fails to accept any input string. On input $a_1 a_2 b_1 b_2 a_3 a_4 b_3 b_4$, for example, the recognizer proceeds as above up to line 6, but then rejects the input, since no scan move is possible on b_1.[5]

2 Securing the correct prefix property by adding redundant subgoals

In order to produce a prefix-correct recognition algorithm by magic-sets rewriting, it is necessary to ensure that in the program to be rewritten, the first argument of all extensional predicates is adorned as bound. To achieve this, we need an extra rewriting of the Datalog program corresponding to the given MCFG before applying magic-sets rewriting.

In the Datalog program representing an MCFG, occurrences of variables in the body of a rule come in pairs, with each pair corresponding to an occurrence of a symbol (terminal or string variable) in the head of the corresponding MCFG rule. We

will rewrite the Datalog program in such a way that the modified program satisfies the following property:

- The order of (the first occurrences of) the pairs of variables in the body of a rule correspond to the order of the corresponding symbol occurrences in the MCFG rule.

This will make sure that the first arguments of all extensional predicates are adorned as bound.[6]

In order to achieve this, we split each 4-ary intensional predicate $R(i,j,k,l)$ into two predicates, $R_1(i,j)$ and $R(i,j,k,l)$. The predicate $R(i,j,k,l)$ retains its original meaning, while the new predicate $R_1(i,j)$ intuitively means $\exists kl.R(i,j,k,l)$. Where an old rule has $R(i,j,k,l)$ in its right-hand side, the new rule has $R_1(i,j)$ and $R(i,j,k,l)$ in its right-hand side; the positions of $R_1(i,j)$ and $R(i,j,k,l)$ will be dictated by the positions of the symbols corresponding to (i,j) and (k,l) in the MCFG rule. Since $R_1(i,j)$ is derivable whenever $R(i,j,k,l)$ is, this will not alter the least fixpoint semantics of the rule.

For instance, this procedure rewrites the third rule of the original program (2) as follows:

$$(3) \quad P(i,l,m,p) :\!- a_1(i,j), P_1(j,k), a_2(k,l),$$
$$a_3(m,n), P(j,k,n,o), a_4(o,p).$$

---

[6]This assumes a normal form for MCFGs characterized by the following condition:

- If $A(t_1, \ldots, t_r) :\!- B_1(x_{1,1}, \ldots, x_{1,r_1}), \ldots, B_m(x_{m,1}, \ldots, x_{m,r_m})$ is a rule, then $t_1 \ldots t_r \in (\Sigma \cup X)^* x_{i,j} (\Sigma \cup X)^* x_{i,k} (\Sigma \cup X)^*$ implies $j < k$, where $X = \{\, x_{i,j} \mid 1 \le i \le m, 1 \le j \le r_i \,\}$.

This normal form corresponds to what Villemonte de la Clergerie (2002a; 2002b) called *ordered simple RCG*.

$S(i, m) :- P_1(i, j),\ Q_1(j, k),\ P(i, j, k, l),\ Q(j, k, l, m).$
$P_1(i, k) :- aux_2(i, k).$
$P(i, k, l, n) :- aux_2(i, k),\ a_3(l, m),\ a_4(m, n).$
$aux_2(i, k) :- a_1(i, j),\ a_2(j, k).$
$P_1(i, l) :- aux_3(i, j, k, l).$
$P(i, l, m, p) :- aux_3(i, j, k, l),\ a_3(m, n),\ P(j, k, n, o),$
$\qquad a_4(o, p).$
$aux_3(i, j, k, l) :- a_1(i, j),\ P_1(j, k),\ a_2(k, l).$
$Q_1(i, k) :- aux_4(i, k).$
$Q(i, k, l, n) :- aux_4(i, k),\ b_3(l, m),\ b_4(m, n).$
$aux_4(i, k) :- b_1(i, j),\ b_2(j, k).$
$Q_1(i, l) :- aux_5(i, j, k, l).$
$Q(i, l, m, p) :- aux_5(i, j, k, l),\ b_3(m, n),\ Q(j, k, n, o),$
$\qquad b_4(o, p).$
$aux_5(i, j, k, l) :- b_1(i, j),\ Q_1(j, k),\ b_2(k, l).$

Figure 3: Rewritten Datalog program.

Note the correspondence with the MCFG rule:

$$(4)\quad P(\ a_1\ x_1\ a_2\ ,\quad a_3\ x_2\ a_4\ ) :- P(x_1, x_2).$$
$$i\quad j\quad k\quad l\qquad m\quad n\quad o\quad p$$

A rule for P_1 is obtained from (3) by discarding the last three subgoals, which pertain to string positions in the second argument of the head of (4):

$$(5)\quad P_1(i, l) :- a_1(i, j),\ P_1(j, k),\ a_2(k, l).$$

We then fold the common part of (5) and (3), creating an auxiliary predicate aux_3 (the subscript indicates the rule number from the original program):

$P_1(i, l) :- aux_3(i, j, k, l).$
$P(i, l, m, p) :- aux_3(i, j, k, l),\ a_3(m, n),$
$\qquad\qquad P(j, k, n, o),\ a_4(o, p).$
$aux_3(i, j, k, l) :- a_1(i, j),\ P_1(j, k),\ a_2(k, l).$

The above description is for 2-MCFGs, but the procedure is applicable to the Datalog program representing any MCFG. In the general case, a $2m$-ary predicate $R(i_1, \ldots, i_{2m})$ is split into m predicates, $R_1(i_1, i_2), \ldots, R_{m-1}(i_1, \ldots, i_{2m-2})$, $R(i_1, \ldots, i_{2m})$, and $m - 1$ auxiliary predicates are introduced, one for each R_i. We call this rewriting procedure *redundancy introduction*.

The result of applying redundancy introduction to the program (2) is in Figure 3. Figure 4 shows the adornments. Note that the adornments on the boldface predicate occurrences in Figure 4 are adjusted to "less bound" patterns in order to satisfy the *unique binding property*. This is justified by

$1: S^{bf}(i, m) :- P_1^{bf}(i, j),\ Q_1^{bf}(j, k),\ P^{bbbf}(i, j, k, l),$
$\qquad Q^{bbbf}(j, k, l, m).$
$2: P_1^{bf}(i, k) :- aux_2^{bf}(i, k).$
$3: P^{bbbf}(i, k, l, n) :- \boldsymbol{aux}_{\boldsymbol{2}}^{bf}(i, k),\ a_3^{bf}(l, m),$
$\qquad\qquad a_4^{bf}(m, n).$
$4: aux_2^{bf}(i, k) :- a_1^{bf}(i, j),\ a_2^{bf}(j, k).$
$5: P_1^{bf}(i, l) :- aux_3^{bfff}(i, j, k, l).$
$6: P^{bbbf}(i, l, m, p) :- \boldsymbol{aux}_{\boldsymbol{3}}^{bfff}(i, j, k, l),\ a_3^{bf}(m, n),$
$\qquad\qquad P^{bfff}(j, k, n, o),\ a_4^{bf}(o, p).$
$7: aux_3^{bfff}(i, j, k, l) :- a_1^{bf}(i, j),\ P_1^{bf}(j, k),\ a_2^{bf}(k, l).$
$8: Q_1^{bf}(i, k) :- aux_4^{bf}(i, k).$
$9: Q^{bbbf}(i, k, l, n) :- \boldsymbol{aux}_{\boldsymbol{4}}^{bf}(i, k),\ b_3^{bf}(l, m),\ b_4^{bf}(m, n).$
$10: aux_4^{bf}(i, k) :- b_1^{bf}(i, j),\ b_2^{bf}(j, k).$
$11: Q_1^{bf}(i, l) :- aux_5^{bfff}(i, j, k, l).$
$12: Q^{bbbf}(i, l, m, p) :- \boldsymbol{aux}_{\boldsymbol{5}}^{bfff}(i, j, k, l),\ b_3^{bf}(m, n),$
$\qquad\qquad Q^{bbbf}(j, k, n, o),\ b_4^{bf}(o, p).$
$13: aux_5^{bfff}(i, j, k, l) :- b_1^{bf}(i, j),\ Q_1^{bf}(j, k),\ b_2^{bf}(k, l).$

Figure 4: Adorned version of the program in Figure 3.

viewing, for instance, $\boldsymbol{aux}_{\boldsymbol{2}}^{bf}(i, k)$ as an abbreviation for $aux_2^{bf}(i, k')$, $k' =^{bb} k$.[7] Generalized supplementary magic-sets rewriting applied to Figure 4 results in Figure 5.

The following shows the trace of running the chart recognizer using the program in Figure 5 on input $a_1 a_2 a_3 a_4$:

1.	$m\_S(0)$	INITIALIZE
2.	$m\_P_1(0)$	PREDICT, r_1, 1
3.	$m\_aux_2(0)$	PREDICT, r_5, 2
4.	$m\_aux_3(0)$	PREDICT, r_7, 2
5.	$sup_{4.1}(0, 1)$	SCAN, r_{22}, 3, $a_1(0, 1)$
6.	$sup_{7.1}(0, 1)$	SCAN, r_{26}, 4, $a_1(0, 1)$
7.	$m\_P_1(1)$	PREDICT, r_{10}, 6
8.	$m\_aux_2(1)$	PREDICT, r_5, 7
9.	$m\_aux_3(1)$	PREDICT, r_7, 7
10.	$aux_2(0, 2)$	SCAN, r_{39}, 5, $a_2(1, 2)$
11.	$P_1(0, 2)$	COMPLETE, r_{37}, 2, 10
12.	$sup_{1.1}(0, 2)$	COMPLETE, r_{17}, 1, 11
13.	$m\_Q_1(2)$	PREDICT, r_2, 12
14.	$m\_aux_4(2)$	PREDICT, r_{11}, 13
15.	$m\_aux_5(2)$	PREDICT, r_{13}, 13

The algorithm correctly rejects the input without making any SCAN moves on a_3. If the input is

---

[7] For the sake of simplicity, we defer explicit use of equality until Section 4.

$r_1: m\_P_1(i) :- m\_S(i).$

$r_2: m\_Q_1(j) :- sup_{1.1}(i, j).$

$r_3: m\_P(i, j, k) :- sup_{1.2}(i, j, k).$

$r_4: m\_Q(j, k, l) :- sup_{1.3}(i, j, k, l).$

$r_5: m\_aux_2(i) :- m\_P_1(i).$

$r_6: m\_aux_2(i) :- m\_P(i, k, l).$

$r_7: m\_aux_3(i) :- m\_P_1(i).$

$r_8: m\_aux_3(i) :- m\_P(i, l, m).$

$r_9: m\_P(j, k, n) :- sup_{6.2}(i, j, k, l, m, n).$

$r_{10}: m\_P_1(j) :- sup_{7.1}(i, j).$

$r_{11}: m\_aux_4(i) :- m\_Q_1(i).$

$r_{12}: m\_aux_4(i) :- m\_Q(i, k, l).$

$r_{13}: m\_aux_5(i) :- m\_Q_1(i).$

$r_{14}: m\_aux_5(i) :- m\_Q(i, l, m).$

$r_{15}: m\_Q(j, k, n) :- sup_{12.2}(i, j, k, l, m, n).$

$r_{16}: m\_Q_1(j) :- sup_{13.1}(i, j).$

$r_{17}: sup_{1.1}(i, j) :- m\_S(i), P_1(i, j).$

$r_{18}: sup_{1.2}(i, j, k) :- sup_{1.1}(i, j), Q_1(j, k).$

$r_{19}: sup_{1.3}(i, j, k, l) :- sup_{1.2}(i, j, k), P(i, j, k, l).$

$r_{20}: sup_{3.1}(i, k, l) :- m\_P(i, k, l), aux_2(i, k).$

$r_{21}: sup_{3.2}(i, k, l, m) :- sup_{3.1}(i, k, l), a_3(l, m).$

$r_{22}: sup_{4.1}(i, j) :- m\_aux_2(i), a_1(i, j).$

$r_{23}: sup_{6.1}(i, j, k, l, m) :- m\_P(i, l, m), aux_3(i, j, k, l).$

$r_{24}: sup_{6.2}(i, j, k, l, m, n) :- sup_{6.1}(i, j, k, l, m),$
$\qquad\qquad\qquad a_3(m, n).$

$r_{25}: sup_{6.3}(i, l, m, o) :- sup_{6.2}(i, j, k, l, m, n),$
$\qquad\qquad\qquad P(j, k, n, o).$

$r_{26}: sup_{7.1}(i, j) :- m\_aux_3(i), a_1(i, j).$

$r_{27}: sup_{7.2}(i, j, k) :- sup_{7.1}(i, j), P_1(j, k).$

$r_{28}: sup_{9.1}(i, k, l) :- m\_Q(i, k, l), aux_4(i, k).$

$r_{29}: sup_{9.2}(i, k, l, m) :- sup_{9.1}(i, k, l), b_3(l, m).$

$r_{30}: sup_{10.1}(i, j) :- m\_aux_4(i), b_1(i, j).$

$r_{31}: sup_{12.1}(i, j, k, l, m) :- m\_Q(i, l, m), aux_5(i, j, k, l).$

$r_{32}: sup_{12.2}(i, j, k, l, m, n) :- sup_{12.1}(i, j, k, l, m),$
$\qquad\qquad\qquad b_3(m, n).$

$r_{33}: sup_{12.3}(i, l, m, o) :- sup_{12.2}(i, j, k, l, m, n),$
$\qquad\qquad\qquad Q(j, k, n, o).$

$r_{34}: sup_{13.1}(i, j) :- m\_aux_5(i), b_1(i, j).$

$r_{35}: sup_{13.2}(i, j, k) :- sup_{13.1}(i, j), Q(j, k).$

$r_{36}: S(i, m) :- sup_{1.3}(i, j, k, l), Q(j, k, l, m).$

$r_{37}: P_1(i, k) :- m\_P_1(i), aux_2(i, k).$

$r_{38}: P(i, k, l, n) :- sup_{3.2}(i, k, l, m), a_4(m, n).$

$r_{39}: aux_2(i, k) :- sup_{4.1}(i, j), a_2(j, k).$

$r_{40}: P_1(i, l) :- m\_P_1(i), aux_3(i, j, k, l).$

$r_{41}: P(i, l, m, p) :- sup_{6.3}(i, l, m, o), a_4(o, p).$

$r_{42}: aux_3(i, j, k, l) :- sup_{7.2}(i, j, k), a_2(k, l).$

$r_{43}: Q_1(i, k) :- m\_Q_1(i), aux_4(i, k).$

$r_{44}: Q(i, k, l, n) :- sup_{9.2}(i, k, l, m), b_4(m, n).$

$r_{45}: aux_4(i, k) :- sup_{10.1}(i, j), b_2(j, k).$

$r_{46}: Q_1(i, l) :- m\_Q(i), aux_5(i, j, k, l).$

$r_{47}: Q(i, l, m, p) :- sup_{12.3}(i, l, m, o), b_4(o, p).$

$r_{48}: aux_5(i, j, k, l) :- sup_{13.2}(i, j, k), b_2(k, l).$

Figure 5: The result of applying generalized supplementary magic-sets rewriting to the program in Figure 4.

$a_1 a_2 b_1 b_2 a_3 a_4 b_3 b_4$ instead, the execution of the algorithm continues as follows:

16.	$sup_{10.1}(2, 3)$	SCAN, r_{30}, 14, $b_1(2, 3)$
17.	$sup_{13.1}(2, 3)$	SCAN, r_{34}, 15, $b_1(2, 3)$
18.	$m\_Q_1(3)$	PREDICT, r_{16}, 17
19.	$m\_aux_4(3)$	PREDICT, r_{11}, 18
20.	$m\_aux_5(3)$	PREDICT, r_{13}, 18
21.	$aux_4(2, 4)$	SCAN, r_{45}, 16, $b_2(3, 4)$
22.	$Q_1(2, 4)$	COMPLETE, r_{43}, 13, 21
23.	$sup_{1.2}(0, 2, 4)$	COMPLETE, r_{18}, 12, 22
24.	$m\_P(0, 2, 4)$	PREDICT, r_3, 23
25.	$sup_{3.1}(0, 2, 4)$	COMPLETE, r_{20}, 24, 10
26.	$sup_{3.2}(0, 2, 4, 5)$	SCAN, r_{21}, 25, $a_3(4, 5)$
27.	$P(0, 2, 4, 6)$	SCAN, r_{38}, 26, $a_4(5, 6)$
28.	$sup_{1.3}(0, 2, 4, 6)$	COMPLETE, r_{19}, 23, 27
29.	$m\_Q(2, 4, 6)$	PREDICT, r_4, 28
30.	$sup_{9.1}(2, 4, 6)$	COMPLETE, r_{28}, 29, 21
31.	$sup_{9.2}(2, 4, 6, 7)$	SCAN, r_{29}, 30, $b_3(6, 7)$
32.	$Q(2, 4, 6, 8)$	SCAN, r_{44}, 31, $b_4(7, 8)$
33.	$S(0, 8)$	COMPLETE, r_{36}, 28, 32

Needless to say, the program that we obtain with our method has room for optimization. For instance, rules of the form $m\_aux(i) :- R(i, j, k)$ are useless in the presence of $m\_aux(i) :- R_1(i)$, so they can be safely removed. Nevertheless, the recognizer produced by our method is always correct and satisfies the correct prefix property without any such fine-tuning.

3 Correctness of the method

It is easy to prove that the Datalog program **P** that we obtain from an MCFG G after redundancy introduction and magic-sets rewriting is correct in the sense that for any string $a_1 \ldots a_n$,

$$\mathbf{P} \cup \{m\_S(0), a_1(0, 1), \ldots, a_n(n - 1, n)\} \vdash S(0, n)$$
$$\text{iff} \quad a_1 \ldots a_n \in L(G).$$

Since the initial Datalog program is correct (in the sense of the above biconditional with $m\_S(0)$

omitted) and magic-sets rewriting preserves correctness (modulo $m\_S(0)$), it suffices to prove that the redundancy introduction transformation preserves correctness.

Let $\mathbf{P}$ be a Datalog program representing a 2-MCFG and let $\mathbf{P'}$ be the result of applying redundancy introduction to $\mathbf{P}$. Let R be any 4-ary intensional predicate in $\mathbf{P}$, D be an extensional database, and c, d, e, f be constants in D. It is easy to see that

$$\mathbf{P'} \cup D \vdash R(c,d,e,f) \quad \text{implies} \quad \mathbf{P'} \cup D \vdash R_1(c,d),$$

and using this, we can prove by straightforward induction that

$$\mathbf{P} \cup D \vdash R(c,d,e,f) \quad \text{iff} \quad \mathbf{P'} \cup D \vdash R(c,d,e,f).$$

The general case of m-MCFGs is similar.

It is also easy to see that our control algorithm is complete with respect to any Datalog program $\mathbf{P}$ obtained from an MCFG by redundancy introduction and magic-sets rewriting. Observing that all facts derivable from $\mathbf{P}$ together with $\{m\_S(0), a_1(0,1), \ldots, a_n(n-1, n)\}$ have the form $R(i_1, \ldots, i_m)$ where $i_1 \leq \cdots \leq i_m$, and rules involving an extensional predicate a all have the form $P(\ldots, j) :\!- R(\ldots, i), a(i,j)$, we can prove by induction that our control algorithm generates all derivable facts $R(i_1, \ldots, i_m)$ before making any scan moves on a_{i_m+1}.

It remains to show the correct prefix property. We call an MCFG *reduced* if every nonterminal denotes a non-empty relation on strings. Let $\mathbf{P}$ be the Datalog program obtained by applying redundancy introduction to a program representing a reduced 2-MCFG. By the correspondence between magic-sets rewriting and *SLD-resolution* (Brass, 1995), it suffices to show that SLD-resolution (with the leftmost selection function) using program $\mathbf{P}$ has a property which corresponds to prefix-correctness.

Let Γ and Δ denote negative clauses, and let $\square$ denote the empty clause. We write

$$\Gamma \overset{\mathbf{P},D}{\Longrightarrow} \Delta$$

to mean that there exists an SLD-derivation starting from goal Γ and ending in goal Δ, using rules in $\mathbf{P}$ and *exactly* the facts in D as input clauses. We call D a *string database* if D is isomorphic to $\{a_1(0,1), \ldots, a_n(n-1, n)\}$. It is easy to see that if $S(0,x) \overset{\mathbf{P},D}{\Longrightarrow} \Gamma$, then D is a string database.

Theorem 1. *If* $S(0, x) \overset{\mathbf{P},D}{\Longrightarrow} \Gamma$, *then* $\Gamma \overset{\mathbf{P},D'}{\Longrightarrow} \square$ *for some* D' *such that* $D \cup D'$ *is a string database.*

This is the desired property corresponding to prefix-correctness. The theorem can be proved with the help of the following lemma.

Lemma 2. *Let* R *be a 4-ary intensional predicate in* $\mathbf{P}$. *For every string database* D *and constants* c, d *in* D *such that* $\mathbf{P} \cup D \vdash R_1(c, d)$, *if* e *is a constant not in* D, *there exists a string database* D' *whose constants are disjoint from those of* D *such that* $\mathbf{P} \cup D \cup D' \vdash R(c, d, e, f)$ *for some constant* f *in* D'.

Again, the general case of m-MCFGs can be treated similarly.

4 Application to tree-adjoining grammars

So far, we have implicitly assumed that the empty string ϵ does not appear as an argument in the head of MCFG rules. Since ϵ can be eliminated from any MCFG generating an ϵ-free language (Seki et al., 1991), this is not an essential restriction, but it is often convenient to be able to handle rules involving ϵ directly, as is the case with 2-MCFGs representing TAGs. To translate an MCFG rule with ϵ into a Datalog rule, we use range-restricted equality as an extensional predicate. For example, a 2-MCFG rule

$$A(x, \epsilon) :\!- B(x).$$

is translated into Datalog as follows:[8]

$$A(i, j, k, l) :\!- B(i, j), k = l.$$

Rewritten Datalog programs will now involve equality. We continue to represent the input string $a_1 \ldots a_n$ as an extensional database $\{a_1(0,1), \ldots, a_n(n-1, n)\}$, but modify our control algorithm slightly:

Chart recognizer control algorithm (revised)
Same as before, except for the following two steps:

1. (INITIALIZE) Initialize the chart to the empty set, the agenda to $\{m\_S(0), 0 = 0\}$, and i to 0.

2. (c) iii. If the agenda is empty, reject the input; otherwise increment i, and then add the fact $i = i$ to the agenda.

---

[8]Since equality is treated as an extensional predicate, rules like this are *safe* in the sense that they can derive ground facts only.

To obtain an $O(n^6)$ prefix-correct Earley recognizer for TAGs by our method, we translate each nonterminal node of an elementary tree into a 2-MCFG rule. For each such node M, the 2-MCFG has a distinct nonterminal symbol M, whose arity is either 2 or 1 depending on whether the node M dominates the foot node or not.

Let M be a node dominating a foot node having children $L^1, \ldots, L^j, N, R^1, \ldots, R^k$, of which N is the child on the path to the foot node. For each elementary tree γ with root node T that can adjoin into M, the 2-MCFG has the rule

(6) $\quad M(w_1 x_1 \ldots x_j z_1, z_2 y_1 \ldots y_k w_2) :-$
$\qquad T(w_1, w_2),\ L^1(x_1), \ldots, L^j(x_j),\ N(z_1, z_2),$
$\qquad R^1(y_1), \ldots, R^k(y_k).$

If adjunction is optional at M, the 2-MCFG also has the rule

$M(x_1 \ldots x_j z_1, z_2 y_1 \ldots y_k) :-$
$\qquad L^1(x_1), \ldots, L^j(x_j),\ N(z_1, z_2),\ R^1(y_1), \ldots, R^k(y_k).$

Let F be a foot node. For each elementary tree γ with root node T that can adjoin into F, the 2-MCFG has the rule

$F(w_1, w_2) :- T(w_1, w_2).$

If adjunction is optional at F, the 2-MCFG also has the rule

$F(\epsilon, \epsilon).$

We omit the other cases, but they are all straightforward.

The translation into Datalog of the 2-MCFG thus obtained results in a variant of Lang's Horn clause axiomatization of TAGs (discussed by Johnson (1994)). For example, consider (6) with $j = k = 2$:

(7) $\quad M(w_1 x_1 x_2 z_1, z_2 y_1 y_2 w_2) :- T(w_1, w_2),\ L^1(x_1),$
$\qquad L^2(x_2),\ N(z_1, z_2),\ R^1(y_1),\ R^2(y_2).$

The Datalog representation of (7) is the following:

(8) $\quad M(i, m, n, r) :- T(i, j, q, r),\ L^1(j, k),\ L^2(k, l),$
$\qquad N(l, m, n, o),\ R^1(o, p),\ R^2(p, q).$

Redundancy introduction rewrites (8) into three rules:

(9) $\quad M_1(i, m) :- aux(i, j, l, m).$
$\qquad M(i, m, n, r) :- aux(i, j, l, m),\ N(l, m, n, o),$
$\qquad\qquad R^1(o, p),\ R^2(p, q),\ T(i, j, q, r).$
$\qquad aux(i, j, l, m) :- T_1(i, j),\ L^1(j, k),\ L^2(k, l),$
$\qquad\qquad N_1(l, m).$

$m\_aux(i) :- m\_M_1(i).$
$m\_aux(i) :- m\_M(i, m, n).$
$m\_N(l, m, n) :- sup_{2.1}(i, j, l, m, n).$
$m\_R^1(o) :- sup_{2.2}(i, j, m, n, o).$
$m\_R^2(p) :- sup_{2.3}(i, j, m, n, p).$
$m\_T(i, j, q) :- sup_{2.4}(i, j, m, n, q).$
$m\_T_1(i) :- m\_aux(i).$
$m\_L^1(j) :- sup_{3.1}(i, j).$
$m\_L^2(k) :- sup_{3.2}(i, j, k).$
$m\_N_1(l) :- sup_{3.3}(i, j, l).$

$sup_{2.1}(i, j, l, m, n) :- m\_M(i, m, n),\ aux(i, j, l, m).$
$sup_{2.2}(i, j, m, n, o) :- sup_{2.1}(i, j, l, m, n),\ N(l, m, n, o).$
$sup_{2.3}(i, j, m, n, p) :- sup_{2.2}(i, j, m, n, o),\ R^1(o, p).$
$sup_{2.4}(i, j, m, n, q) :- sup_{2.3}(i, j, m, n, p),\ R^2(p, q).$
$sup_{3.1}(i, j) :- m\_aux(i),\ T_1(i, j).$
$sup_{3.2}(i, j, k) :- sup_{3.1}(i, j),\ L^1(j, k).$
$sup_{3.3}(i, j, l) :- sup_{3.2}(i, j, k),\ L^2(k, l).$

$M_1(i, m) :- m\_M_1(i),\ aux(i, j, l, m).$
$M(i, m, n, r) :- sup_{2.4}(i, j, m, n, q),\ T(i, j, q, r).$
$aux(i, j, l, m) :- sup_{3.3}(i, j, l),\ N_1(l, m).$

Figure 6: The result of applying generalized supplementary magic-sets rewriting to the three rules in (9).

Finally, the generalized supplementary magic-sets rewriting yields the rules in Figure 6. Each rule in Figure 6 involves at most 6 variables, while the arity of predicates is at most 5. It is easy to see that this holds in general; it follows that the time and space complexity of the recognizer for TAGs produced by our method is $O(n^6)$ and $O(n^5)$, respectively.

5 Comparison with previous approaches

Prefix-correct Earley-like recognizers for MCFGs have been presented before (Matsumura et al., 1989; Harkema, 2001; Albro, 2002; Villemonte de la Clergerie, 2002a; Villemonte de la Clergerie, 2002b). The recognizer obtained by our method seems to be slightly different from each of them, but the main advantage of our approach lies not in the resulting recognizer, but in *how* it is obtained. Unlike previous approaches, we borrow a well-known and well-understood technique from deductive database theory, namely magic-sets rewriting, to automatically *derive* an Earley-style recognizer. Since the parsing schema for Earley's algorithm can be regarded as a special case of generalized supplementary magic-sets rewriting, there is a precise sense in which our recognizer may be called an *Earley* recognizer. We have used an ad hoc but simple and easy-to-understand rewriting (redundancy introduction) to secure the correct prefix property, and it is the only step in our approach specifically tailor-made for MCFGs.

The application of our method to TAGs in turn uses a completely straightforward encoding of TAGs into Datalog programs (via 2-MCFGs), which is close to Lang's Horn clause axiomatization. (Lang's encoding itself can be used to the same effect.) The resulting recognizer for TAGs is prefix-correct and runs in time $O(n^6)$ and space $O(n^5)$, which is the same as the best known bound for prefix-correct recognizers for TAGs (Nederhof, 1999). The behavior of our recognizer on Nederhof's (1999) example roughly corresponds to that of Nederhof's recognizer, but there is a significant difference between the two in the indices involved in some of the items. More importantly, unlike Nederhof's, our recognizer is a special case of a more general construction, and the time and space complexity bounds are obtained without any fine-tuning.

Since it involves very little non-standard technique, we believe that our method is easier to understand and easier to prove correct than previous approaches. For this reason, we also hope that this work serves useful pedagogical purposes.

References

Albro, Daniel M. 2002. An Earley-style parser for multiple context-free grammars. Unpublished manuscript, UCLA.

Arikawa, Setsuo, Takeshi Shinohara, and Akihiro Yamamoto. 1992. Learning elementary formal systems. *Theoretical Computer Science*, 95(1):97–113.

Beeri, Catriel and Raghu Ramakrishnan. 1991. On the power of magic. *Journal of Logic Programming*, 10(3–4):255–299.

Brass, Stefan. 1995. Magic sets vs. SLD-resolution. In Eder, J. and L. A. Kalinichenko, editors, *Advances in Databases and Information Systems*, pages 185–203. Springer, Berlin.

Groenink, Annius. 1997. *Surface without Structure*. Ph.D. thesis, Utrecht University.

Harkema, Hendrik. 2001. *Parsing minimalist languages*. Ph.D. thesis, UCLA.

Johnson, Mark. 1994. Logical embedded push-down automata in tree-adjoining grammar parsing. *Computational Intelligence*, 10(4):495–505.

Kanazawa, Makoto. 2007. Parsing and generation as Datalog queries. In *Proceedings of the 45th Annual Meeting of the Association for Computational Linguistics*, pages 176–183.

Matsumura, Takashi, Hiroyuki Seki, Mamoru Fujii, and Tadao Kasami. 1989. Some results on multiple context-free grammars. *IEICE Technical Report*, COMP 88–78:17–26. In Japanese.

Nederhof, Mark-Jan. 1999. The computational complexity of the correct-prefix property for TAGs. *Computational Linguistics*, 25(3):345–360.

Seki, Hiroyuki, Takashi Matsumura, Mamoru Fujii, and Tadao Kasami. 1991. On multiple context-free grammars. *Theoretical Computer Science*, 88(2):191–229.

Shieber, Stuart M., Yves Schabes, and Fernando C. N. Pereira. 1995. Principles and implementations of deductive parsing. *Journal of Logic Programming*, 24(1–2):3–36.

Sikkel, Klaas. 1997. *Parsing Schemata*. Springer, Berlin.

Smullyan, Raymond M. 1961. *Theory of Formal Systems*. Princeton University Press, Princeton, N.J.

Ullman, Jeffrey D. 1989a. Bottom-up beats top-down in Datalog. In *Proceedings of the Eighth ACM Symposium on Principles of Database Systems*, pages 140–149.

Ullman, Jeffrey D. 1989b. *Principles of Database and Knowledge-Base Systems. Volume II: The New Technologies*. Computer Science Press, Rockville, M.D.

Villemonte de la Clergerie, Éric. 2002a. Parsing MCS languages with thread automata. In *Proceedings of the Sixth International Workshop on Tree Adjoining Grammar and Related Frameworks (TAG+6)*, pages 101–108.

Villemonte de la Clergerie, Éric. 2002b. Parsing mildly context-sensitive languages with thread automata. In *Proceedings of the 19th International Conference on Computational Linguistics*, pages 1–7.

Factorizing Complementation in a TT-MCTAG for German

Timm Lichte
Emmy-Nother-Nachwuchsgruppe
SFB 441
University of Tübingen
`timm.lichte@uni-tuebingen.de`

Laura Kallmeyer
Emmy-Nother-Nachwuchsgruppe
SFB 441
University of Tübingen
`lk@sfs.uni-tuebingen.de`

Abstract

TT-MCTAG lets one abstract away from the relative order of co-complements in the final derived tree, which is more appropriate than classic TAG when dealing with flexible word order in German. In this paper, we present the analyses for sentential complements, i.e., wh-extraction, that-complementation and bridging, and we work out the crucial differences between these and respective accounts in XTAG (for English) and V-TAG (for German).

1 Introduction

Classic TAG is known to offer rather limited (Becker et al., 1991) and unsatisfying ways to account for flexible word order in languages such as German. The descriptive overhead is immediately evident: Every possible relative order of co-complements of a verb, has to be covered by an extra elementary tree. To give an example from German, the verb *vergisst* (forgets) with two complements would receive two elementary trees in order to license the verb final configurations in (1), not mentioning the other extra elementary trees that are necessary for verb-second position.

(1) a. *dass Peter ihn heute vergisst*
 b. *dass ihn Peter heute vergisst*
 c. *dass ihn heute Peter vergisst*
 d. *dass heute ihn Peter vergisst*
 e. ...
 ('that Peter forgets him/it today')

While classic TAG seems to be appropriate for dealing with fixed word order languages and structural case (i.e., rudimentary case inflection), it is somehow missing the point when applied to free word order languages with rich case inflection.

This work addresses the modelling of complementation in German by means of TT-MCTAG, a recently developed derivative of Multi-Component TAG (MCTAG), that uses tree tuples as elementary structures. In contrast to classic TAG, we are able to abstract away from the relative order of co-complements in the final derived tree. Consequently, the TT-MCTAG account of complementation does not seem to be available for strict word order languages such as English, if complement-argument linking is performed on the basis of pre-derivational, lexical structures.

Therefore, a part of this survey will deal with the comparison with XTAG (XTAG Research Group, 2001), a rich TAG for English. Focussing on wh-extraction, we can observe a trade-off between the extent of word order flexibility and the size of the lexicon. Another comparison is dedicated to V-TAG (Rambow, 1994), which follows a strategy similar to TT-MCTAG, but chooses a different path to constrain locality. The effects of this choice can be clearly observed with bridging constructions.

We thus restrict ourselves to sentential complements, namely wh-extraction, that-complementation and bridging. The assigned analyses are parts of an extensive grammar for German, GerTT (German TT-MCTAG), that is currently being implemented using TT-MCTAG.[1] A parser is also available as part of the TuLiPA framework (Parmentier et al., 2008).[2]

---

[1] `http://www.sfb441.uni-tuebingen.de/emmy-noether-kallmeyer/gertt/`
[2] `http://sourcesup.cru.fr/tulipa/`

Proceedings of The Ninth International Workshop on Tree Adjoining Grammars and Related Formalisms
Tübingen, Germany. June 6-8, 2008.

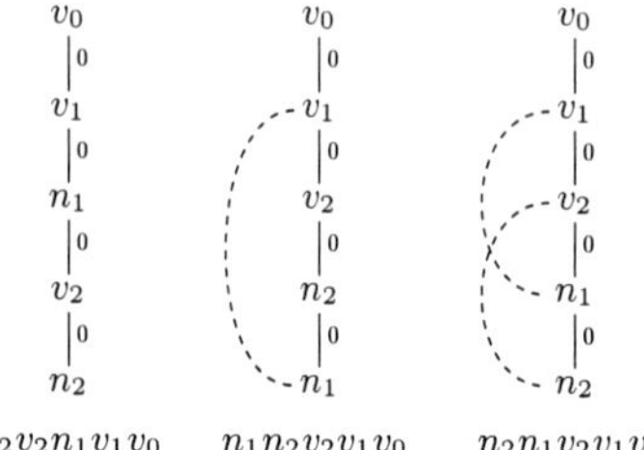

Some derivation trees and corresponding strings (node sharing relations are depicted as dotted edges):

$$n_2 v_2 n_1 v_1 v_0 \qquad n_1 n_2 v_2 v_1 v_0 \qquad n_2 n_1 v_2 v_1 v_0$$

Figure 1: Sample TT-MCTAG

2 k-**TT-MCTAG**

In TT-MCTAG, elementary structures are made of tuples of the form $\langle \gamma, \{\beta_1, ..., \beta_n\}\rangle$, where $\gamma, \beta_1, ..., \beta_n$ are elementary trees in terms of TAG (Joshi and Schabes, 1997). More precisely, γ is a lexicalized elementary tree while $\beta_1, ..., \beta_n$ are auxiliary trees. During derivation, the β-trees have to attach to the γ-tree, either directly or indirectly via node sharing (Kallmeyer, 2005). Roughly speaking, node sharing terms an extended locality, that allows β-trees to also adjoin at the roots of trees that either adjoin to γ themselves, or that are again in a node sharing relation to γ. In other words, an argument β must be linked by a chain of root adjunction to an elementary tree that adjoins to β's head γ.

As an example, consider the TT-MCTAG in Fig. 1. A derivation in this grammar necessarily starts with γ_v. We can adjoin arbitrarily many copies of γ_{v_1} or γ_{v_2}, always to the root of the already derived tree. Concerning the respective argument trees β_{n_1} and β_{n_2}, they must either adjoin immediately to the root of the correponding γ_{v_i} or their adjunction can be delayed. In this case they adjoin later to the root and we say that they stand in a node sharing relation to the corresponding γ_{v_i}. As a result we obtain all strings where an arbitrary

sequence of v_i ($1 \leq i \leq 2$) precedes a v_0 and for each of the v_i ($1 \leq i \leq 2$), there is a unique correponding argument n_i in the string that precedes this v_i. In terms of dependencies, we obtain all permutations of the n_i, i.e., a language displaying everything from nested to cross-serial dependencies.

TT-MCTAG are further restricted, such that at each point of the derivation the number of pending β-trees is at most k. This subclass is also called k-TT-MCTAG. TT-MCTAG in general are NP-complete (Søgaard et al., 2007) while k-TT-MCTAG are mildly context-sensitive (Kallmeyer and Parmentier, 2008).

3 Principles of Complementation

3.1 Basic assumptions

The linguistic understanding of a tuple is that of a head (the γ-tree) and its subcategorization frame (the β-trees). More precisely, the β-trees contain a substitution node, where the complement is inserted. Another way to incorporate complements is to have a footnote in the head tree. This is exploited in, e.g., coherent constructions and bridging constructions. A TT-MCTAG account of scrambling and coherent constructions has been presented in Lichte (2007). Because of the nature of node sharing, subsitution establishes strong islands for movement, while adjunction widens the domain of locality.

In contrast to XTAG, we completely omit empty categories (e.g. traces, PRO) in syntactic description. This follows from rejecting a base word order for German, as well as dealing with argument raising and control only in the semantics.[3] As an example, consider the elementary tree tuples for (1) in Fig. 2 and the (TAG) derivation tree for (1)a.

In this derivation, none of the arguments adjoins immediately to their head *vergisst* but both stand in a node sharing relation to it.

Besides verb-final (V3) trees as in Fig. 2, there are also verb-second (V12) trees for finite verbs that contain two verbal positions: the left bracket (position of the verb) and the right bracket (sometimes containing, e.g., particles). See Fig. 3 for the *vergisst* tuple in verb-second sentences such as (2).

---

[3]This is linguistically supported, e.g., by Sag and Fodor (1994) and Culicover and Wilkins (1986).

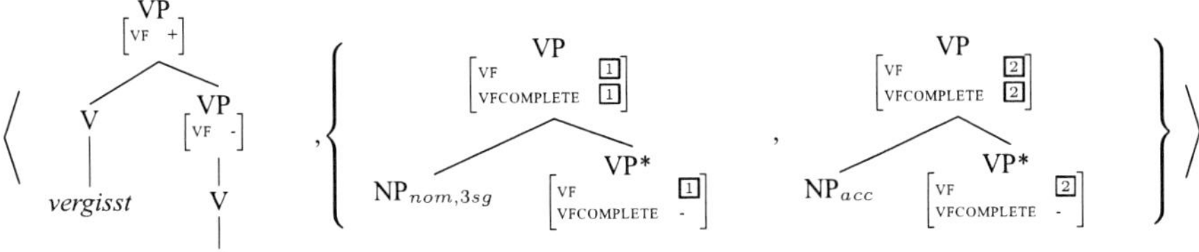

Figure 3: V12 tree tuple for *vergisst* as in (2)

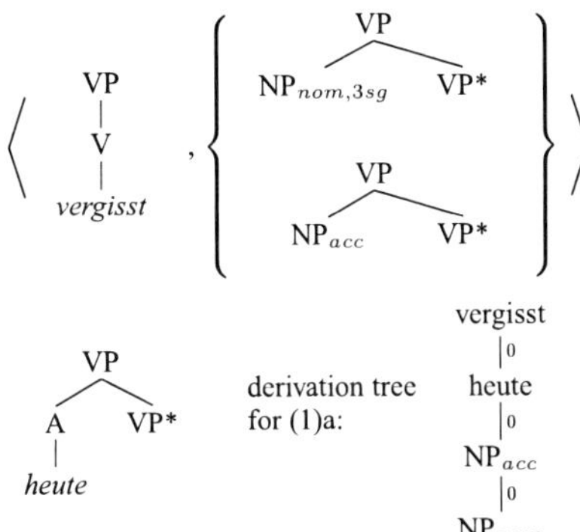

Figure 2: Tree tuples and derivation tree for (1)

(2) a. *Peter vergisst ihn*
    Peter forgets him
   b. *ihn vergisst Peter*
    him forgets Peter

A feature VF for *vorfeld* indicates whether a VP node dominates the left bracket and therefore belongs to the vorfeld. If this is the case, then we must adjoin exactly one tree to this VP node since the vorfeld is always filled by exactly one constituent. This is guaranteed by the feature VFCOMPLETE that indicates whether the vorfeld is already filled. A vorfeld-adjoining argument tree switches this feature from $-$ to $+$.

3.2 Raising, auxiliaries and control

In our grammar, raising verbs and auxiliaries do not have a subject argument tree. Instead, the subject comes with the embedded infinitival. In this, we follow the choices of the XTAG grammar. Control verbs, however, have a subject. The argument identity between the controller and the subject of the embedded infinitive is established via a special feature that is then used within semantic computation.

Because of the difference between raising and control, we have to deal with verbs embedding an infinitive with subject (raising, auxiliaries, ECM verbs) and verbs embedding an infinitive without subject. This is more complicated than in XTAG since the presence of a subject cannot be seen from the verb tree, the subject argument tree being a separate auxiliary tree. Therefore we need a feature SUBJ that indicates whether a verb has a subject. Furthermore, the infinitive can have different forms, captured by the feature STAT for status: It can be a bare infinitive (STAT 1) an infinitive with *zu* (STAT 2) or a participle (STAT 3).

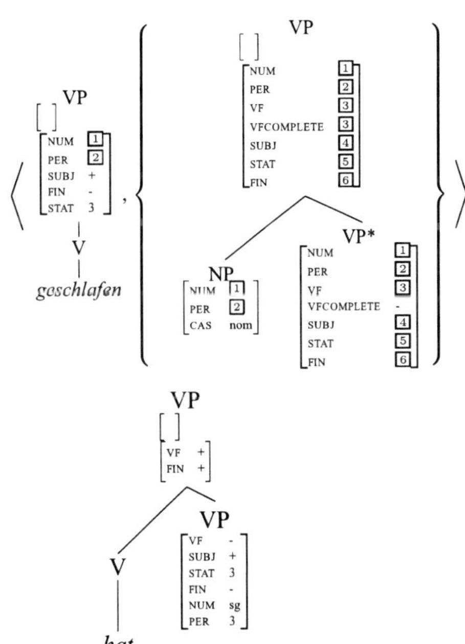

Figure 4: Analysis of auxiliaries

(3) *Peter hat geschlafen*
   Peter has slept

As an example, Fig. 4 shows the trees for *hat* and

geschlafen in (3). In V2 auxiliary constructions such as (3), the left bracket is contributed by a separate auxiliary tree instead of being fixed within the tuple of the main verb. We must make sure that the auxiliary is recognized as left bracket and that there is exactly one element occupying the vorfeld, i.e., preceding the left bracket. This can be done by setting the feature VF − at the foot node and + at the root. The feature VFCOMPLETE on the argument trees works then exactly as in the case where the left bracket comes with the main verb.

A further issue to take into account is the agreement between subject and verb. Since we have a free word order language, we do not know where on the verbal spine the subject comes in. Therefore we need to percolate the subject agreement feature along the entire verbal spine to be unified with the auxiliary verb agreement features.

3.3   PP and sentential argument trees

Concerning the morphological form an argument can take (a NP, a PP or a sentential argument), we do not distinguish between these at the level of the category of the argument slot. Rather, their specific properties are treated within appropriate features (e.g., CASE). This can be achieved by assigning to the mopho-syntactic category (CAT) of argument slots either an underspecified value or a disjunction of category labels.[4] As a result, the same tree-family can be used for all verbs taking the same number of arguments. The selection of a preposition for one of the arguments is done via the case feature.

Furthermore, in our grammar, the family of a verb does not contain extra tree tuples for wh-extraction. Instead, the wh-element has a nominal category and can be substituted into a nominal argument tree. This accounts for the facts that wh-elements distribute similarly to non-wh NPs, see (4).

(4) a.   *Peter hat wen   heute gesehen*
      Peter has whom_WH today seen

    b.   *wen   hat Peter wann gesehen*
        whom_WH has Peter when seen

---

[4]Both strategies are supported by the metagrammar framework XMG (Duchier et al., 2004), but not yet by the TuLiPA parser (Parmentier et al., 2008). Therefore, in our current implementation of the grammar, only NP and PP arguments are treated uniformly, both of them having the category NP.

The underspecification of argument categories and the fact that wh-extraction does not require special tree truples considerably decreases the number of verb families that are needed compared to grammars such as XTAG. From our experience with implementing the grammar we have the impression that this is an advantage for the grammar writer.

The choice to treat sentential and nominal arguments alike means in particular that sentential complements are added by substitution and therefore constitute islands for scrambling. However, an exceptional case are bridge verbs (see next section).

4   Sentential Complements

We present the analysis of sentential complements for German, that have a finite verb in clause-final position (V3). Nonfinite sentential complementation is ignored throughout the paper.

In German, V3 sentences serve as source for subordinate clauses, that are marked by certain elements in sentence-initial position, e.g., a wh-pronoun, a relative pronoun, or a complementizer. To model this fact, we introduce the feature S-TYPE, which indicates the sentence type via a complex value. Fig. 5 presents the schema of S-TYPE and its specification in the tree tuple of *vergisst*. Note that marking is enforced by the top-bottom mismatch of MARKED in the root node of the head tree.

4.1   Free relatives and embedded questions

Free relatives and embedded questions consist of V3 sentences that start with a relative pronoun or a wh-pronoun, respectively. Examples are given in (5).

(5) a.   *den   heute Peter bestohlen   hat*
      whom_REL today Peter stolen_from has

    b.   *wen   heute Peter bestohlen   hat*
      whom_WH today Peter stolen_from has
      ('from whom Peter has stolen')

The corresponding constructions in English are commonly said to involve *wh-extraction*. Note that, in contrast to English, German lacks do-support and preposition stranding altogether. The analyses of free relatives and embedded questions in Fig. 6 only differ with respect to the terminal and the MARKING value in the elementary trees of

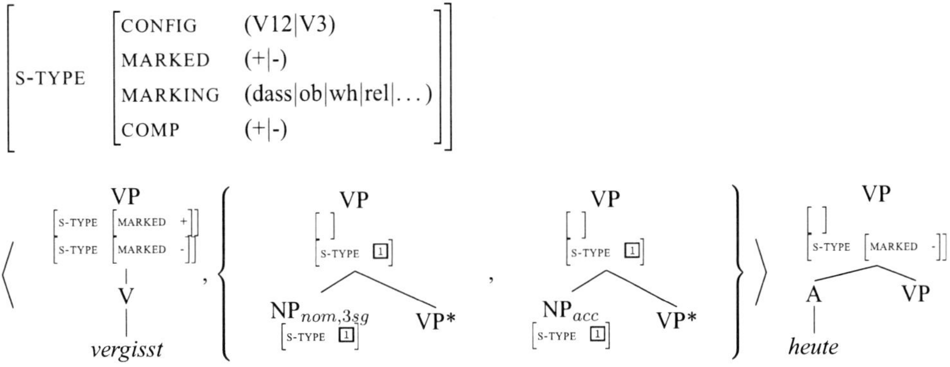

Figure 5: Use of the features STYPE and MARKED

the respective pronouns. Both substitute into a regular complement slot, and both have the MARKED feature set to +, which suffices to resolve the feature conflict in the VP projection.

4.2 Complementized sentences

Complementized sentences consist of V3 sentences that have a complementizer in initial position, e.g., *dass* (that), *ob* (whether), and *wenn* (if). An example is given in (6).

(6) a. *dass ihn heute Peter vergisst*
    that him today Peter forgets
  b. **dass dass ihn heute Peter vergisst*
  c. **dass ihn vergisst heute Peter*

Two pitfalls have to be avoided: stacked complementizers as in (6)b, and V12 configurations as in (6)c. Considering Fig. 7, the first pitfall is avoided by using the feature COMP, that indicates whether complementation already took place. To account for the second one, the feature CONFIG specifies the topological configuration of the underlying sentence.

4.3 Bridge verbs

Bridge verbs allow for the extraction of constituents from the complementized sentential complement, see (7).

(7) a. *Wen glaubst du, dass Peter heute*
    Whom think_2SG you, that Peter today
    vergisst?
    forgets

  b. *?Wer glaubst du, dass ihn heute*
    Who think_2SG you, that him today
    vergisst?
    forgets

  c. **Wen magst du, dass Peter heute*
    Whom like_2SG you, that Peter today
    vergisst?
    forgets

  d. **Du glaubst wen, dass Peter heute*
    You think_2SG whom, that Peter today
    vergisst?
    forgets

In order to derive the example sentence in (7), the tree tuple from Fig. 8 has to be attached to some derived tree such as in Fig.7, but where the accusative object is still pending. Due to the adjunction of the bridge verb, the pending complement is able to adjoin at its root node via node sharing. The VF feature makes sure that only one pending complement can attach higher.

The long extraction of the subject in (7)b is claimed to be ungrammatical in English (*that-trace effect*). If this would also hold for German (which is rejected by several authors, see Featherston (2003)), we would have to introduce further features indicating the type of the complement. As it is now, the bridge verb is agnostic towards the material that is adjoined at its root. The contrast between bridge verbs and non-bridge verbs in (7)c could be explained by the absence of bridging tree tuples for non-bridge verbs. Long-distance extraction to a non-initial position, as in (7)d, is ruled out since the lower-right VP node is no root and therefore not shared.

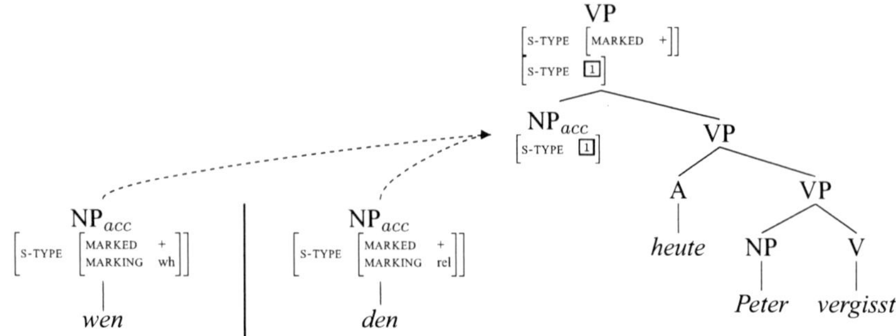

Figure 6: Wh-pronouns and relative pronouns

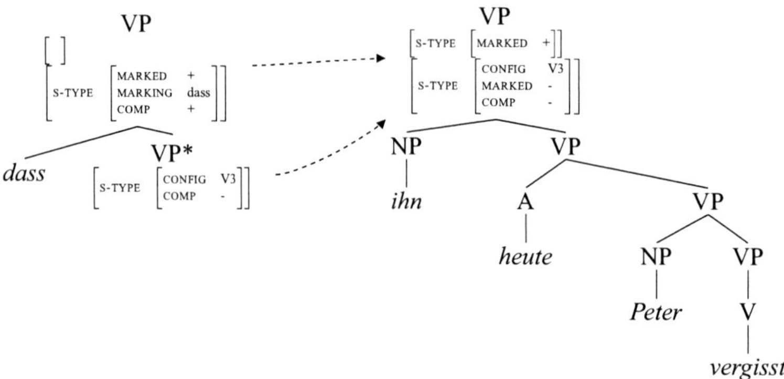

Figure 7: Complementizers

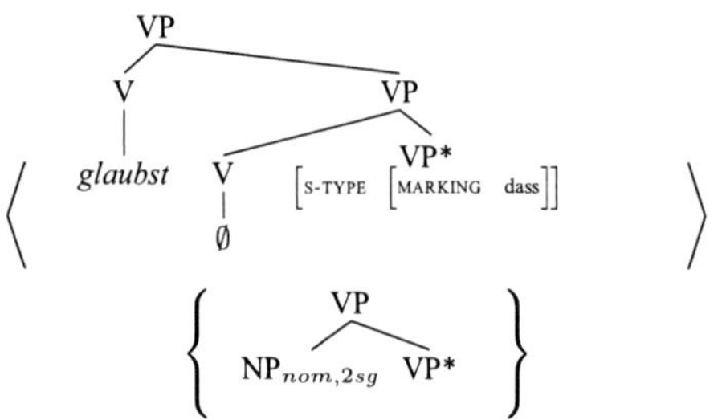

Figure 8: Bridge verbs

5 Extraction in XTAG

The principal discrepancy between XTAG and our grammar is the way of encoding the relative order between complements: using TAG, XTAG determines the relative order of complements in elementary trees. Consequently, deviations from the canonical order of complements have to be explicitly anticipated by providing extra trees in the grammar. This can be prominently observed with wh-extraction phenomena, where potentially every complement can be extracted. Thus, focussing merely on wh-extraction, a verb with n complements receives $n + 1$ elementary trees in XTAG, such as the one for object extraction in Fig. 9.[5] In our grammar based on TT-MCTAG, however, there is exactly one tree tuple for each verb and its subcategorization frame.

Nesson and Shieber (2007) consider a tree-local MCTAG account to reduce the set of extraction trees in XTAG by introducing tree sets that contain the extracted complement and its trace in separate trees. This, however, only moves the inherent ambiguity to the representation of the nouns, which does not seem to be more preferable to us.

6 Comparison to V-TAG

TT-MCTAG's nearest relative certainly is V-TAG from Rambow (1994), also designed for flexible word order phenomena in German. Superficially,

---

[5]We ignore preposition stranding here, since it does not exist in German. Furthermore, we deal with sentential complements in terms of direct objects.

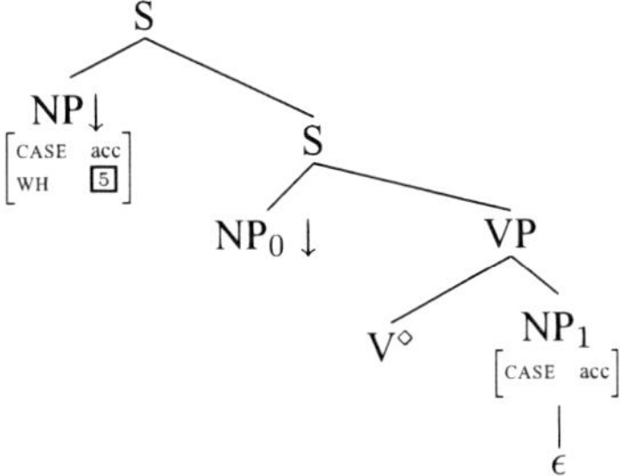

Figure 9: Feature reduced XTAG tree for object extraction (Fig. 15.1 therein)

their elementary structures look quite similar, as Fig. 10 shows. Technically, however, the limitation of non-locality is accomplished in different ways: where TT-MCTAG refers to the derivation tree using the notion of shared nodes, V-TAG makes use of *dominance links* and *integrity constraints* in the derived tree.

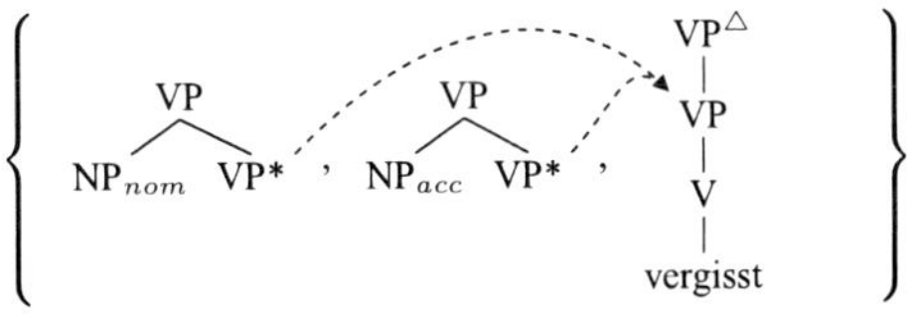

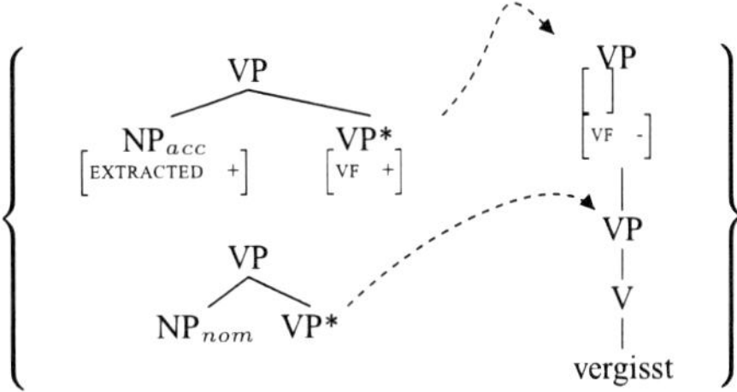

(dotted arrows = dominance links, △ = integrity constraint)

Figure 10: V-TAG tree set for *vergisst* ('forgets')

Most of the presented analyses for sentential complements can be easily mapped onto V-TAG variants, while preserving the idea of factorizing complementation. There is, however, one crucial exception: The analysis for bridging constructions cannot be borrowed directly, since, within V-TAG, it is not possible to express that the VP root node is accessible for a complement of the sentential complement, while the lower VP node is not accessible. Hence, in order to exclude (7)d while keeping an analysis that factors arguments into separate auxiliary trees, one needs different argument trees for complements that might be scrambled and complements that are extracted. The latter might, e.g., be forced to adjoin to a node with VF = +, as shown in Fig.11. However, the necessary removing of the integrity constraint on the VP root of the verbal tree would allow a movement of the non-extracted complement into the mittelfeld of the bridge verb as in (8). This is something that cannot happen with TT-MCTAG since the mittelfeld

node of the bridge verb is not accessible via node sharing for arguments of the embedded verb.

(8)*Wen   glaubst   Peter du,   dass heute
     Whom think_2SG Peter you, that today
     vergisst?
     forgets

Figure 11: Possible V-TAG tree set for extraction with factored complements

Of course, in order to analyse bridge verbs with extraction in V-TAG, there is always the possibility to have the extracted argument and its verbal head in the same elementary tree; only the (possibly scrambled) other complements are in separate argument trees. Then the integrity constraint on the upper VP node can be maintained and examples (7) and (8) are analysed correctly.

In general one can say that formalisms such as V-TAG (and also DSG (Rambow et al., 2001)) have to model locality constraints explicitly since the derivation itself in these formalisms is not constrained by any locality requirement. As a result, an analysis that factors complementation the way we propose it within TT-MCTAG seems less easily available. Furthermore, the fact that locality constraints follow from the TT-MCTAG formalism and need not be explicitly stipulated is in our view an advantage of this formalism.[6]

7 Discussion

As already mentioned, a key idea of our grammar is the factorization of argument slots in separate auxiliary trees. As a result, we need considerably less elementary tree sets per family than standard TAG. Furthermore, since we treat prepositional, sentential and nomial arguments alike, the number of tree set families reduces as well. From our current experience with the development of the grammar, we feel that this is an advantage for grammar

___
[6]We might of course encounter cases where the TT-MCTAG locality is too restrictive.

implementation. Concerning parsing, we have to take into account all possible combinations of the trees in our tuples. In this respect, the factorization of course only shifts the task of building constituent structures for subcategorization frames to a different part of the system.

k-TT-MCTAG is mildly context-sensitive and, furthermore, we suspect that it is a proper subclass of set-local MCTAG. Recently, Chen-Main and Joshi (2007) discussed the fact that in actual analyses, only a very small part of the possibilities provided by multicomponent TAG extensions (e.g., tree-local and set-local MCTAG) is used. Consequently, the proposed MCTAGs don't correspond to the actual need for linguistic descriptions. We hope that k-TT-MCTAG with its rather strong locality might be a further step towards the identification of the class of grammar formalisms suitable for natural language processing.

Acknowledgments

The work presented here was funded by the Emmy-Noether program of the DFG.

We would like to thank three anonymous reviewers whose comments helped to considerably improve the paper. Furthermore, we are indebted to the TuLiPA-team, in particular Yannick Parmentier, Wolfgang Maier and Johannes Dellert. Without the TuLiPA parser, the development of our German TT-MCTAG would not have been possible.

References

Becker, Tilman, Aravind K. Joshi, and Owen Rambow. 1991. Long-distance scrambling and tree adjoining grammars. In *Proceedings of ACL-Europe*.

Chen-Main, Joan and Aravind Joshi. 2007. Multicomponent Tree Adjoining Grammars, Dependency Graph Models, and Linguistic Analyses. In *ACL 2007 Workshop on Deep Linguistic Processing*, pages 1–8, Prague, Czech Republic, June. Association for Computational Linguistics.

Culicover, Peter W. and Wendy Wilkins. 1986. Control, PRO, and the projection principle. *Language*, 62(1):120–153.

Duchier, Denys, Joseph Le Roux, and Yannick Parmentier. 2004. The Metagrammar Compiler: An NLP Application with a Multi-paradigm Architecture. In *Second International Mozart/Oz Conference (MOZ'2004)*.

Featherston, Sam. 2003. That-trace in German. *Lingua*, 1091:1–26.

Joshi, Aravind K. and Yves Schabes. 1997. Tree-adjoining grammars. In Rozenberg, G. and A. Salomaa, editors, *Handbook of Formal Languages*, volume 3, pages 69–124. Springer, Berlin, New York.

Kallmeyer, Laura and Yannick Parmentier. 2008. On the relation between Multicomponent Tree Adjoining Grammars with Tree Tuples (TT-MCTAG) and Range Concatenation Grammars (RCG). In *Proceedings of the 2nd International Conference on Language and Automata Theory and Applications LATA*, Tarragona, Spain, March.

Kallmeyer, Laura. 2005. Tree-local multicomponent tree adjoining grammars with shared nodes. *Computational Linguistics*, 31:2:187–225.

Lichte, Timm. 2007. An MCTAG with tuples for coherent constructions in German. In *Proceedings of the 12th Conference on Formal Grammar*. Dublin, Ireland, 4-5 August 2007.

Nesson, Rebecca and Stuart Shieber. 2007. Extraction phenomena in synchronous TAG syntax and semantics. In Wu, Dekai and David Chiang, editors, *Proceedings of the Workshop on Syntax and Structure in Statistical Translation*. Rochester, New York, 26 April 2007.

Parmentier, Yannick, Laura Kallmeyer, Wolfgang Maier, Timm Lichte, and Johannes Dellert. 2008. TuLiPA: A syntax-semantics parsing environment for mildly context-sensitive formalisms. In *Proceedings of TAG+9*.

Rambow, Owen, K. Vijay-Shanker, and David Weir. 2001. D-Tree Substitution Grammars. *Computational Linguistics*.

Rambow, Owen. 1994. *Formal and Computational Aspects of Natural Language Syntax*. Ph.D. thesis, University of Pennsylvania, Philadelphia. IRCS Report 94-08.

Sag, Ivan A. and Janet Dean Fodor. 1994. Extraction without traces. In *Proceedings of the Thirteenth Annual Meeting of the West Coast Conference on Formal Linguistics*, pages 365–384, Stanford. CSLI Publications.

Søgaard, Anders, Timm Lichte, and Wolfgang Maier. 2007. The complexity of linguistically motivated extensions of tree-adjoining grammar. In *Recent Advances in Natural Language Processing 2007*, Borovets, Bulgaria.

XTAG Research Group. 2001. A Lexicalized Tree Adjoining Grammar for English. Technical report, Institute for Research in Cognitive Science, University of Pennsylvania, Philadelphia, PA.

Lambek Grammars, Tree Adjoining Grammars
and Hyperedge Replacement Grammars

Richard Moot

LaBRI(CNRS), INRIA Bordeaux SO & Bordeaux University

351, cours de la Libération

33405 Talence, France

Richard.Moot@labri.fr

Abstract

Two recent extension of the non-associative Lambek calculus, the Lambek-Grishin calculus and the multimodal Lambek calculus, are shown to generate class of languages as tree adjoining grammars, using (tree generating) hyperedge replacement grammars as an intermediate step. As a consequence both extensions are mildly context-sensitive formalisms and benefit from polynomial parsing algorithms.

1 Introduction

Joshi et al., (1991) have shown that many independently proposed mildly context-sensitive grammar formalisms — combinatory categorial grammars, head grammars, linear indexed grammars and tree adjoining grammars (TAGs) — generate the same class of string languages.

For the Lambek calculus **L** (Lambek, 1958), Pentus (1995) has shown that **L** grammars generate only context-free languages. Two recent incarnations of Lambek grammars have sought to extend the generative capacity the Lambek calculus: the *multimodal* Lambek calculus $\mathbf{NL}\diamondsuit_\mathcal{R}$ (Moortgat, 1997) and the *Lambek-Grishin* calculus **LG** (Moortgat, 2007). Both of these systems use the non-associative Lambek calculus **NL** (Lambek, 1961), for which polynomial algorithms exist (de Groote, 1999; Capelletti, 2007), as their base, but add interaction principles to augment the descriptive power. While both systems have been shown to handle linguistic phenomena for which no satisfactory Lambek calculus analysis exists, little is

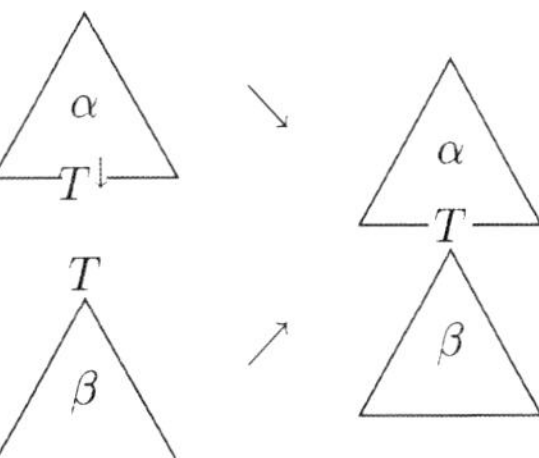

Figure 1: Substitution

known about the exact class of languages generated by either system or about the complexity cost of adding these interaction principles.

In the current paper I shown that both $\mathbf{NL}\diamondsuit_\mathcal{R}$ and **LG** generate the same class of languages as TAGs, using hyperedge replacement grammars as an intermediate step.

2 Tree Adjoining Grammars and Hyperedge Replacement Grammars

Tree Adjoining Grammars (Joshi and Schabes, 1997) combine trees using the operations of *substitution* (shown in Figure 1) which replaces a nonterminal leaf $T^\downarrow$ by a tree with root T and *adjunction* (shown in Figure 2) which replaces and internal node A by a tree with root node A and foot node A^*.

Formally, TAGs are defined as follows.

Definition 1 *An TAG is a tuple* $\langle \Sigma, N_S, N_A, \mathcal{I}, \mathcal{A} \rangle$ *such that*

- Σ, N_S *and* N_A *and three disjoint alphabets of terminals, substitution nonterminals and adjunction nonterminals respectively, I will use upper case letters* $T, U, \ldots$ *and of course*

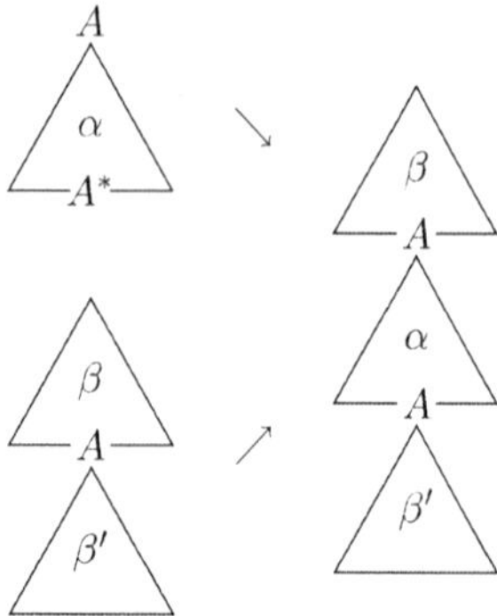

Figure 2: Adjunction

the distinguished start symbol S to stand for members of N_S whereas I will use upper case letters $A, B, \ldots$ for members of N_A.

- *$\mathcal{I}$ is a finite set of initial trees,*

- *$\mathcal{A}$ is a finite set of auxiliary trees.*

The trees in $\mathcal{I} \cup \mathcal{A}$ are called the elementary trees.
Trees are subject to the following conditions:

- *the root nodes of all initial trees are members of N_S,*

- *the root nodes of all auxiliary trees are members of N_A,*

- *every auxiliary tree has exactly one leaf which is a member of N_A. This leaf is called the* foot node,

- *all other leaves of elementary trees are members of $N_S \cup \Sigma$.*

A TAG satisfying the additional condition that all elementary trees have exactly one terminal leaf is called a lexicalized *tree adjoining grammar (LTAG). This leaf is called the* lexical anchor,

In addition, a TAG is allowed to specify constraints on adjunction. Let $A \in N_A$ and let t be the set of auxiliary trees with root node A and foot node A^*. A node A in a elementary tree α is said to have selective adjunction *in case it specifies a subset $t' \subsetneq t$ of trees which are allowed to adjoin at this node. The special case where $t' = \emptyset$ is called* null adjunction. *Finally, a node can specify* obligatory adjunction *where an auxiliary tree has to be adjoined at the node.*

The only difference with the standard definition of tree adjoining grammars (Joshi and Schabes, 1997) is the use of separate alphabets for auxiliary and substitution nonterminals. In addition to making the substitution marker $T^{\downarrow}$ and the foot node marker A^* technically superfluous, this will make the different embedding results which follow slightly easier to prove.

Definition 2 *An LTAG' grammar G is an LTAG satisfying the following additional conditions.*

- *all internal nodes of elementary trees have exactly two daughters,*

- *every adjunction node either specifies the null adjunction or the obligatory adjunction constraint without any selectional restrictions,*

- *every adjunction node is on the path from the lexical anchor to the root of the tree.*

The definition of LTAG' is very close to the definition of *normal* or *spinal form* LTAGs used by Joshi et al. (1991) and by Vijay-Shanker and Weir (1994) to show correspondence between LTAGs and combinatory categorial grammars, so it should be no surprise it will serve as a way to shown inclusion of tree adjoining languages in multimodal and Lambek-Grishin languages. The only difference is that the adjunction nodes are required to be on the path from the root to the *lexical anchor* instead of the foot node.

Lemma 3 *For every LTAG grammar G there is a weakly equivalent LTAG' grammar G'.*

Proof (sketch) The proof is analogous to the proof of Vijay-Shanker and Weir (1994). □

A *hypergraph* is a set of *hyperedges*, portrayed as an edge label in a rectangular box, which can be incident to any number of vertices. These connections are portrayed by lines (called 'tentacles') labelled $0, \ldots, n$ (the selectors) for a hyperedge of arity $n + 1$. A *hyperedge replacement grammar* (Engelfriet, 1997; Drewes et al., 1997) replaces a hyperedge with a nonterminal symbol by a hypergraph.

The rank of a terminal or nonterminal symbol is the number of its tentacles. The rank k of a HR grammar is the maximum number of tentacles of a nonterminal symbol. We will be particularly interested in HR grammars of rank two (HR_2) even

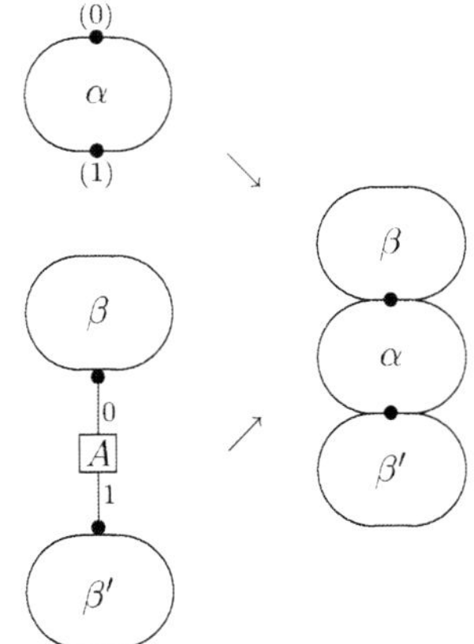

Figure 3: Hyperedge Replacement

though we do use *terminal* nodes with multiple edges.

Figure 3 shows an example of hyperedge replacement for a nonterminal A of rank two. It is attached to two vertices, represented by fat dots, with selectors 0 and 1 respectively. If $A \to \alpha$ is a rule in the HR grammar, we can replace the hyperedge A by first deleting it, then identifying the external node (0) of α with the node which was connected to tentacle 0 and external node (1) of α with the node which was connected to tentacle 1. The similarity with Figure 2 should be striking. Note however, that since the grammatical objects of hyperedge replacement grammars are *hypergraphs*, β and β' need not be disjoint. In fact, even the two tentacles are allowed to reach the same vertex. However, when we restrict the right hand sides of rules to be trees[1] then, as we will see in Lemma 5, hyperedge replacement and adjunction will correspond exactly.

There are several ways to represent trees in HR grammars, but the following will turn out to be convenient for our applications. A node with label A and n daughters[2] is represented as a hyperedge A with $n + 1$ tentacles, with tentacle 0 pointing towards the parent node and tentacles $1, \ldots, n$ selecting its daughters from left to right.

Definition 4 *A hypergraph H is a (hyper-)tree iff every node in H is incident to two hyperedges, once by a selector 0 and once by a selector > 0,*

---

[1]This is $TR(HR_{tr})$ from (Engelfriet and Maneth, 2000).

[2]We assume here that all occurrences of A have the same number of daughters, which we can accomplish by a simple renaming, if necessary.

except the root node, which is incident to a single hyperedge by selector 0.

Lemma 5 HR_2 *grammars generating trees and TAG grammars are strongly equivalent.*

Proof (sketch) From TAG to HR_2, we start with a TAG G and categorise the different adjunction nodes, introducing new symbols whenever two nodes labelled by the same symbol of N_A either select a different set of trees or differ with respect to obligatory adjunction to obtain a TAG G' which is equivalent to G up to a relabelling of the members of N_A.

Now let t be an initial tree with root node T in G', we transform it into a hypertree t' corresponding to Definition 4, with each adjunction point replaced by a unary branch with the nonterminal A corresponding to the adjunctions possible at the node and each leaf U marked for substitution replaced by a nonterminal leaf U and add rule $T \to t'$ to the HR grammar.

Each of the members of $A \in N_A$ in G' has a set of auxiliary trees t assigned to it as well as an indication of whether or not adjunction is obligatory. For each $\alpha \in t$ we add a rule $A \to \alpha$ to the grammar. In addition, if adjunction is not obligatory we add a rule $A \to \bullet$, eliminating the nonterminal hyperedge.

Now every adjunction corresponds to a hyperedge replacement as shown in Figure 3 and every substitution to the same figure, but with both the 1 tentacle and the β' subtree removed.

From HR_2 to TAG we use the fact that we generate a tree and that all nonterminals are of rank ≤ 2.

Suppose A is a nonterminal of rank two and $A \to \alpha$ is a rule in the HR_2 grammar G. In case α is a single node $\bullet$ we mark all adjunctions of a nonterminal A as optional in the grammar. If not, we add the auxiliary tree α' which we obtain from α by labelling the external node (0) by A and the external node (1) by A^* to the TAG.

Suppose T is a nonterminal of rank one and $T \to t$ is a rule in G. By Definition 4, in order for this rule to be productive the single external node has to be the root. We label the root by T and add the resulting tree as initial tree to the TAG. Again, it is easy to see that every hyperedge replacement of a nonterminal of rank 1 corresponds to a substitution and every hyperedge replacement of rank 2

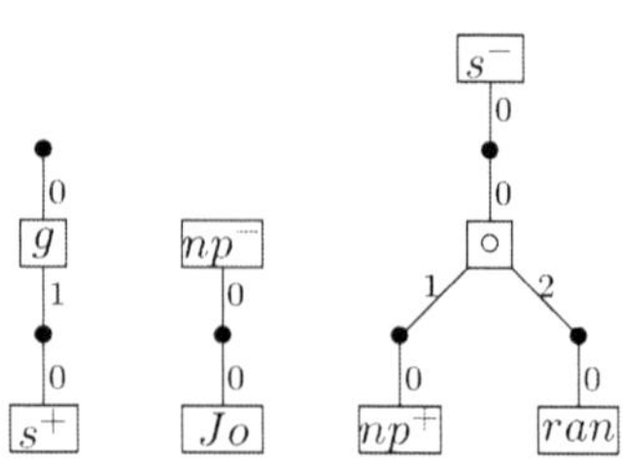

Figure 4: AB lexicon

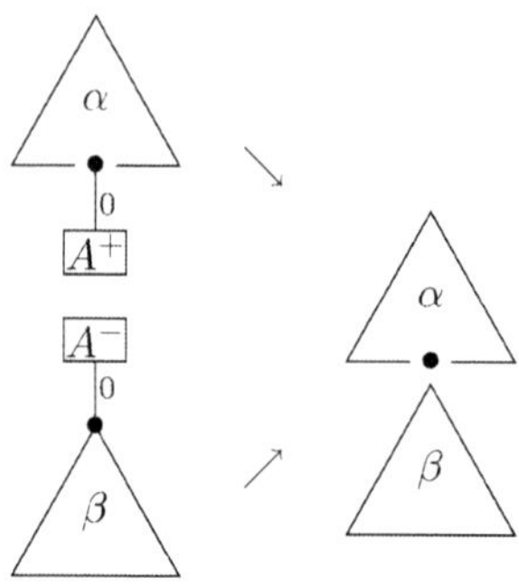

Figure 5: The axiom rule

corresponds to an adjunction in the generated TAG grammar.   □

3 Lambek Grammars

Before talking about Lambek grammars, seen from a hypergraph perspective, it is useful to first show a lexicon for AB grammars. Figure 4 shows a trivial AB lexicon for the phrase 'Jo ran'. As usual in categorial grammars, we distinguish between positive and negative occurrences of atomic formulas.[3]

The tree on the left indicates that the goal formula g of this grammar is a positive s atomic formula. The lexical entry for 'ran' indicates it is looking for an np to its left to produce an s, whereas the entry for 'Jo' simply provides an np. Note that because of the extra unary hyperedge at the root nodes, the two lexical trees are not trees according to Definition 4. I will refer to them as *typed* trees.

The axiom rule (Figure 5) shows how positive and negative formulas of the same type cancel each-other out by identifying the nodes selected by the two unary hyperedges. The resemblance with the substitution operation in Figure 1 should be clear, though we do not require α and β to be disjoint: instead we require that an AB *derivation* — a set of applications of the axiom rule — ends in a (non-typed) tree where all leaves are labelled by terminal symbols.

With respect to Lambek grammars, we are primarily interested in two recent extensions of it, the multimodal Lambek calculus with two modes in-

teracting by means of the mixed associativity and mixed commutativity structural rules (Moortgat, 1997) and the Lambek-Grishin calculus with the Grishin class IV interactions (Moortgat, 2007).

Extending the AB hypergraph calculus in this way involves adding new constructors and graph contractions which eliminate them. This moves the hypergraph calculus (or at least the intermediate structures in the derivations) further away from trees, but we will continue to require that the result of connecting and contracting the graph will be a (non-typed) tree. Contractions will correspond to the logical rules $[R/_i]$, $[L\bullet_i]$ and $[R\backslash_i]$ in the $\mathbf{NL}\Diamond_{\mathcal{R}}$ case and to the logical rules $[L\oslash]$, $[R\odot]$ and $[L\oslash]$ in the $\mathbf{LG}$ case. The contraction for $[L\bullet]$ is shown in the middle and on the right of Figure 6.

An additional constraint on the trees will be that in only contains mode 0 in the $\mathbf{NL}\Diamond_{\mathcal{R}}$ case and that it doesn't contain the 'inverse' Grishin structural connective ';' in the $\mathbf{LG}$ case. This has as a consequence that in any proof, the Grishin connectives and the connectives for mode 1 can only occur in pairs.

The calculus sketched here is just a hypergraph interpretation of the proof nets for the multimodal Lambek calculus of Moot and Puite (2002) and their extension to $\mathbf{LG}$ of Moot (2007), who show that it is sound and complete with respect to the sequent calculus.

As we have seen, it is trivial to model the substitution operation: in this respect substitution is modelled in a way which is equivalent up to notational choices to the work on partial proof trees (Joshi and Kulick, 1997).

Figure 7 shows how to model the adjunction operation, with the solution for $\mathbf{NL}\Diamond_{\mathcal{R}}$ on the left and

---

[3]Negative formulas correspond to resources we have and positive formulas correspond to resources we need. Think of A^+ as being similar to $A^\downarrow$.

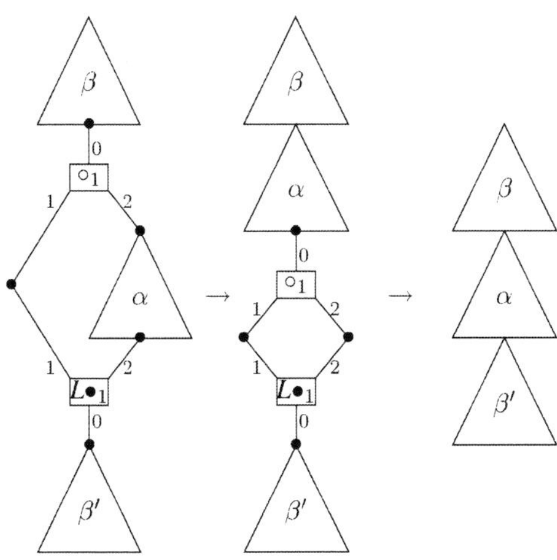

Figure 6: A contraction and structural rules for simulating adjunction

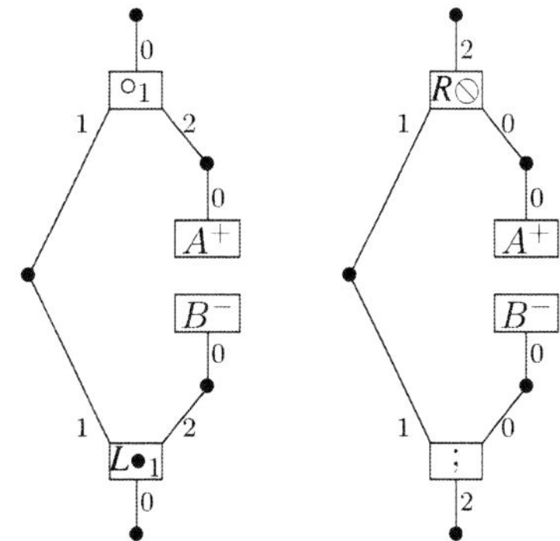

Figure 7: Lambek hypergraphs for adjunction

the solution for **LG** on the right.

Figure 6 shows how this allows us to adjoin a hypergraph corresponding to an auxiliary tree to this adjunction point. After two axiom rules, we will have the structure shown on the left. The mixed associativity and commutativity structural rules allow us to move the $\circ_1$ hyperedge down the tree until we have the structure shown in the middle. Finally, we apply the contraction, deleting the $\circ_1$ and $L\bullet_1$ edges and identifying the two nodes marked by selector 0 to obtain the structure on the right. Remark how these steps together perform an adjunction operation. For the sake of efficiency we will usually not apply the structural rules explicitly. Instead, we will use a generalised contraction, which moves directly from the left of the figure to the structure on the right.

Lemma 6 *If G is an LTAG' grammar, then there exists a strongly equivalent $NL\diamondsuit_{\mathcal{R}}$ grammar G' and a strongly equivalent LG grammar G''.*

Proof (sketch) For each lexical tree t of G we construct a lexical tree t' in G' and a lexical tree t'' in G'', translating every adjunction point by the left hand side of Figure 7 for G' and by its right hand side for G''.

Now let d be a LTAG' derivation using grammar G. We translate this derivation into an $NL\diamondsuit_{\mathcal{R}}$ derivation d' and an **LG** derivation d'' as follows:

- Whenever we substitute a tree with root T for a leaf $T^{\downarrow}$ we perform the corresponding axiom connection in d' and d'', as shown in Figure 5.

- Whenever we adjoin a tree with root A and foot A^* we perform the A axiom for the root node, the B axiom for the foot node followed by the generalised contraction shown in Figure 6.

In order to show we generate *only* the LTAG' derivations we have to show that no other combination of axioms will produce a proof net. Given the separation of non-terminals into N_S and N_A as well as the contraction requirement this is trivial. $\square$

To complete the proofs, we show that there is an HR grammar G' generating the hypergraphs corresponding to the proofs of an **LG** or **NL**$\diamondsuit_{\mathcal{R}}$ grammar G, that is to say the grammar G' generates sequences of lexical graphs which, using axiom connections and generalised contractions contract to a tree.

Lemma 7 *If G is a Lambek Grammar, then there exists a strongly equivalent HR_2 grammar G'.*

Proof (sketch) Let G be a **NL**$\diamondsuit_{\mathcal{R}}$ or an **LG** grammar. We generate a hyperedge replacement grammar H of rank two which generate all proof nets, that is to say all lexical graphs which by means of axiom connections and generalised contractions convert to a tree. Conceptually, we can think of this HR grammar as operating in three phases:

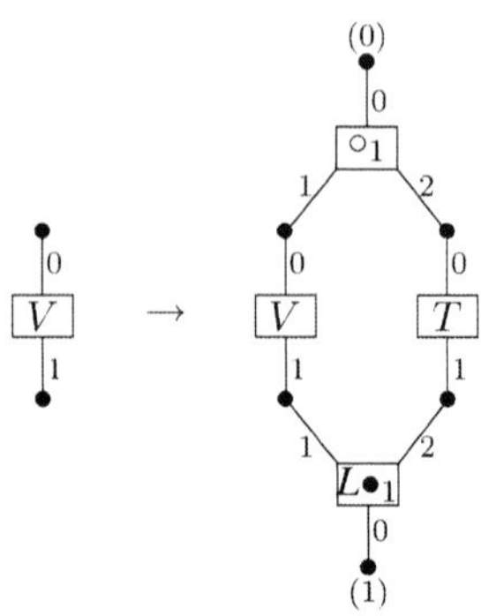

Figure 8: Lambek grammar as HR grammar — adjunction

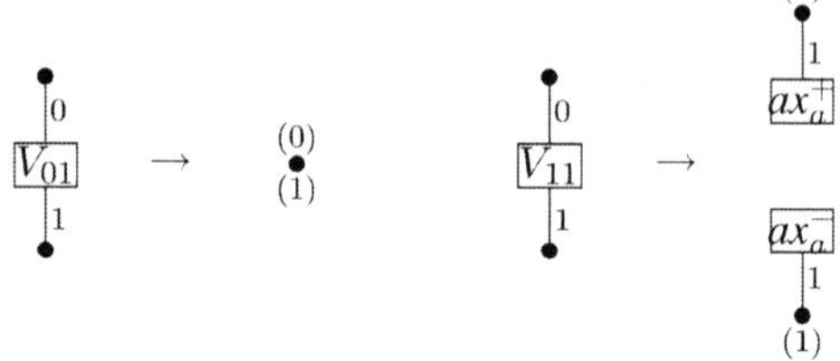

Figure 9: Lambek grammar as HR grammar — flow/axiom

1. Expand T (tree) nonterminals to generate *all* binary branching trees with V (vertex) nonterminals between all branches.

2. Expand V nonterminals to perform generalised expansions, that is to say inverse contractions, as shown in Figure 8.

3. Erase the V nonterminals which correspond to 'flow' formulas and disconnect the V nonterminals which correspond to axioms and as shown in Figure 9.

Now, given a sequence of lexical graphs, a total matching of the positive and negative axiomatic formulas and a sequence s of generalised contractions contracting this proof net to a tree we can generate an HR derivation d by induction on the length of s. The induction hypothesis is that during steps 1 and 2 we always have a hypergraph corresponding to the proof net $\mathcal{P}$ which has a V edge for every vertex in $\mathcal{P}$.

In case s is 0, there are no expansions and we already a binary tree with a V edge for every vertex in it. Since the T rules allow us to generate any binary branching tree, G can generate this tree as well. For every V edge in the tree which is the result of an axiom rule, we apply its inverse, shown in Figure 9 on the right, and we erase all other V edges as shown on the left of the same figure.

In case $s > 0$, we know by induction hypothesis that the hypergraph representation of the proof net we are constructing has a V edge for each of the vertices in the proof net. Because each subtree of the hypergraph has started as a T edge, this

is true of the α subtree as well. We rearrange the HR derivation in such a way that all expansions of the T edge into α occur at the end, then insert the expansion shown in Figure 8 just before this sequence. The result is a valid HR derivation of a hypergraph which contracts to the same tree as the proof net. $\qquad\square$

Figure 10 summarises the different inclusions with their corresponding lemma's.

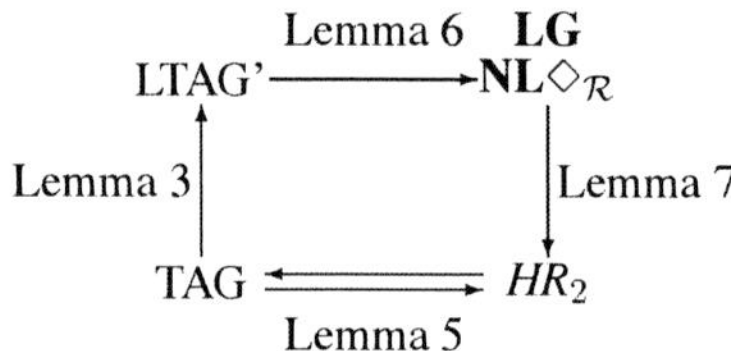

Figure 10: A summary of the previous lemma's

The following corollary follows immediately.

Corollary 8 *$NL\diamond_{\mathcal{R}}$ and **LG** grammars generate mildly context-sensitive languages.*

4 Polynomial Parsing

The strong correspondence between Lambek grammars and hyperedge replacement grammars does not immediately give us polynomial parsing for Lambek grammars: as shown in (Drewes et al., 1997) for example, even hyperedge replacement grammars of rank 2 can generate NP complete graph languages, such as the Hamiltonian path problem. Lautemann (1990) presents a (very abstract) version of the well-known Cocke, Kasami and Younger algorithm for context-free string grammars (Hopcroft and Ullman, 1979) for hyperedge replacement grammars and presents two ways of obtaining polynomial complexity, the first of which will interest us here. It uses the

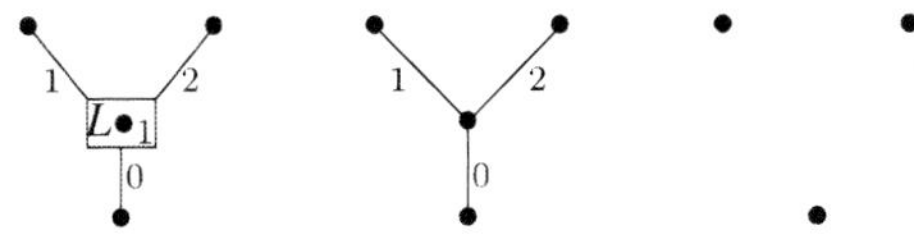

Figure 11: s-separability of the bipartite graph corresponding to a proof net

notion of s-separability, which corresponds to the maximum number of connected components in a graph when s vertices are deleted.

Theorem 9 (Lautemann (1990)) *If HR grammar G is of rank s and s-$sep_{L(G)} = O(1)$ then $L(G) \in LOGCFL$[4].*

Corollary 10 *For any sentence length w, $NL\Diamond_{\mathcal{R}}$ and LG grammars are in LOGCFL.*

Proof Lautemann discusses HR grammars generating graph languages and not hypergraph languages. However, this is not a real restriction given that we can interpret a hypergraph as a bipartite graph with the vertices corresponding to the vertices in the hypergraph as one partition and the hyperedges as the second partition. Figure 11 shows this interpretation of the leftmost graph in the middle of the figure. On the right, we can see how deleting the central vertex, corresponding to the hyperedge in the original graph on the left, results in (at most) three distinct components. The rank of the hyperedge replacement grammar for proof nets is two. Finally, for a sentence with w words, we start with w disjoint lexical graphs. Therefore, deleting two vertices from w disjoint graphs produces at most $w + 6$ disjoint graphs.   □

It is slightly unsatisfactory that this complexity result uses the number of words in the sentence w as a constant, though it seems possible to eliminate the constant by using a slightly more specific algorithm.

Pentus (2006) has shown that the associative Lambek calculus **L** is NP complete. The reason deleting a vertex from an $NL\Diamond_{\mathcal{R}}$ or **LG** hypergraph gives at most three different hypergraphs is

because we work with a non-associative system. Although Moot and Puite (2002) show that associativity is easily accommodated in the proof net calculus, it results in a system without upper bound on the number of daughters which a node can have. Therefore, deleting a vertex from an **L** hypergraph can result in an unbounded number of connected components.

5   Discussion and Future Work

When looking at the proof of Lemma 5, it is clear that HR_1 grammars generate substitution only TAGs, whereas HR_2 grammars generate TAGs. The tree generating power of HR grammars increases with the maximum rank of the grammar. For example, it is easy to generate the non-TAG language $a^n b^n c^n d^n e^n f^n$ using nonterminals of rank 3. In general, Engelfriet and Maneth (2000) show that $TR(HR_{tr})$, the set of tree languages generated by hyperedge replacement grammar such that the right hand side of all rules is a (hyper-)tree is equal to CFT_{sp}, the context-free tree grammars which are simple in the parameters, ie. without copying or deletion of trees, which is a different way of stipulating the linear and non-erasing constraint on linear context-free rewrite systems (LCFRS) (Vijay-Shanker et al., 1987).

Weir (1992) shows that *string generating* hyperedge replacement grammars generate the same languages as LCFRS and multi-component tree adjoining grammars (MCTAGs). All this suggests a possible extension of the current results relating tree generating HR grammars of rank > 2 to MC-TAGs and LCFRS.

With respect to $NL\Diamond_{\mathcal{R}}$, it seems possible to extend the current results, increasing the number of modes to generate richer classes of languages, possibly the same classes of languages as those generated by LCFRS and MCTAGs. For **LG**, such extensions seem less evident. Indeed, an appealing property of **LG** is that we do not need different modes, but if we are willing to add different modes to **LG** then extensions of the classes of languages generated seem possible.

An interesting consequence of the translations proposed here is that they open the way for new parsing algorithms of Lambek grammars. In addition, compared to earlier work like that of Moortgat and Oehrle (1994), they give radically new ways of implementing phenomena like Dutch verb

---

[4]LOGCFL is the complexity class of of problems which are log-space reducible to the decision problems for context-tree grammars. Vijay-Shanker et al., (1987) show that linear context-free rewrite systems and multicomponent TAGs are also in this complexity class.

clusters in $\mathbf{NL}\Diamond_{\mathcal{R}}$.

6 Conclusions

$\mathbf{NL}\Diamond_{\mathcal{R}}$ and **LG** are mildly context-sensitive formalisms and therefore benefit from the pleasant properties this entails, such as polynomial parsability. TAGs and HR grammars, because of the simplicity of their basic operations, have played a central role in establishing this correspondence.

References

Capelletti, Matteo. 2007. *Parsing with Structure-Preserving Categorial Grammars*. Ph.D. thesis, Utrecht Institute of Linguistics OTS.

de Groote, Philippe. 1999. The non-associative Lambek calculus with product in polynomial time. In Murray, N. V., editor, *Automated Reasoning With Analytic Tableaux and Related Methods*, volume 1617 of *Lecture Notes in Artificial Intelligence*, pages 128–139. Springer.

Drewes, Frank, Annegret Habel, and Hans-Joerg Kreowski. 1997. Hyperedge replacement graph grammars. In Rozenberg, Grzegorz, editor, *Handbook of Graph Grammars and Computing by Graph Transformations*, volume I, pages 95–162. World Scientific.

Engelfriet, Joost and Sebastian Maneth. 2000. Tree languages generated by context-free graph grammars. In *Theory and Applications of Graph Transformations*, volume 1764 of *Lecture Notes in Computer Science*, pages 15–29. Springer.

Engelfriet, Joost. 1997. Context-free graph grammars. In Rosenberg, Grzegorz and Arto Salomaa, editors, *Handbook of Formal Languages 3: Beyond Words*, pages 125–213. Springer, New York.

Hopcroft, John E. and Jeffrey D. Ullman. 1979. *Introduction to Automata Theory, Languages and Computation*. Addison-Wesley, Reading, Massachussets.

Joshi, Aravind and Seth Kulick. 1997. Partial proof trees as building blocks for a categorial grammar. *Linguistics and Philosophy*, 20(6):637–667.

Joshi, Aravind and Yves Schabes. 1997. Tree-adjoining grammars. In Rosenberg, Grzegorz and Arto Salomaa, editors, *Handbook of Formal Languages 3: Beyond Words*, pages 69–123. Springer, New York.

Joshi, Aravind, Vijay Shanker, and David Weir. 1991. The convergence of mildly context-sensitive grammar formalisms. In Sells, Peter, Stuart Shieber, and Thomas Wasow, editors, *Foundational Issues in Natural Language Processing*, pages 31–82. MIT Press, Cambridge, Massachusetts.

Lambek, Joachim. 1958. The mathematics of sentence structure. *American Mathematical Monthly*, 65:154–170.

Lambek, Joachim. 1961. On the calculus of syntactic types. In Jacobson, R., editor, *Structure of Language and its Mathematical Aspects, Proceedings of the Symposia in Applied Mathematics*, volume XII, pages 166–178. American Mathematical Society.

Lautemann, Clemens. 1990. The complexity of graph languages generated by hyperedge replacement. *Acta Informatica*, 27(5):399–421.

Moortgat, Michael and Richard T. Oehrle. 1994. Adjacency, dependency and order. In *Proceedings 9th Amsterdam Colloquium*, pages 447–466.

Moortgat, Michael. 1997. Categorial type logics. In van Benthem, Johan and Alice ter Meulen, editors, *Handbook of Logic and Language*, chapter 2, pages 93–177. Elsevier/MIT Press.

Moortgat, Michael. 2007. Symmetries in natural language syntax and semantics: the Lambek-Grishin calculus. In *Proceedings of WoLLIC 2007*, volume 4567 of *LNCS*, pages 264–284. Springer.

Moot, Richard and Quintijn Puite. 2002. Proof nets for the multimodal Lambek calculus. *Studia Logica*, 71(3):415–442.

Moot, Richard. 2007. Proof nets for display logic. Technical report, CNRS and INRIA Futurs.

Pentus, Mati. 1995. Lambek grammars are context free. In *Proceedings of the Eighth Annual IEEE Symposium on Logic in Computer Science*, pages 429–433, Montreal, Canada.

Pentus, Mati. 2006. Lambek calculus is NP-complete. *Theoretical Computer Science*, 357(1):186–201.

Vijay-Shanker, K. and David Weir. 1994. The equivalence of four extensions of context free grammars. *Mathematical Systems Theory*, 27(6):511–546.

Vijay-Shanker, K., David Weir, and Aravind Joshi. 1987. Characterizing structural descriptions produced by various grammatical formalisms. In *Proceedings of the 25th Annual Meeting of the Association for Computational Linguistics*, pages 104–111, Stanford, California. Association for Computational Linguistics.

Weir, David. 1992. Linear context-free rewriting systems and deterministic tree-walking transducers. In *Proceedings of the 30th Annual Meeting of the Association for Computational Linguistics*, pages 136–143, Morristown, New Jersey. Association for Computational Linguistics.

Synchronous Vector TAG for Syntax and Semantics: Control Verbs, Relative Clauses, and Inverse Linking

Rebecca Nesson
School of Engineering
and Applied Sciences
Harvard University
nesson@seas.harvard.edu

Stuart Shieber
School of Engineering
and Applied Sciences
Harvard University
shieber@seas.harvard.edu

Abstract

Recent work has used the synchronous tree-adjoining grammar (STAG) formalism to demonstrate that many of the cases in which syntactic and semantic derivations appeared to be divergent could be handled elegantly through synchronization. This research has provided syntax and semantics for diverse and complex linguistic phenomena. However, certain hard cases push the STAG formalism to its limits, requiring awkward analyses or leaving no clear solution at all. In this paper a new variant of STAG, synchronous vector TAG (SV-TAG), and demonstrate that it has the potential to handle hard cases such as control verbs, relative clauses, and inverse linking, while maintaining the simplicity of previous STAG syntax-semantics analyses.

1 Introduction

As first described by Shieber and Schabes (1990), *synchronous tree-adjoining grammar* (STAG) can be used to provide a semantics for a TAG syntactic analysis by taking the tree pairs to represent a syntactic analysis synchronized with a semantic analysis. Recent work has used the STAG formalism to demonstrate that many of the cases in which syntactic and semantic derivations appeared to be divergent could be handled elegantly through synchronization. This research has provided syntax and semantics for such diverse and complex linguistic phenomena as relative clauses[1] (Han, 2006;

Nesson and Shieber, 2006), nested quantifiers (Nesson and Shieber, 2006), wh-questions (Nesson and Shieber, 2006; Nesson and Shieber, 2007), in-situ wh-questions (Nesson and Shieber, 2007), it-clefts (Han and Hedberg, 2006), and topicalization (Nesson and Shieber, 2007). In these analyses the constraints of the tree-local or set-local MCTAG formalisms have played a critical role in permitting the available semantic readings while ruling out the unavailable ones. This research has demonstrated the value of synchronous grammars for characterizing the syntactic-semantic interface by showing how much more could be done using this simple mechanism than previously thought.

The analysis of nested quantifiers presented by Nesson and Shieber (2006) exemplifies this. Consider the sentence:

(1) Two politicians courted every person at some fundraiser.

We use the synchronous set-local MCTAG grammar in Figure 1 to analyze sentence (1).[2] We depart from traditional TAG notation by labeling adjunction sites explicitly with boxed numbers. The node labels we use in the semantics indicate the semantic types of the phrases they dominate.

Although a nested quantifier may take scope over the quantifier within which it is nested (so-called "inverse linking") not all permutations of scope orderings of the quantifiers are available (Joshi et al., 2003). In particular, the *every* > *two* > *some* reading is ill-formed (Hobbs and

---

[1]Both published analyses fail to predict all available scope readings for some sentences. This paper presents a relative clause analysis that addresses this shortcoming.

[2]An alternative analysis exists in which the prepositional phrase modifies the main verb. This derivation is still available and is distinct from the problem case that appears in the literature and that we discuss here.

Proceedings of The Ninth International Workshop on Tree Adjoining Grammars and Related Formalisms
Tübingen, Germany. June 6-8, 2008.

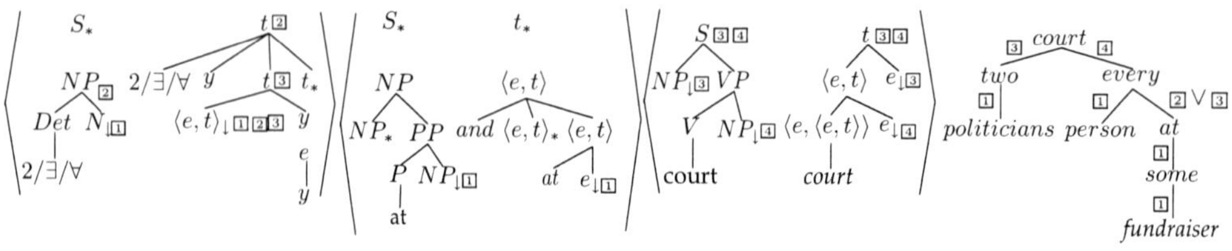

Figure 1: Grammar and derivation for sentence (1): "Two politicians courted every person at some fundraiser." Note that we make use of a higher-order conjunction operation here (and elsewhere), which conjoins properties "pointwise" in the obvious way.

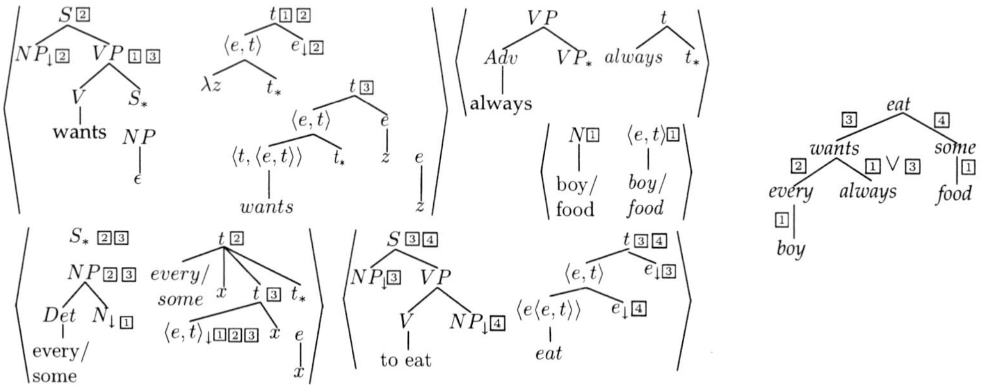

Figure 2: Synchronous TL-MCTAG grammar and derivation for sentence (2): "Every boy always wants to eat some food."

Shieber, 1987), and the $some > two > every$ reading, while formally expressible has been claimed to be not semantically available (Fodor, 1982; Horn, 1974).[3] In our analysis, because the nested quantifier is introduced through the prepositional phrase, which in turn modifies the noun phrase containing the nesting quantifier, the two quantifiers already form a set that operates as a unit with respect to the rest of the derivation. Without any further stipulation, all and only the attested four readings are generated.

However, the simplicity and constrained nature of the STAG approach brings with it serious challenges of expressivity. Certain hard cases push the STAG formalism to its limits, requiring awkward analyses or leaving no clear solution at all.

In this paper we define a new variant of STAG, synchronous vector TAG (SV-TAG), and demonstrate that it has the potential to handle hard cases

such as control verbs, relative clauses, and inverse linking, while maintaining the simplicity of previous STAG syntax-semantics analyses.

2 Difficult Cases for STAG Syntax and Semantics

The elegance of the STAG analysis is encouraging. However, certain cases seem to require more flexibility than the previous analysis, couched in tree- and set-local MCTAG, provides. For instance, as mentioned above, some accounts (VanLehn, 1978; Hobbs and Shieber, 1987) indicate that a fifth scope reading is possible in sentences like sentence (1). We illustrate the limitations of STAG with two further examples involving the semantics of control verbs and relative clauses.

2.1 Control Verbs

Consider the sentence:

(2) Every boy always wants to eat some food.

---

[3] But see the study by VanLehn (1978) for a contrary view on which this reading is merely dispreferred. We return to this issue later.

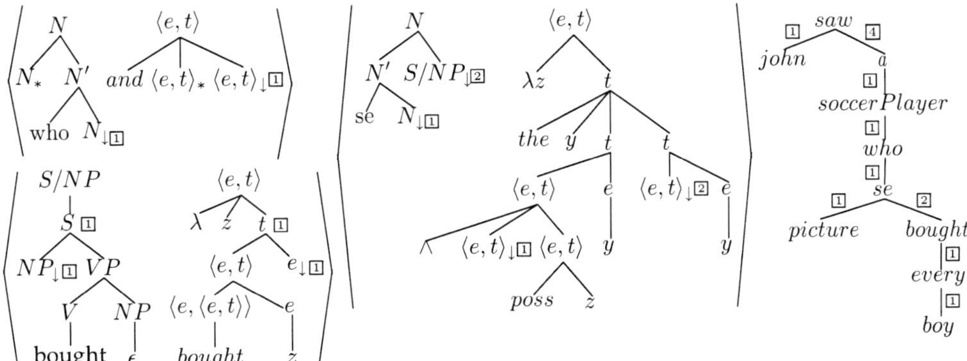

Figure 3: Additional grammar and derivation for sentence (3): "John saw a soccer player whose picture every boy bought." The tree sets for nouns, quantifiers, and the verb *saw* have the same structure as those in Figure 2.

With appropriate context, sentence (2) can produce the scope ordering $always > some > every > wants$.[4] However, a straightforward STAG analysis of the sentence produces a derivation that is incompatible with this reading. Both the derivation of the sentence and the elementary trees for *wants* and *always* are given in Figure 2. If *always* adjoins at link ① and *every* adjoins at link ③ they become indivisibly attached to each other and *some* cannot intervene between them. If *always* adjoins at link ③ instead, the scope reading $every > some > always > wants$ will be produced. But there is no way to generate the reading $always > some > every > wants$. In order to produce this reading the scope of *every* and the scope of *always* must be prevented from becoming attached to each other before they multiply adjoin with *some* at the root of *eat*.

2.2 Relative Clauses

Consider the sentence:

(3) John saw a soccer player whose picture every boy bought.

In this sentence *every* can outscope the implicit quantifier in *whose*, giving the reading where each boy bought a different picture of the soccer player.[5] However, as shown in Figure 3, because

every adjoins to *bought* and *bought* substitutes into *whose* below the scope of *whose*, there is no way for the scope of *every* to attach above *whose*. As with the earlier problems, what is required is the ability to delay the attachment scope of *every* to allow it to attach higher in the derived tree.

These examples demonstrate that STAG requires further development to be able to express the full range of readings that quantificational phenomena generate.

3 Synchronous Vector-TAG

A simple solution to this problem would merely relax the set-locality of the semantic MCTAG in the presented grammar. However, this introduces at least two problems. First, the complexity of non-local MCTAG is prohibitive. Second, by eliminating set-locality, the readings generated become extremely hard to control. To remedy these problems, we propose the use of vector TAG (Rambow, 1994), a computationally more tractable and expressively more controllable multicomponent TAG formalism as the base formalism to synchronize.

A Vector-TAG (V-TAG) is a 5-tuple (N, T, S, V) where N and T are disjoint sets of nonterminal and terminal symbols, respectively; $S \in N$ is the start symbol; and V is a set of sets of trees, called vectors.[6] The vectors in V

---

[4]The problem arising from sentence 2 was pointed out to us by Maribel Romero and students at the University of Pennsylvania.

[5]The problematic characteristics of this example were pointed out to us by Chung-hye Han.

[6]In Rambow's original definition the sets in V were partitioned into two sets, V_I and V_A, where the sets in V_I were constrained to include at most one initial tree, and the sets in

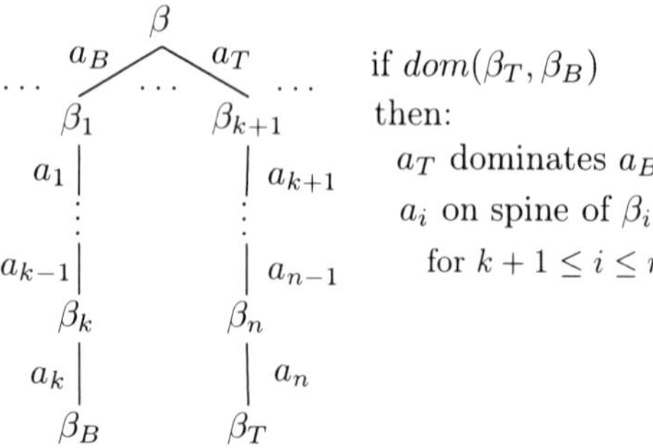

if $dom(\beta_T, \beta_B)$
then:
$\quad a_T$ dominates a_B
$\quad a_i$ on spine of β_i,
$\qquad$ for $k + 1 \le i \le n$

Figure 4: Schematic diagram of a V-TAG derivation tree.

possess dominance links. For a vector $\tau \in V$ the dominance links form a binary relation dom over the set of nodes in the trees of τ such that if $dom(\eta_1, \eta_2)$, then η_1 is the foot node of an auxiliary tree in τ, and η_2 is any node in any tree of τ. A *strict* V-TAG is one in which all trees in a vector are connected to each other via dominance links. We use an even stronger constraint in the analyses presented here in which the dominance links in a vector must form a total order over the trees. We call the unique tree in the vector that does not dominate any other tree the *foundation tree*. We distinguish individual trees in a vector with subscripts numbered from 0 starting with the foundation tree.

A derivation in a V-TAG is defined as in TAG. There is no locality requirement or other restriction on adjunction except that if one tree from a vector is used in a derivation, all trees from that vector must be used in the derivation.[7] In addition, all adjunctions must respect the dominance relations in that a node η_1 that dominates a node η_2 must appear on the path from η_2 to the root of the derived tree. If a tree with foot η_1 multiply adjoins at the same location as a tree containing a node η_2 that is dominated by η_1, the tree containing with η_1 must appear higher in the derived tree. Rambow (1994) defines integrity constraints

for V-TAG that limit the locations where trees in a vector may adjoin. An *integrity constraint* placed on a node in an elementary tree dictates that the node may not be on the path between two nodes connected by a dominance link.

The derivation tree for a V-TAG may be constructed just as for an MCTAG or STAG where the nodes of the tree are the tree sets and the branches of the tree are labeled with the links at which the synchronized operations take place or the address of the adjunction in the case of a non-foundation tree. The base derivation tree can also be elaborated to give a clearer picture of the relationships between individual trees. In an elaborated derivation tree each tree in a vector is represented explicitly and subscripted to indicate its place in the total order of its vector.

In an elaborated derivation tree the non-foundation trees of a vector do not have to be children of the same tree as the foundation tree of their vector. However, the dominance constraints of the vectors must be respected. Well-formedness can be checked on an elaborated derivation tree by finding the nearest common ancestor of any two trees connected by a dominance link and checking that the address on the branch leading to the dominating tree dominates the address leading to the dominated tree and that each tree along the path from the dominating tree to the common ancestor adjoins along the spine. Figure 4 gives a schematic example of a well-formed elaborated derivation tree.

We define a synchronous V-TAG (SV-TAG) as a set of triples, $\langle v_L, v_R, \frown \rangle$ where v_L and v_R are V-TAG vectors and $\frown$ is a linking relation between nodes in v_L and v_R. A pair (or pair of sets) of trees within each vector are distinguished as the foundation trees. A *foundation adjunction* occurs when the foundation trees drawn from the left and right vectors of $\langle v_L, v_R, \frown \rangle$ adjoin at linked locations in some other vector $\langle v'_L, v'_R, \frown' \rangle$. In contrast to tree-local or set-local MCTAG in which every adjunction site must be marked with a link in order for a tree set to adjoin, in SV-TAG only the adjunction sites where the foundation trees adjoin are marked explicitly with links. The remainder of the trees in v_L and v_R are free to adjoin anywhere in the left and right derived trees, respectively, so long as they obey the constraints of their dominance links. Practically, this definition constrains synchronized

---

V_A contained only auxiliary trees. We relax the requirements of and distinction between these two sets of sets to allow sets of any combination of initial and auxiliary trees including sets with more than one initial tree.

[7] The definition of V-TAG is very similar to that of non-local MCTAG as defined by Weir (1988) except that in non-local MCTAG all trees from a tree set are required to adjoin simultaneously.

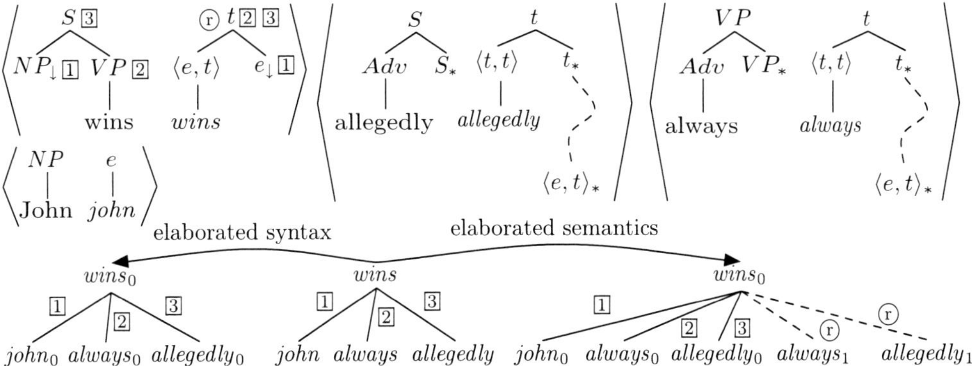

Figure 5: An grammar and derivation trees for sentence (4): "Allegedly John always wins." In the elaborated derivation trees the non-foundation trees are connected with a dashed line. The circled link is simply a shorthand for an address in the tree, not true links in the grammar.

V-TAG vectors to have one synchronized operation with the remainder of the trees adjoining with the usual unconstrained non-locality of V-TAG.

An SV-TAG can be characterized as *simple*, *tree-local*, *set-local* or *non-local* depending on the number and orientation of the link locations in the grammar. If each link has only one location in the left and right grammars then the SV-TAG is called *simple* because the foundation adjunctions on each side of the grammar follow the constraints of a TAG. If links have multiple locations that occur all within one tree on each side of the grammar then the SV-TAG may be termed *tree-local*. When links occur in multiple trees within a vector the SV-TAG is called *set-local* and if link locations of a single link occur in multiple vectors then the SV-TAG is called *non-local*. Although it is possible for foundation trees to occur anywhere in the total order over the trees of a vector, in this analysis we consider only grammars in which the foundation trees do not dominate any other trees in their vector.

Unlike set-local and tree-local MCTAG which are known to be NP-hard to parse (Søgaard et al., 2007), lexicalized V-TAG can be parsed in polynomial time (Rambow, 1994; Kallmeyer, 2007). Although SV-TAG recognition is also NP-hard due to the complexity introduced by synchronization, related work on synchronous unordered vector grammar with dominance links suggests that for a given *simple* SV-TAG grammar a polynomial time tree-to-forest translation algorithm may exist that permits a parse of the syntax of a sentence to

be translated into the forest of corresponding semantic trees (or vice versa) (Rambow and Satta, 1996). As with all synchronous-grammar-based analyses, the derivation tree still provides an underspecified representation for the semantics.

3.1 The Derivation Tree

In the STAG model of syntax and semantics the derivation tree is the interface between the two as well as the means for capturing underspecification in the semantics. An SV-TAG permits greater freedom for divergence between syntax and semantics because rather than requiring all trees in a set to be synchronized, in SV-TAG only the foundation trees are synchronized. As a result, underspecification in the SV-TAG model extends beyond multiple adjunction producing different derived trees from the derivation tree. In SV-TAG the additional underspecification results from the locations at which the non-foundation trees ultimately attach. Although the base derivation tree still serves as the connection between the syntactic and semantic derivations and the interface through which they constrain each other, an elaborated derivation tree can help clarify the available readings on each side of the grammar. An example of a grammar, derivation, and elaborated derivation for the following sentence is given in Figure 5.

(4) Allegedly John always wins.

Sentence (4) permits only one reading in which *allegedly* outscopes *always*. This constraint is de-

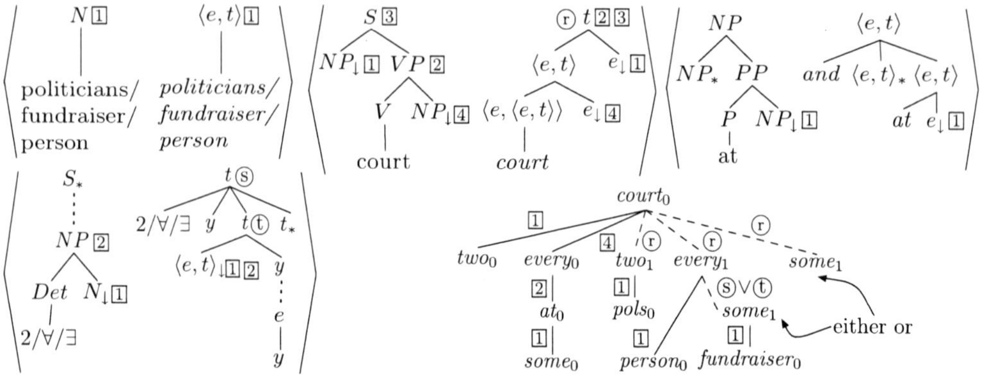

Figure 6: SV-TAG grammar and elaborated semantic derivation for sentence (1): "Two politicians courted every person at some fundraiser." Note that there are three possible locations where $some_1$ can adjoin. If it multiply adjoins at ⓡ it must adjoin higher than $every_1$ to satisfy its dominance constraint.

termined by the order of attachment of the adverb trees along the VP spine. To enforce this constraint in the semantics we can require that the non-foundation trees of the adverbs attach in the same order as the foundation trees in the shared derivation tree.[8]

4 Applying SV-TAG to the Hard Cases

The additional flexibility provided by SV-TAG permits analysis of the difficult control verb and relative clause examples presented above while still providing a satisfactory analysis of the inverse linking example.

4.1 Inverse Linking

Figure 6 gives a SV-TAG grammar and elaborated semantic derivation tree for sentence (1). The elementary tree sets are similar to the ones presented above except that we have removed the S_* and t_* trees from the elementary tree set for the prepositions *at* and removed all of the non-foundational link locations. The syntactic derivation is straightforward and is presented implicitly in the elaborated derivation tree. The semantic derivation merits closer examination. The tree containing the bound variable of *some* in the semantics foundationally adjoins into *at* at link $\boxed{1}$. The scope tree of *some* is free to adjoin anywhere along the path to the root of the derived tree. It has no site at which

to adjoin into the *at* tree, so it must adjoin higher in the derivation tree. The scope tree of *some* may adjoin into either of the two t nodes on the path to the root of the *every* tree while still respecting its dominance link. Adjoining at these two positions will indivisibly connect the scopes of *every* and *some* in both orders as in the STAG analysis of this sentence presented earlier. However, the scope part of *some* does not have to adjoin at these nodes. When *every* foundationally adjoins into *court*, the scope part of *some* will become free to adjoin anywhere between the root of the scope part of *every* and the root of the derivation. Since the only location available for the scope parts of *every*, *two*, and *some* can adjoin are at the root of *court*, this will produce the fifth scope reading in which *two* intervenes between *some* and *every*. The sixth scope reading is prevented by the dominance link requiring the foot of the scope tree of *some* to dominate the bound variable of *some*.

It is interesting to note that the disputed fifth reading requires the scope part of *some* to travel several steps up the derivation tree. Whether there is any relationship between the relative obscurity of this scope reading and the necessity of passing the scope of *some* two levels up the tree may be explored in future work.

4.2 Control Verbs

Figure 7 presents an SV-TAG grammar and the elaborated semantic derivation tree for sentence (2). As with the previous example, the syn-

---

[8]In the case of two adverbs multiply adjoining at the same location we can require that the order of attachment be consistent across syntax and semantics to produce the same result.

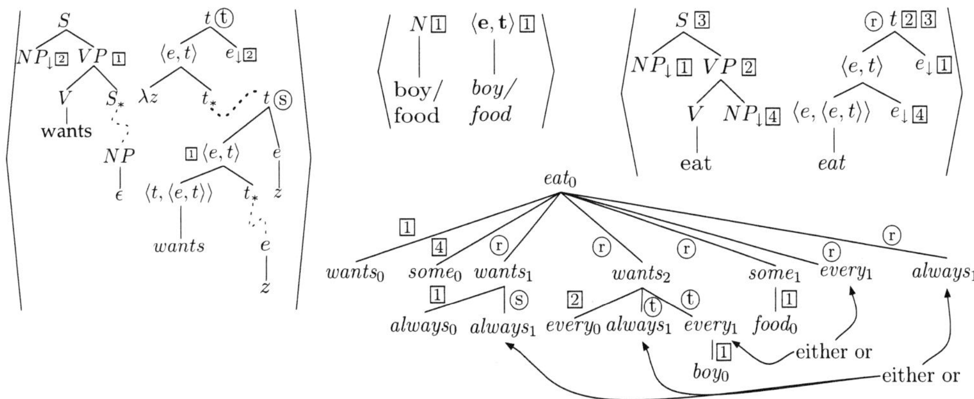

Figure 7: SV-TAG grammar and elaborated semantic derivation tree for sentence (2): "Every boy always wants to eat some food." The tree pair for *always* is as in Figure 5 and the trees for the quantifiers are as in Figure 6.

tactic derivation is straightforward. In the semantics, SV-TAG allows us to produce all six orderings between the quantifiers as well as the de dicto and de re readings of *want*. Both *always* and *every* foundationally adjoin into *wants*. The readings in which *always* and *every* are indivisibly attached to each other as well as the reading in which *some* intervenes between *every* and *always* can be produced by adjoining the dominating trees of *always* and *every* into t nodes of the *wants* tree. The reading in which *some* intervenes between *always* and *every* is produced by the scope parts of *always* and *some* multiply adjoining at the root of *eat*.

Because the scope part of *always* is not part of its foundation it can attach above other scopetakers that attach along the *VP* spine. However, constraints such as the one suggested for sentence (4) may be used to disallow this.

4.3 Relative Clauses

The SV-TAG grammar and derivation tree in Figure 8 achieve the reading that could not be achieved in STAG. Note that the grammar differs only in that the links have been reduced to foundation links. The scope part of *every* is able to pass up through *bought* and is available to adjoin at either of the t nodes in the implicit quantifier in the *se* tree.

Without any constraint the scope part of *every* may continue higher in the derivation to multiply adjoin with the scope of *a* at the root of *saw*. This

violates the linguistic generalization that quantifiers may not take scope above a relative clause that contains them. An integrity constraint placed at the root of the *se* semantic tree blocks the scope part of *every* from escaping the relative clause.

5 Conclusion

This paper demonstrates that certain hard cases for synchronous TAG syntax and semantics, such as control verbs, can be successfully analyzed using SV-TAG, a synchronous variant of V-TAG defined herein. SV-TAG maintains the simplicity inherent in the synchronous grammar approach to modeling the syntax-semantics interface, provides the derivation tree as an underspecified representation of the semantics, and is likely to be efficient to process.

References

Fodor, Janet D. 1982. The mental representation of quantifiers. In Peters, S. and E. Saarinen, editors, *Processes, Beliefs, and Questions*, pages 129–164. D. Reidel.

Han, Chung-Hye and Nancy Hedberg. 2006. Piedpiping in relative clauses: Syntax and compositional semantics based on synchronous tree adjoining grammar. In *Proceedings of the 8th International Workshop on Tree Adjoining Grammars and Related Formalisms (TAG+ 8)*, pages 41–48, Sydney, Australia.

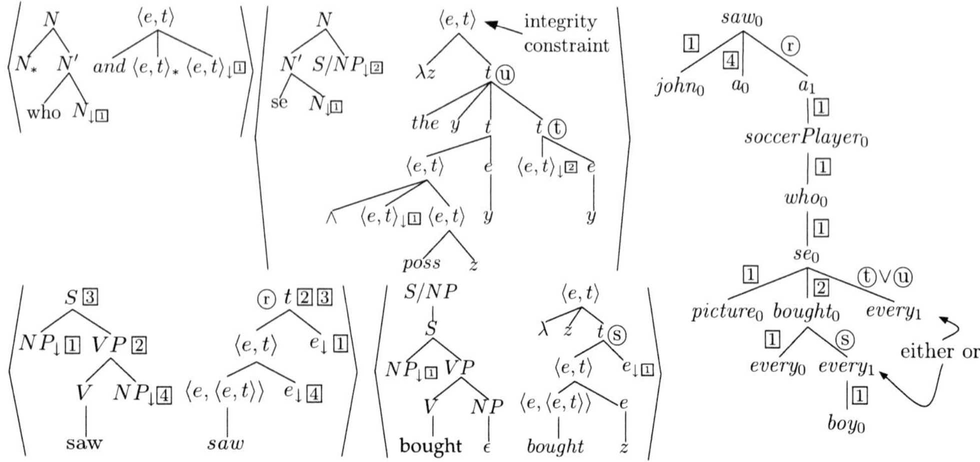

Figure 8: SV-TAG grammar and derivation tree for sentence (3): "John saw a soccer player whose picture every boy bought." Tree sets for nouns and quantifiers are as in earlier figures.

Han, Chung-Hye. 2006. A tree adjoining grammar analysis of the syntax and semantics of it-clefts. In *Proceedings of the 8th International Workshop on Tree Adjoining Grammars and Related Formalisms (TAG+ 8)*, pages 33–40, Sydney, Australia.

Hobbs, Jerry and Stuart M. Shieber. 1987. An algorithm for generating quantifier scopings. *Computational Linguistics*, 13(1-2):47–63.

Horn, G. M. 1974. *The Noun Phrase Constraint*. Ph.D. thesis, University of Massachusetts, Amherst, Massachusetts.

Joshi, Aravind K., Laura Kallmeyer, and Maribel Romero. 2003. Flexible composition in LTAG: Quantifier scope and inverse linking. In Harry Bunt, Ielka van der Sluis and Roser Morante, editors, *Proceedings of the Fifth International Workshop on Computational Semantics IWCS-5*, pages 179–194, Tilburg, January.

Kallmeyer, Laura. 2007. A declarative characterization of different types of multicomponent tree adjoining grammars. In Georg Rehm, Andreas Witt, Lothar Lemnitzer, editor, *Datenstrukturen für linguistische Ressourcen und ihre Anwendungen - Proceedings der GLDV-Jahrestagung 2007*, pages 111–120. Gunter Narr Verlag, Tuebingen University, April.

Nesson, Rebecca and Stuart M. Shieber. 2006. Simpler TAG semantics through synchronization. In *Proceedings of the 11th Conference on Formal Grammar*, Malaga, Spain, 29–30 July.

Nesson, Rebecca and Stuart M. Shieber. 2007. Extraction phenomena in synchronous tag syntax and semantics. In *Proceedings of the Workshop on Syntax and Structure in Statistical Translation*, Rochester, NY, April.

Rambow, Owen and Giorgio Satta. 1996. Synchronous models of language. In Joshi, Aravind K. and Martha Palmer, editors, *Proceedings of the Thirty-Fourth Annual Meeting of the Association for Computational Linguistics*, pages 116–123, San Francisco. Morgan Kaufmann Publishers.

Rambow, Owen. 1994. Formal and computational aspects of natural language syntax. PhD Thesis, Department of Computer and Information Science, University of Pennsylvania.

Shieber, Stuart M. and Yves Schabes. 1990. Synchronous tree-adjoining grammars. In *Proceedings of the 13th International Conference on Computational Linguistics*, volume 3, pages 253–258, Helsinki.

Søgaard, Anders, Timm Lichte, and Wolfgang Maier. 2007. On the complexity of linguistically motivated extensions of tree-adjoining grammar. In *Recent Advances in Natural Language Processing 2007*.

VanLehn, Kurt. 1978. Determining the scope of English quantifiers. Technical Report 483, MIT Artificial Intelligence Laboratory, Cambridge, MA.

Weir, David. 1988. Characterizing mildly context-sensitive grammar formalisms. PhD Thesis, Department of Computer and Information Science, University of Pennsylvania.

The use of MCTAG to Process Elliptic Coordination

Djamé Seddah
Lallic / Université Paris-Sorbonne
Alpage / Inria Rocquencourt
Paris, France
djame.seddah@paris-sorbonne.fr

Abstract

In this paper, we introduce a formalization of various elliptical coordination structures within the Multi-Component TAG framework. Numerous authors describe elliptic coordination as parallel constructions where symmetric derivations can be observed from a desired predicate-argument structure analysis. We show that most famous coordinate structures, including zeugma constructions, can be analyzed simply with the addition of a simple synchronous mechanism to the MCTAG framework .

1 Introduction

We assume the reader to be familiar with the TAG framework (Joshi, 1987) and with Multi-Component TAG (MCTAG, (Weir, 1988)). We will focus on the analysis of elliptical coordination and zeugma construction in French. The main goal of this work is to build a syntax-semantic interface based on an acyclic dependency graphs obtained through MCTAG's derivation and a simple synchronous mechanism. Knowing that pure LTAG cannot handle coordination with ellipsis without adding new notions of derivation and new operations (e.g. conjoin operation in (Sarkar and Joshi, 1996b)), we propose to use a enhanced version of MC-TAG for the processing of these structures. To the best of our knowledge, this is the first time that such a proposal is made within this framework. In this paper, we first discuss some of our examples, then we explore divergences of analysis between some elided predicates of a coordination and we finally present, using oriented synchronization links, our MC-TAG proposals going from Non-Local MCTAG (NL-MCTAG) solutions to unlexicalized Tree-Local MCTAG (TL-MCTAG) ones. We conclude by showing that our proposal can deal with a wide range of coordinations using a uniform framework.

2 A Parallel Derivation Structure?

We want our model to be able to deal not only with simple coordinations without any ellipsis, but also with a wide range of non-trivial ones, including gapping (1a), and zeugmas (1d,e). We will focus on gapping coordination and zeugma construction here. For the remainder of this paper, zeugma construction are defined in the sense of the rhetorical construction *syllepsis* when two words are *inappropriately linked together* (Lascarides et al., 1996), where *inappropriately* means that either there is a mismatch between two different subcategorization frames (1d,e) or between two different semantic interpretations with respect to their compositional status (1d). In that interpretation, zeugma constructions are not a rare epiphenomenon. Since Coordination of Unlike Categories (henceforth CUC) actually involves a subcategorization frame mismatch between conjuncts (Sag et al., 1985; Jorgensen and Abeillé, 1992), we treat them jointly with zeugma.

The coordination schema we use is of the form $\boxed{S \rightarrow S\ Conj\ S}$. We will not describe NP coordination here.

2.1 Symmetrical Derivations

In order to process sentences (1a-1g), we consider that any lexeme which is erased in an elliptic coordination can be modeled by an empty lexeme, written ε, which fills the other member of the coordination. This analysis is not new by itself but if we want to obtain dependency graphs such as Fig. 2 or Fig. 3, we must agree that the elided part is more abstract than a lexical coindexation. Actually, to obtain the derivation graph in Fig. 2 we have to anchor the empty element to the tree schemata (N0VN1) anchored by the realized verb.

Proceedings of The Ninth International Workshop on Tree Adjoining Grammars and Related Formalisms
Tübingen, Germany. June 6-8, 2008.

a) Jean aime$_i$ Marie et Paul ε_i Virginie *John loves Mary and Paul Virginia* Predicate elision
b) Marie fabrique ε_i et Pierre vend des crêpes$_i$ *Mary cooks and Peter sells pancakes* Right node raising
c)Marie$_i$ cuit ε_j et ε_i vend des crêpes$_j$ *Mary cooks and sells pancakes* Left object and right node raising
d) Napoleon prit$_i$ du poids et ε_i beaucoup de pays *Napoleon gained weight and [conquered] a lot of countries* Zeugma construction
e) Jean est un républicain et fier de l'être *John is a republican and proud of it* Coordination of unlike category
f) Paul$_i$ mange une pomme et ε_i achète des cerises *Paul eats an apple and buys cherries* Right subject elision
g) Mary admires ε_i and Sue thinks she likes Peter$_i$ "Unbounded right node raising" (Milward, 1994)

Figure 1: Examples of elliptic constructions

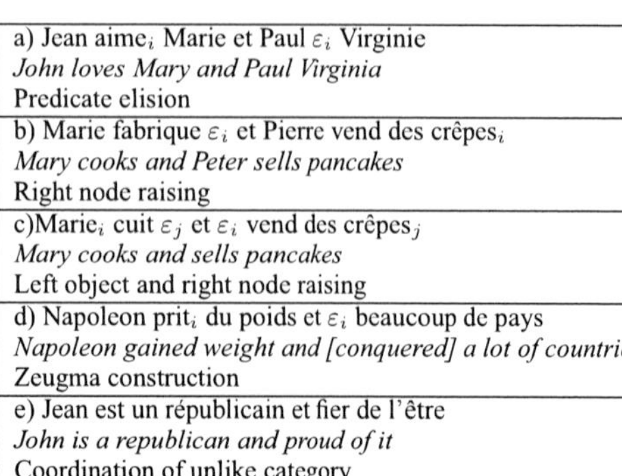

Derived Tree   Derivation Graph

Figure 2: Derived tree and Derivation Graph for sentence 1a

This anchoring of an empty element leads to an unrealized instance of an elementary tree which will be substituted in the rightmost node of the coordination elementary tree (i.e. CET). Cases of Right Node Raising lead to the creation of a dependency link between the realized argument in the rightmost part of the CET and its unrealized counterpart. The idea is to have the same main parallel set of derivations in both parts of the CET (regardless of possible adjunction, see sentence 1g where the tree anchored by "thinks" can be an auxiliary tree of the form N0VS* which will adjoin on the root of the elementary tree N0VN1 anchored by "like").

2.2 Asymmetrical Derivations

It would be possible to handle elliptic coordination with (extended) TAG if both sides of a coordination had parallel derivations (Sarkar and Joshi, 1996a; Seddah and Sagot, 2006). In the case of CUC, the elementary trees which should have been coordinated, following their anchors coindexations, are not of the same type. For exam-

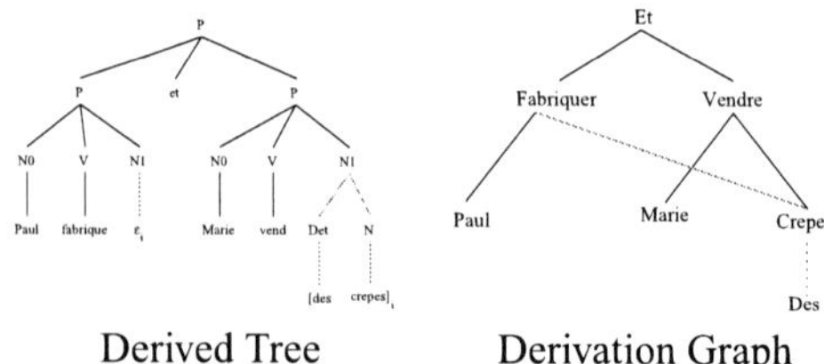

Derived Tree   Derivation Graph

Figure 3: Derived tree and Derivation Graph for sentence 1b

ple, in sentence (1e) the realized verb anchors a N0VN1 tree whereas its unrealized counterpart anchors a N0VAdj one. Therefore a tree schema copy as suggested by (Seddah and Sagot, 2006) cannot really be applied.[1] In case of pure zeugma construction such as in (1e), the mismatch is even more pronounced because in French "prendre du poids" is a multi word expression meaning "to gain weight". In LTAG this expression would lead to an initial tree with "[prendre]" as a main anchor and "du poids" as co-anchors, so the resulting tree will be similar to an intransitive N0V tree. The rightmost part of the coordination, on the contrary, can be paraphrased as "[Napoleon conquered] a lot of countries" which can be analyzed with a regular N0VN1 tree in a strictly compositional manner. Hence, using a parallelism of derivation is not sufficient to obtain a proper derivation structure. The CCG framework and its elegant handling of gapping (Steedman, 1990) does not handle these mismatches without difficulty, see (Sag et al., 1985) or (Jorgensen and Abeillé, 1992) as well for solutions based on features subsumption and complex category constraints.

3 MCTAG Analysis

In this section, we briefly present MCTAG as the framework in which we propose several ways to process elliptic coordination. A formal definition of our MCTAG is given section 3.6.

3.1 Introduction to MCTAG

The term "Multi-Component Tree Adjunct Grammar" (MCTAG, (Joshi, 1987; Weir, 1988)) describes a class of descriptive formalisms which extend the derivational generative power (Becker

---

[1] As suggested by an anonymous reviewer, CUC could be handled by (Sarkar and Joshi, 1996a) using "node contraction" on both argument nodes and anchors.

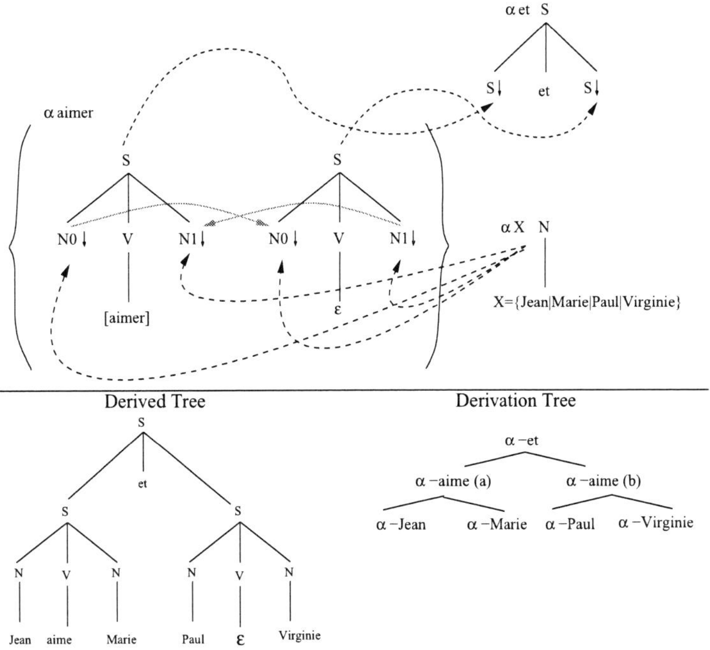

Figure 4: Sketch of analysis : "Jean aime Marie et Paul Virignie"

et al., 1992; Schuler et al., 2000) of Tree Adjunct Grammars by allowing sets of trees, as a whole unit, to be part of a derivation step. Several types of MCTAG can be defined based on how the trees in a set adjoin into various nodes. If all nodes belong to the same elementary tree, MC-TAGs are qualified as Tree-Local [TL-MCTAG], if all nodes belong to the same set, MCTAGs are Set-Local [SL-MCTAG] and Non-Local MCTAG [NL-MCTAG] otherwise. All of these MCTAG's subclasses have a stronger generative capacity than TAG and it shall be noted that TL-TAG has the same weak and strong generative power (Weir, 1988). TL and SL-MCTAG can be parsed in a polynomial time (Boullier, 1999; Villemonte de La Clergerie, 2002) whereas NL-MCTAG's parsing is known to be NP-Complete (Rambow and Satta, 1992). Following (Kallmeyer, 2005), we define a MCTAG, M, as a regular TAG, G, with an additional set of tree sets where each tree set is a subset of G's elementary trees.

As opposed to (Weir, 1988), (Kallmeyer, 2005) defines the MCTAG derivations to appear as the ones from the underlying TAG. This means that if a tree set γ, composed of elementary trees γ_i, is

derived into a tree set γ', the derivation tree will display every derivation instead of a link between γ' and γ. Thus, in order to allow more precise compositional analysis of coordination with ellipsis via the derivation tree, we adopt this view and for each tree set we add a set, S_L, of oriented links between substitution leaf nodes of its elementary trees. These links provide the means to share arguments between elementary trees inside a tree set.

3.2 Simple case : two Conjuncts

The main idea of our proposal is to include an unrealized tree in a set where the argument nodes are linked from the realized tree to the other one. This constitutes an extension to regular MC-TAG where no constraints of this type are defined. If we restrict the type of MCTAG to be Tree-Local then both trees must be substituted on the same elementary tree. Thus, as the tree schemas are the same, this will ensure that the set of derivations in both sides of the coordination will be parallelized. The dashed arrows in figure 4 exist to force argument position to be linked. An arrow must be oriented to prevent analysis of sentences such as :

"* [ε_i] aime Marie et Jean$_i$ aime Virginie". In order to allow regular substitution on linked nodes, a precedence order must be added: Regular substitution on a linked node will always have precedence over linked substitution (w.r.t to feature constraints if any).

Moreover, if some constraints on the application order of the trees are not defined, nothing will prevent the unrealized tree schema to be substituted on the leftmost part of the coordination. The model will thus overgenerate on sentences such as "* _Jean [ε_i] Marie et Paul aime_$_i$ _Virginie_"[2]. Looking at the analysis provided in figure 4 where all coordinated trees of the tree set are substituted in the same elementary tree (i.e. α-et), it is obvious that the mechanism presented in this paper for gapping coordination with two conjuncts needs only the generative power of Tree Local MCTAG (Weir, 1988). Nevertheless, in the case of multiple gapping coordination such as "Paul aime Marie, Jacques Virginie et Paul Caroline" the question is to know if it is possible to provide an analysis which maintains simple compositional analysis without multiplying the number of elementary tree sets.

3.3 General Case : n Conjuncts with $n > 2$

The method proposed for the particular case of two conjuncts is formally simple and can be implemented relatively easily on top of an existing TAG Parser. However, the case of multiple conjuncts of the type $\boxed{S_1, S_2, S_3, ...\text{and } S_N}$ brings in the necessity of handling as many unrealized trees inside a tree set as conjuncts members of the coordination. We present in section 3.3 our method to handle multiple unrealized trees in a tree set without having an exponential number of elementary tree sets in our grammar. For the presentation of the general case, this technical aspect is not needed. For the moment, let us assume that the grammar provides the correct tree set and the correct number of unrealized trees.

Non-local MCTAG proposal An intuitive method in the _spirit_ of the general TAG framework would consist in handling the recursive nature of the conjuncts members using the adjunction of an auxiliary tree anchored by a comma ($\beta-',')$ which

would adjoin on the root of the initial tree (α-et) anchored by the conjunction (see Fig. 5) whereas the n-th member of the coordination would substitute in the left-hand side node of $\beta-','$. We restrict the auxiliary trees $\beta-','$ to adjoin only on the root of α-et or on the root of another instance of $\beta-','$.

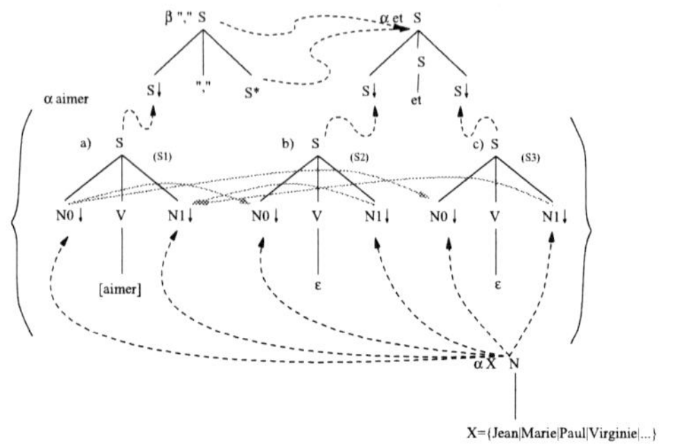

Abstract Derivation tree (predicates only)

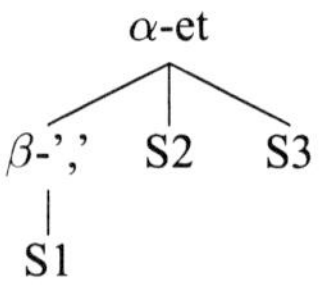

Figure 5: NL-MCTAG Derivations : S_1, S_2 and S_3

The problem with this analysis is that the formalism we use must be Non-local MCTAG (NL-MCTAG, (Weir, 1988)), whose formal power pushes the class of Mildy Context-Sensitive Languages to its upper bound, due to a parsing complexity beyond polynomial complexity (Rambow and Satta, 1992). Moreover, without further constraints on the application order of the derivations, this model overgenerates on sentences of the form $\boxed{* S_1 \text{ and } S_2, S_3}$. One way to restrict this behavior would be to add an internal node labeled S on the spine of the conjunction trees (α-et, β-',') and prevent adjunction of β-',' on its root. Derivations will be correct but the derived trees will be slightly unorthodox.

Set-local MCTAG Solution Let us recall that in SL-TAG every derivation from a tree set must occur in the same tree set and that a tree from a given tree set cannot be adjoined nor substituted in a tree from the same set. In that case, we propose[3], a tree set which contains the initial tree α-et and the correct number of auxiliary trees β-','. Here, the first

---

[2]Left predicate elision, although rare and somehow questionable in French, can be observed in :"_(?)Paul,ε_i lundi; Jacques,ε_i mardi et Pierre travailleras$_i$ Samedi_" - (?) Paul, monday, Jack Tuesday and Peter will work Saturday-

[3]Following a suggestion from (Danlos L., P.C)

and last trees, named S_1 and S_3 in Fig. 6 are substituted on the leaf nodes of α-et and the intermediate tree (S_2) is substituted on the rightmost node of β-',' which itself is adjoined on the root of S1. Any S_n tree will be handled by recursive adjunction of another instance of β-',' on the root of a tree S_{n-1}.

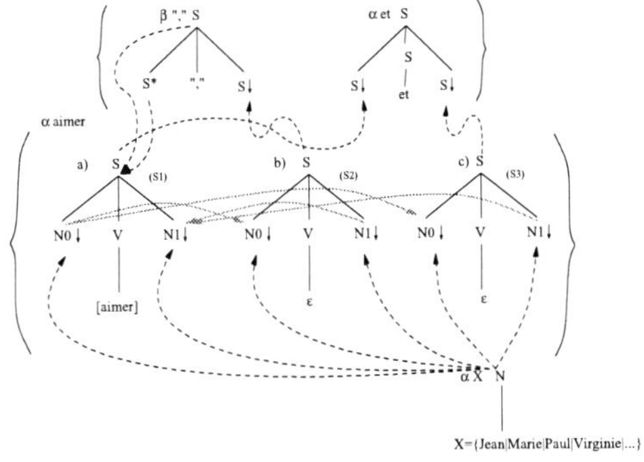

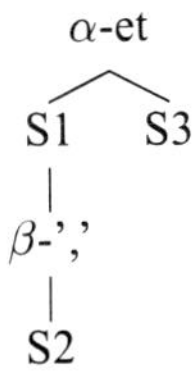

Figure 6: SL-MCTAG Derivations : S_1, S_2 and S_3

For this analysis as well, the same kind of restrictions as for the NL-MCTAG analysis would have to be established.

Dealing with Non Fixed Tree-Set's Cardinality
So far, we assumed that the grammar will provide the correct cardinality of a tree set (namely the correct number of unrealized elementary trees). Obviously, such an assumption cannot stand; it would lead to an exponential amount of elementary tree sets inside the grammar. In (Villemonte de La Clergerie, 2005), the author implements a proposal to handle this growing size problem using regular operators (mainly disjunction, Kleene star, interleaving and optionality) on nodes or subpart of a metagrammar tree description (Vijay-Shanker and Schabes, 1992; Candito, 1996). We argue for the use of the Kleene star and the optionality operator to cope with the potential exponential size of our MCTAG. The tree set α-aimer (Fig. 7) would then contain one main anchored tree, an optional unrealized Kleene starred tree of the form N0VN1

and the argument sharing links between substitution leaf nodes.

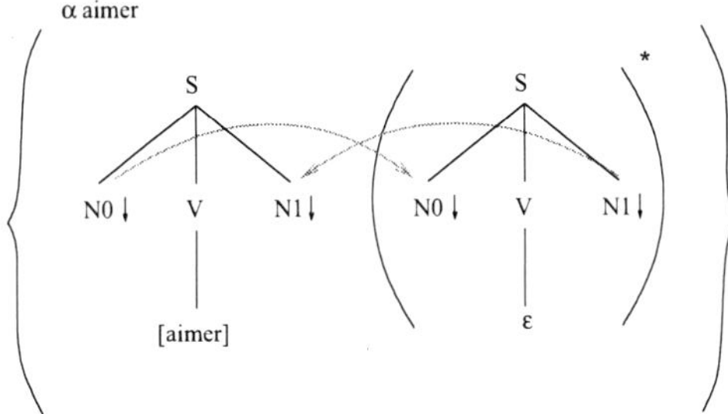

Figure 7: Factorized Tree set for α-aimer

Tree-local MCTAG Proposal Following this path, a straightforward definition of a factorized tree α-et is to insert two optional edges (ended by ',' and S↓) (Fig. 8) between the first two leaves of the tree α-et.

By using the two factorized trees (Fig. 7 & 8), an

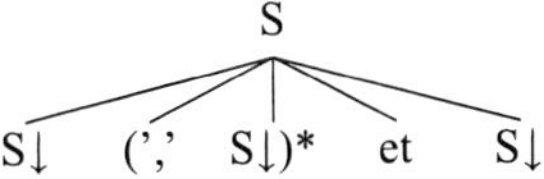

Figure 8: Factorized Tree set for α-et

analysis of gapping coordination with any given number of conjuncts stands in TL-MCTAG ; its logical interpretation is simply a logical *AND* with n arguments.

3.4 Zeugma Construction and CUC

To allow zeugma construction and CUC, we propose a set of trees that includes two different tree schemas, one of them being anchored by the co-indexed lexical element (cf. figure 9) and the other by the empty element. In case of the sentence (1d),

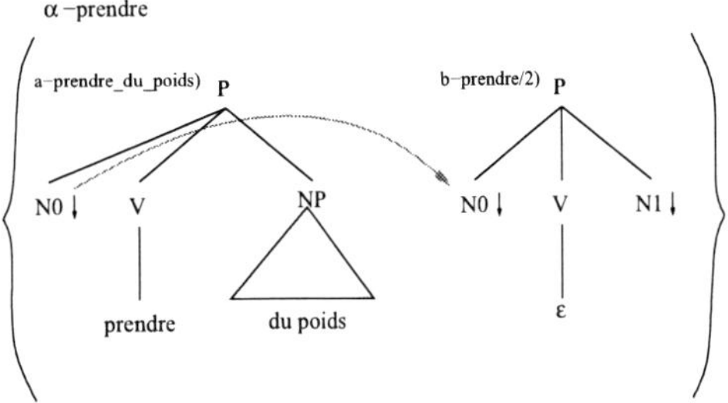

Figure 9: Tree set for α-prendre-du-poids

the tree anchored by "Napoleon" will be substituted on the node N0 of the N0V*prendre-du-poids* and linked to the node N0 of tree schema N0VN1. The rest of the derivations will just be the same as for the regular predicate elision stated before. For CUC, a similar method will operate: the tree set will this time include a N0V[to be]N1 anchored tree and a N0VAdj tree schema.

3.5 Case of Right Node Raising

Right node raising, as in sentence (1b), illustrates perfectly the fact that our model is entirely dependent of the extended domain of locality brought by the use of MCTAG. Being in a same tree set allows two elementary trees to share a "minimal" semantic unit, knowing the main verbal predicate which is elided in one of them. But in a sentence such as *John cooks ε_i and Mary sells beans$_i$*, we definitely have two different elementary trees, the first one having its object realized in the second one. However, if we consider only the set of derivations including the anchoring ones (displayed as special substitution nodes in Fig. 10), we must admit that these trees are indeed very similar and that an oriented link from the anchoring node of the first tree to the anchoring node of the second one could exist. This link would be superseded by an effective "anchoring" derivation on the second tree. If we want to keep the benefit of a direct compositional interpretation of the derivation tree, it suffices to establish that the label of an inner tree will be a variable instantiated to the label of its lexical anchor.

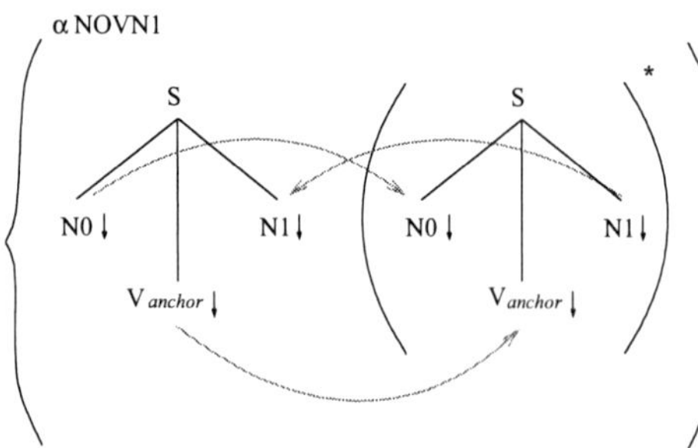

Figure 10: Unlexicalized tree set

To forbid analysis such as "* John cooks$_i$ ε_j and Mary ε_i beans$_j$.", we add a restriction on the set of links (cf. section 3.1) stating that there is a strict alternation between a link from node N1

of a tree γ_i to a node N1 of a tree γ_0 and a link from the main anchoring node (V_{anchor}) of tree γ_0 to the main anchor of the tree γ_i. A side effect of having an oriented link between two anchoring nodes is that it predicts the ungrammaticality of sentences such as "*John Mary and Paul loves Virginia" which were a cause of trouble in the general case. Thus, the main cause of overgeneration is avoided and we can provide a reasonable analysis of many elliptic coordinations without having to choose between the different types of MCTAG. Using this method and tree factorization, sentences with argument order alternation between conjuncts can be processed simply by defining an alternation between two sets of edges in a tree of a tree set, as long as the oriented links continue to point to the correct nodes.[4]

3.6 Definition of MCTAG with Local Synchronous Derivation

Following (Kallmeyer, 2005), we define the formalism used in this paper as MCTAG with Local Synchronous Derivations (MCTAG-Local SD). A MCTAG-Local SD is a tuple $G = \langle I, A, N, T, S, L, R \rangle$ with I being the set of initials trees, A the set of auxiliary trees, N (resp. T) the set of nonterminal (resp. terminal) labels, S the set of elementary tree sets, L the set of oriented links between two leaf nodes of two different elementary trees of a tree set of S and R the set of application constraints of L. $G_{TAG} = \langle I, A, N, T \rangle$ is the underlying TAG whose derivations constitute the backbone of MCTAG-Local SD derivation tree. We define the local synchronous derivation. Let Γ be the tree set with γ_i and γ_0 as its trees. γ_0 is called the main anchor tree. Let L_Γ be the set of tuples $\langle N_L, N_R \rangle$ with a tuple characterizing an oriented link from N_L to N_R with N_L the site node of a derivation and N_R a site node of a derivation in another tree of the same tree set. Let R_Γ be the set of restrictions of L_Γ.

1) if an instance of an elementary tree γ' is derived (by substitution or mandatory adjunction) on a node N_L of a tree γ_i

2) if there exists a node N_R of γ_j such that $\langle N_L, N_R \rangle$ is a valid oriented link of L_Γ

3) if no derivation succeeds on the node N_R of γ_j

4) if no derivation exists from a node N_j of a tree

---

[4]Therefore Gorn's address should not be used for node's id as the order of nodes will not be fixed.

γ_j to a node N_i of γ_i such that $\langle N_j, N_i \rangle$ is a valid oriented link of L_Γ (this is a restriction of R)
5) then a derivation of the same instance as the one of the tree γ' (cf. (1)), which substituted to γ_i in N_L, is created in the node N_R of γ_j.

To define the local-SD of anchoring, let us assume that unrealized trees are tree schemas with a special leaf node labeled "$V_{anchor} \downarrow$" and that each anchor is realized by substituting a special initial tree of root "V_{anchor}" dominating the "real" lexical anchor. Thus, anchoring is realized through substitution and the relevant oriented link is of the form $\langle N_{\gamma_0}, N_{\gamma_j} \rangle$ with N_{γ_0} the leaf node where this special substitution takes place and N_{γ_j} the relevant leaf nodes of the unrealized anchors where the special substitution should have taken place. Therefore, the same process that was valid for the regular local synchronous derivation can be applied. If we need any restriction on which tree should be selected by any anchor, it would suffice to establish a checking function (unification check, subcat. frame checking, type checking...) for each anchoring derivation. We made sure that no linked derivation could occur on already realized substitution node, therefore we can conjecture than the weak generative power of MCTAG is preserved.

4 Related Work

The principal work done on Coordination in the LTAG framework has been done by (Sarkar and Joshi, 1996a). The authors extend the formalism itself by a new operation, the conjoin operation, to provide derivation structures which cannot be obtained by pure (Lexicalized)TAG. Although powerful by allowing node merging and rich derivational structures, this operation leads to a difficult interpretation of the derivation tree in terms of generated languages even though the final derivation tree is actually a derivation graph. The derived tree becomes also a bit difficult to interpret for any classical phrase based linguistic theory. However, this model has been implemented among others by (Banik, 2004) for an interface syntax-semantic framework. Closer to our approach, to process elliptic coordination (Sarkar, 1997) introduces Link-Sharing TAG, a more constrained formalism than Synchronous TAG (Shieber and Schabes, 1990) while belonging to the same family. The main idea is to dissociate dependency from constituency by the use of pairs of trees, one being a regular ele-

mentary trees, the other being a dependency tree. Derivations are shared thanks to a synchronization mechanism over different pairs of the same type (dependency and constituency). On the contrary, our approach builds parallel derivations by simply having trees inside a same tree set and links are built explicitly for the sharing of arguments. Our methods seems to operate on two different axes (vertical vs horizontal) but further analysis will be needed to exploit potential points of convergence.

5 Discussion

The main argument in favor of the use of MC-TAG to process gapping coordination is that using tree sets with unrealized trees allows pure compositional analysis of the resulting derivation tree without the need to capture the missing lexical anchors through different elementary trees. In short, associating realized and unrealized trees in a same tree set allows the handling of parallel derivation structures simply by means of the MCTAG's extended domain of locality and by a few links between argument position. By allowing trees to be described as unlexicalized, we go deeper in the abstraction, resulting in the capacity to handle multiple kinds of elliptic coordinations using a unified framework. Of course losing the advantage of lexicalization may be a huge drawback so one possibility is to keep the main tree of a set (γ_0) lexicalized and during the tree selection we add to a shared derivation forest the "pseudo" derivation proof of an anchoring substitution, thus we maintain illusion of unlexicalization while benefiting from its counterpart. Some questions remain open, in particular, knowing exactly what kind of parsing complexity can we expect from a MCTAG with tree sets of dynamic cardinality? Even if we stick to the TL-MCTAG with Local SD, the parsing complexity is directly related to the number of nodes of a tree set and to its cardinality. Adding a synchronous mechanism even of a limited range, and with restrictions, but over k inner local trees, increases again the parsing complexity.

6 Conclusion

In this paper, we have proposed a simple model of coordination within an extended MCTAG framework. We showed that the extended power of MCTAG permits strict and relaxed parallelism analysis for coordination while allowing the analysis of problematic constructions even within the TL-MCTAG framework. Future work will be oriented toward formal characterization of this promising formalism.

Acknowledgments

We would like to thank Benoît Crabbé, Laurence Danlos, Eric de la Clergerie, Benoît Sagot, Giorgo Satta, Marie Candito and the anonymous reviewers for their comments.

References

Banik, Eva. 2004. Semantics of VP Coordination in LTAG. In *Proceedings of the TAG+7 workshop, Vancouver, Canada, May 20-22*.

Becker, Tilman, Owen Rambow, and Michael Niv. 1992. The derivational generative power of formal systems, or, scrambling is beyond LCFRS. Technical Report IRCS-92-38, Philadelphia, PA.

Boullier, Pierre. 1999. On multicomponent TAG parsing. In *6ème conférence annuelle sur le Traitement Automatique des Langues Naturelles (TALN'99)*, pages 321–326, Cargèse, Corse, France, July.

Candito, Marie-Hélène. 1996. A principle-based hierarchical representation of ltags. In *Proceedings of the 16th conference on Computational linguistics*, pages 194–199, Morristown, NJ, USA. Association for Computational Linguistics.

Jorgensen, Il. and A. Abeillé. 1992. Coordination of "unlike categories" in tag. In *Proceedings of the 2nd TAG Workshop*, Philadelphia, US.

Joshi, Aravind K. 1987. Introduction to tree adjoining grammar. In Manaster-Ramer, A., editor, *The Mathematics of Language*. J. Benjamins.

Kallmeyer, Laura. 2005. A declarative characterization of a declarative characterization of multicomponent tree adjoining grammars. In *Proceedings of Traitement automatique des langues Naturelles - TALN'05*, Dourdan, France.

Lascarides, Alex, Ann Copestake, and Ted Briscoe. 1996. Ambiguity and coherence. *Journal of Semantics*, 13(1):41–65.

Milward, David. 1994. Non-constituent coordination: Theory and practice. In *Proceedings of the 15th International Conference on Computational Linguistics (COLING94)*, Kyoto.

Rambow, Owen and Giorgo Satta. 1992. Formal properties of non-locality. In *Proceedings of the 2nd International Workshop on Tree Adjoining Grammar*, Philadelpia, Pennsylvania.

Sag, Ivan A., Gerald Gazdar, Thomas Wasow, and Steven Weisler. 1985. Coordination and how to distinguish categories. *Natural Language and Linguistic Theory*, 3(2):117–171.

Sarkar, A. and A. Joshi. 1996a. Handling coordination in a tree adjoining grammar. Technical report, Dept. of Computer and Info. Sc., Univ. of Pennsylvania, Philadelphia, PA.

Sarkar, Anoop and Aravind Joshi. 1996b. Coordination in tree adjoining grammars: Formalization and implementation. In *COLING'96, Copenhagen*, pages 610–615.

Sarkar, A. 1997. Separating Dependency from Constituency in a Tree Rewriting System. pages 153–160, Saarbruecken, Germany.

Schuler, William, David Chiang, and Mark Dras. 2000. Multi-component tag and notions of formal power. In *ACL '00: Proceedings of the 38th Annual Meeting on Association for Computational Linguistics*, pages 448–455, Morristown, NJ, USA. Association for Computational Linguistics.

Seddah, Djamé and Benoît Sagot. 2006. Modeling and analysis of elliptic coordination by dynamic exploitation of derivation forests in LTAG parsing. In *Proceedings of TAG+8*, Sydney, Australia.

Shieber, Stuart and Yves Schabes. 1990. Synchronous Tree Adjoining Grammars. In *COLING*, volume 3, pages 253–260, Helsinki.

Steedman, Marc. 1990. Gapping as constituant coordination. *Linguistic and Philosophy*, 13:207–264.

Vijay-Shanker, K. and Yves Schabes. 1992. Structure sharing in lexicalized tree-adjoining grammars. In *Proceedings of the 14th conference on Computational linguistics*, pages 205–211, Morristown, NJ, USA. Association for Computational Linguistics.

Villemonte de La Clergerie, Éric. 2002. Parsing mildly context-sensitive languages with thread automata. In *Proc. of COLING'02*, August.

Villemonte de La Clergerie, Éric. 2005. From metagrammars to factorized TAG/TIG parsers. In *Proceedings of the Fifth International Workshop on Parsing Technology (IWPT'05)*, pages 190–191, Vancouver, Canada, October.

Weir, David Jeremy. 1988. *Characterizing mildly context-sensitive grammar formalisms*. Ph.D. thesis, Philadelphia, PA, USA. Supervisor-Aravind K. Joshi.

Plasticity of grammatical recursion in German learners of Dutch

Douglas J. Davidson & Peter Indefrey
F.C. Donders Centre for Cognitive Neuroimaging
Max Planck Institute for Psycholinguistics
Nijmegen, The Netherlands
`doug.davidson@mpi.nl, peter.indefrey@mpi.nl`

Abstract

We examined the multilingual comprehension and learning of cross-serial and embedded constructions in German-speaking learners of Dutch using magnetoencephalography (MEG). In several experimental sessions, learners performed a sentence-scene matching task with Dutch sentences including two different verb orders (Dutch or German verb order). The results indicated a larger evoked response for the German order relative to the Dutch order over frontal sensors after three months, but not initially. The response implies that sensitivity to violations of verb order remains plastic into adulthood.

1 Introduction

Psycholinguistic studies have examined cross-serial and embedded complement clauses in West Germanic in order to distinguish between different types of working memory models of human sentence processing (Bach, Brown, & Wilson 1986; Joshi, 1990), and this contrast has been important in applications of Tree-Adjoining Grammar (Joshi, 1985). Many language users are bilingual in German and Dutch, suggesting that they maintain knowledge akin to a synchronized grammar (Shieber and Schabes, 1990). Psycholinguistic studies of production, using syntactic priming, suggest that syntactic representations from L1 and L2 can influence each other during production (Harsuiker and Pickering, 2007). However, these effects seem to be limited to structures where word order is shared. Also, it is not yet well understood how bilingual users comprehend or acquire complement structures. For example, adult language users may have difficulty adopting the verb order preference of another language if it is not consistent with their first language. In principle, this could be the case when German-speaking learners of Dutch learn to adopt the verb order preference of Dutch in infinitival embedded clauses because German does not permit the same verb orders as Dutch (see Section 2.1).

Adult plasticity in the use of these constructions is investigated here by examining the response of German-speaking learners of Dutch using magnetoencephalography (MEG), a measurement technique that can reveal the electrophysiological response to grammatical violations. Recent work has shown that electrophysiology is sensitive to learning-related changes in adult language learners (Mueller et al 2005; Osterhout et al. 2006). The hypothesis under investigation is that the ability to adapt to different forms of recursion remains plastic in adulthood.

1.1 Linguistic and Computational Models of Grammatical Complexity

Representational work has been concerned with the distinction between crossed and nested dependencies in recursive structures from both linguistic and computational perspectives. We will first detail the descriptive and theoretical linguistic background. In Standard German complement clauses, the first verbal head has the most local NP as its dependent, as in (1) versus (2); note that the sentences are similar to the materials used in the experiment described later.

(1)   ...*dass   wir   das   Kreuz   das   Dreieck*
      ...that we   the   cross   the   triangle
      berühren   lassen
      touch   let
      'that we let the cross touch the triangle'

(2)   *...*dass wir das Kreuz das Dreieck lassen*
      berühren

The German constituent order of a complement clause, $NP_1NP_2NP_3V_2V_1$. Note that in this structure, the verb cluster V_2V_1 is ordered so that the most-embedded verb, V_2 (*berühren*), is first. The dependency between the object NP_3 and V_2 is therefore the shortest, while the dependency between the subject NP_1 and V_1 is the longest.

In contrast to German, Standard Dutch licenses a crossed dependency, as shown in (3–4), with the same interpretation as the earlier German examples. In this construction, the sequence of verbs in the complement clause is V_1V_2, e.g., (*laten raken*). The first-encountered verbal head, V_1, is to be matched to its dependency higher in the constituent structure, NP_1, crossing over the other dependents.

(3)   *...*dat   wij   het   kruis   de   driehoek*
      ...that we   the   cross   the   triangle
      raken   laten
      touch   let
      'that we let the cross touch the triangle'

(4)   ...*dat wij het kruis de driehoek laten raken*

The comparison between German and Dutch complement clauses has been influencial in the development of formal language models with higher generative capacity (Shieber, 1985; Joshi, 2004). Specifically, the crossed dependencies in Dutch and other languages in the West Germanic family cannot be modeled using context-free grammars (Evers, 1975; Shieber, 1985). The constrast between these structures has been addressed by diverse linguistic frameworks that have varying representational assumptions (Bobaljik, 2004; Kroch & Santorini, 1991; Evers, 1975). Joshi and collegues have shown that a number of linguistic frameworks can be grouped into the mildly context sensitive languages (Joshi, 1985; Joshi, Vijay-Shanker, & Weir, 1991). The capacity of LTAG to model the crossing dependency has led, in turn,

to an algorithmic analysis of the time and memory requirements necessary to parse the crossing and embedded verb orders (Joshi, 1990). This analysis predicts that the Dutch crossing structure is easier to recognize because verbs can be individually linked to their dependent arguments in a queue, rather than first encoding the series of verbs into a (stack-like) working memory as in German (Joshi, 1990).

On the face of it, the difference between Dutch and German embedded constructions with respect to formal language properties might lead one to expect a relatively high threshold for acquiring these constructions in a second language or borrowing them in language contact settings. However, this assumption is not supported by the considerable synchronic and diachronic variability among the West Germanic languages and/or dialects (Barbiers et al. in press; Pauwels, 1953; Wurmbrand, 2004). For example, the embedded clause construction is found in Frisian and the cross-serial construction is found in Swiss German. Also note that both Dutch and German allowed either order earlier in their language histories. During the 14th century, Early New High German permitted either the nested or crossed verb orders but Modern German does not (Sapp, 2006). The substantial dialectal and diachronic variation in the use of these structures would suggest that the subordinate clause verb order is relatively susceptible to change.

1.2   Working Memory Processing Models

Within psycholinguistics, processing models of complexity (Gibson, 1998; Lewis, 1996; Gordon et al., 2002) have addressed why some structures appear to be more difficult to parse or interpret than others in comprehension. They also address why, in some extreme cases, certain types of grammatical sentences seem to be impossible to process, even when the constructions are unambiguous and involve only two or three clauses. In most cases, these theories employ a complexity metric as a linking assumption. This complexity metric associates strings and hypothesized grammatical representations with processing difficulty and breakdown.

Dependency locality theory (DLT; Gibson, 1989) proposes that the processing cost of a linguistic construction depends on how the construction consumes working memory storage or computational resources. The DLT proposal is that the processing cost of a construction increases proportional to the number of incomplete syntactic dependencies that must be held in working memory before they are resolved. This type of resource cost is strongly influenced by the locality of the head and a dependent, such that longer-distance dependencies between a head and a dependent incur a greater resource cost. A second type of cost is incurred when new discourse entities must be set up in a discourse model. Other models of linguistic processing complexity emphasize interference in working memory as a potential source of processing difficulty (Lewis, 1996; Gordon et al. 2002). In these accounts, the number of open dependencies of the same type (e.g., the same grammatical case) will determine processing difficulty, other factors held constant.

The contrast between crossed versus embedded dependencies has been used to support these models. Bach et al. (1986) had separate groups of Dutch and German native speakers rate the comprehensibility, as well as answer paraphrase questions, concerning sentences similar to those in (1-2), but with an increasing number of verbs. They observed equivalent question answering performance for both Dutch and German participants for the constructions using two verbs, but differences between the two language groups for higher levels of embedding and more verbs. With three or more verbs, Dutch participants made fewer errors with the Dutch cross-serial construction than the German participants made with the German embedded construction. Also, the Dutch subjects rated the (three-verb) cross-serial construction easier to process than the Germans rated the German (three-verb) embedded construction. These differences have been taken as evidence first, that the cross-serial construction is easier to process than the embedded construction, and second, that human parsing does not employ a stack-based working memory for linguistic material, but rather a queue-like working memory, because a stack-like architecture would not have predicted the advantage for Dutch. Joshi (1990) has argued that the performance differences observed by Bach *et al.* (1986) could be accounted for by representational assumptions as well.

The DLT account (Gibson, 1998) of these find-

ings assumes that syntactic categories that are predicted first will accrue a greater memory cost because they must be maintained in working memory. In Dutch, this cost is initially higher because the first verb of a three-verb cluster closes a longer-distance dependency than the corresponding German version of the sentence. However, because this dependency is closed, the other verbs can be processed with less cost. In the German version, the first verb of the cluster closes a short-distance dependency, but the other dependencies must be kept active in working memory. Later in the German verb cluster the longer distance dependency is resolved with a higher cost. Thus, in the DLT account the linear order of the verbs allows Dutch to distribute integration costs over the verb cluster more equally than in the German version, which concentrates the higher–cost dependencies near the end of the verb cluster.

The difference between fewer versus more embeddings was also investigated by Kaan and Vasić (2004), who investigated reading times of Dutch subjects presented with two- and three-verb versions of the Dutch cross-serial dependency. They showed that average reading times increased at the first verb of the three-verb constructions relative to the two-verb constructions, and in addition, that the type of NP presented in the pre-verbal string affected integration at the verb. They concluded that a storage component like that proposed in Gibson (1998) along with a role for interference proposed by Gordon et al. (2001) would best account for the reading time data.

In the TAG-based processing model of the Bach et al. data, an embedded pushdown automaton and a complexity metric are proposed. Joshi (1990) proposed a complexity metric to express the amount of memory (or time) required to recognize sentences with the automaton, similar to the complexity metric(s) proposed by Gibson (1998). The distinguishing feature of the model is that multiple memory stores ("stacks of stacks") are used to store intermediate parse results during the recognition of multiple-clause embeddings, rather than a single (pushdown) store. The automaton is able to use the patterns of symbols in the multiple stores to recognize certain types of extended projections. These projections are able to capture the crossing dependencies found in Dutch in such a way that clause relationships are recognized at each verb in Dutch, but crucially, only at the end of the verb sequence in German. Thus, the Joshi (1990) account formalizes the explanation for the processing differences between Dutch and German, and provides a linking hypothesis between the linguistic representation and the complexity metrics.

The above models, while offering a detailed account of performance parameters observed in controlled experimental settings, nevertheless abstract away from the fact that linguistic function is implemented in networks of neurons arranged in the cerebral cortex that is subject to experience-dependent change. Some work within psycholinguistics has addressed learning linguistic complexity. In artificial neural network approaches, grammatical knowledge is modeled with a network for string sequences, termed a simple recurrent network (SRN), rather than a symbolic grammar. Christiansen and Chater (1999) addressed the cross-serial versus embedded contrast with this approach, and have also argued that approaches like the SRN have important properties such as experience-dependent plasticity and robustness to non-ideal input. However, Grüning (2006) has recently argued that models of sequences consistent with embedded constructions are arguably *simpler* than systems that model sequences consistent with cross-serial dependencies, which is not completely consistent with the behavioral data reviewed above. However there are few experimental data on human learning of these types of structures, so it is not yet clear which human learning patterns these networks (or symbolic approaches) would be expected to model.

In the population-based approach of Niyogi (2006) a learner hears a grammar selected from a *population* of individuals (who may speak somewhat different languages). One major distinction between this approach and that of the SRN is that it models the population of speakers as a dynamical system rather than an individual. This approach is relevant for the present experiment because the approach assumes a model of grammatical plasticity in which (hypothesized) grammars become stable (Niyogi, 2006, pp. 187-189). It is not yet clear whether aspects of grammar such as verb order constraints should be viewed as either stable or plastic in such a model.

While artificial neural network models of lin-guistic processing offer an account of how linguistic complexity might arise in networks of threshold-based processing units, they nonetheless abstract away from realistic details of electrophysiological responses usually modeled within psychophysiology and neuroscience, and more importantly, how those electrophysiological responses change with experience. SRN models emphasize the role of experience-dependent change in response to statistics of the input, but there have been few attempts to link these hypotheses to physical neural systems.

2 Method

The present experiment attempts to make this link by examining the electrophysiological response of learners over time (see Davidson & Indefrey, submitted). In three experimental sessions spanning their initial acquisition of Dutch in an intensive Dutch course, German learners performed a sentence-scene matching task with Dutch sentences including two different verb constituent orders (Dutch verb order, German verb order). In addition they rated the grammaticality of similar constructions in a separate rating task. The sessions took place over a period of three months (at the start of the course, at two weeks, and at three months after the start of the course).

2.1 Participants and Materials

The participants ($n = 13$) were all over 18 years old. The materials consisted of sentences that described a simple scene involving geometric objects. Half of the sentences contained a verb order consistent with Dutch (crossing dependencies, 5) and half consistent with German (embedded dependencies, 6).

(5) *Je   zal   zien   dat   wij   het   rode   kruis*
    You will see   that we   the   red   cross
    de   blauwe   driehoek   <u>laten</u>   raken
    the   blue   triangle   let   touch
    'You will see that we let the red cross touch the blue triangle'

(6) *Je zal zien dat wij het rode kruis de blauwe driehoek <u>raken</u> laten*

In addition to the MEG task, the learners also rated the acceptability of sentences with a similar structure as the examples, but different words.

A control group ($n = 25$) of native Dutch speakers also rated the same sentences, but were not scanned with the MEG.

2.2 Procedure, Recordings, and Analysis

MEG signals were recorded in a magnetically-shielded room using a CTF system equipped with 151 axial gradiometers (VSM Tech Ltd., CTF Systems, Coquitlam, B. C., Canada), at a sampling rate of 1 kHz, low-pass filtered at 150 Hz during acquisition. The MEG provides a measure of magnetic field fluctuations due to electrical activity of synchronized post-synaptic potentials (Hämäläinen et al., 1993), analogous to EEG. The planar gradient of the sensor activity was derived to increase the spatial sensitivity of the measure. The data were analyzed with a clustering algorithm and tested for significance using randomization tests (Maris and Oostenveld, 2007). The analysis tested the null hypothesis of no differential violation response to the verb orders in each of the sessions. The behavioural data were analyzed using a mixed effect model (Baayen et al., 1986). For contrasts, posterior density intervals (HPD_d) were computed to assess whether the distribution of the parameter of interest is likely to include zero.

3 Results

3.1 Behavioural Classification

Figure 1 shows that the Dutch control participants rated the Dutch verb order as acceptable, and the German verb order as unacceptable, as expected. The German learners initially rated the sentences that were incompatible with German grammar as unacceptable, but over time rated the sentences as acceptable as the Dutch-speaking control group. Similarly, they rated the sentences compatible with German grammar more acceptable at the start of acquisition but less so later in acquisition, again approximating the Dutch control group's rating.

A direct comparison of the ratings for the German versus the Dutch order showed that the learners rated the Dutch order worse at the first session ($d = 1.15$, $HPD_d = 0.25, 2.02$), equal in the second session ($d = -0.90$, $HPD_d = -2.18, 0.36$, includes zero), and the German order worse in the last ($d = -2.54$, $HPD_d = -3.79, -1.30$).

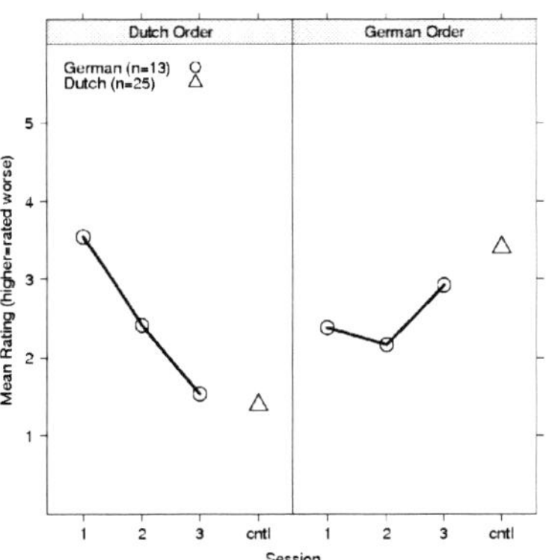

Figure 1: Average of median ratings of sentences following the German and Dutch verb orders.

3.2 Event-Related Fields

The average planar gradient of the evoked field to the initial verb within the cluster revealed a larger evoked response for the German order relative to the Dutch order over frontal sensors after two weeks, but not initially. At the second and third test sessions there was a significantly larger amplitude response for the German order compared to the Dutch order; session 2: $sumT = 32.72$, $p = 0.0073$, 12 sensors; session 3: $sumT = 72.88$, $p = 0.0006$, 25 sensors. Figures 2 and 3 show the topography of the response at sessions one and three for a time window of 0.2 to 0.4 s after the onset of the initial verb.

4 Discussion

The experiment reported here presented Dutch complement clause constructions to beginning German learners of Dutch over several sessions. This was done to examine how learners respond to different verb cluster orders of Dutch sentences as knowledge and proficiency of Dutch is acquired. The sentences were arranged to contrast two verb orders. One construction was a violation of Dutch grammar, which required a cross-serial dependency between verbs and their dependents. The other construction was a violation of German grammmar (were it applied to the Dutch sentences), which does not permit cross-serial dependencies, but instead requires the strict embed-

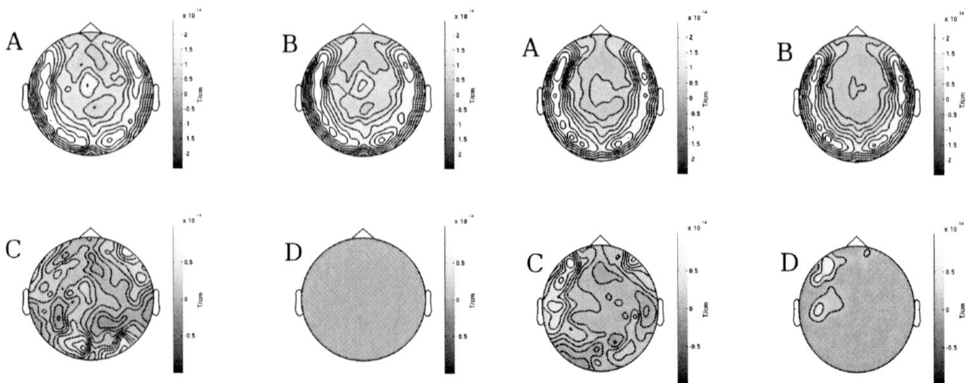

Figure 2: Topography of the average planar gradient of the event-related fields (0.2 to 0.4 s) for the German and Dutch verb orders in initial session. A. German order, B. Dutch order, C. German-Dutch contrast, D. statistically significant difference (none present).

Figure 3: Topography of the average planar gradient of the event-related fields (0.2 to 0.4 s) for the German and Dutch verb orders after three months. A. German order, B. Dutch order, C. German-Dutch contrast, D. statistically significant differences.

ding of verbs and their dependents.

The behavioural and electrophysiological results suggest that cortical responses to verb order preferences in complement clauses can change within three months after the onset of adult language learning, implying that this aspect of grammatical processing remains plastic into adulthood. The primary implication of this result is that the preference for crossed versus the embedded order is relatively flexible. This is in contrast to the assumptions of some theoretical models of language change (Labov, 2007), which assume that adult acquisition is relatively slow and error-prone. However, it must be stressed that Dutch and German are similar in many other respects, so it is likely that the learners in the present study acquired proficiency at a faster rate than learners with a different L1.

The results reported here have several implications for representational and processing models. Work on formal grammar has highlighted the distinction between crossed versus nested dependencies because of the implications that these structures have for different families of mathematical grammars. The existence of crossed dependencies like those in Dutch imply that grammars that are more expressive than context free grammars are

necessary in order to successfully model linguistic grammatical patterns. Although this property is fundamental for frameworks which attempt to find a proper structural description of human languages using a constrained formal system, the formal distinction between context free and context sensitive grammars does not, in itself, imply that crossed dependencies are more complex to process, or more complex to learn. The work on processing reviewed in the Introduction in fact suggests that crossed dependencies are in fact easier for comprehenders to parse than nested dependencies. The results presented here add to this literature by showing that crossing dependencies can be acquired in a relatively short period of time by adult learners, at least when other aspects of the L1 are similar (e.g., Germanic).

Our findings of fast L2 verb order acquisition suggest a need for a bilingual model of crossed and nested dependencies. A formal framework for modeling the correspondences between different grammatical systems has been proposed by Shieber (Shieber & Schabes, 1990). In this *Synchronous* Tree-Adjoining Grammar (STAG), a transfer lexicon is used to map pairs of elementary trees to one another in two separate TAGs. One advantage of such a framework is that the same modeling advantages found in TAG can be used in modeling correspondences between grammatical systems. In TAG, lexical items are associated with elementary trees to model local dependencies (factoring dependencies and recursion; Joshi, 1990). In the case of German and Dutch, pairs of elementary trees with inverted verb orders would be associated with each other in the transfer lexicon. Learning the Dutch verb order when the L1 is German would consist of learning that a subset of Dutch verbs (non-finite verbs, causative verbs, perception verbs) requires an inverted order in a complement clause. The links in the STAG transfer lexicon would model the fact that bilingual or learning speakers know that the meaning of the Dutch version of the sentence is the same as the German version, with a different verb order. A model of this type may account for the relative speed at which the learners acquired the Dutch order.

The present study, along with several other recent findings in the EEG literature (Osterhout et al. 2006; Mueller et al. 2005), offers evidence that the representational capacity of adult language users can change quickly during adult language learning. However, resource-based psycholinguistic models of processing complexity like those reviewed in the introduction have not yet addressed how the grammatical or representational resources used to parse complex sentences can change with language experience. Future modeling efforts could be directed at jointly modeling how grammatical representations are learned under resource limitations. An interesting modeling issue concerns how a network model (e.g., Christiansen & Chater, 1999) could learn to be sensitive to both the German and Dutch verb orders in the same speaker. Note that Dutch permits both verb orders, depending on finiteness of the verbs involved, so it appears to be necessary to address this issue in order to model single languages as well. Also, the work reported here has not explored the extent to which learning the Dutch verb order impacts processing of German sentences, or how long the sensitivity to verb order differences remains in the absence of direct experience with Dutch. Future empirical work could address these issues by examining behavioral or electrophysiological indices of parsing complexity in proficient German-Dutch bilinguals, as well as learners who are no longer active users of Dutch.

References

Baayen, R. H., Davidson, D. J. & Bates, D. M. in press. Mixed-effects modelling with crossed random effects for subjects and items. *Journal of Memory and Language.*

Bach, E., Brown, C. & Marslen–Wilson, W. D. 1986. Crossed and nested dependencies in Dutch and German: A psycholinguistic study. *Language and Cognitive Processes, 1*(4), 249–262.

Barbiers *et al.* (in press). *Syntactic Atlas of Dutch Dialects. Volume 2: Auxiliaries, verbal clusters, and negation.* Amsterdam, Amsterdam University Press.

Bobaljik, J. D. 2004. Clustering theories. In *Verb clusters: A study of Hungarian, German, and Dutch,* Eds. K. É. Kiss and H. van Riemsdijk, Pp. 121-146. Amsterdam/Philadelphia: John Benjamins Publishing Company.

Christiansen, M. H. & Chater, N. 1999. Toward a connectionist model of recursion in human linguistic performance, *Cognitive Science, 23,* 157–205.

Evers, A. 1975. *The transformational cycle in Dutch and German.* PhD Dissertation. University of Utrecht. Distributed by the Indiana University Linguistics Club, Bloomington, IL.

Davidson, D. J. & Indefrey, P. (submitted). Electrophysiological responses to crossed versus nested structures in German learners of Dutch.

Gibson, E. 1998. Linguistic complexity: Locality of syntactic dependencies. *Cognition, 68,* 1 76.

Gordon, P. C., Hendrick, R., & Levine, W. H. 2002. Memory-load interference in syntactic processing. *Psychological Science, 13,* 425–430.

Grüning, A. 2006. Stack-like and queue-like dynamics in recurrent neural networks. *Connection Science, 18,* 23–42.

Hämäläinen, M. Hari, R., Ilmoniemi, R., Knuutila, J., & Lounasmaa, O. V. 1993. Magnetoencephalography: Theory, instrumentation, and applications to non-invasive studies of signal processing in the human brain. *Reviews in Modern Physics, 65,* 413–497.

Hartsuiker, R. J. & Pickering, M. J. 2007. Language integration in bilingual sentence production. *Acta Psychologica,* doi:10.1016/j.actpsy.2007.08.005.

Joshi, A. K. 1990. Processing crossed and nested dependencies: An automaton perspective on psycholinguistic results. *Language and Cognitive Processes, 5,* 1–27.

Joshi, A. K. 1985. Tree adjoining grammars: How much context-sensitivity is required to provide reasonable structural descriptions? In D. Dowty, L. Karttunen, and A. Zwicky (eds.) *Natural Language Processing: Psycholinguistic, Computational, and Theoretical Perspectives.*, Cambridge University Press, New York.

Joshi, A. K. 2004. Starting with complex primitives pays off: Complicate locally, simplify globally. *Cognitive Science, 28*, 637–668.

Joshi, A. K., Vijay-Shanker, K., & Weir, D. 1991. The convergence of mildly context sensitive grammar formalisms. In P. Sells, S. Shieber & T. Wasow (Eds), Foundational Issues in Natural Language Processing. MIT Press, Cambridge, Massachusetts, pages 31–81.

Kaan, E. & Vasić, N. 2004. Cross-serial dependencies in Dutch: Testing the influence of NP type on processing load. *Memory & Cognition, 32*, 175–184.

Kroch, A. S. & Santorini, B. 1991. The derived constituent structure of the West Germanic verb-raising construction. In R. Freidin (Ed.) *Principles and Parameters in Comparative Grammar.* MIT Press, Cambridge, Mass.

Labov, W. 2007. Transmission and diffusion. *Language, 83*, 344–387.

Lewis, R. L. 1996. Interference in short-term memory: The magical number two (or three) in sentence processing. *Journal of Psycholinguistic Research, 25*, 93–113.

Maris, E. & Oostenveld, R. 2007. Nonparametric statistical testing of EEG- and MEG-data. *Journal of Neuroscience Methods, 164* (1), 177–190.

Mueller, J. L., Hahne, A., Fujii, Y., & Friederici, A. D. 2005. Native and nonnative speakers' processing of a miniature version of Japanese as revealed by ERPs. *Journal of Cognitive Neuroscience, 17*(8), 1229–1244.

Niyogi, P. 2006. *The computational nature of language learning and evolution.* MIT Press.

Pauwels, A. 1953. *De plaats van hulpwerkwoord, verleden deelwoord en infinitief in de Nederlandse bijzin.* Leuven, Symons. [The position of the auxiliary, past participle, and infinitive in the Dutch subordinate clause.]

Osterhout, L., McLaughlin, J., Pitkänen, I., Frenck-Mestre, C. & Molinaro, N. 2006. Novice learners, longitudinal designs, and event-related potentials: A means for exploring the neurocognition of second language processing. *Language Learning, 56*, 199–230.

Sapp, C. D. 2006. *Verb order in subordinate clauses from Early New High German to Modern German.* Unpublished PhD dissertation. Indiana University.

Shieber, S. 1985. Evidence against the context-freeness of natural language. *Linguistics and Philosophy, 8*, 333–343.

Shieber, S. & Schabes, Y. 1990. Synchronous Tree Adjoining Grammars. *Proceedings of the 13th International Conference on Computational Linguistics (COLING 90)*, Helsinki, Finland.

Wurmbrand, S. 2004. West Germanic verb clusters: The empirical domain. In *Verb clusters: A study of Hungarian, German, and Dutch*, Eds. K. É. Kiss and H. van Riemsdijk, Pp. 43-85. Amsterdam/Philadelphia: John Benjamins Publishing Company.

Reflexives and TAG Semantics

Robert Frank
Department of Cognitive Science
Johns Hopkins University
3400 N. Charles Street
Baltimore, MD 20910, USA
rfrank@jhu.edu

Abstract

Nesson and Shieber (2006) argue that the synchronous TAG (STAG) formalism provides an empirically adequate, yet formally restrictive solution to the problem of associating semantic interpretations with TAG derivations. In this paper, I further explore this approach, focusing on the semantics of reflexives. I find that STAG indeed permits a simple analysis of core cases of reflexives. This analysis does not, however, easily extend to contexts in which the reflexive and its antecedent are arguments of distinct elementary trees. I consider three possible extensions to the analysis which remedy these difficulties.

1 Introduction

The TAG community has recently witnessed an explosion of research into the problem of assigning semantic interpretations to TAG derivations. One line of work, beginning with Shieber and Schabes (1990), uses the synchronous TAG (STAG) formalism to build syntactic and logical form representations in parallel. The second type of proposal, put forward originally by Kallmeyer and Joshi (2003) and refined and extended in Kallmeyer and Romero (2008), exploits a unification operation defined over semantic feature structures associated with elementary trees to produce a Minimal Recursion Semantics representation. Nesson and Shieber (2006) argue that because the STAG proposal makes use of no additional machinery beyond the TAG formalism itself, it provides a more restrictive solution to the problem of semantic interpretation. To the degree that STAG is adequate

to the task, one should then prefer it, as it holds out the possibility for providing explanatory accounts of semantic phenomena, much as TAG's restrictiveness has been shown to yield explanatory accounts of syntactic phenomena (Kroch, 1987; Frank, 2002). In this paper, I explore the question of STAG's adequacy, focusing on the phenomenon of reflexive interpretation.

As is well-known, reflexives are referentially dependent elements which are interpreted through their relation with a syntactically local antecedent. This syntactic sensitivity has led to analyses of the distribution of reflexives in terms of a syntactic constraint on the establishment of a syntactic correlate of the antecedent-reflexive relation (i.e., indexations), most famously the Binding Theory of Chomsky (1981). An alternative approach, explored by Partee and Bach (1984) and in much work since, assumes that anaphoric dependencies are instead established during the process of computing a semantic interpretation. The essential idea in such treatments is that reflexives are higher order functions over (transitive) predicates, decreasing the arity of the predicate by one and identifying the semantic value of two of the predicate's arguments via lambda abstraction.

(1) $[\![\text{himself}]\!] = \lambda P_{\langle e,\langle e,t \rangle \rangle} \lambda x. P(x, x)$

2 An STAG analysis

We can mimic this semantic treatment of reflexives in STAG by using the elementary tree set given in Figure 1a. The multicomponent tree set includes, on the syntactic side, trees corresponding to the reflexive and its antecedent, constrained to stand in a syntactic c command relation. This is identical to the assumptions of Ryant and Schef-

Proceedings of The Ninth International Workshop on Tree Adjoining Grammars and Related Formalisms
Tübingen, Germany. June 6-8, 2008.

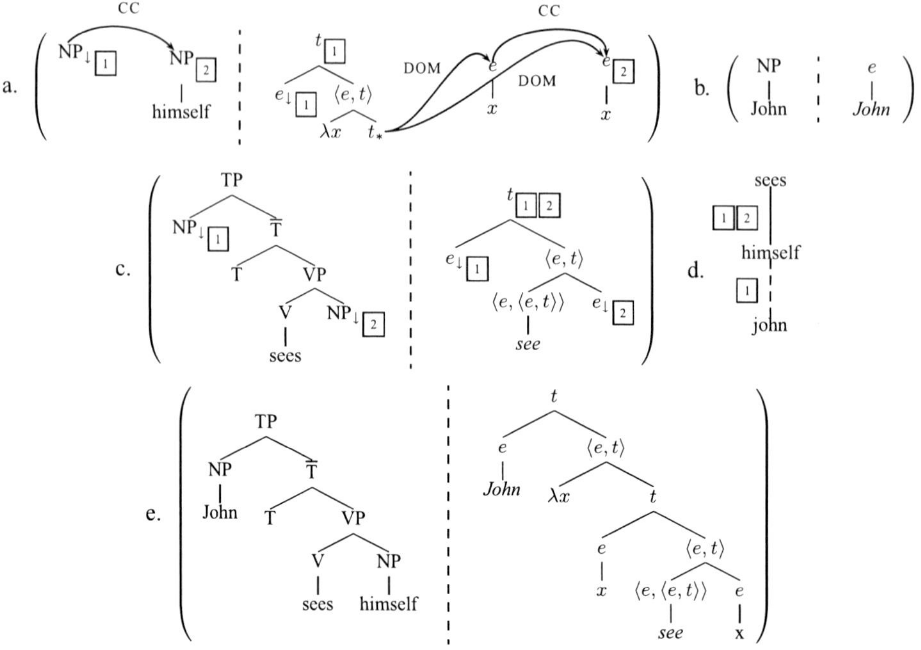

Figure 1: Elementary trees for (a) reflexives, (b) type e nominals, and (c) transitive predicates; (d) is the derivation tree for *John sees himself*, and (e) is the derived tree.

fler (2006) who propose an analysis of reflexives in the unification-based framework. On the semantic side, the tree set includes one tree that represents an instance of function application and lambda abstraction and two other trees, each an instance of the variable over which abstraction has taken place, constrained to stand in the relevant c-command and dominance relations. This tree set and the other trees depicted in Figure 1b and c can be employed in the tree-local derivation represented by the derivation tree in Figure 1d to produce the derived trees in Figure 1e. In this derivation, the antecedent first substitutes into the reflexive elementary tree, and the result then composes into the verbally headed elementary tree.

This type of derivation works equally well with quantified subjects. For such a case, I assume the semantic representation of the quantifier familiar from other STAG-based semantics work, shown in Figure 2a. To generate such an example, we follow the derivation depicted in Figure 2b. First, the quantifier combines first with reflexive: on the syntax side the NP tree representing the quantifier substitutes into the degenerate NP

tree from the reflexive's tree set, while on the semantic side, the t-recursive auxiliary tree from the quantifier interpretation adjoins to the root of the t-recursive auxiliary from the reflexive interpretation and the e-rooted variable substitutes into the substitution slot in the same tree, thereby satisfying tree-locality. (Another derivation with adjoining to the foot rather than to the root would also satisfy tree-locality, but would violate the dominance restriction imposed by the quantifier tree set that ensures variable binding.) The resulting multi-component set is then combined with the verbally-headed elementary tree, as in the previous derivation, to produce the derived trees in Figure 2c.

This analysis extends to examples with reflexives embedded in non-quantificational picture-NPs:

(2)   John bought the picture of himself.

To derive such a case, we need only adjoin the pair of trees depicted in Figure 3a, representing the head of the picture-NP, to the root of the reflexive-headed NP tree and its semantic analog. The derivation for (2) then continues just as in Figure 1.

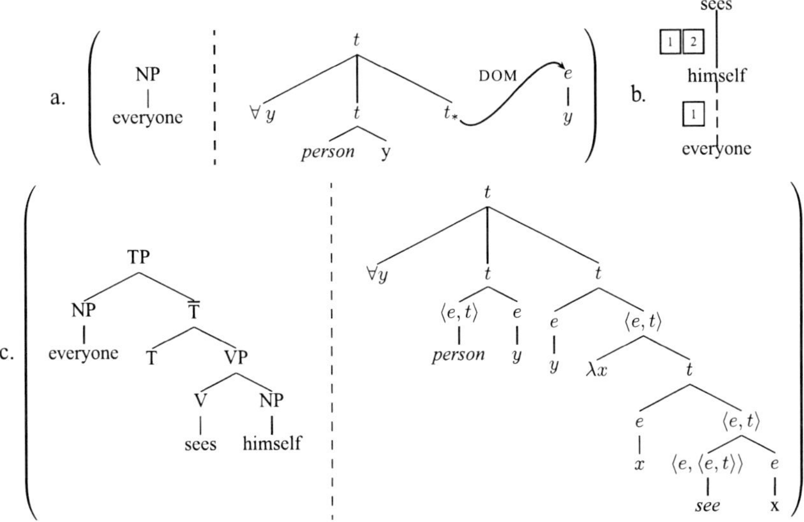

Figure 2: Derivation for quantifier-bound reflexives in *everyone sees himself*: (a) quantifier elementary trees, (b) derivation tree, (c) derived trees

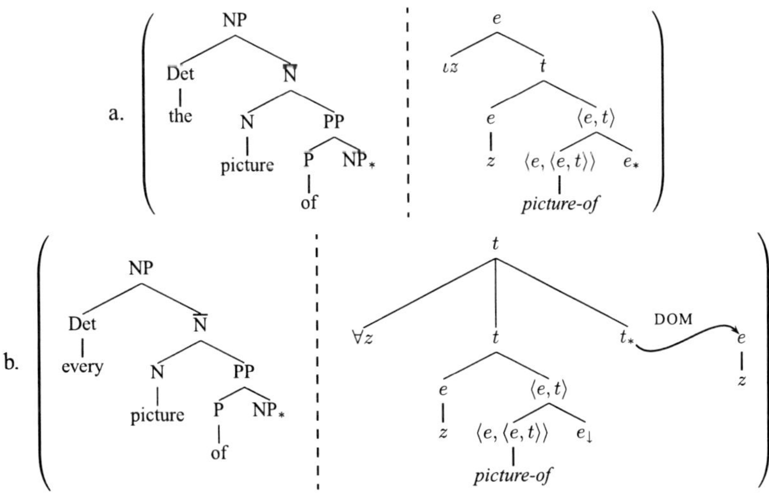

Figure 3: Elementary trees for picture NPs: (a) *e*-type, and (b) quantificational

One might object that the synchronous elementary tree set I have associated with the reflexive in Figure 1a is incompatible with the TAG version of the theta criterion (Frank, 2002), according to which all non-projected nodes need to be licensed via some predicate-argument relation and all arguments must be represented as a non-projected node. Under the reasonable assumption that this constraint applies to syntactic and semantic elementary tree sets alike, just as it applies to individual elementary trees, it is not clear how the syntactic and semantic elementary tree sets that represent the reflexive can be both well-formed: the syntactic set includes a single non-projected node (corresponding to the NP that is the antecedent of the reflexive), while the semantic set includes two (the substitution node of type e and the foot node of type t). This distinction suggests that the TAG theta criterion should more properly be understood as the reflection of a more general constraint on the expression of grammatical dependencies in elementary trees or tree sets, whether syntactic or semantic. The relevant dependency in the case of the syntactic representation of the reflexive is the relation established with its antecedent. The semantic dependencies, in contrast, are those that can be read off of the semantic interpretation in (1): the reflexive denotes a relation between an individual and a predicate and it is these that are realized as non-projected argument slots in this tree set.[1]

Divergences between the syntactic and semantic dependents will be found quite widely in functional elements whose denotations are taken to be higher order functions. Such elements will include quantifiers, reflexives, measure heads, relative pronouns and wh-phrases. In the case of lexical predicates, the syntactic and semantic dependents will tend to be better aligned though even here there may be divergences. The landing site of a wh-phrase that has undergone wh-movement to a higher clause might be thought of as a kind of syntactic dependent to the higher clause, and indeed the treatments of 'long' movement by Frank and Kroch (1995) and Frank (2002) in which the wh-phrase is substituted into such a position can be thought of as adopting this perspective. Similarly, one might be tempted to represent in the syntactic side of a synchronous grammar the case dependency between a finite raising verb and its subject or between an ECM verb and the subject of its complement clause (cf. Carroll et al. (2000)), while maintaining the standard set of dependencies on the semantic side. Pursuing this line of analysis raises a host of issues that lie beyond the scope of the current work.

This STAG analysis has a couple of significant advantages over compositional treatments using meanings like the one in (1). First of all, it avoids the need to multiply interpretations for the reflexive when it occurs as the dative argument of ditransitive predicates or with different antecedents. To derive the interpretive possibilities in (3) and (4), the different interpretations shown below each example must be assigned to the reflexive.

(3) Mary showed John himself in the mirror.
$$[\![\text{himself}]\!] = \lambda P_{\langle e,\langle e,\langle e,t\rangle\rangle\rangle}\lambda x\lambda y.P(y,x,x)$$

(4) John showed Mary himself in the mirror.
$$[\![\text{himself}]\!] = \lambda P_{\langle e,\langle e,\langle e,t\rangle\rangle\rangle}\lambda x\lambda y.P(y,x,y)$$

Under the STAG analysis, both of these interpretations can be derived from the single reflexive tree set in Figure 1. The difference between the different binding possibilities depends on the locus of substitution for the degenerate NP elementary tree from the reflexive tree set, and correspondingly the locus of substitution for the lambda-bound variable, whether into the patient or goal argument slots.

Secondly, the syntactic locality of the reflexive-antecedent relation derives not from a stipulation on semantics of the reflexive, but rather from the local nature of the TAG derivation. In contrast, using a semantic calculus using a denotation for the reflexive such as (1) as well as the operation of function composition, one could compute an interpretation of type $\langle e,\langle e,t\rangle\rangle$ for the word sequence *thinks that Mary admires*. As Szabolcsi (1987) notes, such a unit could then be combined with the reflexive and subject NP to yield a long-distance interpretation for the reflexive, an inter-

---

[1]Note that the predicate that is an argument of the reflexive is of type t in the TAG tree set, as opposed to the type $\langle e,\langle e,t\rangle\rangle$ in (1). This is a result of the flexibility afforded by multi-component composition as compared to function application in the more standard semantic calculus. It would be interesting to see whether such felxibility would allow us to restrict the types of all non-projected argument nodes to base (as opposed to function) types. Such a restriction would, if it can be maintained, impose substantial restrictions on possible interpretations for lexical elements.

pretation that must be blocked via some additional stipulation.[2]

3 Moving beyond clausemates

Attractive as this analysis is, it has two shortcomings if it is to serve as a demonstration of the viability of STAG semantics in this domain. First of all, so long as the strictures of tree-local (or even set-local) MCTAG are maintained, the analysis cannot be extended to cases of reflexives embedded in quantificational picture NPs like the following:

(5) John bought every picture of himself.

The derivation of such an example will not involve the e-type tree set for the picture NP in Figure 3a, but must instead use the quantificational tree set in Figure 3b. This tree set cannot however be combined with the reflexive tree set in a tree-local or even set local fashion. On the one hand, the reflexive trees cannot both adjoin or substitute into the *picture* tree on the syntactic side, since the latter provides no position for the antecedent. The reverse combination can proceed on the syntactic side of the derivation, where the picture NP tree adjoins to the root of the reflexive-headed NP. However, on the semantic side this do not work out, since this NP is linked only to the e-type variable tree, which can host either adjoining of the t-recursive auxiliary tree or substitution of type e variable. Note that even if the root of the reflexive NP were linked to the root of the t-recursive auxiliary tree, allowing for the scope to be established, the derivation would still fail because of the absence of a slot for substitution of the variable introduced by the picture-NP tree. Both of these failures arise from the same source, neither the reflexive nor the picture-NP tree include structural representation of the predicate one of whose semantic arguments needs to be quantified over, and one of whose syntactic arguments needs to serve as the antecedent for the reflexive.

We need not necessarily despair at this aspect of our analysis. On the basis of examples like (6) and (7), Pollard and Sag (1992) and Reinhart and Reuland (1993) have argued that reflexives inside

of picture-NPs are in fact exempt from the usual syntactically-defined locality conditions on reflexive interpretation.

(6) Bill_i finally realized that if The Times was going to print [that picture of himself_i with Gorbachev] in the Sunday edition, there might be some backlash.

(7) Lucie_i said that (you agreed that) a picture of herself_i would be nice on that wall.

These authors argue that the interpretation of reflexives in picture-NP contexts is determined by pragmatically defined conditions.

Even if we suppose that this is correct, this is not enough to avoid difficulties entirely, as there is another pair of constructions that leads to problems: raising and ECM.

(8) John seems to himself to be the best candidate.

(9) John considers himself to be the best candidate.

Let us turn first to raising. Under the usual TAG derivation of a raising sentence like (8), the raising verb is represented by an auxiliary tree that lacks a position for a subject. This lack of a subject position immediately causes a problem when we attempt to combine the reflexive tree set with the raising auxiliary of which it is an argument, as there is no position that serve as the attachment site for the degenerate NP tree (see Figure 1a), and therefore we cannot retain either tree- or set-locality.[3]

There are a number of possible lines of analysis we might pursue here. I will outline each briefly, but space prevents me from deciding among them. The first involves a rethinking of the TAG syntactic analysis of raising, along the lines envisioned in the previous section, so that the syntactic representation of the raising verb's elementary tree would indeed include a representation of its syntactic dependent, the subject. This would permit the incor-

---

[2]Szabolcsi (1987) argues that the lack of locality built into the reflexive's semantics is desirable in order to deal with cases of long-distance anaphors (Koster and Reuland, 1991). Clearly, my current proposal does not extend to such cases, and must treat them via a different mechanism.

[3]For such reasons, Ryant and Scheffler (2006) in their analysis of reflexives exploit the flexible composition operation, thereby losing much of the constraint that the TAG formalism imposes on derivations. (Kallmeyer and Romero, 2007) demonstrate that this problem can be avoided by taking the antecedent component of the syntactic representation of the reflexive to adjoin to VP rather than NP. This move requires however the introduction of a regimen of feature passing of antecedent features.

poration of both halves of the reflexive's (syntactic) tree set into this the raising predicate's tree set. I will leave this option unexplored, because of the broad implications it would have on the treatment of locality in raising constructions more generally.

A second option involves taking the combination of the raising predicate and the reflexive experiencer to be the result of a lexical process, so that this combination was represented via a single elementary tree set. As seen in Figure 4, this tree set would have two components in the syntactic half to incorporate the representation of the reflexive's antecedent. This tree set could be adjoined into an infinitival clause to produce the appropriate syntax and interpretation. Such a lexicalist analysis of reflexives could in fact be applied to the monoclausal and picture NP cases discussed earlier, as well as to ECM.[4]

Unlike the first two possibilities which retain the same two part elementary tree set for the reflexive, a third analytic option alters this assumption. Specifically, this analysis adopts the considerably simpler view of reflexive syntax and semantics represented in Figure 5a, according to which the syntactic representation of of a reflexive is a single NP elementary tree, and the interpretation is variable of type e. When this reflexive is substituted into a raising auxiliary tree, the identity of the variable with which it is associated is percolated to the root of the raising auxiliary, as in the tree in Figure 5b. To accomplish the binding of this variable, I assume that the syntax and logical form associated with a simple clause are both somewhat more complex than we have been assuming, but in a manner that has independent motivation (see Figure 5c). On the syntax side, I take the subject to be generated within VP and raised to its surface position. On the semantics side, this structural assumption translates into a lambda-bound variable that is saturated by the surface subject (Heim and Kratzer, 1998). Because the VAR feature ensures the identity of the reflexive variable and the lambda bound variable, the reflexive variable will be bound once the raising auxiliary adjoins into the infinitival clause. A similar analysis will work for the ECM case as well, using the pair of trees in Figure 6 as the representation for the ECM predicate.

The VAR feature, if it is to fit with the feature system of TAG as usually understood, can take only one of a finite set of values.[5] In fact, such a bound on the number of distinct variables that can be present in an STAG-derived logical form is already imposed upon us by the fact that these logical forms are constructed from a TAG, which by definition may contain only a finite set of elementary trees. The restriction to a bounded number of distinct variables does not, of course, rule out the generation of sentences with unbounded complexity, so long as variables can be "reused". Because of the bounded nature of reflexive binding, the restriction will not cause any difficulties as the domain over which a reflexive can be bound is limited. What the restriction does rule out is, for instance, sentences with interactions between unboundedly many quantifiers and variables bound by them. As the number of such quantifier-pronoun pairings increases, such sentences become ever more difficult to comprehend, and it is therefore a rather thorny theoretical question as to whether such examples ought to be generated by the grammar (Joshi et al., 2000).

References

Carroll, John, Nicolas Nicolov, Olga Shaumyan, Martine Smets, and David Weir. 2000. Engineering a wide-coverage lexicalized grammar. In *Proceedings of the 5th International Workshop on Tree Adjoining Grammars and Related Frameworks*, pages 55–60, Paris.

Chomsky, Noam. 1981. *Lectures on Government and Binding*. Foris, Dordrecht.

Frank, Robert and Anthony Kroch. 1995. Generalized

---

[4]The ECM cases raise a problem as they might allow locality to be circumvented by repeated adjoining to the root of the syntactic tree representing the infinitival clause, hosting the reflexive. I leave this issue open for future work. Interestingly, such an issue does not arise in the case of raising, as the $\bar{\text{T}}$ recursion of the raising auxiliary prevents the introduction of an intervening antecedent even under repeated adjoining of auxiliary trees, without resort to intermediate traces. Interestingly, this analysis correctly predicts that intervening experiencers should not count as potential intervening binders.

    (i)   John$_i$ seems to Mary to appear to himself$_i$ to be the best candidate.

---

[5]This is a respect in which the feature unification exploited in work in TAG semantics is different from that that has traditionally been used in TAG syntax. And it is in this sense that the kind of feature unification I am exploiting is distinctly less powerful than that used by Kallmeyer and Romero (2007).

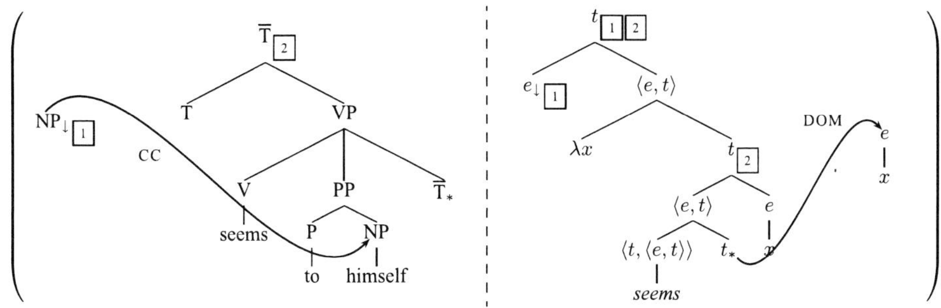

Figure 4: Elementary trees for composed reflexive-raising predicate

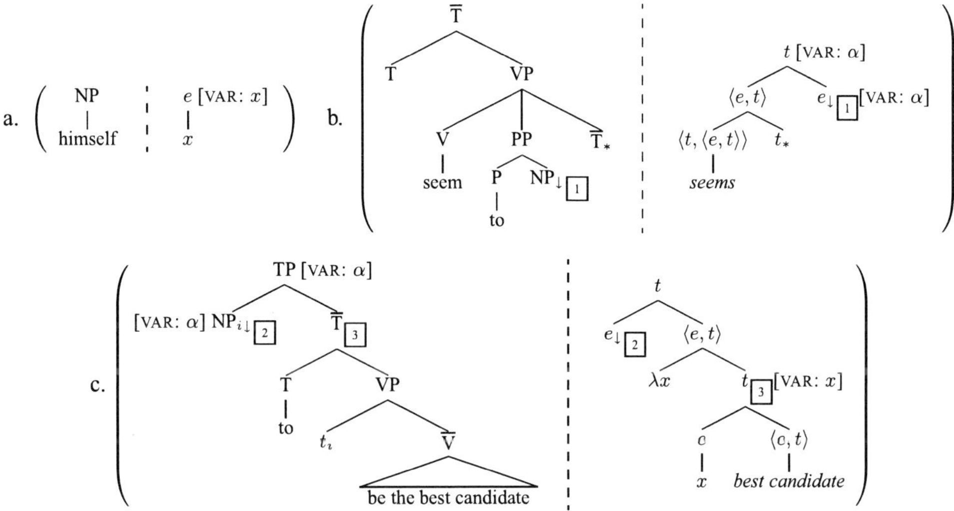

Figure 5: Elementary trees for raising derivation with VAR feature passing

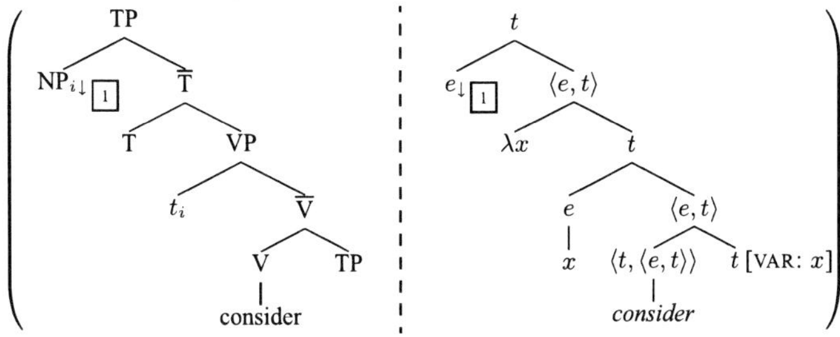

Figure 6: Elementary trees for ECM derivation with VAR feature passing

transformations and the theory of grammar. *Studia Linguistica*, 49(2):103–151.

Frank, Robert. 2002. *Phrase Structure Composition and Syntactic Dependencies*. MIT Press, Cambridge, MA.

Han, Chung-hye. 2007. Pied-piping in relative clauses: Syntax and compositional semantics using synchronous tree adjoining grammar. *Research on Language and Computation*, 5(4):457–479.

Heim, Irene and Angelika Kratzer. 1998. *Semantics in Generative Grammar*. Blackwell, Oxford.

Joshi, Aravind K., Tilman Becker, and Owen Rambow. 2000. Complexity of scrambling: A new twist on the competence-performance distinction. In Abeillé, Anne and Owen Rambow, editors, *Tree Adjoining Grammars: Formalisms, Linguistic Analysis and Processing*, pages 167–181. CSLI Publications, Stanford, CA.

Kallmeyer, Laura and Aravind K. Joshi. 2003. Factoring predicate argument and scope semantics: Underspecified semantics with LTAG. *Research on Language and Computation*, 1:3–58.

Kallmeyer, Laura and Maribel Romero. 2007. Reflexives and reciprocals in LTAG. In Geertzen, Jereon, Elias Thijsse, Harry Bunt, and Amanda Schiffrin, editors, *Proceedings of the Seventh International Workshop on Computational Semantics (IWCS-7)*, pages 271–282, Tilburg.

Kallmeyer, Laura and Maribel Romero. 2008. Scope and situation binding in LTAG using semantic unification. *Research on Language and Computation*, 6(1):3–52.

Koster, Jan and Eric Reuland, editors. 1991. *Long-Distance Anaphora*. Cambridge University Press, Cambridge.

Kroch, Anthony. 1987. Unbounded dependencies and subjacency in a tree adjoining grammar. In Manaster-Ramer, Alexis, editor, *The Mathematics of Language*, pages 143–172. John Benjamins, Amsterdam.

Nesson, Rebecca and Stuart M. Shieber. 2006. Simpler TAG semantics through synchronization. In Winter, Shuly, editor, *Proceedings of the 11th conference on Formal Grammar*, pages 129–142. CSLI Publications.

Partee, Barbara and Emmon Bach. 1984. Quantification, pronouns, and VP anaphora. In Groenendijk, Jeroen, Theo M.V. Janssen, and Martin Stockhof, editors, *Truth, Interpretation and Information*, pages 99–130. Foris Publications, Dordrecht.

Pollard, Carl and Ivan Sag. 1992. Anaphors in English and the scope of binding theory. *Linguistic Inquiry*, 23.

Reinhart, Tanya and Eric Reuland. 1993. Reflexivity. *Linguistic Inquiry*, 24:657–720.

Ryant, Neville and Tatjana Scheffler. 2006. Binding of anaphors in LTAG. In *Proceedings of the 8th International Workshop on Tree Adjoining Grammar and Related Formalisms (TAG+8)*, pages 65–72. Association for Computational Linguistics.

Shieber, Stuart and Yves Schabes. 1990. Synchronous tree adjoining grammars. In *Proceedings of the 13th International Conference on Computational Linguistics*, volume 3, pages 253–258, Helsinki.

Szabolcsi, Anna. 1987. Bound variables in syntax (are there any?). In Groenendijk, Jeroen, Martin Stockhof, and Fred Veltman, editors, *Proceedings of the 6th Amsterdam Colloquium*, pages 331–353, Amsterdam. Institute for Logic, Language and Information.

Modeling Mobile Intention Recognition Problems with Spatially Constrained Tree-Adjoining Grammars

Peter Kiefer
Laboratory for Semantic Information Technologies
University of Bamberg
`peter.kiefer@uni-bamberg.de`

Abstract

The problem of inferring an agent's intentions from her spatio-temporal behavior is called *mobile intention recognition problem*. Using formal grammars we can state these problems as parsing problems. We argue that context-free formalisms are not sufficient for important use cases. We introduce *Spatially Constrained Tree-Adjoining Grammars* which enrich TAGs with knowledge about the structure of space, and about how space and intentions are connected.

1 Introduction

The interaction possibilities between a mobile user and her device are often restricted. Mobile usage scenarios, such as navigation (Krüger et al., 2004), location-based gaming (Schlieder et al., 2006), and maintenance work (Kortuem et al., 1999), imply that the user's haptic and cognitive resources (Baus et al., 2002) are bound by a specific task. In these situations we would desire a system that somehow 'guesses' the user's information needs and presents the information automatically. The system must have a complex model of the intentions that are possible in a specific use case, and find an intention which consistently explains the user's behavior (*intention recognition problem*, IR).

In literature, the IR problem is also known as *plan recognition (PR) problem* (Carberry, 2001). It can be seen as the problem of revealing the hidden structural regularities that underlie an agent's sequence of behaviors. Formal grammars are often used to describe structural regularities, not only in natural language processing (NLP), but also in

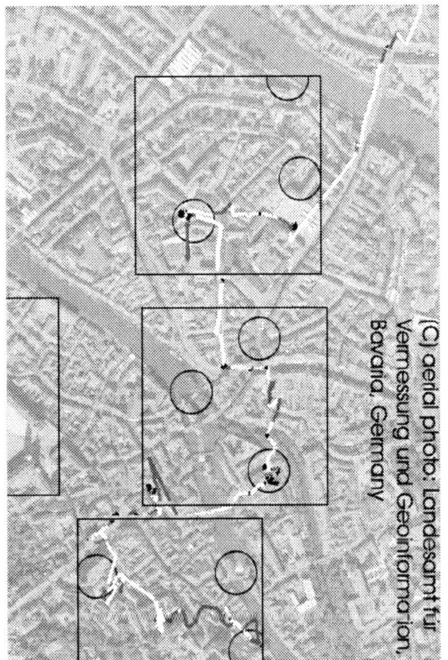

Figure 1. Spatio-temporal behavior in a location-based game: what are the user's intentions?

areas like computer vision (Chanda and Dellaert, 2004), and action recognition (Bobick and Ivanov, 1998). Consequently, formal grammars were also considered for PR/IR (Pynadath, 1999). Recent work has drawn parallels between NLP and PR/IR and argued that the expressiveness of context-free grammars (CFG) is not sufficient for important use cases (Geib and Steedman, 2007; Kiefer and Schlieder, 2007).

This paper continues this line of research by proposing mobile IR problems as an application area for Tree-Adjoining Grammars (TAG). We first explain which steps are necessary to state a

Proceedings of The Ninth International Workshop on Tree Adjoining Grammars and Related Formalisms
Tübingen, Germany. June 6-8, 2008.

mobile IR problem as parsing problem (section 2). We make the point that this problem class is special because mobile behavior happens in space and time. Section 3 introduces *Spatially Constrained Tree-Adjoining Grammars* (SCTAG), and explains how they can be used to model complex intention-space-relations elegantly. We close with an overview on related work (section 4) and an outlook on our future research (section 5).

2 Mobile intention recognition with formal grammars

2.1 Bridging the gap

One implication of spatio-temporality is that the gap between sensor input (e.g. position data from a GPS device) and high-level intentions (e.g. *'find a restaurant'*) is extremely large. To bridge this gap, we use a multi-level architecture with the level of *behaviors* as intermediate level between *position* and *intention*. We process a stream of (lat/lon)-pairs as follows:

1. *Preprocessing* The quality of the raw GPS data is improved. This includes removing points with zero satellites, and those with an impossible speed.

2. *Segmentation* The motion track is segmented at the border of regions, and when the spatio-temporal properties (e.g. speed, direction) of the last n points have changed significantly (Stein and Schlieder, 2005).

3. *Feature Extraction* Each segment is analyzed and annotated with certain features, like speed and curvature (Schlieder and Werner, 2003).

4. *Classification* Using these features, each motion segment is classified to one *behavior*. We can use any mapping function from feature vector to behaviors, for instance realized as a decision tree.

As output we get a stream of behaviors. In the example from Fig. 2 we distinguish the following spatio-temporal behaviors: riding (b_r), standing (b_0), sauntering (b_s), curving (b_c), and slow-curving (b_{cs}). In other use cases we might as well have non spatio-temporal behaviors, like manual user input. We call an IR problem a *mobile* one if at least some behaviors are spatio-temporal ones.

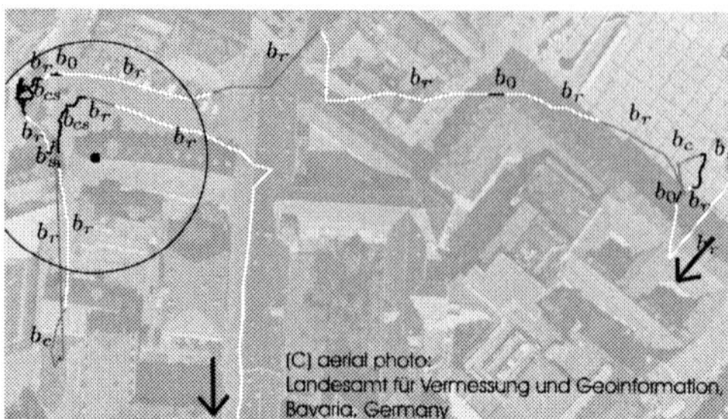

Figure 2: Spatio-temporal behavior sequence in the first region.

The track from Figures 1 and 2 was recorded in the location-based game CityPoker. In the scope of this paper, we will only roughly introduce the rules of this game whenever needed. For a complete description, refer to (Schlieder, 2005). The reason why this game is especially suited as exemplary use case is that CityPoker is played by bike at high speed.

2.2 Parsing behavior sequences

The stream of behaviors described above serves as input to a parsing algorithm. Using behaviors as terminals and intentions as non-terminals, we can write rules of a formal grammar that describe the intentions of an agent in our domain. Most plan recognition approaches have followed a hierarchical structure of plans/intentions (e.g. (Kautz and Allen, 1986; Geib and Goldman, 2003)). In CityPoker, for instance, a player will certainly have the intention to *Play*. At the beginning of each game, the members of a team discuss their strategy. Playing in CityPoker means exchanging cards in several cache regions, so we model a sequence of intentions as follows: $GotoRegion$ $HandleRegion$, $GotoRegion$ $HandleRegion$, and so on. In the cache region players find themselves a comfortable place to stand, answer a multiple-choice question, and select one out of three caches, depending on their answer. In the cache, they search a playing card which is hidden in the environment (see the behavior sequence in Fig. 2).

A context-free production system for CityPoker is listed in Fig. 3[1]. The choice of the formalism de-

---

[1] Rules with a right-hand side of the form $(symbol_1|...|symbol_n)^+$ are a simplified notation for 'an arbitrary sequence of $symbol_1, ..., symbol_n$, but at least one of them'.

pends on the requirements of the use case. As argued in (Schlieder, 2005), most intention recognition use cases need at least the expressiveness of a CFG. A typical example is leaving the same number of regions as entered before ($enter^n leave^n$). We can find the currently active intention in the parse tree by choosing the non-terminal which is direct parent of the current behavior.

2.3 Spatially Grounded Intentional Systems

Up to here we have largely ignored the spatial aspect of mobile intention recognition. We have used space in the preprocessing, but the last subsection was nothing but a simple CFG with intentions and behaviors. Now we will see how space can help us to reduce ambiguity. Consider the two parse trees in Fig. 4: both are possible for the behavior sequence from Fig. 2. In the upper one the agent has entered the circular cache and is searching for the cards. In the bottom one the agent is in the region and still searching for the cache. Obviously, the upper one can only occur if the behaviors are located in a cache. This is the basic idea of *Spatially Grounded Intentional Systems* (SGIS) (Schlieder, 2005): SGIS are context-free production systems with the extension that each rule is annotated with a number of regions in which it is applicable. We call this the *spatial grounding* of rules. For instance, a *HandleCache* intention is grounded in all regions of type *cache*. We modify all rules accordingly. An SGIS rule for the original rule (12) would look like follows:

$$HandleCache \rightarrow$$
$$SearchCards \quad DiscussStrategy$$
$$[grounding : cache_{1,1}, ..., cache_{5,3}]$$

This reduces the number of possible rules applicable at each position in the behavior sequence, thus avoiding many ambiguities. For parsing in SGIS we replace the pure behavior stream $(beh_1, beh_2, beh_3, ...)$ by a stream of behavior/region pairs: $((beh_1, reg_1), (beh_2, reg_2), (beh_3, reg_3), ...)$. Each behavior is annotated with the region in which it occurs. Also the non-terminals in the parse tree are annotated with a region *(Intention, region)*, with the meaning that all child-intentions or child-behaviors of this intention must occur in that region. SGIS are a short form of writing rules of the following form (where

Symbol can be an intention or a behavior):

$$(Intention, reg_x) \quad \rightarrow$$
$$(Symbol_1, reg_x) \quad ... \quad (Symbol_n, reg_x)$$

That means, we cannot write rules for arbitrary combinations of regions. In addition, we require that another rule can only be inserted at an intention $Symbol_i$ if the region of the other rule is (transitive) child in the partonomy, i.e. in the above rule we can only insert productions with a region reg_y $part\_of$ reg_x (which includes the same region: reg_y.equals(reg_x)). SGIS have been designed for partonomially structured space. The nesting of rules follows closely the nesting of regions and sub-regions in the spatial model. The CityPoker partonomy is structured as follows: the game_area contains five rectangular cache_regions, each of which in turn contains three caches (see Fig. 1.

3 A 'Spatialized' TAG

3.1 Spatial constraints

SGIS support a partonomial structure between regions, i.e. only *part_of* relations exist. In general, a lot more topological relations are possible, like *touches, disjunct, identical*, or *north-of*. Examples can be found in the literature on geographic information science (Egenhofer and Franzosa, 1991). This restriction of SGIS hinders us from expressing frequently occurring use cases. Consider the motion track in Fig. 2: the agent enters the cache, shows some searching behavior, and then temporarily leaves the circular cache to the south. Knowing the whole motion track we can decide that this is an *AccidentalLeave* intention, and not a *ChangePlan* intention[2]. It is not necessary that the intermediate intention, let us call it *Confused*, is located in the parent cache_region of the cache. Finally, entering just *any* cache is not sufficient for an *AccidentalLeave* intention, but we require that cache to be the same as left before.

---

[2]A player in CityPoker who has given a wrong answer to the quiz will be searching at the wrong cache and probably give up after some time. He will then head for one of the other caches. The *ChangePlan* intention was omitted in Fig. 3 for reasons of clarity.

Production Rules for CityPoker

$$
\begin{aligned}
Play &\rightarrow DiscussStrategy\ Continue &(1)\\
DiscussStrategy &\rightarrow b_0 &(2)\\
Continue &\rightarrow \varepsilon \mid GotoRegion\ HandleRegion\ Continue &(3)\\
GotoRegion &\rightarrow (b_r|b_0|b_c)^+ &(4)\\
HandleRegion &\rightarrow SelectCache\ GotoCache\ HandleCache &(5)\\
SelectCache &\rightarrow FindParkingPos\ AnswerQuiz &(6)\\
FindParkingPos &\rightarrow (b_r|b_c|b_{cs})^+ &(7)\\
AnswerQuiz &\rightarrow b_0 &(8)\\
GotoCache &\rightarrow (SearchWayToC\ |NavigateTowardsC)^+ &(9)\\
SearchWayToC &\rightarrow (b_0|b_{cs}|b_s)^+ &(10)\\
NavigateTowardsC &\rightarrow (b_r|b_c)^+ &(11)\\
HandleCache &\rightarrow SearchCards\ DiscussStrategy &(12)\\
SearchCards &\rightarrow (CrossCache|DetailSearch)^+ &(13)\\
CrossCache &\rightarrow (b_r)^+ &(14)\\
DetailSearch &\rightarrow (b_0|b_{cs}|b_s|b_c)^+ &(15)
\end{aligned}
$$

Figure 3: Context-free production rules for intention recognition in CityPoker.

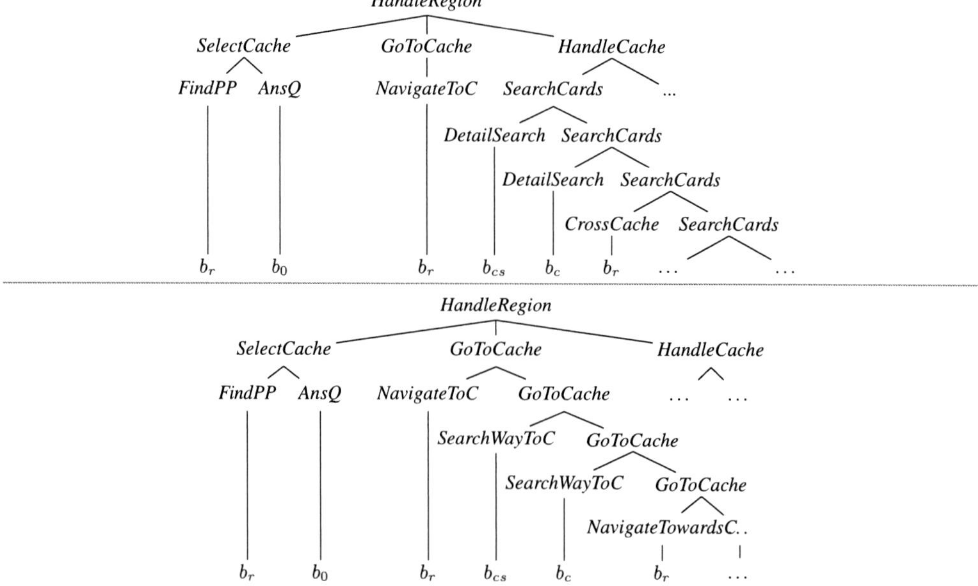

Figure 4: Parsing ambiguity if we had no spatial knowledge (see track from Fig. 2). Through spatial disambiguation in SGIS we can decide that the bottom parse tree is correct.

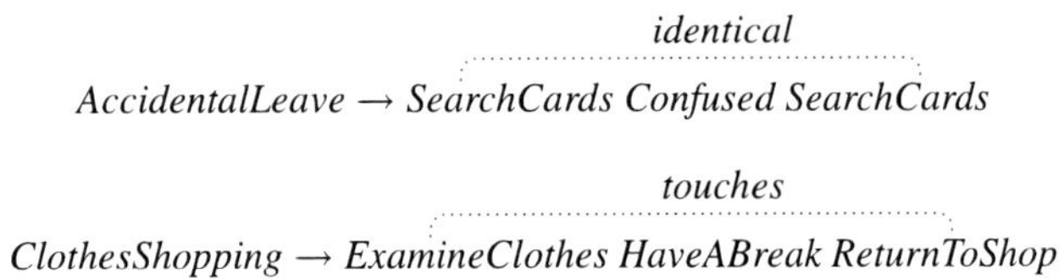

identical

$AccidentalLeave \rightarrow SearchCards\ Confused\ SearchCards$

touches

$ClothesShopping \rightarrow ExamineClothes\ HaveABreak\ ReturnToShop$

Figure 5: Two examples for spatial constraints in context-free production rules.

identical   *identical*

$HandleRegion\ HandleRegion\ RevisitRegion\ HandleRegion\ RevisitRegion$

Figure 6: Sequence of intentions with crossing spatial constraints.

We would need the following rule

$$(AccidentalLeave, cache_{1,1}) \rightarrow$$
$$(SearchCards, cache_{1,1}),$$
$$(Confused, [unconstrained]),$$
$$(SearchCards, cache_{1,1})$$

We cannot formulate this in SGIS, but still it makes no sense to write rules for pairs of (intention, region). What we would need to formalize the *accidental leaving pattern* elegantly is displayed in Fig. 5, top. We can easily find other examples of the pattern 'a certain behavior/intention occurs in a region which has a spatial relation r to another region where the agent has done something else before'. For instance, we can find use cases where it makes sense to detect a $ReturnToX$ intention if the agent has forgotten the way back to some place. We could define this as 'the agent shows a searching behavior in a region which *touches* a region she has been to before', see Fig. 5, bottom.

3.2 Cross-dependencies: a parallel to NLP

Two or more 'return to region' intentions can easily be crossed, see Fig. 6. In a real CityPoker game this can happen for tactical reasons. Players in CityPoker do not necessarily change a playing card although they have found it. They memorize the types of cards they have found and their exact position, and continue in the game. For a number of reasons it might make sense to change in another cache_region first. Sometimes they return to that cache_region at some time later in the game to change a card (without the effort of answering the quiz, cache search, and so on). What we need for

this *crossed return to region pattern* is a possibility to create *cross-dependencies*.

3.3 Spatially Constrained TAGs

To express the spatial dependencies described above, we take TAGs as defined in (Joshi and Schabes, 1997) with links as described in (Joshi, 1985), and enhance them by spatial knowledge.

Definition: A Spatially Constrained Tree-Adjoining Grammar is defined as $SCTAG = (TAG, R, SR, GC, NLC)$, where

- $TAG = (I, B, IT, AT, S)$, defined over intentions I, and behaviors B.

- R is a set of regions

- SR is a set of spatial relations, where each relation $r \subseteq R \times R$

- $GC \subseteq (IT \cup AT) \times R$ is a set of grounding constraints

- NLC is a set of spatial non-local constraints. Each constraint has a type from the spatial relations SR and is defined for two nodes in one tree from $IT \cup AT$.

Adjoining and substitution on an SCTAG work as in (Joshi and Schabes, 1997). The grounding constraints allow us to state that an elementary tree may only be located in a certain number of regions. The non-local constraints, on the other hand, allow us to state that the region of one symbol in an elementary tree must have a certain spatial relation to the region of another symbol in the same elementary tree.

As in SGIS, the terminals and non-terminals at the time of writing an SCTAG are not pairs of (symbol, region), but simply behaviors and intentions. This supports the intuition of a knowledge engineer who first writes the decomposition of intentions to sub-intentions, and in a second step annotates spatial knowledge.

Figure 7 lists part of a SCTAG that handles the re-visisting of cache_regions in CityPoker. Non-local spatial constraints are displayed as dotted lines. A complete grammar for this use case would convert all context-free rules from Fig. 3 to trees and add them to the grammar. This step is trivial. Figure 8 demonstrates how cross-dependencies evolve through two adjoining operations.

3.4 Parsing of SCTAG

For parsing a spatially constrained grammar, we modify Joshi's existing Early-like parsing algorithm (Joshi and Schabes, 1997). Like the original Earley parser for CFG, this parser works on charts in which the elementary constructs of the grammar are kept. In Joshi's parser the 'Earley dot' traverses trees and not Strings. In our case, we additionally store for each symbol in each chart entry the set of regions in which it may occur, i.e. when inserting a new chart entry we resolve the spatial constraints by a simple look-up in the spatial relation table.

The parser works in four steps: scan, predict, complete, and adjoin. We modify the scan operation. The scan operation reads the next symbol from the input and matches it with the chart entries. Although we write our SCTAG rules on intentions and behaviors, we get pairs of *(symbol, region)* during parsing. We first execute scan using *symbol*, as in the original parser, and then use the *region* information to throw away those regions in our chart entries that are not consistent with the *region* information. As soon as a symbol in a chart entry has an empty set of possible regions we throw away the chart entry.

Although we do not provide a formal description of the parser in this paper, it should be clear that adding spatial constraints to such a parser will not make it slower but faster. The reason is that spatial constraints give us more predictive information. 'Any algorithm should have enough information to know which tokens are to be expected after a given left context' (Joshi and Sch-

abes, 1997, p.36). Knowing the spatial context of left-hand terminals we can throw away those hypotheses that are not consistent with the spatial constraints. A formal description of the parser, as well as an evaluation, will be issue of future publications.

4 Related Work

Approaches for IR differ in the way possible intentions are represented. A number of formalisms has been proposed for modeling the mental state of an agent, ranging from finite state machines (Dee and Hogg, 2004) to complex cognitive modeling architectures, like the ACT-R architecture (Anderson et al., 2004). With formal grammars, which are between these two extremes, we try to keep the balance between expressiveness and computational complexity. Another important line of research in IR are approaches based on probabilistic networks, e.g. (Bui, 2003; Liao et al., 2007).

For the classification of segments in Fig. 2 we used a simple decision tree. The set of behavior types we are interested in was chosen manually. An automatic detection of motion patterns is the concern of the spatio-temporal data mining community, see e.g. (Laube et al., 2004).

Spatial constraints are also dealt with in multimodel interfaces supporting sketching, like the nuSketch system (Forbus et al., 2001). Speech recognition provides help 'for stating what spatial relationships are essential versus accidental' (p. 5).

5 Outlook

As a next step we will specify the parsing algorithm for SCTAG formally, and implement it for a mobile device. In this paper we treated all spatial relations as arbitrary relations, without using the formal properties of these relations for inference (like transitivity). Adding temporal constraints could also be worthwhile.

References

Anderson, J.R., D. Bothell, M.D. Byrne, S. Douglass, C. Lebiere, and Y. Qin. 2004. An integrated theory of the mind. *Psychological Review*, 111(4):1036–1060, October.

Baus, J., A. Krueger, and W. Wahlster. 2002. A resource-adaptive mobile navigation system. In

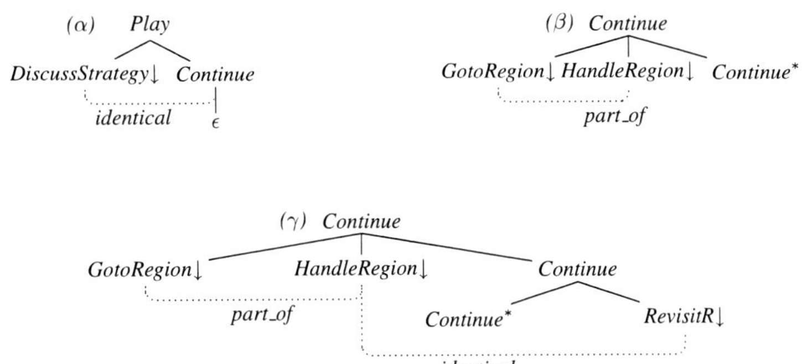

Figure 7: Initial tree (α) and auxiliary trees (β and γ) in a SCTAG for CityPoker.

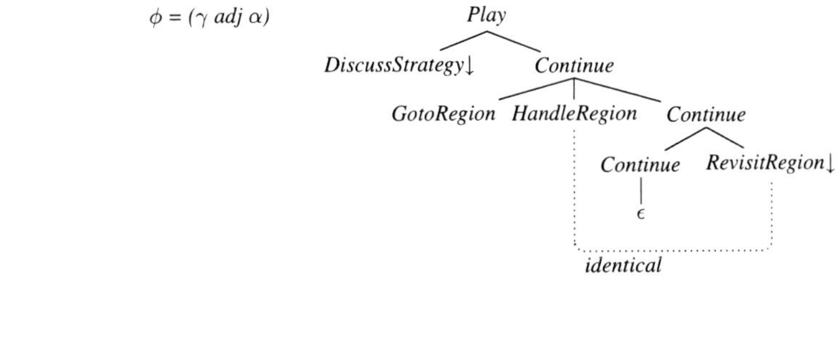

Figure 8: Adjoining in an SCTAG can lead to cross-dependencies of constraints. Non-crossing spatial constraints are omitted for reasons of clarity.

Proc. 7th International Conference on Intelligent User Interfaces, pages 15–22, San Francisco, USA. ACM Press.

Bobick, A.F. and Y.A. Ivanov. 1998. Action recognition using probabilistic parsing. In *Proc. of the Conference on Computer Vision and Pattern Recognition*, pages 196–202.

Bui, Hung H. 2003. A general model for online probabilistic plan recognition. In *Proceedings of the International Joint Conference on Artificial Intelligence (IJCAI)*.

Carberry, Sandra. 2001. Techniques for plan recognition. *User Modeling and User-Adapted Interaction*, 11(1-2):31–48.

Chanda, Gaurav and Frank Dellaert. 2004. Grammatical methods in computer vision: An overview. Technical Report GIT-GVU-04-29, College of Computing, Georgia Institute of Technology, Atlanta, GA, USA, November. ftp://ftp.cc.gatech.edu/pub/gvu/tr/2004/04-29.pdf.

Dee, H.M. and D.C. Hogg. 2004. Detecting inexplicable behaviour. In *Proceedings of the British Machine Vision Conference*, pages 477–486. The British Machine Vision Association.

Egenhofer, Max J. and Robert D. Franzosa. 1991. Point-set topological relations. *International Journal of Geographical Information Systems*, 5(2):161–174.

Forbus, Kenneth D., Ronald W. Ferguson, and Jeffery M. Usher. 2001. Towards a computational model of sketching. In *Proceedings of the 6th international conference on Intelligent user interfaces*, pages 77–83, New York, USA. ACM.

Geib, Christopher W. and Robert P. Goldman. 2003. Recognizing plan/goal abandonment. In *Proceedings of the Eighteenth International Joint Conference on Artificial Intelligence (IJCAI)*, pages 1515–1517.

Geib, Christopher W. and Mark Steedman. 2007. On natural language processing and plan recognition. In *Proceedings of the 20th International Joint Conference on Artificial Intelligence (IJCAI)*, pages 1612–1617.

Joshi, Aravind K. and Yves Schabes. 1997. Tree-adjoining grammars. In Rozenberg, G. and A. Salomaa, editors, *Handbook of Formal Languages*, volume 3, pages 69–124. Springer, Berlin, New York.

Joshi, A. K. 1985. Tree adjoining grammars: How much context-sensitivity is required to provide reasonable structural descriptions? In Dowty, D. R., L. Karttunen, and A. M. Zwicky, editors, *Natural Language Parsing: Psychological, Computational, and Theoretical Perspectives*, pages 206–250. Cambridge University Press, Cambridge.

Kautz, Henry and James F. Allen. 1986. Generalized plan recognition. In *Proc. of the AAAI conference 1986*.

Kiefer, Peter and Christoph Schlieder. 2007. Exploring context-sensitivity in spatial intention recognition. In *Workshop on Behavior Monitoring and Interpretation, 40th German Conference on Artificial Intelligence (KI-2007)*, pages 102–116. CEUR Vol-296. ISSN 1613-0073.

Kortuem, G., M. Bauer, and Z. Segall. 1999. Netman: The design of a collaborative wearable computer system. *Mobile Networks and Applications*, 4(1):49–58, March.

Krüger, A., A. Butz, C. Müller, C. Stahl, R. Wasinger, K.-E. Steinberg, and A. Dirschl. 2004. The connected user interface: realizing a personal situated navigation service. In *Proc. of the 9th international Conference on Intelligent User Interfaces*, pages 161–168. ACM Press.

Laube, Patrick, Marc van Krefeld, and Stephan Imfeld. 2004. Finding remo - detecting relative motion patterns in geospatial lifelines. In *Developments in Spatial Data Handling, Proceedings of the 11th International Symposium on Spatial Data Handling*, pages 201–215.

Liao, Lin, Donald J. Patterson, Dieter Fox, and Henry Kautz. 2007. Learning and inferring transportation routines. *Artificial Intelligence*, 171(5-6):311–331.

Pynadath, David V. 1999. *Probabilistic Grammars for Plan Recognition*. Ph.D. thesis, The University of Michigan.

Schlieder, Christoph and Anke Werner. 2003. Interpretation of intentional behavior in spatial partonomies. In *Spatial Cognition III, Routes and Navigation, Human Memory and Learning, Spatial Representation and Spatial Learning*, volume 2685 of *Lecture Notes in Computer Science*, pages 401–414. Springer.

Schlieder, C., P. Kiefer, and S. Matyas. 2006. Geogames - designing location-based games from classic board games. *IEEE Intelligent Systems*, 21(5):40–46, Sep/Oct.

Schlieder, Christoph. 2005. Representing the meaning of spatial behavior by spatially grounded intentional systems. In *GeoSpatial Semantics, First International Conference*, volume 3799 of *Lecture Notes in Computer Science*, pages 30–44. Springer.

Stein, Klaus and Christoph Schlieder. 2005. Recognition of intentional behavior in spatial partonomies. In *ECAI 2004 Worskhop 15: Spatial and Temporal Reasoning (16th European Conference on Artificial Intelligence)*.

Across-the-Board Extraction in Minimalist Grammars

Gregory M. Kobele
Institut für deutsche Sprache und Linguistik
Humboldt-Universität zu Berlin
kobele@rz.hu-berlin.de

Abstract

Minimalist grammars cannot provide adequate descriptions of constructions in which a single filler saturates two mutually independent gaps, as is commonly analyzed to be the case in parasitic gap constructions and other across-the-board extraction phenomena. In this paper, I show how a simple addition to the minimalist grammar formalism allows for a unified treatment of control and parasitic gap phenomena, and can be restricted in such a way as to account for across-the-board exceptions to the coordinate structure constraint. In the context of standard constraints on movement, the weak generative capacity of the formalism remains unaffected.

1 Introduction

Minimalist grammars (MGs) (Stabler, 1997) are a mildly context-sensitive grammar formalism (Michaelis, 2001), which provide a rigorous foundation for some of the main ideas of the minimalist program (Chomsky, 1995). There are two basic structure building operations, binary **merge** and unary **move**.

In typical analyses of linguistic phenomena, operator–variable chains (in the sense of a quantifier and its bound variable; $\forall x.\phi[x]$) are analyzed in terms of first merger of the operator into a position where its variable is ultimately to appear (resulting in something like $\phi[\forall]$), and then moving the operator into its scope-taking position, leaving a bound 'trace' in the moved-from position (result-

ing in the desired $\forall x.\phi[x]$).[1]

Now, although minimalist grammars can capture naturally various kinds of non-local dependencies in this way, something needs to be added to the system to allow it to account for apparent non-resource-sensitive behaviour. Pursuing the logical formula metaphor introduced above, MGs can define only (closed) *linear* formulae, where each variable is bound by a distinct quantifier, and each quantifier binds exactly one variable. However, the phenomena of control and parasitic gaps both involve a single filler being associated with multiple gaps—in other words, the 'chains' here are tree-structured (see fig.1).[2]

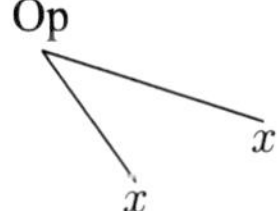

Figure 1: The filler-gap dependencies exemplified by parasitic gaps

In this paper, we show how slash-feature percolation, as adapted to MGs by Kobele (2007), allows for a straight-forward implementation of

---

[1] This non-compositional description of the intermediate derivational steps is for the imagination only. Compositional semantics for this kind of analysis are easy to provide (see Kobele (2006)), as it is after all just the familiar Cooper-storage (Cooper, 1983) writ funny.

[2] For the sake of perspicuity, I am ignoring multiple movements of the same subexpression, as occurs in the analysis of passivization followed by wh-movement, as in a sentence like *Who did John think t was kissed t*. The distinguishing characteristic which sets the control/parasitic gap type phenomena apart from this kind of multiple movement is that in this case each movement is to a c-commanding position in the derived structure—such movement chains have the shape of strings, whereas those of the parasitic gap variety are trees.

Proceedings of The Ninth International Workshop on Tree Adjoining Grammars and Related Formalisms
Tübingen, Germany. June 6-8, 2008.

Sag's (1983) analysis of parasitic gap phenomena in the minimalist framework, while preserving the weak generative capacity of the formal system. This analysis extends immediately to control. Other cases of such non-resource-sensitive phenomena, such as well-known exceptions to the coordinate structure constraint, fall out as well, although a (weak generative capacity preserving) extension to the minimalist grammar type-system is needed to account for some of the familiar restrictions on such movements.

2 Slash-feature percolation and MGs

In the minimalist tradition, where long distance dependencies are mediated via movement, across-the-board extraction out of a conjunct as in 1 is sometimes thought to be derived from an intermediate structure of the form below:

1. Who did John meet and Susan kiss?

$$[_S \ John \ meet \ who] \ and \ [_S \ Susan \ kiss \ who]$$

In order for this kind of analysis to work, some mechanism must be in place to ensure the identity of both moving elements—identity of *derived structure*, not merely of category (as suggested by example 2).

2. *Which bank did John rob or Susan walk along?

Crucially, this mechanism is not reducible to ellipsis in this framework, as it must allow a single resource (the trigger for movement residing in the COMP position) to meet the requirements of multiple expressions (the features on each of the wh-words)—ellipsis is not standardly assumed to have this character.

A simple way around this problem is to introduce the ATB-moved element *after* conjoining the two clauses together. To implement this idea, we adopt the mechanism of slash-feature percolation, as adapted to MGs by Kobele (2007). (Slash-feature introductions are represented in the below as traces.)

$$[_S \ John \ meet \ t] \ and \ [_S \ Susan \ kiss \ t]$$

The change required to Kobele's system is to allow *identical slash-features* to be *unified*, instead of crashing the derivation of an expression. (This is simply Sag's (1983) GPSG analysis adapted to this framework.) An MG expression can be represented as a tuple of categorized structures (each element of this tuple corresponds to a moving treelet). In order to make the link with LCFRSs, a finite upper bound needs to be placed on the length of such a tuple. Stabler proposes that no two treelets may have the same first feature (this amounts to a strict version of Chomsky's Shortest Move Constraint). Kobele maintains this assumption in his enriched MG system as well, forcing missing (i.e. 'slashed') expressions to behave in the same way as real ones. Our proposal builds on the fact that slashed expressions, unlike moving expressions, have no internal structure. Thus, there arises no computational problem in comparing two slash-features—it is an atomic operation. Specifically, we claim that in order to avoid shortest move violations, identical slash-features may be unified with one another. A specific instance of the **merge** operation is given in figure 2. An expression of the form (John meet : S), $\langle$d -k -q, -w$\rangle$ indicates that it is selectable as a tensed sentence (S), and that it is missing an element of type d -k -q -w (a +wh noun phrase), but that it has satisfied the first three dependencies (d -k -q) of this expression. As the expression it is merged with in this figure is missing the very same type of element, they are identified in the result. This contrasts with the situation in which one (or both) of the wh-phrases is already present, as in figure 3. In this case, the resulting expression has two subexpressions (the slashed expression $\langle$d -k -q, -w$\rangle$ and the wh-phrase (who, -w)) with the same active first feature (-w), violating the shortest move constraint.

3 Control and Parasitic Gaps

With this slight relaxation of resource sensitivity with respect to hypotheses, we are able to account for control (3) and parasitic gap constructions (4) in terms of across the board movement.

3. John wanted to kiss Susan.

4. Who did John want to kiss before meeting?

Essentially, slash-feature unification gives us the ability to have limited *sideward* movement in the sense of Nunes (2004). The analysis here of ATB

$$\frac{(\text{and Susan kiss}\ :\ =\text{S S}),\ \langle \text{d -k -q},\ -\text{w}\rangle \qquad (\text{John meet}\ :\ \text{S}),\ \langle \text{d -k -q},\ -\text{wh}\rangle}{(\text{John meet and Susan kiss}\ :\ \text{S}),\ \langle \text{d -k -q},\ -\text{w}\rangle}$$

Figure 2: Unification of hypotheses avoids crash

$$\frac{(\text{and Susan kiss}\ :\ =\text{S S}),\ \langle \text{d -k -q},\ -\text{w}\rangle \qquad (\text{John meet}\ :\ \text{S}),\ (\text{who},\ -\text{w})}{(\text{John meet and Susan kiss}\ :\ \text{S}),\ \langle \text{d -k -q},\ -\text{w}\rangle,\ (\text{who},\ -\text{w})}$$

Figure 3: An SMC violation

movement and of parasitic gaps can be seen as a (clear and precise) variant of Nunes'.[3]

3.1 Control

The treatment of control as (a form of) movement agrees in spirit with recent developments in the minimalist tradition (Hornstein, 2001; Kobele, 2006), but its unification with *ATB* movement forces us to make the base position of the controller not c-command the base position of the controllee. Instead, the controller must raise to a position which c-commands the controllee, as sketched in figure 4.

$$[_{VP}\ [_{V'}\ \text{t}\ ]\ [_{S}\ldots \text{t}\ldots]\ ]$$

Figure 4. Control as ATB Movement

In the context of minimalist grammars, this movement is naturally identified with movement for case (to an object agreement position—AgrOP). The treatment of control as a form of movement obviates the need for the empty category PRO, and thus of mysterious indices relating controllee and controller. Instead, 'PRO' is simply a trace in a theta-position, coindexation is replaced by chain formation, and the effects of the 'control module' need to be enforced via standard constraints on movement.

A fragment for English which implements these ideas is given as figure 5. The fragment is the same as the one given in Kobele (2006) (which is to say that this treatment of control is broadly compatible with other standard analyses), except that base positions of sentential complements and arguments in obligatory control verbs have been altered so as to conform to the anti-c-command condition imposed by this analysis of control.[4]

This grammar gets both subject and object control constructions, as in 5 and 6 below.

5. John promised Mary to shave every barber.

6. John persuaded Mary to shave every barber.

The object control case is perhaps the most surprising, as the object (in 6, *Mary*) is supposed to move outside of the VP, and yet clearly follows the verb. The basic idea of the analysis of such cases is that movement for case does indeed put the object to the left of the verb, but that subsequent head movement of the verb (broadly following Chomsky's (1957) affix hopping analysis of the English auxiliary system) remedies the situation. The choice of controller (whether subject or object) in the sentences 5 and 6 above is determined by whether the sentential complement is merged before or after the base position of the subject. If before, there is no subject slash-feature to be unified with the slash-feature in the sentential complement, and thus subject control is impossible. If after, then the SMC ensures that the object must already have checked its case (as the more

---

[3]The difference is, of course, that here the phonological content of the ATB-moved expression is not present at its base positions, whereas in Nunes' system, it is. The present treatment of control in terms of ATB movement cannot analyze purported cases of 'backward control' (Polinsky and Potsdam, 2006) as such.

[4]Due to space limitations, only intuitions about relevant aspects of this grammar will be attempted to be conveyed here. The interested reader is invited to consult Kobele (2006) for definitions and examples. The fragment deals with raising, expletive *it*, control, passivization, and quantifier scope, in a way that neatly derives the ban on super-raising, and the tensed-clause-boundedness of QR.

that::=S s

will::=perf +k +q S	have::=en perf	be::=ing prog
-s::=>perf +k +q S	-en::=>prog en	-ing::=>v ing
-ed::=>perf +k +q S	ε::=>prog perf	ε::=>v prog
to::=perf s	be::=pass v	-en::=>V pass

	ε::=>V +k =d +q v	
arrive::=d v	devour::=d V	
	shave::=d V	
seem::=s v	expect::=s V	expect::=d =s v
	want::=s V	want::=d =s v
	hope::=S V	hope::=d =s v
persuade::=d =s V		
promise::=s =d V	promise::=d +k =d =s +q v	

ε::=>v =z v   it::z -k

George::d -k -q	the::=n d -k -q	ointment::n
John::d -k -q	every::=n d -k -q	abbot::n
Mary::d -k -q	some::=n d -k -q	barber::n

Figure 5: A grammar for English A movement (slightly modified from Kobele (2006))

recently merged subject has case requirements of its own), and thus slash-features of the sentential complement have only the slash-features of the matrix subject to unify with.

3.2 TAG Approaches to Control

Both Kroch and Joshi (1985) as well as the XTAG project (2001) make use of the empty category PRO to mediate control relations between argument positions. In the XTAG project use is made of equations in feature structures, which allow for lexical determination of binding relationships. Restrictions on the relative positions of controller and controllee, as well as on the realization of PRO is governed by formalism external constraints on elementary trees.

The Multi-dominance TAG system of Chen-Main (2006) seems able to implement a PRO-less theory of control, along the lines proposed in Hornstein (2001). Her account of node contraction as being constrained by derivational locality might provide a principled (formalism internal) account of the configurational relation between controller and controllee.

3.3 Parasitic Gaps

In summary, this extension to MGs gives us a formal system in which fillers can be associated with multiple gaps in certain circumstances. Evaluation of the linguistic applicability of such a formalism needs to be done with respect to the kinds of analyses that it makes available. We continue to assume the analysis of English given as figure 5. We have sketched the implementation of obligatory control present in this fragment above. Parasitic gaps (of the form in 4) require an analysis of gerundival adjuncts, which we will treat here as vP adjuncts (i.e. they appear after the logical subject, if any, is introduced), which we will analyze in terms of the **adjoin** operation formalized in Frey and Gärtner (2002).[5] A gerundival adjunct is headed by a

---

[5]Another option is to explicitly control the direction of merger (via merge-left (x=) and merge-right (=x) features), and then to mediate adjunction via an empty lexical item ε::=>v =pg v, where prepositions heading gerundival adjuncts are assigned the type =g pg. The basic problem is that the verb needs to remain accessible for future affixal operations, and that the gerundival adjunct needs to appear to the right of the vP. With the 'standard' antisymmetric treatment of the linear order of merged elements (first-merged object to the right, all others to the left) embedded in classical MGs, this is not so easily done, as in order for the verb to remain accessible to future head movement operations, it must

prepositional element which selects a gerundive clause (before::=g ≈v), and a gerundive clause is simply what you get if instead of merging a tense marker (like will::=perf +k +q S or to::=perf s) you merge *-ing* (-ing::=>perf g). At the vP level (and at the perfP level), a clause will have a DP waiting to check its case (-k) and scope (-q) features (the logical subject, if the clause is in the active voice, and the logical object, otherwise). In order to avoid a violation of the SMC, both this DP in the vP and the DP in the prepositional gerundive adjunct must be slashed expressions (of the form ⟨d, -k -q⟩) which are identified, resulting in a control configuration. A parasitic gap configuration arises when the object of the prepositional gerundive clause and of the vP are slashed as well (of the form ⟨d -k -q, -w⟩). Note that this analysis accounts for the well-known fact that A movement (passive or raising) does not license parasitic gaps (as in 7): the object in the prepositional genitive has had its case and scope features checked, and thus can only survive as a slashed expression if it is moving again (say, to check a *wh* feature). For this reason it will not be unifiable with an A moving expression, which is looking next to check its case feature. Of course, a sentence like 7 can be made grammatical by passivizing the gerundive adjunct clause (as in 8), thereby taking it out of the parasitic gap construction type.

7. *Susan was kissed before meeting.

8. Susan was kissed before being met.

There are many properties of the parasitic gap construction that this analysis does not account for (see the collection Culicover and Postal (2001)), but it does capture some interesting properties in a simple way, without changing the weak generative capacity of the system (the proof of this is essentially the same as the one given in Michaelis (2001)—it is a consequence of the fact that the number of possible hypotheses are upper-bounded by the number of distinct licensee (-x) features in the grammar (due to the SMC)).

The ability to license parasitic gaps, as mentioned briefly above, has often been used as a diagnostic to distinguish between A and A-bar movement types. The analysis of parasitic gaps given

here suggests that the fact that only A-bar (i.e. *wh*) movements license parasitic gaps can be explained in purely configurational terms, i.e. without positing some occult connection between movement types and the parasitic gap phenomenon. This has, as far as this analysis is on the right track, serious ramifications for analyses of phenomena (such as scrambling), which have used parasitic gap licensing properties to argue that these phenomena involve a particular dependency type. This perspective on parasitic gaps also makes the fact that in certain languages A movements can license parasitic gaps unsurprising.

3.4 Parasitic Gaps in TAGs

Kroch and Joshi (1985) account for parasitic gap constructions as in 4 by taking as elementary trees biclausal structures. They note that they make a grammatical distinction between sentences like 4 on the one hand, and sentences like 9 on the other, where the parasitic gap is embedded in a subordinate clause inside of the prepositional gerund introducing it.

9. What did John devour without bothering to shave?

They are forced into this position by their treatment of gerunds as non-syntactically derived words. If one retreated to a post-syntactic view of morphology, whereby the terminal items in elementary trees were thought of not as concrete words but rather as abstract lexemes, whose ultimate realization were determined in part by their syntactic context, then as long as the 'gerundivizing' feature were above a clausal adjunction site, and the verb below it, sentences such as 9 would be generable. Thus, this aspect of Kroch and Joshi's analysis seems almost an accidental property.

A more fundamental difference between the Kroch and Joshi proposal and the one presented here lies in the number of gaps which can be associated with a single overt operator. As their strategy is to extend the size of elementary trees so that all gaps and binders are contained within them, they are forced to the position that there is a fixed upper bound on the number of parasitic gaps that can be dependent on one operator. In the present theory, parasitic gaps can be recursively embedded inside others, and thus there is predicted to be no principled upper bound on the number of gaps

---

be merged first, and thus the merger of the gerundival adjunct places it erroneously to the left of the vP.

what::d -k -q -w   before::=g ≈v   -ing::=>perf g
ε::=>S +w c   without::=g ≈v

Figure 6: Extending the grammar in fig. 5 to get parasitic gap constructions

a single filler can fill. A sentence distinguishing these two proposals is given below as 11 (where Kroch and Joshi's original proposal of two is taken as the cut-off point).

10. What did Mary take without paying for?

11. What did Mary intend to return after taking without paying for?

Unfortunately, neither sentence 9 nor sentence 11 are the 'clear cases' (Chomsky, 1956) that one should base linguistic theories on. As such, their ultimate grammatical status will have to wait an independent validation of one or the other syntactic theory.

4   Coordinate Structures

Although slash-feature identification seems to capture the basic effect of ATB movement (as noted by Sag), the prototypical ATB construction (as in 1) involves extraction out of a conjunction, and is constrained in ways that we currently do not account for (in particular, extraction must be out of *both* conjuncts). To implement these constraints, we need a way to block movement out of an expression, and to ensure that the slash-features of both conjuncts are identical. As a first step, we build this in to the category system in the following way. First, we add a diacritic on category features (c^*) which permits them to be selected only if they have no moving elements (this can be implemented as a restriction on the domain of the **merge** operation, and allows for the simple statement of a certain kind of island constraint). To be able to ensure that the slash-features of two different selected items are identical, we need to more drastically revise the minimalist category system. We want to assign the following type to *and*:

$$=S^\alpha =S^\alpha \ S^*$$

The interpretation of the superscripted material is as the slash-features of the selected expression, and the fact that both superscripts are identical on both selection features indicates that both

selected expressions must have the same slash-features.[6] At least intuitively, a link may be drawn between this extension of the minimalist grammar type-system, and the addition of local-constraints (Kroch and Joshi, 1985) to tree-adjoining grammars.

Chen-Main (2006) further develops the system introduced in Sarkar and Joshi (1996) to deal with conjunction in TAGs. So long as the contractible nodes in any given derived tree are bounded in advance, it seems as though a strategy like the one pursued here could be extended to her system. The elementary tree for *and* would have equations on each of its two substitution nodes stating that, *after* substitution and subsequent internal *and*-tree internal contractions, the remaining contractible nodes in each subtree are identical. The remaining contractible nodes in each subtree would need to be identified with an identical partner in the other subtree, so as to ensure that later 'movement' be truly across the board.

5   Conclusion

Slash-feature percolation is straightforward to add to the minimalist grammar formalism, and amounts to relaxing the requirement that an expression must be derivationally present before it can begin satisfying dependencies. This paper has tried to show that adding slash-feature percolation to MGs allows for interesting and revealing analyses of what I have been calling across-the-board extraction phenomena, analyses which co-exist well with other analyses of different grammatical phenomena. Indeed, it seems not implausible that slash-feature percolation (which, in MGs, acts upon the regular derivation trees) is simply addable to TAGs as well (but on the level of the derived tree), and can make similar analytical options available as it does for MGs, and CFGs.

---

[6]This is like passing the same stack of indices to two nonterminals in an indexed grammar. The essential difference is that our 'stacks' are bounded in size (due to the SMC). This fact makes this enrichment of the type system weakly innocuous. Note that this very same constraint is stateable in GPSG, without any increase in generative capacity.

References

Chen-Main, Joan. 2006. *On the generation and linearization of multi-dominance structures*. Ph.D. thesis, Johns Hopkins.

Chomsky, Noam. 1956. Three models for the description of language. *IRE Transactions on Information Theory*, 2(3):113–124.

Chomsky, Noam. 1957. *Syntactic Structures*. Mouton, The Hague.

Chomsky, Noam. 1995. *The Minimalist Program*. MIT Press, Cambridge, Massachusetts.

Cooper, Robin. 1983. *Quantification and Syntactic Theory*. D. Reidel, Dordrecht.

Culicover, Peter W. and Paul M. Postal, editors. 2001. *Parasitic Gaps*, volume 35 of *Current Studies in Linguistics*. MIT Press.

Frey, Werner and Hans-Martin Gärtner. 2002. Scrambling and adjunction in minimalist grammars. In Jäger, Gerhard, Paola Monachesi, Gerald Penn, and Shuly Wintner, editors, *Proceedings of Formal Grammar 2002*, pages 41–52.

Hornstein, Norbert. 2001. *Move! A Minimalist Theory of Construal*. Blackwell.

Kobele, Gregory M. 2006. *Generating Copies: An investigation into structural identity in language and grammar*. Ph.D. thesis, University of California, Los Angeles.

Kobele, Gregory M. 2007. A formal foundation for A and A-bar movement in the minimalist program. In Kracht, Marcus, Gerald Penn, and Edward P. Stabler, editors, *Mathematics of Language 10*. UCLA.

Kroch, Anthony S. and Aravind K. Joshi. 1985. The linguistic relevance of tree adjoining grammar. Technical Report MS-CIS-85-16, Department of Computer & Information Science, University of Pennsylvania.

Michaelis, Jens. 2001. *On Formal Properties of Minimalist Grammars*. Ph.D. thesis, Universität Potsdam.

Nunes, Jairo. 2004. *Linearization of Chains and Sideward Movement*, volume 43 of *Linguistic Inquiry Monographs*. MIT Press, Cambridge, Massachusetts.

Polinsky, Maria and Eric Potsdam. 2006. Expanding the scope of control and raising. *Syntax*, 9(2):171–192, August.

Sag, Ivan A. 1983. On parasitic gaps. *Linguistics and Philosophy*, 6:35–45.

Sarkar, Anoop and Aravind K. Joshi. 1996. Coordination in tree adjoining grammars: Formalization and implementation. In *Proceedings of the 16th International Conference on Computational Linguistics (COLING)*, pages 610–615, Copenhagen, Denmark.

Stabler, Edward P. 1997. Derivational minimalism. In Retoré, Christian, editor, *Logical Aspects of Computational Linguistics*, volume 1328 of *Lecture Notes in Computer Science*, pages 68–95. Springer-Verlag, Berlin.

XTAG Research Group. 2001. A lexicalized tree adjoining grammar for English. Technical Report IRCS-01-03, IRCS, University of Pennsylvania.

TuLiPA: A syntax-semantics parsing environment for mildly context-sensitive formalisms

Yannick Parmentier
CNRS - LORIA
Nancy Université
F-54506, Vandœuvre, France
parmenti@loria.fr

Laura Kallmeyer
SFB 441
Universität Tübingen
D-72074, Tübingen, Germany
lk@sfs.uni-tuebingen.de

Wolfgang Maier
SFB 441
Universität Tübingen
D-72074, Tübingen, Germany
wo.maier@uni-tuebingen.de

Timm Lichte
SFB 441
Universität Tübingen
D-72074, Tübingen, Germany
timm.lichte@uni-tuebingen.de

Johannes Dellert
SFB 441 - SfS
Universität Tübingen
D-72074, Tübingen, Germany
jdellert@sfs.uni-tuebingen.de

Abstract

In this paper we present a parsing architecture that allows processing of different mildly context-sensitive formalisms, in particular Tree-Adjoining Grammar (TAG), Multi-Component Tree-Adjoining Grammar with Tree Tuples (TT-MCTAG) and *simple* Range Concatenation Grammar (RCG). Furthermore, for tree-based grammars, the parser computes not only syntactic analyses but also the corresponding semantic representations.

1 Introduction

The starting point of the work presented here is the aim to implement a parser for a German TAG-based grammar that computes syntax and semantics. As a grammar formalism for German we chose a multicomponent extension of TAG called TT-MCTAG (Multicomponent TAG with Tree Tuples) which has been first introduced by Lichte (2007). With some additional constraints, TT-MCTAG is mildly context-sensitive (MCS) as shown by Kallmeyer and Parmentier (2008).

Instead of implementing a specific TT-MCTAG parser we follow a more general approach by using Range Concatenation Grammars (RCG) as a pivot formalism for parsing MCS languages. Indeed the generative capacity of RCGs lies beyond MCS, while they stay parsable in polynomial time (Boullier, 1999). In this context, the TT-MCTAG (or TAG) is transformed into a strongly equivalent RCG that is then used for parsing. We have implemented the conversion into RCG, the RCG

parser and the retrieval of the corresponding TT-MCTAG analyses. The parsing architecture comes with graphical input and output interfaces, and an XML export of the result of parsing. It is called TuLiPA (for "Tübingen Linguistic Parsing Architecture") and is freely available under the GPL.[1] Concretely, TuLiPA processes TT-MCTAGs and TAGs encoded in the XML format of the XMG (eXtensible MetaGrammar) system of Duchier et al. (2004).

In this paper, we present this parsing architecture focusing on the following aspects: first, we introduce the TT-MCTAG formalism (section 2). Then, we present successively the RCG formalism (section 3) and the conversion of TT-MCTAG into RCG (section 4). Section 5 shows how RCG is parsed in practice. Eventually, we present the retrieval of TT-MCTAG derivation structures (section 6), the computation of semantic representations (section 7) and optimizations that have been added to speed up parsing (section 8).

2 TT-MCTAG

TT-MCTAGs (Lichte, 2007) are multicomponent TAGs (MCTAG) where the elementary tree sets consist of one lexicalized tree γ, the *head tree* and a set of auxiliary trees $\beta_1, ..., \beta_n$, the *argument trees*. We write these sets as tuples $\langle \gamma, \{\beta_1, ..., \beta_n\} \rangle$. During derivation, the argument trees have to attach to their head, either directly or indirectly via *node sharing*. The latter means that they are linked by a chain of root-adjunctions to a tree adjoining to their head.

---

[1] http://sourcesup.cru.fr/tulipa/

(1)   ... dass es der Mechaniker zu reparieren verspricht
   ... that it the mechanic to repair promises
   '... that the mechanic promises to repair it'

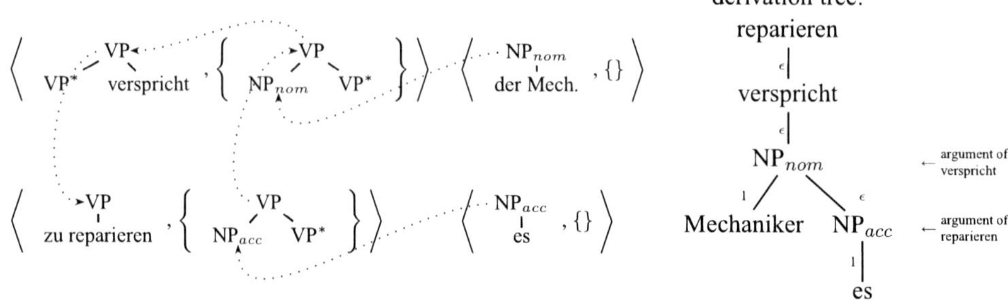

Figure 1: TT-MCTAG analysis of (1)

Definition 1 (TT-MCTAG) *An MCTAG $G = \langle I, A, N, T, \mathcal{A} \rangle$ is a TT-MCTAG iff*

1. *every $\Gamma \in \mathcal{A}$ has the form $\{\gamma, \beta_1, \ldots, \beta_n\}$ where γ contains at least one leaf with a terminal label, the* head tree, *and $\beta_1, \ldots, \beta_n$ are auxiliary trees, the* argument trees. *We write such a set as a tuple $\langle \gamma, \{\beta_1, \ldots, \beta_n\}\rangle$.*

2. *A derivation tree D for some $t \in L(\langle I, A, N, T\rangle)$ is licensed as a TAG derivation tree in G iff D satisfies the following conditions (MC) ("multicomponent condition") and (SN-TTL) ("tree-tuple locality with shared nodes"):*

  (a) **(MC)** *There are k pairwise disjoint instances $\Gamma_1, \ldots, \Gamma_k$ of elementary tree sets from $\mathcal{A}$ for some $k \geq 1$ such that $\bigcup_{i=1}^{k} \Gamma_i$ is the set of node labels in D.*

  (b) **(SN-TTL)** *for all nodes $n_0, n_1, \ldots, n_m$, $m > 1$, in D with labels from the same elementary tree tuple such that n_0 is labelled by the head tree: for all $1 \leq i \leq m$: either $\langle n_0, n_i\rangle \in \mathcal{P}_D{}^2$ or there are $n_{i,1}, \ldots, n_{i,k}$ with auxiliary tree labels such that $n_i = n_{i,k}$, $\langle n_0, n_{i,1}\rangle \in \mathcal{P}_D$ and for $1 \leq j \leq k - 1$: $\langle n_{i,j}, n_{i,j+1}\rangle \in \mathcal{P}_D$ where this edge is labelled with ϵ.*

TT-MCTAG has been proposed to deal with free word order languages. An example from German is shown in Fig. 1. Here, the NP_{nom} auxiliary tree

---

[2]For a tree γ, $\mathcal{P}_\gamma$ is the parent relation on the nodes, i.e., $\langle x, y\rangle \in \mathcal{P}_\gamma$ for nodes x, y in γ iff x is the mother of y.

adjoins directly to *verspricht* (its head) while the NP_{acc} tree adjoins to the root of a tree that adjoins to the root of a tree that adjoins to *reparieren*.

For a more extended account of German word order using TT-MCTAG see Lichte (2007) and Lichte and Kallmeyer (2008).

TT-MCTAG can be further restricted, such that at each point of the derivation the number of pending β-trees is at most k. This subclass is also called k-TT-MCTAG.

Definition 2 (k-TT-MCTAG) *A TT-MCTAG $G = \langle I, A, N, T, \mathcal{A}\rangle$ is of rank k (or a k-TT-MCTAG for short) iff for each derivation tree D licensed in G:*

  (TT-k) *There are no nodes n, $h_0, \ldots, h_k$, $a_0, \ldots, a_k$ in D such that the label of a_i is an argument tree of the label of h_i and $\langle h_i, n\rangle, \langle n, a_i\rangle \in \mathcal{P}_D^{+}$ for $0 \leq i \leq k$.*

TT-MCTAG in general are NP-complete (Søgaard et al., 2007) while k-TT-MCTAG are MCS (Kallmeyer and Parmentier, 2008).

3   RCG as a pivot formalism

The central idea of our parsing strategy is to use RCG (Boullier, 1999; Boullier, 2000) as a pivot formalism.

Definition 3 (RCG) *A RCG is a tuple $G = \langle N, T, V, S, P\rangle$ such that a) N is an alphabet of predicates of fixed arities; b) T and V are disjoint alphabets of terminals and of variables; c) $S \in N$ is the start predicate (of arity 1) and d) P is a finite set of clauses*

$$A_0(x_{01}, \ldots, x_{0a_0}) \rightarrow \epsilon,$$

or

$$A_0(x_{01}, \ldots, x_{0a_0}) \rightarrow$$
$$A_1(x_{11}, \ldots, x_{1a_1}) \ldots A_n(x_{n1}, \ldots, x_{na_n})$$
with $n \geq 1$, $A_i \in N$, $x_{ij} \in (T \cup V)^*$ and a_i being the arity of A_i.

Since throughout the paper we use only positive RCGs, whenever we say "RCG", we actually mean "positive RCG".[3] An RCG with maximal predicate arity n is called an RCG of arity n.

When applying a clause with respect to a string $w = t_1 \ldots t_n$, the arguments in the clause are instantiated with substrings of w, more precisely with the corresponding ranges.[4] The instantiation of a clause maps all occurrences of a $t \in T$ in the clause to an occurrence of a t in w and consecutive elements in a clause argument are mapped to consecutive ranges.

If a clause has an instantiation wrt w, then, in one derivation step, the left-hand side of this instantiation can be replaced with its right-hand side. The language of an RCG G is $L(G) = \{w \mid S(\langle 0, |w| \rangle) \overset{*}{\Rightarrow} \epsilon \text{ wrt } w\}$.

A sample RCG is shown in Fig. 2.

RCG: $G = \langle \{S, A, B\}, \{a, b\}, \{X, Y, Z\}, S, P \rangle$
$\quad S(X\,Y\,Z) \rightarrow A(X, Z)\,B(Y),$
$\quad A(a\,X, a\,Y) \rightarrow A(X, Y), A(\epsilon, \epsilon) \rightarrow \epsilon,$
$\quad B(b\,X) \rightarrow B(X), B(\epsilon) \rightarrow \epsilon.$
Input: $w = aabaa$.
Derivation:

$S(X\,Y\,Z) \rightarrow A(X,Z)\,B(Y)$

$\langle 0, 2 \rangle \langle 2, 3 \rangle \langle 3, 5 \rangle \quad \langle 0, 2 \rangle \langle 3, 5 \rangle \langle 2, 3 \rangle$
$\quad aa \quad b \quad aa \quad\quad aa \quad aa \quad b$
yields $S(\langle 0, 5 \rangle) \Rightarrow A(\langle 0, 2 \rangle, \langle 3, 5 \rangle)B(\langle 2, 3 \rangle)$.

$B(b\,X) \rightarrow B(X) \quad\quad$ and $B(\epsilon) \rightarrow \epsilon$

$\langle 2, 3 \rangle \langle 3, 3 \rangle \langle 3, 3 \rangle$
$\quad b \quad\;\, \epsilon \quad\;\, \epsilon$
yield $A(\langle 0, 2 \rangle, \langle 3, 5 \rangle)B(\langle 2, 3 \rangle) \Rightarrow$
$\quad A(\langle 0, 2 \rangle, \langle 3, 5 \rangle)B(\langle 3, 3 \rangle) \rightarrow A(\langle 0, 2 \rangle, \langle 3, 5 \rangle)$.

$A(a\,X\,a\,Y) \rightarrow A(X,Y)$

$\langle 0, 1 \rangle \langle 1, 2 \rangle \langle 3, 4 \rangle \langle 4, 5 \rangle \langle 1, 2 \rangle \langle 4, 5 \rangle$
$\quad a \quad\;\, a \quad\;\, a \quad\;\, a \quad\;\, a \quad\;\, a$
yields $A(\langle 0, 2 \rangle, \langle 3, 5 \rangle) \Rightarrow A(\langle 1, 2 \rangle, \langle 4, 5 \rangle)$.

$A(a\,X\,a\,Y) \rightarrow A(X,Y) \quad\quad$ and $A(\epsilon, \epsilon) \rightarrow \epsilon$

$\langle 1, 2 \rangle \langle 2, 2 \rangle \langle 4, 5 \rangle \langle 5, 5 \rangle \langle 2, 2 \rangle \langle 5, 5 \rangle$
$\quad a \quad\;\, \epsilon \quad\;\, a \quad\;\, \epsilon \quad\;\, \epsilon \quad\;\, \epsilon$
yield $A(\langle 1, 2 \rangle, \langle 4, 5 \rangle) \Rightarrow A(\langle 2, 2 \rangle, \langle 5, 5 \rangle) \Rightarrow \epsilon$

Figure 2: Sample RCG

---

[3]The negative variant allows for negative predicate calls of the form $\overline{A}(\alpha_1, \ldots, \alpha_n)$. Such a predicate is meant to recognize the complement language of its positive counterpart, see Boullier (2000).

[4]A range $\langle i, j \rangle$ with $0 \leq i < j \leq n$ corresponds to the substring between positions i and j, i.e., to $t_{i+1} \ldots t_j$.

4 Transforming TT-MCTAG into RCG

The transformation of a given k-TT-MCTAG into a strongly equivalent simple RCG is an extension of the TAG-to-RCG transformation proposed by Boullier (1999). The idea of the latter is the following: the RCG contains predicates $\langle \alpha \rangle(X)$ and $\langle \beta \rangle(L, R)$ for initial and auxiliary trees respectively. X covers the yield of α and all trees added to α, while L and R cover those parts of the yield of β (including all trees added to β) that are respectively to the left and the right of the foot node of β. The clauses in the RCG reduce the argument(s) of these predicates by identifying those parts that come from the elementary tree α/β itself and those parts that come from one of the elementary trees added by substitution or adjunction. An example is shown in Fig. 3.

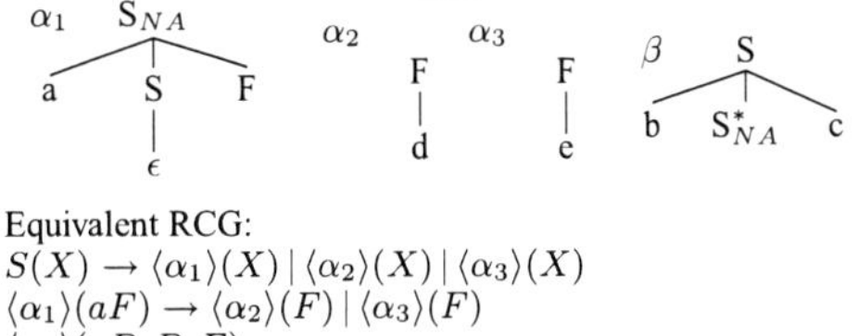

Equivalent RCG:
$S(X) \rightarrow \langle \alpha_1 \rangle(X) \mid \langle \alpha_2 \rangle(X) \mid \langle \alpha_3 \rangle(X)$
$\langle \alpha_1 \rangle(aF) \rightarrow \langle \alpha_2 \rangle(F) \mid \langle \alpha_3 \rangle(F)$
$\langle \alpha_1 \rangle(aB_1B_2F) \rightarrow$
$\quad \langle \beta \rangle(B_1, B_2)\langle \alpha_2 \rangle(F) \mid \langle \beta \rangle(B_1, B_2)\langle \alpha_3 \rangle(F)$
$\langle \beta \rangle(B_1b, cB_2) \rightarrow \langle \beta \rangle(B_1, B_2)$
$\langle \alpha_2 \rangle(d) \rightarrow \epsilon \quad \langle \alpha_3 \rangle(e) \rightarrow \epsilon \quad \langle \beta \rangle(b, c) \rightarrow \epsilon$

Figure 3: A TAG and an equivalent RCG

For the transformation from TT-MCTAG into RCG we use the same idea. There are predicates $\langle \gamma \ldots \rangle$ for the elementary trees (not the tuples) that characterize the contribution of γ. We enrich these predicates in a way that allows to keep track of the "still to adjoin" argument trees and constrain thereby further the RCG clauses. The pending arguments are encoded in a list that is part of the predicate name. The yield of a predicate corresponding to a tree γ contains not only γ and its arguments but also arguments of predicates that are higher in the derivation tree and that are adjoined below γ via node sharing. In addition, we use branching predicates adj and sub that allow computation of the possible adjunctions or substitutions at a given node in a separate clause.

As an example see Fig. 4. The first clause states that the yield of the initial α_{rep} consists of the left and right parts of the root-adjoining tree wrapped around *zu reparieren*. The adj predicate takes care

$$\langle \alpha_{rep}, \emptyset \rangle (L\ zu\ reparieren\ R) \rightarrow \langle adj, \alpha_{rep}, \epsilon, \{\beta_{acc}\} \rangle (L, R)$$
$$\langle adj, \alpha_{rep}, \epsilon, \{\beta_{acc}\} \rangle (L, R) \rightarrow \langle \beta_{acc}, \emptyset \rangle (L, R) \mid \langle \beta_v, \{\beta_{acc}\} \rangle (L, R)$$
$$\langle \beta_{acc}, \emptyset \rangle (L\ X, R) \rightarrow \langle adj, \beta_{acc}, \epsilon, \emptyset \rangle (L, R) \langle sub, \beta_{acc}, 1 \rangle (X)$$
$$\langle sub, \beta_{acc}, 1 \rangle (X) \rightarrow \langle \alpha_{es}, \emptyset \rangle (X) \qquad \langle \alpha_{es}, \emptyset \rangle (es) \rightarrow \epsilon$$
$$\langle \beta_v, \{\beta_{acc}\} \rangle (L, verspricht\ R) \rightarrow \langle adj, \beta_v, \epsilon, \{\beta_{nom}, \beta_{acc}\} \rangle (L, R)$$

Figure 4: Some clauses of the RCG corresponding to the TT-MCTAG in Fig. 1

of the adjunction at the root (address ϵ). It states that the list of pending arguments contains already β_{acc}, the argument of α_{rep}. According to the second clause, we can adjoin either β_{acc} (while removing it from the list of pending arguments) or some new auxiliary tree β_v.

The general construction goes as follows: We define the decoration string σ_γ of an elementary tree γ as in Boullier (1999): each internal node has two variables L and R and each substitution node has one variable X (L and R represent the left and right parts of the yield of the adjoined tree and X represents the yield of a substituted tree). In a top-down-left-to-right traversal the left variables are collected during the top-down traversal, the terminals and variables of substitution nodes are collected while visiting the leaves and the right variables are collected during bottom-up traversal. Furthermore, while visiting a foot node, a separating "," is inserted. The string obtained in this way is the decoration string.

1. We add a start predicate S and clauses $S(X) \rightarrow \langle \alpha, \emptyset \rangle (X)$ for all $\alpha \in I$.

2. For every $\gamma \in I \cup A$: Let L_p, R_p be the left and right symbols in σ_γ for the node at position p if this is not a substitution node. Let X_p be the symbol for the node at position p if this is a substitution node. We assume that $p_1, \ldots, p_k$ are the possible adjunction sites, $p_{k+1}, \ldots, p_l$ the substitution sites in γ. Then the RCG contains all clauses
$$\langle \gamma, LPA \rangle (\sigma_\gamma) \rightarrow$$
$$\langle adj, \gamma, p_1, LPA_{p_1} \rangle (L_{p_1}, R_{p_1})$$
$$\ldots \langle adj, \gamma, p_k, LPA_{p_k} \rangle (L_{p_k}, R_{p_k})$$
$$\langle sub, \gamma, p_{k+1} \rangle (X_{p_{k+1}}) \ldots \langle sub, \gamma, p_l \rangle (X_{p_l})$$
such that

- If $LPA \neq \emptyset$, then $\epsilon \in \{p_1, \ldots, p_k\}$ and $LPA \subseteq LPA_\epsilon$, and
- $\bigcup_{i=0}^{k} LPA_{p_i} = LPA \cup \Gamma(\gamma)$ where $\Gamma(\gamma)$ is either the set of arguments of γ (if γ is a head tree) or (if γ is an argument itself), the empty set.

3. For all predicates $\langle adj, \gamma, dot, LPA \rangle$ the RCG contains all clauses
$$\langle adj, \gamma, dot, LPA \rangle (L, R) \rightarrow$$
$$\langle \gamma', LPA' \rangle (L, R)$$
such that γ' can be adjoined at position dot in γ and

- either $\gamma' \in LPA$ and $LPA' = LPA \setminus \{\gamma'\}$,
- or $\gamma' \notin LPA$, γ' is a head (i.e., a head tree), and $LPA' = LPA$.

4. For all predicates $\langle adj, \gamma, dot, \emptyset \rangle$ where dot in γ is no OA-node, the RCG contains a clause $\langle adj, \gamma, dot, \emptyset \rangle (\epsilon, \epsilon) \rightarrow \epsilon$.

5. For all predicates $\langle sub, \gamma, dot \rangle$ and all γ' that can be substituted into position dot in γ the RCG contains a clause $\langle sub, \gamma, dot \rangle (X) \rightarrow \langle \gamma', \emptyset \rangle (X)$.

5 RCG parsing

The input sentence is parsed using the RCG computed from the input TT-MCTAG via the conversion algorithm introduced in the previous section. Note that the TT-MCTAG to RCG transformation is applied to a subgrammar selected from the input sentence[5], for the cost of the conversion is proportional to the size of the grammar (all licensed adjunctions have to be computed while taking into account the state of the list of pending arguments).[6]

The RCG parsing algorithm we use is an extension of Boullier (2000). This extension concerns (i) the production of a shared forest and (ii) the use of constraint-based techniques for performing some subtask of RCG parsing.

---

[5]In other terms, the RCG conversion is done *on-line*.

[6]We do not have a proof of complexity of the conversion algorithm yet, but we conject that it is exponential in the size of the grammar since the adjunctions to be predicted depend on the adjunctions predicted so far and on the auxiliary trees adjoinable at a given node.

RCG: **RCG Derivation wrt** aab**:**

$$
\begin{aligned}
C_0 \quad & S(XYZ) && \rightarrow && A(X,Y)B(Z) \\
C_1 \quad & A(aX, aY) && \rightarrow && A(X,Y) \\
C_2 \quad & A(aX, aY) && \rightarrow && B(X)B(Y) \\
C_3 \quad & B(\epsilon) && \rightarrow && \epsilon \\
C_4 \quad & B(b) && \rightarrow && \epsilon \\
C_5 \quad & A(\epsilon, \epsilon) && \rightarrow && \epsilon
\end{aligned}
$$

RCG shared forest:

$$
\begin{aligned}
C_0(X := a, Y := a, Z := b) \quad &\rightarrow \quad (\, C_1(X := \epsilon, Y := \epsilon) \vee C_2(X := \epsilon, Y := \epsilon)\,) \quad \wedge \quad C_4 \\
C_1(X := \epsilon, Y := \epsilon) \quad &\rightarrow \quad C_5 \\
C_2(X := \epsilon, Y := \epsilon) \quad &\rightarrow \quad C_3 \wedge C_3
\end{aligned}
$$

Figure 5: RCG derivation and corresponding shared forest.

5.1 Extracting an RCG shared forest

Boullier (2000) proposes a recognition algorithm relying on two interdependent functions: one for instantiating predicates, and one for instantiating clauses. Recognition is then triggered by asking for the instantiation of the start predicate with respect to the input string. An interesting feature of Boullier's algorithm lies in the tabulation of the (boolean) result of predicate and clause instantiations. In our parsing algorithm, we propose to extend this tabulation so that not only boolean values are stored, but also the successful clause instantiations for the RHS of each instantiated clause. In other terms, we use a 3-dimensional tabulation structure, where entries are of the following form:

$$
\Gamma[(i, \vec{\rho})][f_q^{\vec{\rho}}][j] := (i_x, \vec{\rho_x})
$$

Γ being a table storing the clause identifier and arguments $i_x, \vec{\rho_x}$ corresponding to the instantiation of the jth RHS predicate of the clause i with the qth binding of arguments $\vec{\rho}$.

As a consequence of this extension, after parsing a shared forest can be straightforwardly extracted from the table of clause instantiations. This shared forest is represented by a context-free grammar, following Billot and Lang (1989). See Fig. 5 for an example.

5.2 Using constraints to instantiate predicates

A second extension of Boullier's algorithm concerns the complex task of clause instantiation. During RCG parsing, for each clause instantiation, all possible bindings between the arguments

of the LHS predicate and (a substring of) the input string must be computed. The more ranges with free boundaries the arguments of the LHS predicate contains, the more expensive the instantiation is. Boullier (2000) has shown that the time complexity of a clause instantiation is $\mathcal{O}(n^d)$, where n is length of the input string, and d is the arity of the grammar (maximal number of free range boundaries). To deal with this high time complexity, Boullier (2000) proposes to use some predefined specific predicates[7] whose role is to decrease the number of free range boundaries.

In our approach, we propose to encode the clause instantiation task into a *Constraint Satisfaction Problem* (CSP). More precisely, we propose to use constraints over finite sets of integers to represent the constraints affecting the range boundaries. Indeed, these constraints over integers offer a natural way of encoding constraints applied on ranges (*e.g.* linear order).

Let us briefly introduce CSPs. In a CSP, a problem is described using a set of variables, which take their values in a given domain. Constraints are then applied on the values these variables can take in order to narrow their respective domain. Finally, one (or all) solution(s) to the problem are searched for, that is to say some (or all) assignment(s) of values to variables while respecting the constraints are searched for. One particularly interesting subclass of CSPs are those that can be stated in terms of constraints on variables ranging over finite sets

---

[7] E.g. a *length* predicate is used to limit the length of the subpart of input string covered by a range.

of non-negative integers. For such CSPs, there exist several implementations offering a wide range of constraints (arithmetic, boolean and linear constraints), and efficient solvers, such as the *Gecode* library[8] (Schulte and Tack, 2006).

In this context, the underlying idea of computing range instantiations as a CSP is the following. We use the natural order of integers to represent the linear order of ranges. More precisely, we compute all possible mappings between position indices in the input string (positive integers) and free range boundaries in the arguments of (the LHS predicate of) the clause to instantiate (variables taking their values in $[0..n]$, n being the length of the input sentence). Note that, within a given argument of a predicate to instantiate, a range of type *constant* can be considered as a constraint for the values the preceding and following range boundaries can take, see the example Fig. 6 (x_i are variables ranging over finite sets of integers and c_j are constants such that $c_j = j$).

(LHS-)Predicate instantiation:
$P(aXY dZ) \quad \leftrightarrow \quad P(abcdef)$

Constraint-based interpretation:
$$P(x_0 \quad a \quad x_1 \ X \ x_2 \ Y \ x_3 \quad d \quad x_4 \ Z \ x_5) \quad \leftrightarrow$$
$$P(c_0 \quad a \quad c_1 \ b \ c_2 \ c \ c_3 \quad d \quad c_4 \ e \ c_5 \ f \ c_6)$$

$$\begin{cases} i \leq j \quad \Rightarrow \quad x_i \leq x_j & \text{(linear order)} \\ x_0 = c_0 \quad x_5 = c_6 & \text{(extern boundaries)} \\ x_1 = c_1 \quad x_3 = c_3 \quad x_4 = c_4 & \text{(anchor constraints)} \end{cases}$$

(here x_2 is the only free range boundary, and can take 3 values, namely c_1, c_2 or c_3)

Figure 6: Constraint-based clause instantiation.

The gain brought by CSP-based techniques remains to be evaluated. So far, it has only been observed empirically between 2 versions of the parser. Nonetheless constraints offer a natural framework for dealing with ranges.[9]

Eventually, note that the extensions introduced in this section do not affect the time complexity of Boullier's algorithm, which is $\mathcal{O}(|G|n^d)$, $|G|$ being the size of the grammar, d its degree, and n the length of the input string.

---

[9]The question of whether feature constraints should be used at this stage or not is discussed in section 6.

6 Retrieving TT-MCTAG derivation structures

As previously mentioned, the result of RCG-parsing is an RCG shared forest. In order to extract from this forest the TT-MCTAG derivation structure (namely the derivation and derived trees), we must first interpret this RCG forest to get the underlying TAG forest, and then expand the latter.

6.1 Interpreting the RCG shared forest

The interpretation of the RCG forest corresponds to performing a traversal of the forest while replacing all *branching* clauses (i.e. clauses whose LHS predicate is labeled by *adj* or *sub*) by the *tree* clause they refer to in the table of clause instantiation. In other terms, each instantiated branching clause is replaced by the tree clause corresponding to its unique RHS-predicate (see Fig. 7).

$$\langle \alpha_{rep}, \emptyset \rangle (es\ der\ Mech\ zu\ rep\ versp) \rightarrow$$
$$\langle adj, \alpha_{rep}, \epsilon, \{\beta_{acc}\} \rangle (es\ der\ Mech, versp)$$

$$\langle adj, \alpha_{rep}, \epsilon, \{\beta_{acc}\} \rangle (es\ der\ Mech, versp) \rightarrow$$
$$\langle \beta_{versp}, \{\beta_{acc}\} \rangle (es\ der\ Mech, versp)$$

$$\langle \beta_{versp}, \{\beta_{acc}\} \rangle (es\ der\ Mech, versp) \rightarrow$$
$$\langle adj, \beta_{versp}, \epsilon, \{\beta_{acc}, \beta_{nom}\} \rangle (es\ der\ Mech., \epsilon)$$

Figure 7: Relation between clause instantiations and TT-MCTAG derivation (using the TT-MCTAG in Fig. 1).

The result of this interpretation of the RCG shared forest is the TT-MCTAG shared forest, i.e. a factorized representation of all TT-MCTAG derivations as a context-free grammar. The extraction of this TT-MCTAG forest is done in a single traversal of the RCG forest (i.e. of the table of clause instantiations) starting from the clause whose LHS predicate is the start predicate. Since the predicate names contain the tree identifiers they refer to, no lookup in the grammar is needed. As a consequence, the time complexity of the extraction of the TT-MCTAG forest is bound by the size of the table of clause instantiations.

Note that (i) we do not expand the alternatives resulting from syntactic ambiguity at this stage, and (ii) both the RCG and TT-MCTAG derivation forests have been computed without taking the feature structures into account. The motivation is to delay the cost of unification to the final step of expansion of the TT-MCTAG forest. Indeed, the word order constraints encoded in the RCG have possibly rejected many ungrammatical structures for which the cost of feature unification would have been wasted time. It would be interesting to experiment whether we would benefit or not from using feature structures as additional constraints on clause instantiation in practice.

6.2 Expanding the TAG shared forest

Finally, from this TT-MCTAG derivation forest, we can extract all derivation trees, and then compute the corresponding derived trees.

This task amounts to traversing the forest in a top-down-fashion, using the information in the encountered nodes (referring to elementary trees) to gradually assemble derivation trees. Some nodes in the forest encode a syntactic ambiguity (disjunctive node), in which case we make a copy of the current derivation tree and apply one of the alternative options to each of the trees before following each branch through. This behavior is easy to implement using a FIFO queue. A few control mechanisms check for integrity of the derivation trees during the process. We end up with a set of derivation trees in an XML DOM format that can either be displayed directly in the GUI or exported in an XML file.

For reasons of flexibility, we chose to rely on an XML DOM internal representation for all the steps of derived tree building. Indeed, this enables each of the derivation steps to be displayed directly in the GUI. Feature unification also happens at this point, allowing for a graphical illustration of feature clashes in the parse tree in debug mode.

7 Computing semantics

The parsing architecture introduced here has been extended to support the syntax/semantics interface of Gardent and Kallmeyer (2003). The underlying idea of this interface is to associate each tree with flat semantic formulas. The arguments of these formulas are unification variables co-indexed with features labelling the nodes of the syntactic tree. During derivation, trees are combined via adjunction and/or substitution, each triggering the unifi-

cations of the feature structures labelling specific nodes. As a result of these unifications, the arguments of the semantic formulas associated with the trees involved in the derivation get unified. In the end, each derivation/derived tree is associated with a flat semantic representation corresponding to the union of the formulas associated with the elementary trees that have been used. An example is given in Fig. 8.

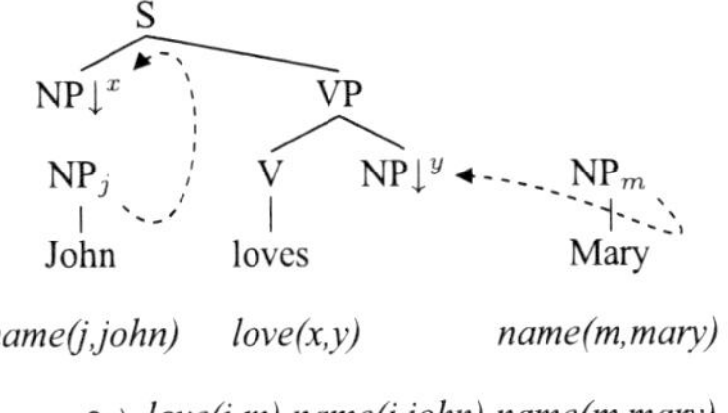

Figure 8: Semantic calculus in Feature-Based TAG.

In our system, the integration of the semantic support has only required 2 extensions, namely (i) the extension of the tree objects to include semantic formulas, and (ii) the extension of the construction of the derived tree so that the semantic formulas are carried until the end and updated with respect to the feature-structure unifications performed.

8 Optimizations

The parsing architecture presented here can host several optimizations. In this section, we present two examples of these. The first one concerns lexical disambiguation, the second one RCG parsing.

Lexical disambiguation becomes a necessity because, for each token of the input sentence, there may be many candidate elementary trees, each of these being used in the RCG conversion, thus leading to a combinatorial explosion for longer sentences.[10] We tackled this problem using the technique introduced in Bonfante et al. (2004). The idea behind their approach is to encode all the possible combinations of elementary trees in an automaton. For this purpose, elementary trees are first reduced to sets of polarity values depending on the *resources* and *needs* they represent (a substitution or foot node refers to a need for a certain category, while a root node corresponds to a re-

---

[10]Recall that all licensed adjunctions are predicted.

source). For example, an S elementary tree with two places for NP substitution has an NP polarity of -2 and an S polarity of +1.Using this representation, every candidate elementary tree is represented by an edge in an automaton built by scanning the input sentence from left to right. The polarity of a path through the automaton is the sum of all the polarities of the edges encountered on the way. While building this automaton, we determine all the paths with a neutral polarity for every category but the parsed constituent's category (whose polarity is +1). Such a path encodes a set of elementary trees that could contribute to a valid parse. As a consequence, the parser only has to consider for RCG conversion, combinations for a small number of tree sets. This approach makes the search space for both RCG conversion and RCG parsing much more manageable and leads to a significant drop in parsing time for some long sentences.

The second optimization concerns RCG parsing, which can have a high cost in cases where there are many free range boundaries. We can decrease the number of such boundaries by adding a constraint preventing range variables referring to substitution nodes from being bound to ϵ.

9   Conclusion and future work

In this paper, we introduced a parsing environment using RCG as a pivot formalism to parse mildly context-sensitive formalisms such as TT-MCTAG. This environment opens the way to multi-formalism parsing. Furthermore, its modular architecture (RCG conversion, RCG parsing, RCG shared forest interpretation) made it possible to extend the system to perform additional tasks, such as semantic calculus or dependency structure extraction. The system is still being developed, but is already used for the development of a TT-MCTAG for German (Kallmeyer et al., 2008). Future work will include experiments with off-line conversion of TT-MCTAG and generalization of branching clauses to reduce the size of the RCG and thus to improve (RCG) parsing time.

References

Billot, Sylvie and Bernard Lang. 1989. The Structure of Shared Forests in Ambiguous Parsing. In *27th Annual Meeting of the Association for Computational Linguistics*, pages 143–151.

Bonfante, Guillaume, Bruno Guillaume, and Guy Perrier. 2004. Polarization and abstraction of grammatical formalisms as methods for lexical disambiguation. In *Proceedings of 20th International Conference on Computational Linguistics (CoLing 2004)*, pages 303–309.

Boullier, Pierre. 1999. On TAG and Multicomponent TAG Parsing. Rapport de Recherche 3668, Institut National de Recherche en Informatique et en Automatique (INRIA).

Boullier, Pierre. 2000. Range concatenation grammars. In *Proceedings of the Sixth International Workshop on Parsing Technologies (IWPT 2000)*, pages 53–64.

Duchier, Denys, Joseph Le Roux, and Yannick Parmentier. 2004. The Metagrammar Compiler: An NLP Application with a Multi-paradigm Architecture. In *Second International Mozart/Oz Conference (MOZ'2004)*.

Gardent, Claire and Laura Kallmeyer. 2003. Semantic Construction in FTAG. In *EACL 2003, 10th Conference of the European Chapter of the Association for Computational Linguistics*, pages 123–130.

Kallmeyer, Laura and Yannick Parmentier. 2008. On the relation between Multicomponent Tree Adjoining Grammars with Tree Tuples (TT-MCTAG) and Range Concatenation Grammars (RCG). In *Proceedings of the 2nd International Conference on Language and Automata Theory and Applications LATA*, pages 277–288.

Kallmeyer, Laura, Timm Lichte, Wolfgang Maier, Yannick Parmentier, and Johannes Dellert. 2008. Developing a TT-MCTAG for German with an RCG-based parser. In *Proceedings of the Sixth International Conference on Language Resources and Evaluation (LREC 2008)*. To appear.

Lichte, Timm and Laura Kallmeyer. 2008. Factorizing Complementation in a TT-MCTAG for German. In *Proceedings of the The Ninth International Workshop on Tree Adjoining Grammars and Related Formalisms (TAG+9)*.

Lichte, Timm. 2007. An MCTAG with tuples for coherent constructions in German. In *Proceedings of the 12th Conference on Formal Grammar*.

Schulte, Christian and Guido Tack. 2006. Views and iterators for generic constraint implementations. In *Recent Advances in Constraints (2005)*, volume 3978 of *Lecture Notes in Artificial Intelligence*, pages 118–132. Springer-Verlag.

Søgaard, Anders, Timm Lichte, and Wolfgang Maier. 2007. The complexity of linguistically motivated extensions of tree-adjoining grammar. In *Recent Advances in Natural Language Processing 2007*.

A Metagrammar for Vietnamese LTAG

Lê Hồng Phương
LORIA/INRIA Lorraine
Nancy, France
lehong@loria.fr

Nguyễn Thị Minh Huyền
Hanoi University of Science
Hanoi, Vietnam
huyenntm@vnu.edu.vn

Azim Roussanaly
LORIA/INRIA Lorraine
Nancy, France
azim@loria.fr

Abstract

We present in this paper an initial investigation into the use of a metagrammar for explicitly sharing abstract grammatical specifications for the Vietnamese language. We first introduce the essential syntactic mechanisms of the Vietnamese language. We then show that the basic subcategorization frames of Vietnamese can be compactly represented by classes using the XMG formalism (eXtensible MetaGrammar). Finally, we report on the implementation the first metagrammar producing verbal elementary trees recognizing basic Vietnamese sentences.

1 Introduction

Metagrammars (MG) have recently emerged as a means to develop wide-coverage LTAG for well-studied languages like English, French and Italian (Candito, 1999; Kinyon, 2003). MGs help avoid redundancy and reduce the effort of grammar development by making use of common properties of LTAG elementary trees.

We present in this paper an initial investigation into the use of a metagrammar for explicitly sharing abstract grammatical specifications for the Vietnamese language. We use the eXtensible MetaGrammar (XMG) tool which was developed by Crabbé (Crabbé, 2005; Parmentier and L. Roux, 2005) to compile a TAG for Vietnamese. The built grammar is called **vnMG** and is made available online for free access[1].

Only in recent years have Vietnamese researchers begun to be involved in the domain of natural language processing in general and in the task of parsing Vietnamese in particular. No work on formalizing Vietnamese grammar is reported before (Nguyen et al., 2004). In (Lê et al., 2006), basic declarative structures and complement clauses of Vietnamese sentences have been modeled using about thirty elementary trees, representing as many subcategorization frames. We show in this paper that these basic subcategorization frames can be compactly represented by classes in XMG formalism.

We first introduce the essential syntactic mechanisms of the Vietnamese language. We then show that the basic subcategorization frames of Vietnamese can be compactly represented by classes using the XMG formalism. We then report on the implementation the first metagrammar producing verbal elementary trees recognizing basic Vietnamese sentences, before concluding.

2 Vietnamese Subcategorizations

As for other isolating languages, the most important syntactic information source in Vietnamese is word order. The basic word order is Subject – Verb – Object. A verb is always placed after the subject in both predicative and question forms. In a noun phrase, the main noun precedes the adjectives and the genitive follows the governing noun. The other syntactic means are function words, reduplication, and, in the case of spoken language, prosody (Nguyễn et al., 2006).

From the point of view of functional grammar, the syntactic structure of Vietnamese follows a topic-oriented structure. It belongs to the topic-prominent languages as described by (Li and Thompson, 1976). In those languages, topics are

---

[1] *http://www.loria.fr/~lehong/tools/vnMG.php*

coded in the surface structure and they tend to control co-referentiality. The topic-oriented "double subject" construction is a basic sentence type. For example, "*Cậu ấy khoẻ mạnh, là sinh viên y khoa / He strong, be student medicine*", which means that "*He is strong, he is medicine student*". In Vietnamese, passive voice and cleft subject sentences are rare or non-existent.

In general, Vietnamese predicates may be classified into three types depending on the need of a copula connecting them with their subjects in the declarative and negative forms (Nguyễn, 2004). Complex predicates can be constructed to form co-ordinated predicative structures starting from these basic types of predicates. We present briefly these three types of Vietnamese predicates in the following subsections.

2.1 First Type Predicates

The first type predicates are predicates which connect directly to their subjects without the need of a copula in both of the declarative and negative forms. For example

- Declarative form: *Tôi đọc sách. / I am reading books.*

- Negative form: *Tôi không đọc sách. / I am not reading books.*

These predicates are assumed by verbal phrases or adjectival phrases. The fact that an adjective can be a predicate is a specificity of Vietnamese in comparison with predicates of occidental languages. In English or French for instance, only verbal phrases can be predicates, adjectives in these languages always signify properties of subjects and they are always followed the verb "*to be*" in English or "*être*" in French.

2.2 Second Type Predicates

The second type predicates are predicates which are connected to their subjects by the copula "*là*" in the declarative form and by copulas "*không là*" or "*không phải*", or "*không phải là*" in the negative form. Predicates of this type are rather rich. They can be:

- Nouns or noun phrases: *Tôi là sinh viên. / I am student.*

- Verbs, adjectives, verbal phrases or adjectival phrases: *Van xin là yếu đuối. / Begging is feeble., Học cũng là làm việc / To study is to work.*

2.3 Third Type Predicates

The third type predicates are predicates which connect directly to their subjects in the declarative form; however in the negative form, they are connected to their subjects by a copula. Predicates of this type are usually

- A clause: *Nó vẫn tên là Quýt. / His name is still Quýt.*

- A composition of a numeral and a noun: *Lê này mười ngàn đồng. / This pear costs ten thousand dongs.*

- A composition of a preposition and a noun: *Lúa này của chị Hoa. / This is the rice of Ms. Hoa.*

- An expression: *Thằng ấy đầu bò đầu bướu lắm. / That guy is very stubborn.*

2.4 Subcategorizations

In the first grammar LTAG for Vietnamese presented in (Lê et al., 2006), each subcategorization is represented by the same structure of elementary trees associated with a considered predicate. We view that the suject is subcategorized in the same way like arguments. The verbs anchor thus elementary trees composed of a node for the subject and one or more nodes for each of its essential complements.

We follow the de facto standard that in TAG, in which each subcategorization is represented by a family of elementary trees. We define families of verbal elementary trees in the Table 1.

We present in the next section a metagrammar that generates this set of elementary trees.

3 A Metagrammar for Verbal Trees

The subcategorizations of elementary trees describe only "canonical" constructions of predicative elements without taking into account for relative or question structures. For the purpose of investigation, we constraint ourselves in developing at the first stage only the verb spines and argument realizations shown in the subcategorizations presented in the previous section.

We have developed a XMG metagrammar that consists of 11 classes (or tree fragments). The

Subcategorizations	Families	Examples
Intransitive	$N_0 V$	*ngủ/sleep*
With a nominal complement	$N_0 V N_1$	*đọc/to read*
With a clausal complement	$N_0 V S_1$	*tin/to believe*
With modal complement	$N_0 V_0 V_1$	*mong/to wish*
Ditransitive	$N_0 V N_1 N_2$	*cho/to give*
Ditransitive with a preposition	$N_0 V N_1 O N_2$	*vay/to borrow*
Ditransitive with a verbal complement	$N_0 V_0 N_1 V_1$	*lãnh đạo/to lead*
Ditransitive with an adjectival complement	$N_0 V N_1 A$	*làm/to make*
Movement verbs with a nominal complement	$N_0 V_0 V_1 N_1$	*ra/to go out*
Movement verbs with an adjectival complement	$N_0 V_0 A V_1$	*trở nên/to become*
Movement ditransitive	$N_0 V_0 N_1 V_1 N_2$	*chuyển/to transfer*

Table 1: Subcategorizations of Vietnamese verbs

metagrammar is currently able to produce the same set of elementary trees described in Table 1 including intransitive, transitive, ditransitive families with and/or without optional complements. As an illustration, the declarative transitive structure in Figure 1 can be defined by combining a canonical subject fragment with an active verb and a canonical object fragment.

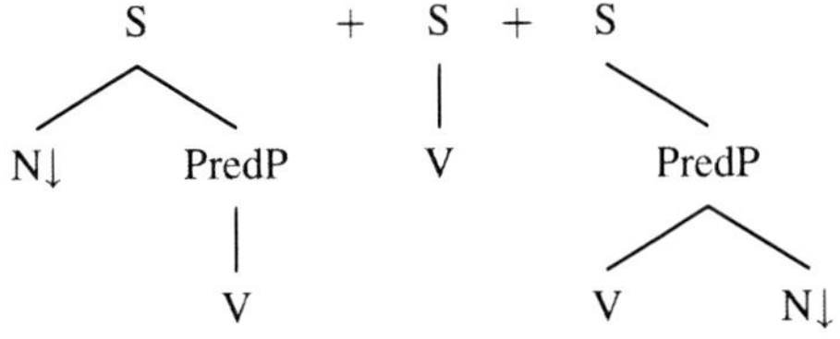

This combination is conveniently expressed by a statement in terms of XMG language as usual:

TransitiveVerb = Subject $\wedge$ ActiveVerb $\wedge$ Object.

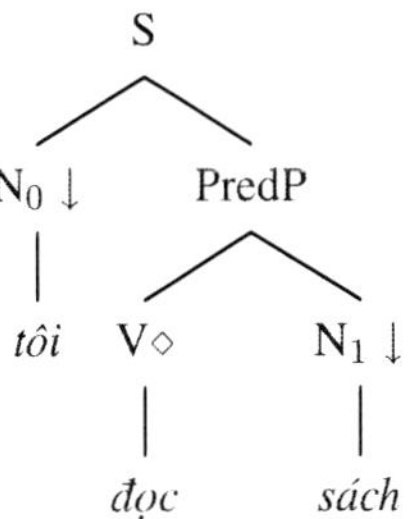

Figure 1: Declarative transitive structure $\alpha n_0 V n_1$

4　Conclusion and Future Work

This paper presents an initial investigation into the use of XMG formalism for developing a first metagrammar producing a LTAG for Vietnamese which recognizes basic verbal constructions. We have shown that the essential subcategorization frames of Vietnamese predicates can be effectively encoded by means of XMG classes while retaining basic properties of the realized verbal trees. This confirms that various syntactic phenomena of Vietnamese can be covered in a Vietnamese MG.

The first evaluation of the MG for Vietnamese is promising but the lexical coverage has to be improved further. Moreover, the grammar coverage needs to be revised by refining the constraints of agrammatical syntactic constructions. Although there are not many tree fragments in the current metagrammar, we find that the current MG over-generates some undesired structures. The MG will also be extended to deal with constructions not yet covered like adjectival and noun phrase constructions. We also intend to generate a test suite to document the grammars and perform realistic evaluations.

There is an existing work on the development of metagrammars for not frequently studied languages like Korean and Yiddish and their relations to a German grammar (Kinyon, 2006). They showed that cross-linguistic generalizations, for example the verb-second phenomenon, can be incorporated into a multilingual MG. We think that a comparison of the Vietnamese MG with this work would be useful. In particular, a study of the relative position of verbs and arguments of Vietnamese and relate it to this work would be benefitial.

References

Marie-Hélène Candito. 1999. *Représentation modulaire et paramétrable de grammaires électroniques lexicalisées : application au français et à l'italien.* Doctoral Dissertation, Université Paris 7.

Benoit Crabbé. 2005. *Représentation informatique de grammaires fortement lexicalisées.* Doctoral Dissertation, Université Nancy 2.

Nguyễn Thị Minh Huyền, Laurent Romary, Mathias Rossignol and Vũ Xuân Lương. 2006. *A Lexicon for Vietnamese Language Processing.* Language Resources and Evaluation, Vol. 40, No. 3–4.

Kinyon A. and Rambow O. 2003. *Using the Meta-Grammar to generate cross-language and cross-framework annotated test-suites.* In Proc. LINC-EACL, Budapest.

Alexandra Kinyon and Carlos A. Prolo. 2002. *A Classification of Grammar Development Strategies.* Proceedings of the Workshop on Grammar Engineering, Taipei, Taiwan.

Kinyon, Alexandra and Rambow, Owen and Scheffler, Tatjana and Yoon, SinWon and Joshi, Aravind K. 2006. *The Metagrammar Goes Multilingual: A Cross-Linguistic Look at the V2-Phenomenon.* Proceedings of the Eighth International Workshop on Tree Adjoining Grammar and Related Formalisms, Sydney, Australia

Lê Hồng Phương, Nguyễn Thị Minh Huyền, Laurent Romary, Azim Roussanaly. 2006. *A Lexicalized Tree-Adjoining Grammar for Vietnamese.* Proceedings of LREC 2006, Genoa, Italia.

Thanh Bon Nguyen, Thi Minh Huyen Nguyen, Laurent Romary, Xuan Luong Vu. 2004. *Developing Tools and Building Linguistic Resources for Vietnamese Morpho-Syntactic Processing.* Proceedings of LREC 2004, Lisbon, Portugal.

Charles N. Li and Sandra A. Thompson. 1976. *Subject and topic: a new typology of language.* In Charles N. Li (ed.). Subject and Topic. London/New York: Academic Press, pp. 457-489..

Yannick Parmentier and Joseph L. Roux. 2005. *XMG: a Multi-formalism Metagrammar Framework.* Proceedings of the Tenth ESSLLI Student Session.

Nguyễn Minh Thuyết and Nguyễn Văn Hiệp. 2004. *Thành phần câu tiếng Việt.* NXB Giáo dục, Hà Nội, Vietnam.

Is Coordination Quantification?

Kevin Lerman* and Owen Rambow†
* Department of Computer Science, † Center for Computational Learning Systems
Columbia University
New York, NY, USA
klerman@cs.columbia.edu, rambow@ccls.columbia.edu

Abstract

We explore the semantics of conjunction using a neo-Davidsonian semantics expressed in a synchronous grammar. We propose to model conjunction as quantification over the set of conjoined entities, and discuss problems that arise in this approach when we have conjoined quantified noun phrases.

1 Introduction

The semantics of conjunction in natural language has proven particularly difficult for formal linguistic theories to model. We present some preliminary work on this problem using synchronous grammars, specifically the SynchUVGDL formalism. We observe similarities between quantification and coordination, and therefore attempt to model the latter as the former. While this reduces the complexity of many simple NP-coordinated sentences, those with quantified NPs prove difficult to model due to the multi-component nature of quantifiers in semantics. We describe our attempts at adopting an underspecified, single-component quantifier to get around this problem, and present the implications of such a representation.

The paper is structured as follows. We first review work in semantics and Tree Adjoining Grammar (TAG), and then briefly present synchronous UVGDL (Section 3). In Section 4, we summarize our approach to modeling semantics using SynchUVGDL, and then discuss the similarities between quantification and conjunction in Section 5 and propose a simple approach. Section 6 presents a serious problem for the proposed approach (the conjunction of quantified NPs), and Section 7 presents our solution.

2 TAG and Semantics

Shieber and Schabes (1990) were the first to propose a syntactic-semantic grammar in the TAG framework, by using synchronous TAG (Synch-TAG). In SynchTAG, two TAGs are linked in such a way that trees in one grammar correspond to trees in the other grammar, and the nodes in corresponding trees are linked. When we substitute or adjoin a tree in a node, then we must substitute or adjoin a corresponding tree in the linked node in the tree in the other grammar. Several different definitions of SynchTAG are possible (Shieber, 1994), and the most interesting definition has the property that the derivation trees for the two derivations in the two synchronized grammars are isomorphic, so that we can talk of a single, TAG-style derivation tree for a SynchTAG. Subsequently, a series of research was published which did not use SynchTAG for semantics, but instead generated a semantic representation during the syntactic derivation, often using feature structures (Kallmeyer, 2002; Kallmeyer and Joshi, 2003; Gardent and Kallmeyer, 2003; M. Romero, 2004). The principal difference is that in this line of work, the semantics is not itself modeled in a TAG.

Recently, Nesson and Shieber (2006; 2007) have revived the approach using SynchTAG. They have shown that a large number of different constructions can be given elegant analyses using a SynchTAG-based analysis. Our work is in this tradition.

3 UVGDL and SynchUVGDL

If TAG can be seen as a partial derivation in a CFG, pre-assembled for convenience, in a UVGDL (Rambow, 1994) the partial derivation is col-

Proceedings of The Ninth International Workshop on Tree Adjoining Grammars and Related Formalisms
Tübingen, Germany. June 6-8, 2008.

lected into one kit, but not actually fully assembled. More technically, in UVGDL, the elementary structures of the grammar are sets of context-free rules which can be augmented with **dominance links**. A dominance link stipulates a relation of (immediate or non-immediate) dominance which must hold in the derived tree structure. Note that despite the formal differences between a TAG and a UVGDL, they share exactly the same notion of extended domain of locality, and both formalisms can be lexicalized; linguistically, an elementary structure in a UVGDL can be used to represent, as in TAG, a lexical head, its (extended) projection, and positions for its arguments. Rambow (1994) shows that the parsing problem (with a fixed grammar) is polynomial in the length of the input sentence, if the UVGDL is lexicalized (as we assume all our grammars are). This formalism can also be seen as a tree description language, with the context-free rules in a set as statements of immediate dominance between one node and one or more daughters (along with constraints on linear precedence among the daughters), the dominance links as statements of dominance (Vijay-Shanker, 1992; Rambow et al., 2001). We choose the rewriting formulation because a synchronous version (SynchUVGDL) was defined by Rambow and Satta (1996) and some initial results on computation were proposed. Specifically, they claim that the parse-to-forest translation problem for a lexicalized SynchUVGDL can be computed in polynomial time.

4 Overview of Semantics with SynchUVGDL

We have been developing a semantic formalism that can be easily modeled using SynchUVGDL (see (Lerman and Rambow, 2008) for details). We adopt the notation of Montague semantics, wherein e is the type of entities, t' is the type of truth values, and for any two types x and y, $< x, y >$ is the type of functions from x's to y's. Our formalism relies heavily on set theory, for example explicitly interpreting $< e, t >$'s as sets rather than as propositions. For instance, Montague semantics might represent *boy* as "boy(x)", a function whose value is true or false depending on whether or not x is a boy. We instead represent *boy* as simply the set of all boys. While this does not alter any truth conditions, the representation is more convenient for this sort of tree-based

formalism. This is because at times a traditional Montague $< e, t >$ such as *boy* must be treated as a function (taking an entity as an argument and returning true iff it is a boy), and at other times it must be treated as a first-order object (when being modified by an adjective such as *tall* to produce a new $< e, t >$ representing "tall-boy"). In certain other formalisms it is easy to underspecify these two cases, but in ours the two views will be directly manifested in the structure of the productions for a word such as *boy* – it either will have a substitution node for an entity and itself be an argument of type t, or it will have no substitution nodes and itself be an argument of type $< e, t >$. Because these two views have different structural representations, we are forced to choose which to use, and generally choose the set representation as being easier to work with under the UVGDL formalism.

Adjectives are then analyzed as functions from sets of entities to "filtered" sets of entities. By way of example, *tall boy* would be represented as "tall(boy)" – "tall()" takes the set of all boys, filters it for those who are tall, and returns a new set consisting of all boys who pass the filter.[1] Note that while we often call these "filters", they are opaque enough to support the semantics of nonintersective adjectives such as *fake*, which would perhaps take a set of entities and yield a new set that contains all entities that appear similar to elements of the argument set, but that nonetheless are not members of the argument set.

The piecewise nature of UVGDL lends itself to neo-Davidsonian semantics, wherein the events denoted by verbs (or possibly by nouns) are treated as first-order objects, akin to entities (we assign them the type of v).[2] Thus, our analysis of verbs and adverbs is nearly identical to that of nouns and adjectives – a verb like *visit* returns the set of all "visit" events, and an adverb like *quickly* would take a set of events (a $< v, t >$) and filter the set for those which were done happily. This is logically equivalent to something like $visit(x) \wedge quickly(x)$, but has more flexibility in representing the meaning of manner adverbs (what is quick

---

[1] Technically, *boy* should be analyzed this way too, as "boy(U)" – a function that takes a set of entities (here, the [U]niverse of all entities) and filters the set for those entities which are boys. In this paper, we will represent this as simply 'boy' for easier reading.

[2] For a detailed discussion of neo-Davidsonian semantics, see (Schein, 2002). The idea is not new; our goal has been to integrate it into a robust syntactic formalism.

depends on the event – Mary quickly batting an eye is different from humanoids quickly spreading through Asia).

Slightly more complicated filters exist to handle verb arguments. For instance, subjecthood is represented as a filter that selects only events which have a certain entity as their agent (or whatever the semantic role of the subject is for the verb). The filter actually comes in two parts: one part that filters a set of events for those that make a certain condition true, and another that specifies that the condition consists of having a certain entity as an agent (see the top left structure in Figure 1). This distinction will become important in the next section. Finally, to preserve the notion that statements are formulas that ultimately resolve to a truth type, an existential quantifier dominates all logic relating to the verb. Thus, the semantics for a statement like *John visited Mary* reads as "There exists an event in the set of (visit events whose subject is John and whose object is Mary)." This matches intuition, as the utterance does not imply any additional detail about the nature of the event being described – just that some event matching this description happened.[3]

Using this formalism, we can with a simple toy grammar (Figure 1) obtain the typical two readings for a sentence like sentence 1 – the one where all the boys visited the same store, and the one where they may have all visited distinct stores (see Figure 2).[4]

(1) Every boy visited a store

Upon inspection, it should become clear that we actually license several additional readings for (1). Because of the argument positions introduced by the semantics for subjecthood and objecthood, the two quantifiers associated with *every boy* and *a store* can actually scope underneath the existential quantifier for the event – in the spots occupied above by "has-agent" and "has-patient". This gives rise to an additional three readings, whose meanings may not be immediately obvious. To make the matter clearer, consider (2).

(2) Every boy lifted-the-piano

---

[3]We do not consider the information contained in the tense of *visited* in this paper

[4]Note that, unlike (Nesson and Shieber, 2006), our semantic trees do not derive a string which represents the semantics; rather, our derived tree itself represents the semantics. Our trees could be easily modified (with additional terminal symbols) to allow for the semantics to be read off as a string. We see no urgent theoretical of practical need for this, however.

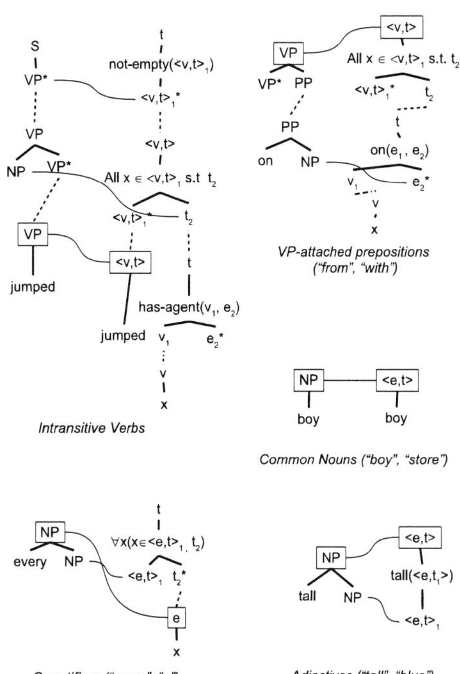

Figure 1: A toy grammar from the Synch-UVGDL framework.

We will treat 'lifted-the-piano' as a simple intransitive verb to simplify our analysis.[5] As is shown in Figure 3, the neo-Davidsonian representation of verbs licenses two readings:

- All the boys gathered around the piano, counted to three, and lifted it together. This corresponds to the reading where ∀ appears directly over 'has-agent'. More technically, "There is a single piano-lifting event, of which all the boys are agents."

- Taking turns, perhaps in a piano-lifting competition, each of the boys lifted the piano. This corresponds to the reading where ∀ is the root of the sentence's semantics. More technically, "For every boy, there exists some piano-lifting event of which he is the subject".

There is actually some debate as to whether the first reading can be obtained with the word "every". See (Winter, 2002) for a detailed discussion.

---

[5]Alternatively, substitute your favorite intransitive verb. We use "lifted-the-piano" because it makes the newly available readings easy to visualize.

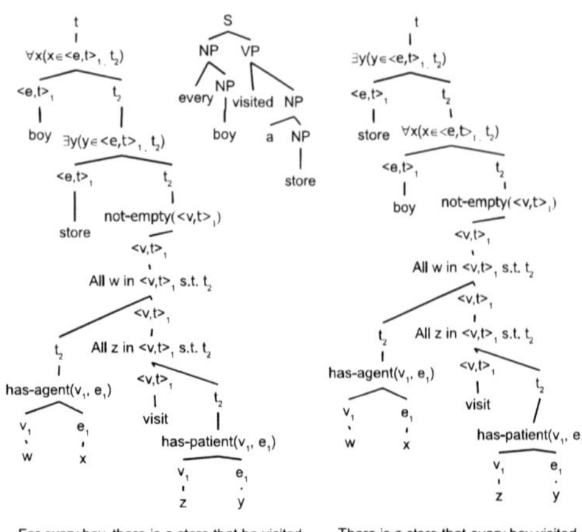

Figure 2: Two readings for *Every boy visited a store*.

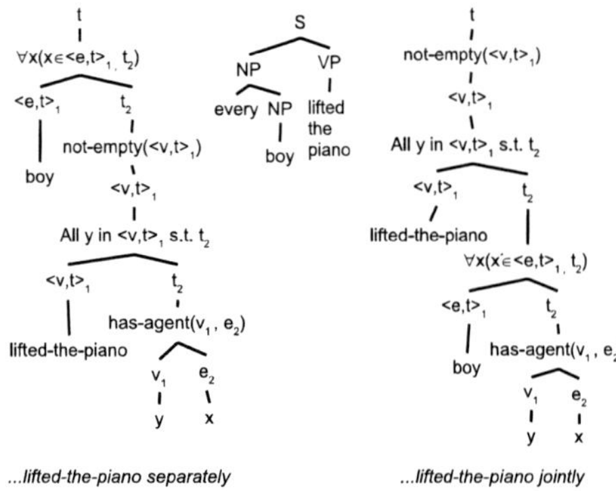

Figure 3: Two meanings for *Every boy lifted a piano*

The precise treatment is beyond the scope of this paper, but if you prefer, replace *every boy* with *all-the boys*, and the readings become readily available.

5 Conjunction as Quantification

The ambiguity in sentence (2) is very similar to a general ambiguity observed when studying conjunction, namely the issue of entity coordination versus sentence coordination. Roughly speaking, it is unclear whether in (2) we are constructing a compound subject out of *every boy*, and applying that subject (containing the set of all boys) to a single event, or if we are constructing many events, each of which has a simple subject. The same ambiguity arises if we substitute a conjunction for the quantifier:

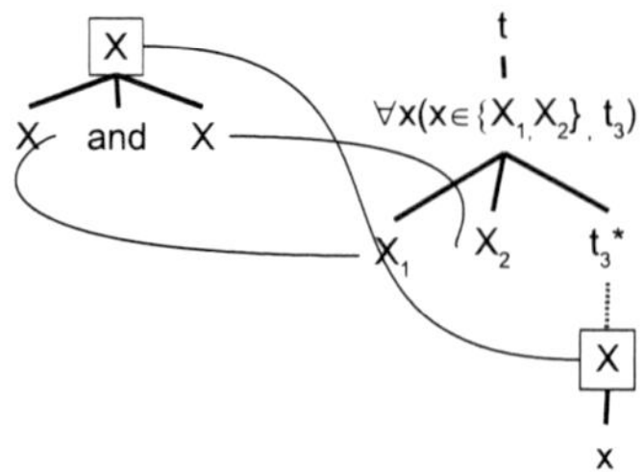

Figure 4: Conjunction modeled as quantification in UVGDL

(3) John and Mary lifted-the-piano

Here it is unclear if we are conjoining at the entity level (John and Mary lifted the piano together) or the sentence level (John lifted the piano and separately, Mary lifted the piano). Devising an analysis of coordination that accounts for both boolean coordination (as in the second case) and entity coordination (as in the first) has been a challenge for many researchers. Sometimes two fundamentally different meanings of words like *and* are proposed to account for this phenomenon: one that conjoins multiple entities or sets of entities into a larger set, and another that conjoins multiple propositions into a single proposition (Partee and Rooth, 1983).

We attempt to construct a single semantic treatment for conjunction by modeling it as quantification over an explicitly defined set (the conjuncts). Following a rough syntactic treatment more or less as suggested by (Sarkar and Joshi, 1996), the semantics for words duplicated across all conjuncts form the "assertion" of this quantifier, and the words specific to the individual conjuncts form the elements of the set to be quantified over (figure 4). Besides eliminating the need to potentially duplicate semantic formulas, this allows the conjuncts to be of any one semantic type, while preserving conjunction as an operation over t-type values. With this analysis, we neatly obtain two readings for *John and Mary lifted-the-piano*, with no duplication of semantic rules and a single analysis of *and* (see Figure 5).

It should be noted that we will require the *entire* semantic components of the words forming the conjuncts – not just their synchronous productions – to scope underneath the conjunction. Conjunction will need to be a sort of island in this sense. Otherwise, we run the risk of having elements of

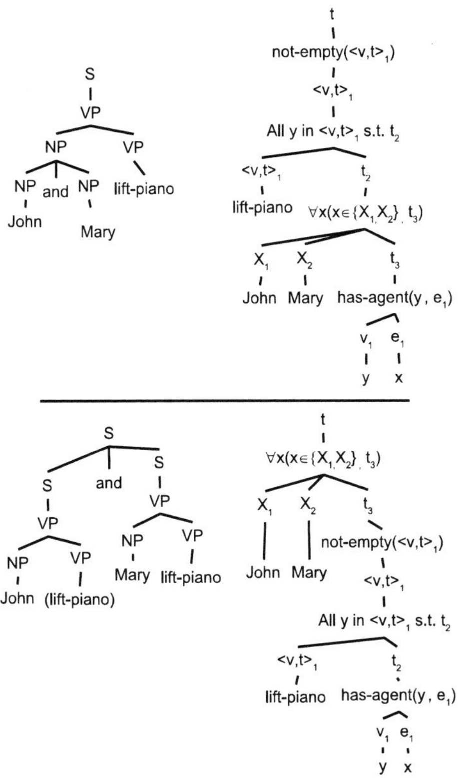

Figure 5: Two analyses for *John and Mary lifted a piano*

one conjunct scope over elements of another.

6 Conjunction Of Quantifiers

Simple sentences such as (3) can be handled very easily with this approach, but we encounter difficulties when we replace *John* and *Mary* with quantified NPs, as in (4).

(4) Every boy and most girls lifted-the-piano

The difficulty comes in the non-contiguous nature of the quantifiers: the individual conjuncts for *every boy* and *most girls* must contain the quantifier, the quantifier restrictor, and the variable the quantifier introduces into its assertion. However, the semantics of *lifted-the-piano* needs to show up in the assertion of the conjunction. This is not possible under the formalism as presented. Approaches that do not have this problem, such as the generalized conjunction of (Partee and Rooth, 1983), instead require conjuncts to be "cast up" and their representations changed depending on the other conjuncts in question – not easily rep-

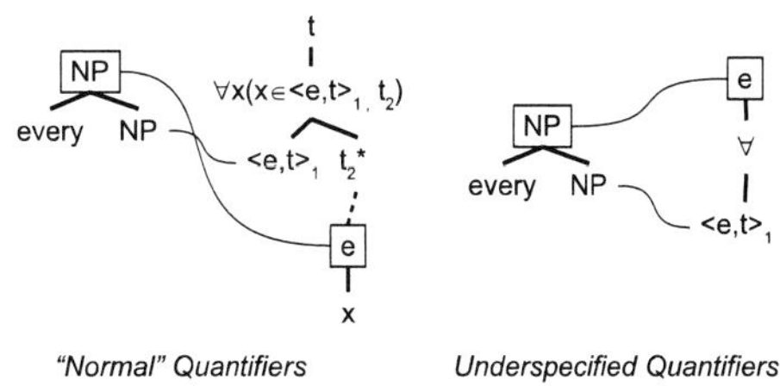

Figure 6: Underspecified quantifiers.

resented within the SynchUVGDL formalism. To handle these cases, we reformulate our quantifiers in such a way that their scope is underspecified, but their form is contiguous.

A quantifier can be viewed as "iterating" through all possible values as given by its restrictor, and seeing what happens when they are substituted in place of the bound variable it introduces in its assertion. The value of the quantifier expression as a whole (true or false) is dependent upon the values observed from its assertion when different possible values are substituted in. Under the SynchUVGDL formalism, formulae are not duplicated, and so quantifiers are able to project only a single copy of their bound variable into their assertion. Furthermore, as per the semantic treatment developed in (Lerman and Rambow, 2008), a quantifier's restrictor is simply a set – it does not contain any instances of the quantifier's bound variable. Thus, we are able to construct an underspecified quantifier as shown in figure 6 – quantifiers with a specified restrictor set, but with no specific assertion (yet).[6]

Intuitively, these underspecified quantifiers may be thought of as "choice functions," selecting an arbitrary element of their restrictor set. In the case of universal quantifiers, the choice function would be something like "pick any" (implying, as per the normal universal quantifier, that the same truth conditions hold for any member of the set). For an existential quantifier, the choice function would be something like "nondeterministically pick a privileged member" (implying that there exists at least one privileged member of whom something is true). These quantifiers are now contiguous, and may be used with our conjunction framework trivially, as seen in figure 7.

---

[6]The notion of underspecifying a quantifier in some manner is not new; as will be shown shortly, this representation is similar to one used in (Hobbs and Shieber, 1987).

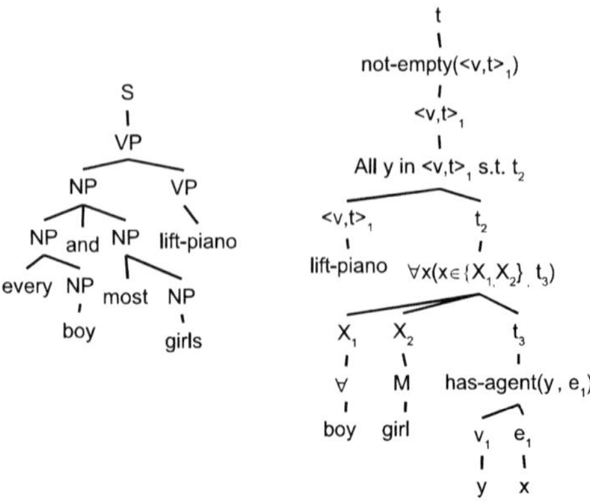

Figure 7: "Every boy and most girls lifted-the-piano [together]" with underspecified quantifiers.

The only challenge arising from this representation is that we have destroyed all notion of quantifier scope. Because quantifiers are now local to their restrictor sets, we are no longer able to distinguish the two common readings of sentences such as "Every boy visited a store." At some level, this is a good thing, as sentences such as these are in fact ambiguous between their two readings. A semantic formula for the meaning of a sentence that doesn't commit to a particular reading is desirable in many cases. However, it is important to be able to produce from this representation the complete set of valid readings for a sentence. As Hobbs and Shieber (1987) and others have pointed out, finding valid scopings is not a trivial task.

7   Restoring Quantifier Scope

Hobbs and Shieber (1987) present an algorithm for finding the valid quantifier scopings in a sentence. Roughly speaking, they iterate through the (currently underspecified) quantifiers of a sentence, in such an order that no quantifier is visited before any other quantifier that dominates it. Each quantifier visited is "moved" to some opaque argument position dominating it, or to the root of the sentence, such that bound variables don't lose their binding. The quantifier and its restrictor are moved, the quantifier "leaves behind" a copy of its bound variable, and whatever logic used to fill that opaque argument (including the left-behind bound variable) become the quantifier's assertion. By choosing a different iteration order, or by choosing different "landing sites" for each quantifier, all possible scope relations can be generated.

If we ignore conjunction for a moment, this algorithm can be applied to the SynchUVGDL framework with almost no modification. After having constructed the semantic tree for a sentence (with underspecified quantifiers), one can iterate through the quantifiers in any order permitted by the Shieber algorithm, and move each to any t-type argument position that dominates it (so long as no variables lose their binding). As before, the quantifier and its restrictor move, the quantifier's bound variable is left behind as a trace, and the logic that used to fill that t position becomes the quantifier assertion. This is facilitated by the structure of fully-specified quantifiers – they take a t-type argument, and are themselves t-type. Thus, the movement operation is essentially adjunction, plus leaving a trace. Because the semantic framework we are working with is neo-Davidsonian, this adaptation of the scope-restoration algorithm enables us to generate the additional single- and multiple-event readings as well, as the introduction of subjects and objects create more arguments of type t in the semantic tree.

Thus, so far the standard SynchUVGDL approach and the approach using underspecified quantifiers (along with the Hobbs-Shieber algorithm for disambiguating scope) are equivalent: in the standard SynchUVGDL approach, the dominance links in the semantics for quantifiers express the potential for extended scope, while the combination of the definition of the formalism (the meaning of dominance links) and the way the semantic side of the SynchUVGDL is constructed determine the actual scope readings. The standard SynchUVGDL approach is declarative, and scope is actually computed using general algorithms for processing SynchUVGDLs, not *ad-hoc* algorithms for scope.

When we introduce conjunction back in, the algorithm must be extended somewhat. First, in the case of coordinating quantified NPs, the quantifier would need to be able to expand to some node within the assertion of the conjunction. That is to say, the conjunction would need to be viewed as iterating through its conjuncts, substituting each into its assertion, then letting any quantifiers expand from its temporary position in the assertion, and then repeating the process with the next one. Crucially, the expansion happens "after" the conjunct has been substituted into the assertion of the conjunction.

- All the boys and most of the girls gathered together around the piano and together lifted it.
- Each of the children individually lifted it.
- All of the boys lifted the piano together, then they left and most of the girls lifted it together.
- All of the boys lifted the piano together, then most of the girls lifted it individually.
- Most of the girls lifted the piano together, then all of the boys lifted it individually.

Figure 8: Readings for *Every boy and most girls lifted-the-piano*

This is necessary because, although we are analyzing conjunctions as having the same structure as quantifiers, they nonetheless quantify over much richer objects. No matter how complex a (normal) quantifier's restrictor may be, it will ultimately yield a set of simple, atomic objects such as entities. Because in the case of conjunction we are quantifying over arbitrary expressions (so arbitrary in fact, that each element of the restrictor set must be vocalized individually, rather than in some compact expression as with a phrase like "every boy"), additional processing may be needed after the elements are substituted into the assertion. While this requires significantly more computation, note that there are tremendously fewer objects to iterate through: whereas a phrase like "every boy" may refer to hundreds or thousands of boys, each element in a conjunction must be vocalized individually, and so we rarely see more than three or four of these in a single sentence.

Additionally, recall that conjunctions must be treated as islands for the semantics of their conjuncts. This property must be retained in the context of quantifier expansion – otherwise we might license readings for (4) wherein the girls lift the piano once for each boy present. So, we prohibit quantifiers from expanding over any conjunctions they may be under. Note that this will never create a problem wherein quantifiers have no place to expand: they expand once they're substituted into the assertion of the conjunction, and the root of the assertion is always of type t.

We see now that the new approach for conjoined quantifiers has no clear equivalent representation in the standard SynchUVGDL approach: this is because the quantifiers are "temporarily" moved into the assertion for expansion, which cannot be replicated in a declarative approach. Thus, these kinds of semantic derivation pose a problem for semantic theories relying entirely on synchronous formalisms.

To this point we have experimented with treating conjunction as quantification, and with an un-

derspecified model of quantification. The next logical step would be to examine the possibility of using the underspecified quantifier model with the quantifier we have introduced for conjunction – in short, underspecified conjunction. If conjunction is made underspecified in the same way as quantification (see figure 9), the semantic trees for sentences with conjunction become much more intuitive. Scope disambiguation would then proceed in the same manner as before – for instance, any quantifiers embedded in a conjunct of a conjunction could only be raised after the conjunction itself did so. The only difference is that conjunction must still be an island for quantifier raising: embedded quantifiers still may not ever scope above the conjunction.

Whereas previously sentences such as *Every boy and most girls lifted-the-piano* had different possible readings depending on the scope selected for *and*, the representation in figure 10 encompasses all 5 possible scope orderings which are summarized in Figure 8. It is, however, unclear whether all five readings really exist. We believe the first two readings are clearly licensed by the sentence, but the last three are somewhat dubious. Intuitively, it seems that the quantifiers *every* and *most* ought to move in parallel, but this behavior is hard to enforce in a way that still makes sense in sentences without such similar NPs (*Every boy and Susan lifted-the-piano*). In our example sentence, the two desired readings could be obtained neatly by declaring the assertion of a conjunction to be "opaque" with respect to quantifiers – they must raise above or below the entire thing (but obviously, stay under the conjunction itself). This would create exactly one reading for each possible position for the conjunction to raise to. It is not clear whether this approach would work in more complex cases.

8 Conclusion

In conclusion, we have explored how we can express the semantics of coordination in a syn-

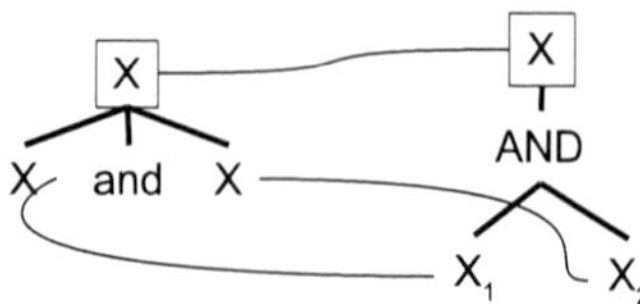

Figure 9: Underspecified conjunction

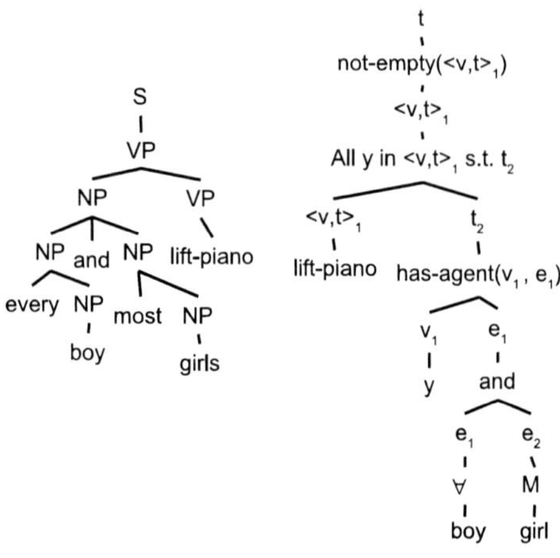

Figure 10: Example derivation with underspecified conjunction

chronous formalism. By modeling conjunction as quantification, we can easily derive the scope ambiguities with respect to the event variable which we see in coordination (do John and Mary lift the piano together, or individually?). We have seen that the conjunction of quantified NPs poses problems that apparently prevent us from expressing scope within the synchronous framework.

References

Gardent, Claire and Laura Kallmeyer. 2003. Semantic construction in F-TAG. In *Tenth Conference of the European Chapter of the Association for Computational Linguistics (EACL'03)*, Budapest, Hungary.

Hobbs, J. R. and S. M. Shieber. 1987. An algorithm for generating quantifier scopings. *Computational Linguistics*, 13:47–63.

Kallmeyer, L. and A. Joshi. 2003. Factoring predicate argument and scope semantics: Underspecified semantics with ltag. *Research on Language and Computation*, 1:3–58.

Kallmeyer, L. 2002. Using an enriched tag derivation structure as basis for semantics. In *Proceedings of the Sixth International Workshop on Tree Adjoining Grammar and Related Frameworks (TAG+6)*, pages 127–136.

Lerman, Kevin and Owen Rambow. 2008. Event semantics in synchronous formalisms. Technical report, Center for Computational Learning Systems, Columbia University.

M. Romero, L. Kallmeyer, O. Babko-Malaya. 2004. Ltag semantics for questions. In *Proceedings of the TAG+7*, pages 186–193, Vancouver.

Nesson, R. and S. Shieber. 2006. Simpler tag semantics through synchronization. In *Proceedings of the 11th Conference on Formal Grammar*, Malaga, Spain.

Nesson, R. and S. Shieber. 2007. Extraction phenomena in synchronous tag syntax and semantics. In *Proceedings of the Workshop on Syntax and Structure in Statistical Translation*, Rochester, New York.

Partee, B. and M. Rooth. 1983. Generalized conjunction and type ambiguity. In Bauerle, R., C. Schwarze, and A von Stechow, editors, *Meaning, use, and the interpretation of language*. Walter de Gruyter, Berlin.

Rambow, Owen and Giorgio Satta. 1996. Synchronous models of language. In *34th Meeting of the Association for Computational Linguistics (ACL'96)*, pages 116–123. ACL.

Rambow, Owen, K. Vijay-Shanker, and David Weir. 2001. D-Tree Substitution Grammars. *Computational Linguistics*, 27(1).

Rambow, Owen. 1994. Multiset-valued linear index grammars. In *32nd Meeting of the Association for Computational Linguistics (ACL'94)*, pages 263–270. ACL.

Sarkar, A. and A. Joshi. 1996. Handling coordination in a tree adjoining grammar. Technical report, Department of Computer and Information Science, University of Pennsylvania, Philadelphia.

Schein, B. 2002. Events and the semantic content of thematic relations. *Logical Form and Language*, page 263344.

Shieber, Stuart and Yves Schabes. 1990. Synchronous tree adjoining grammars. In *Proceedings of the 13th International Conference on Computational Linguistics*, Helsinki.

Shieber, Stuart B. 1994. Restricting the weak generative capacity of Synchronous Tree Adjoining Grammar. *Computational Intelligence*, 10(4):371–385.

Vijay-Shanker, K. 1992. Using descriptions of trees in a Tree Adjoining Grammar. *Computational Linguistics*, 18(4):481–518.

Winter, Y. 2002. Atoms and sets: A characterization of semantic number. *Linguistic Inquiry*, pages 493–505.

Feature Unification in TAG Derivation Trees

Sylvain Schmitz
LORIA, INRIA Nancy Grand Est, France
Sylvain.Schmitz@loria.fr

Joseph Le Roux
LORIA, Nancy Université, France
Joseph.Leroux@loria.fr

Abstract

The derivation trees of a tree adjoining grammar provide a first insight into the sentence semantics, and are thus prime targets for generation systems. We define a formalism, *feature-based regular tree grammars*, and a translation from feature based tree adjoining grammars into this new formalism. The translation preserves the derivation structures of the original grammar, and accounts for feature unification.

1 Introduction

Each sentence derivation in a tree adjoining grammar (Joshi and Schabes, 1997, TAG) results in two parse trees: a *derived tree* (Figure 1a), that represents the phrase structure of the sentence, and a *derivation tree* (Figure 1b), that records how the elementary trees of the grammar were combined. Each type of parse tree is better suited for a different set of language processing tasks: the derived tree is closely related to the lexical elements of the sentence, and the derivation tree offers a first insight into the sentence semantics (Candito and Kahane, 1998). Furthermore, the derivation tree language of a TAG, being a regular tree language, is much simpler to manipulate than the corresponding derived tree language.

Derivation trees are thus the cornerstone of several approaches to sentence generation (Koller and Striegnitz, 2002; Koller and Stone, 2007), that rely crucially on the ease of encoding regular tree grammars, as dependency grammars and planning problems respectively. Derivation trees also serve as intermediate representations from which both derived trees (and thus the linear order information) and semantics can be computed, e.g. with the abstract categorial grammars of de Groote (2002),

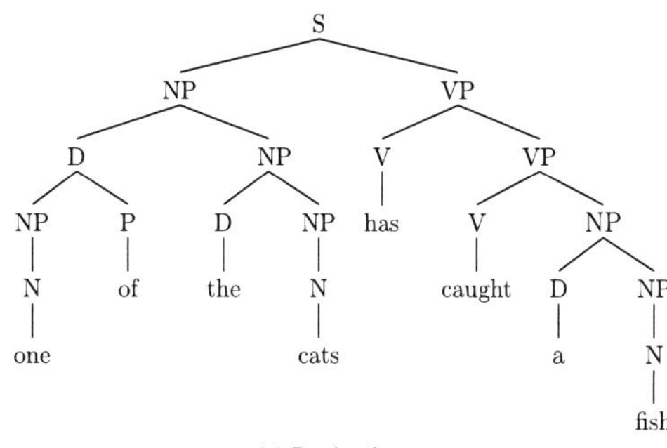

(a) Derived tree.

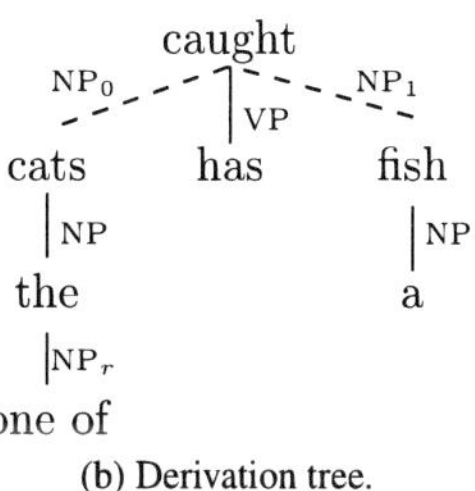

(b) Derivation tree.

Figure 1: Parse trees for "One of the cats has caught a fish." using the grammar of Figure 2.

Pogodalla (2004), and Kanazawa (2007), or similarly with the bimorphisms of Shieber (2006).

Nevertheless, these results do not directly apply to many real-world grammars, which are expressed in a feature-based variant of TAGs (Vijay-Shanker, 1992). Each elementary tree node of these grammars carries two feature structures that constrain the allowed substitution or adjunction operations at this node (see for instance Figure 2). In theory, such structures are unproblematic, because the possible feature values are drawn from finite domains, and thus the number of grammar categories could be increased in order to account for all the possible structures. In practice, the sheer number of structures precludes such a naive im-

Proceedings of The Ninth International Workshop on Tree Adjoining Grammars and Related Formalisms
Tübingen, Germany. June 6-8, 2008.

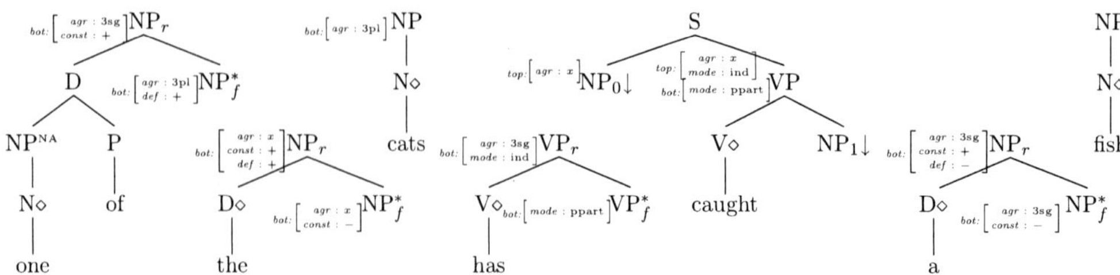

Figure 2: A feature-based tree adjoining grammar. For the sake of clarity, we identify elementary trees with their anchors in our examples.

plementation: for instance, the 50 features used in the XTAG English grammar (XTAG Research Group, 2001) together define a domain containing more than 10^{19} different structures. Furthermore, finiteness does not hold for some grammars, for instance with the semantic features of Gardent and Kallmeyer (2003).

Ignoring feature structures typically results in massive over-generation in derivation-centric systems. We define a formalism, *feature-based regular tree grammars*, that produces derivation trees that account for the feature structures found in a tree adjoining grammar. In more details,

- we recall how to generate the derivation trees of a tree adjoining grammar through a regular tree grammar (Section 2), then

- we define feature-based regular tree grammars and present the translation from feature-based TAG (Section 3); finally,

- we provide an improved translation inspired by left corner transformations (Section 4).

We assume the reader is familiar with the theory of tree-adjoining grammars (Joshi and Schabes, 1997), regular tree grammars (Comon et al., 2007), and feature unification (Robinson, 1965).

2 Regular Tree Grammars of Derivations

In this section, we define an encoding of the set of derivation trees of a tree adjoining grammar as the language of a regular tree grammar (RTG). Several encodings equivalent to regular tree grammars have been described in the literature; we follow here the one of de Groote (2002), but explicitly construct a regular tree grammar.

Formally, a tree adjoining grammar is a tuple $\langle \Sigma, N, I, A, S \rangle$ where Σ is a terminal alphabet, N

is a nonterminal alphabet, I is a set of initial trees α, A is a set of auxiliary trees β and S is a distinguished nonterminal from N. We note γ_r the root node of the elementary tree γ and β_f the foot node of the auxiliary tree β. Let us denote by $\gamma_1, \ldots, \gamma_n$ the *active* nodes of an elementary tree γ, where a substitution or an adjunction can be performed;[1] we call n the *rank* of γ, denoted by $\mathrm{rk}(\gamma)$. We set γ_1 to be the root node of γ, i.e. $\gamma_1 = \gamma_r$. Finally, $\mathrm{lab}(\gamma_i)$ denotes the label of node γ_i.

Each elementary tree γ of the TAG will be converted into a single rule $X \to \gamma(Y_1, \ldots, Y_n)$ of our RTG, such that $\mathrm{rk}(\gamma) = n$ and each of the Y_i symbols represents the possible adjunctions or substitutions of node γ_i. We introduce accordingly two duplicates $N_A = \{X_A \mid X \in N\}$ and $N_S = \{X_S \mid X \in N\}$ of N, and a nonterminal labeling function defined for any active node γ_i with label $\mathrm{lab}(\gamma_i) = X$ as

$$\mathrm{nt}(\gamma_i) = \begin{cases} X_A & \text{if } \gamma_i \text{ is an adjunction site} \\ X_S & \text{if } \gamma_i \text{ is a substitution site} \end{cases} \quad (1)$$

The rule corresponding to the tree "one of" in Figure 2 is then $NP_A \to \text{one of}(NP_A, D_A, P_A, N_A)$, meaning that this tree adjoins into an NP labeled node, and expects adjunctions on its nodes NP_r, D, P, and N. Given our set of elementary TAG trees, only the first one of these four will be useful in a reduced RTG.

Definition 1. The *regular derivation tree grammar* $G = \langle S_S, \mathcal{N}, \mathcal{F}, R \rangle$ of a TAG $\langle \Sigma, N, I, A, S \rangle$ is a RTG with axiom S_S, nonterminal alphabet $\mathcal{N} = N_S \cup N_A$, terminal alphabet $\mathcal{F} = I \cup A \cup$

---

[1] We consider in particular that no adjunction can occur at a foot node. We do not consider null adjunctions constraints on root nodes and feature structures on null adjoining nodes, which would rather obscure the presentation, and we do not treat other adjunction constraints either.

$\{\varepsilon_A\}$ with ranks $\mathrm{rk}(\gamma)$ for elementary trees γ in $I \cup A$ and rank 0 for ε_A, and with set of rules

$$R = \{X_S \to \alpha(\mathrm{nt}(\alpha_1), \dots, \mathrm{nt}(\alpha_n))$$
$$\mid \alpha \in I, n = \mathrm{rk}(\alpha), X = \mathrm{lab}(\alpha_r)\}$$
$$\cup \{X_A \to \beta(\mathrm{nt}(\beta_1), \dots, \mathrm{nt}(\beta_n))$$
$$\mid \beta \in A, n = \mathrm{rk}(\beta), X = \mathrm{lab}(\beta_r)\}$$
$$\cup \{X_A \to \varepsilon_A \mid X_A \in N_A\}$$

$\square$

The ε-rules $X_A \to \varepsilon_A$ for each symbol X_A account for adjunction sites where no adjunction takes place. The RTG has the same size as the original TAG and the translation can be computed in linear time.

Example 2. The reduced regular tree grammar corresponding to the tree adjoining grammar of Figure 2 is then:

$$\langle S_S, \{S_S, VP_S, VP_A, NP_S, NP_A\},$$
$$\{\text{one of}, \text{the}, \text{cats}, \text{has}, \text{caught}, \text{a}, \text{fish}, \varepsilon_A\},$$
$$\{ \ S_S \to \mathrm{caught}(NP_S, VP_A, NP_S),$$
$$NP_S \to \mathrm{cats}(NP_A),$$
$$NP_S \to \mathrm{fish}(NP_A),$$
$$NP_A \to \mathrm{the}(NP_A),$$
$$NP_A \to \mathrm{a}(NP_A),$$
$$NP_A \to \mathrm{one\ of}(NP_A),$$
$$NP_A \to \varepsilon_A,$$
$$VP_A \to \mathrm{has}(VP_A),$$
$$VP_A \to \varepsilon_A\}\rangle$$

$\square$

Let us recall that the derivation relation induced by a regular tree grammar $G = \langle S_S, \mathcal{N}, \mathcal{F}, R \rangle$ relates terms[2] of $T(\mathcal{F}, \mathcal{N})$, so that $t \Rightarrow t'$ holds iff there exists a context[3] C and a rule $A \to a(B_1, \dots, B_n)$ such that $t = C[A]$ and $t' = C[a(B_1, \dots, B_n)]$. The language of the RTG is $L(G) = \{t \in T(\mathcal{F}) \mid S_S \Rightarrow^* t\}$.

One can check that the grammar of Example 2 generates trees with a root labeled with "caught", and three subtrees, the leftmost and rightmost of which labeled with "cats" or "fish" followed by an arbitrary long combination of nodes labeled with "one of", "a" or "the". The central subtree is an

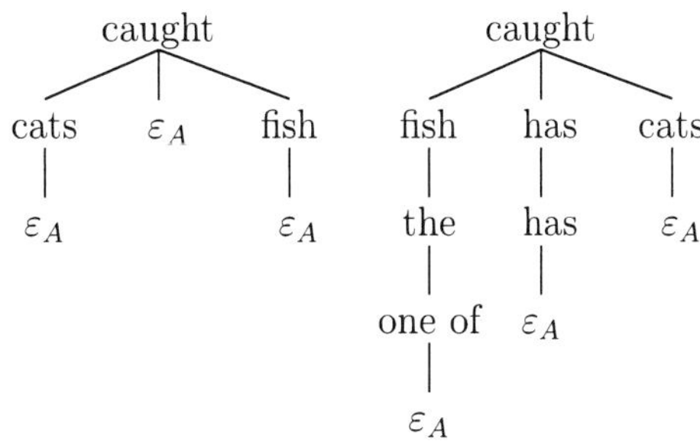

Figure 3: Some trees generated by the regular tree grammar of Example 2.

arbitrary long combination of nodes labeled with "has". Each branch terminates with ε_A. Two of these trees can be seen on Figure 3. Our RTG generates the derivation trees of a version of the original TAG expunged from its feature structures.

3 Unification on TAG Derivation Trees

3.1 Feature-based Regular Tree Grammars

In order to extend the previous construction to feature-based TAGs, our RTGs use combinations of rewrites and unifications—also dubbed *narrowings* (Hanus, 1994)—of terms with variables in $\mathcal{N} \times \mathcal{D}$, where $\mathcal{N}$ denotes the nonterminal alphabet and $\mathcal{D}$ the set of feature structures.[4]

Definition 3. A *feature-based regular tree grammar* $\langle S, \mathcal{N}, \mathcal{F}, \mathcal{D}, R \rangle$ comprises an axiom S, a set $\mathcal{N}$ of nonterminal symbols that includes S, a ranked terminal alphabet $\mathcal{F}$, a set $\mathcal{D}$ of feature structures, and a set R of rules of form $(A, d) \to a((B_1, d'_1), \dots, (B_n, d'_n))$, where $A, B_1, \dots, B_n$ are nonterminals, $d, d'_1, \dots, d'_n$ are feature structures, and a is a terminal with rank n.

The *derivation* relation $\Rightarrow$ for a feature-based RTG $G = \langle S, \mathcal{N}, \mathcal{F}, \mathcal{D}, R \rangle$ relates pairs of terms from $T(\mathcal{F}, \mathcal{N} \times \mathcal{D})$ and u-substitutions, such that $(s, e) \Rightarrow (t, e')$ iff there exist a context C, a rule $(A, d) \to a((B_1, d'_1), \dots, (B_n, d'_n))$ in R with fresh variables in the feature structures, a structure

---

[2] The set of *terms* over the alphabet $\mathcal{F}$ and the set of variables $\mathcal{X}$ is denoted by $T(\mathcal{F}, \mathcal{X})$; $T(\mathcal{F}, \emptyset) = T(\mathcal{F})$ is the set of trees over $\mathcal{F}$.

[3] A *context* C is a term of $T(\mathcal{F}, \mathcal{X} \cup \{x\})$, $x \notin \mathcal{X}$, which contains a single occurrence of x. The term $C[t]$ for some term t of $T(\mathcal{F}, \mathcal{X})$ is obtained by replacing this occurrence by t.

[4] In order to differentiate TAG tree substitutions from term substitutions, we call the latter *u-substitutions*. Given two feature structures d and d' in $\mathcal{D}$, we denote by the u-substitution $\sigma = \mathrm{mgu}(d, d')$ their *most general unifier* if it exists. We denote by $\top$ the most general element of $\mathcal{D}$, and by *id* the identity.

d', and an u-substitution σ verifying

$$s = C[(A, d')], \quad \sigma = \mathsf{mgu}(d, e(d')), \quad e' = \sigma \circ e$$
$$\text{and } t = C[a((B_1, \sigma(d_1')), \dots, (B_n, \sigma(d_n')))].$$

The *language* of G is

$$L(G) = \{t \in T(\mathcal{F}) \mid \exists e, ((S, \top), id) \Rightarrow^* (t, e)\}.$$

$\square$

Features percolate hierarchically through the computation of the most general unifier mgu at each derivation step, while the global u-substitution e acts as an environment that communicates unification results between the branches of our terms.

Feature-based RTGs with a finite domain $\mathcal{D}$ are equivalent to regular tree grammars. Unrestricted feature-based RTGs can encode Turing machines just like unification grammars (Johnson, 1988), and thus we can reduce the halting problem on the empty input for Turing machines to the emptiness problem for feature-based RTGs, which is thereby undecidable.

3.2 Encoding Feature-based TAGs

For each tree γ with rank n, we now create a rule $P \to \gamma(P_1, \dots, P_n)$. A right-hand side pair $P_i = (\mathsf{nt}(\gamma_i), d_i')$ stands for an active node γ_i with feature structure $d_i' = \mathsf{feats}(\gamma_i) = \left[\begin{smallmatrix} top\,:\,top(\gamma_i) \\ bot\,:\,bot(\gamma_i) \end{smallmatrix}\right]$, where $top(\gamma_i)$ and $bot(\gamma_i)$ denote respectively the top and bottom feature structures of γ_i.

The left-hand side pair $P = (A, d)$ carries the *interface* $d = \mathsf{in}(\gamma)$ of γ with the rest of the grammar, such that d percolates the root *top* feature, and the foot *bot* feature for auxiliary trees. Formally, for each initial tree α in I and auxiliary tree β in A, using a fresh variable t, we define

$$\mathsf{in}(\alpha) = \begin{bmatrix} top\,:\,t \\ top\,:\,top(\alpha_r) \end{bmatrix} \tag{2}$$

$$\mathsf{in}(\beta) = \begin{bmatrix} top\,:\,t \\ top\,:\,top(\beta_r) \\ bot\,:\,bot(\beta_f) \end{bmatrix} \tag{3}$$

The interface thus uses the top features of the root node of an elementary tree, and we have to implement the fact that this top structure is the same as the top structure of the variable that embodies the root node in the rule right-hand side. With the same variable t, we define accordingly:

$$\mathsf{feat}(\gamma_i) = \begin{cases} \begin{bmatrix} top\,:\,t \\ bot\,:\,bot(\gamma_r) \end{bmatrix} & \text{if } \gamma_i = \gamma_r \\[2ex] \begin{bmatrix} top\,:\,top(\gamma_i) \\ bot\,:\,bot(\gamma_i) \end{bmatrix} & \text{otherwise} \end{cases} \tag{4}$$

Finally, we add ε-rules $(X_A, \left[\begin{smallmatrix} top\,:\,v \\ bot\,:\,v \end{smallmatrix}\right]) \to \varepsilon_A$ for each symbol X_A in order to account for adjunction sites where no adjunction takes place. Let us denote by $\mathsf{tr}(\gamma_i)$ the pair $(\mathsf{nt}(\gamma_i), \mathsf{feats}(\gamma_i))$.

Definition 4. The feature-based RTG $G = \langle S_S, N_S \cup N_A, \mathcal{F}, \mathcal{D}, R \rangle$ of a TAG $\langle \Sigma, N, I, A, S \rangle$ with feature structures in $\mathcal{D}$ has terminal alphabet $\mathcal{F} = I \cup A \cup \{\varepsilon_A\}$ with respective ranks $\mathsf{rk}(\alpha)$, $\mathsf{rk}(\beta)$, and 0, and set of rules

$$R = \{(X_S, \mathsf{in}(\alpha)) \to \alpha(\mathsf{tr}(\alpha_1), \dots, \mathsf{tr}(\alpha_n))$$
$$\mid \alpha \in I, n = \mathsf{rk}(\alpha), X = \mathsf{lab}(\alpha_r)\}$$
$$\cup \{(X_A, \mathsf{in}(\beta)) \to \beta(\mathsf{tr}(\beta_1), \dots, \mathsf{tr}(\beta_n))$$
$$\mid \beta \in A, n = \mathsf{rk}(\beta), X = \mathsf{lab}(\beta_r)\}$$
$$\cup \{X_A \left[\begin{smallmatrix} top\,:\,t \\ bot\,:\,t \end{smallmatrix}\right] \to \varepsilon_A \mid X_A \in N_A\}$$

$\square$

Example 5. With the grammar of Figure 2, we obtain the following ruleset:

$$S_S\top \to \text{caught}$$
$$\left(NP_S \left[\begin{smallmatrix} top\,:\,[\,agr\,:\,x\,] \end{smallmatrix}\right], VP_A \left[\begin{smallmatrix} top\,:\,\left[\begin{smallmatrix} agr\,:\,x \\ mode\,:\,ind \end{smallmatrix}\right] \\ bot\,:\,[\,mode\,:\,ppart\,] \end{smallmatrix}\right], NP_S\top \right)$$
$$NP_S \left[\begin{smallmatrix} top\,:\,t \end{smallmatrix}\right] \to \text{cats}\left(NP_A \left[\begin{smallmatrix} top\,:\,t \\ bot\,:\,[\,agr\,:\,3pl\,] \end{smallmatrix}\right]\right)$$
$$NP_S \left[\begin{smallmatrix} top\,:\,t \end{smallmatrix}\right] \to \text{fish}(NP_A \left[\begin{smallmatrix} top\,:\,t \end{smallmatrix}\right])$$
$$NP_A \left[\begin{smallmatrix} top\,:\,t \\ bot\,:\,\left[\begin{smallmatrix} agr\,:\,x \\ const\,:\,- \end{smallmatrix}\right] \end{smallmatrix}\right] \to \text{the}\left(NP_A \left[\begin{smallmatrix} top\,:\,t \\ bot\,:\,\left[\begin{smallmatrix} agr\,:\,x \\ const\,:\,+ \\ def\,:\,+ \end{smallmatrix}\right] \end{smallmatrix}\right]\right)$$
$$NP_A \left[\begin{smallmatrix} top\,:\,t \\ bot\,:\,\left[\begin{smallmatrix} agr\,:\,3sg \\ const\,:\,- \end{smallmatrix}\right] \end{smallmatrix}\right] \to \text{a}\left(NP_A \left[\begin{smallmatrix} top\,:\,t \\ bot\,:\,\left[\begin{smallmatrix} agr\,:\,3sg \\ const\,:\,+ \\ def\,:\,- \end{smallmatrix}\right] \end{smallmatrix}\right]\right)$$
$$NP_A \left[\begin{smallmatrix} top\,:\,t \\ bot\,:\,\left[\begin{smallmatrix} agr\,:\,3pl \\ def\,:\,+ \end{smallmatrix}\right] \end{smallmatrix}\right] \to \text{one of}\left(NP_A \left[\begin{smallmatrix} top\,:\,t \\ bot\,:\,\left[\begin{smallmatrix} agr\,:\,3sg \\ const\,:\,+ \end{smallmatrix}\right] \end{smallmatrix}\right]\right)$$
$$NP_A \left[\begin{smallmatrix} top\,:\,v \\ bot\,:\,v \end{smallmatrix}\right] \to \varepsilon_A$$
$$VP_A \left[\begin{smallmatrix} top\,:\,t \\ bot\,:\,[\,mode\,:\,ppart\,] \end{smallmatrix}\right] \to \text{has}\left(VP_A \left[\begin{smallmatrix} top\,:\,t \\ bot\,:\,\left[\begin{smallmatrix} agr\,:\,3sg \\ mode\,:\,ind \end{smallmatrix}\right] \end{smallmatrix}\right]\right)$$
$$VP_A \left[\begin{smallmatrix} top\,:\,v \\ bot\,:\,v \end{smallmatrix}\right] \to \varepsilon_A$$

$\square$

With the grammar of Example 5, one can generate the derivation tree for "One of the cats has caught a fish." This derivation is presented in Figure 4. Each node of the tree consists of a label and of a pair (t, e) where t is a term from $T(\mathcal{F}, \mathcal{N} \times \mathcal{D})$ and e is an environment.[5] In order to obtain fresh variables, we rename variables from the RTG: we reuse the name of the variable in the grammar, prefixed by the Gorn address of the node where the rewrite step takes place. Labels indicate the chronological order of the narrowings in the derivation.

Labels in Figure 4 suggest that this derivation has been computed with a left to right strategy. Of course, other strategies would have led to the same

---

[5]Actually, we only write the change in the environment at each point of the derivation.

result. The important thing to notice here is that the crux of the derivation lies in the fifth rewrite step, where the agreement between the subject and the verb is realized. Substitutions sites are completely defined when all adjunctions in the subtree have been performed. In the next section we propose a different translation that overcomes this drawback.

4 Left Corner Transformation

Derivations in the previous feature-based RTG are not very predictive: the substitution of "cats" into "caught" in the derivation of Figure 1b does not constrain the agreement feature of "caught". This feature is only set at the final ε-rewrite step after the adjunction of "one of", when the top and bottom features are unified. More generally, given a substitution site, we cannot *a priori* rule out the substitution of most initial trees, because their root does usually not carry a top feature.

A solution to this issue is to compute the derivations in a transformed grammar, where we start with the ε-rewrite, apply the root adjunctions in reverse order, and end with the initial tree substitution. Since our encoding sets the root adjunct as the leftmost child, this amounts to a selective left corner transformation (Rosenkrantz and Lewis II, 1970) of our RTG—an arguably simpler intuition than what we could write for the corresponding transformation on derived trees.

4.1 Transformed Regular Tree Grammars

The transformation involves regular tree grammar rules of form $X_S \to \alpha(X_A, ...)$ for substitutions, and $X_A \to \beta(X_A, ...)$ and $X_A \to \varepsilon_A$ for root adjunctions. After a reversal of the recursion of root adjunctions, we will first apply the ε rewrite using a rule $X_S \to \varepsilon_S(X)$ with rank 1 for ε_S, followed by the root adjunctions $X \to \beta(X, ...)$, and finally the substitution itself $X \to \alpha(...)$, with a decremented rank for initial trees.

Example 6. On the grammar of Figure 2, we obtain the rules:

$$
\begin{aligned}
S_S &\to \text{caught}(NP_S, VP_A, NP_S) \\
NP_S &\to \varepsilon_S(NP) \\
NP &\to \text{cats} \\
NP &\to \text{fish} \\
NP &\to \text{the}(NP) \\
NP &\to \text{one of}(NP) \\
VP_A &\to \text{has}(\mathbf{VP}_A) \\
VP_A &\to \varepsilon_A
\end{aligned}
$$

$\square$

Adjunctions that do not occur on the root of an initial tree, like the adjunction of "has" in our example, keep their original translation using $X_A \to \beta(X_A, ...)$ and $X_A \to \varepsilon_A$ rules. We use the nonterminal symbols X of the grammar for root adjunctions and initial trees, and we retain X_S for the initial ε_S rewrite on substitution nodes.

Definition 7. The *left-corner transformed* RTG $G_{\text{lc}} = \langle S_S, N \cup N_S \cup N_A, \mathcal{F}_{\text{lc}}, R_{\text{lc}} \rangle$ of a TAG $\langle \Sigma, N, I, A, S \rangle$ has terminal alphabet $\mathcal{F}_{\text{lc}} = I \cup A \cup \{\varepsilon_A, \varepsilon_S\}$ with respective ranks $\text{rk}(\alpha) - 1$, $\text{rk}(\beta)$, 0, and 1, and set of rules

$$
\begin{aligned}
R_{\text{lc}} = \ & \{X_S \to \varepsilon_S(X) \mid X_S \in N_S\} \\
\cup \ & \{X \to \alpha(\text{nt}(\alpha_2), \ldots, \text{nt}(\alpha_n)) \\
& \quad \mid \alpha \in I, n = \text{rk}(\alpha), X = \text{lab}(\alpha_r)\} \\
\cup \ & \{X \to \beta(X, \text{nt}(\beta_2) \ldots, \text{nt}(\beta_n)) \\
& \quad \mid \beta \in A, n = \text{rk}(\beta), X = \text{lab}(\beta_r)\} \\
\cup \ & \{X_A \to \beta(\text{nt}(\beta_1), \ldots, \text{nt}(\beta_n)) \\
& \quad \mid \beta \in A, n = \text{rk}(\beta), X = \text{lab}(\beta_r)\} \\
\cup \ & \{X_A \to \varepsilon_A \mid X_A \in N_A\}
\end{aligned}
$$

$\square$

Due to the duplicated rules for auxiliary trees, the size of the left-corner transformed RTG of a TAG is doubled at worst. In practice, the reduced grammar witnesses a reasonable growth (10% on the French TAG grammar of Gardent (2006)).

The transformation is easily reversed. We define accordingly the function lc^{-1} from $T(\mathcal{F}_{\text{lc}})$ to $T(\mathcal{F})$:

$$
\text{lc}^{-1}(\varepsilon_S(t)) = \text{s}(t, \varepsilon_A)
$$
$$
\begin{aligned}
\text{s}(\beta(t_1, t_2, ..., t_n), t) \\
&= \text{s}(t_1, \beta(t, f_{\beta_2}(t_2), ..., f_{\beta_n}(t_n))) \\
\text{s}(\alpha(t_1, ..., t_n), t) &= \alpha(t, f_{\alpha_2}(t_1), ..., f_{\alpha_{n+1}}(t_n)) \\
\text{a}(\gamma(t_1, ..., t_n)) &= \gamma(f_{\gamma_1}(t_1), ..., f_{\gamma_n}(t_n))
\end{aligned}
$$
$$
f_{\gamma_i}(t) = \begin{cases} \text{a}(t) & \gamma_i \text{ adjunction site} \\ \text{lc}^{-1}(t) & \gamma_i \text{ substitution site} \end{cases}
$$

We can therefore generate a derivation tree in $L(G_{\text{lc}})$ and recover the derivation tree in $L(G)$ through lc^{-1}.

4.2 Features in the Transformed Grammar

Example 8. Applying the same transformation on the feature-based regular tree grammar, we obtain the following rules for the grammar of Figure 2:

$$
S_S \to \text{caught}
$$
$$
\left(NP_S \left[top : [\, agr : x\,] \right], VP_A \left[\begin{matrix} top : \left[\begin{matrix} agr : x \\ mode : \text{ind} \end{matrix} \right] \\ bot : [\, mode : \text{ppart}\,] \end{matrix} \right], NP_S \right)
$$

$$NP_S\left[top:t\right] \to \varepsilon_S\left(NP\left[\begin{smallmatrix}top:t\\bot:t\end{smallmatrix}\right]\right)$$

$$NP\left[bot:[agr:3\text{pl}]\right] \to \text{cats}$$

$$NP\top \to \text{fish}$$

$$NP\begin{bmatrix}top:t\\bot:\begin{bmatrix}agr:x\\const:+\\def:+\end{bmatrix}\end{bmatrix} \to \text{the}\left(NP\begin{bmatrix}top:t\\bot:\begin{bmatrix}agr:x\\const:-\end{bmatrix}\end{bmatrix}\right)$$

$$NP\begin{bmatrix}top:t\\bot:\begin{bmatrix}agr:3\text{sg}\\const:+\\def:-\end{bmatrix}\end{bmatrix} \to \text{a}\left(NP\begin{bmatrix}top:t\\bot:\begin{bmatrix}agr:3\text{sg}\\const:-\end{bmatrix}\end{bmatrix}\right)$$

$$NP\begin{bmatrix}top:t\\bot:\begin{bmatrix}agr:3\text{sg}\\const:+\end{bmatrix}\end{bmatrix} \to \text{one of}\left(NP\begin{bmatrix}top:t\\bot:\begin{bmatrix}agr:3\text{pl}\\def:+\end{bmatrix}\end{bmatrix}\right)$$

$$VP_A\begin{bmatrix}top:t\\bot:[mode:\text{ppart}]\end{bmatrix} \to \text{has}\left(VP_A\begin{bmatrix}top:t\\bot:\begin{bmatrix}agr:3\text{sg}\\mode:\text{ind}\end{bmatrix}\end{bmatrix}\right)$$

$$VP_A\left[\begin{smallmatrix}top:v\\bot:v\end{smallmatrix}\right] \to \varepsilon_A$$

$$\square$$

Since we reversed the recursion of root adjunctions, the feature structures on the left-hand side and on the root node of the right-hand side of auxiliary rules are swapped in their transformed counterparts (e.g. in the rule for "one of").

This version of a RTG for our example grammar is arguably much easier to read than the one described in Example 5: a derivation has to go through "one of" and "the" before adding "cats" as subject of "caught".

The formal translation of a TAG into a transformed feature-based RTG requires the following variant tr_lc of the tr function: for any auxiliary tree β in A and any node γ_i of an elementary tree γ in $I \cup A$, and with t a fresh variable of $\mathcal{D}$:

$$\text{in}_\text{lc}(\beta) = \begin{bmatrix}top:t\\bot:\text{bot}(\beta_f)\end{bmatrix} \tag{5}$$

$$\text{feats}_\text{lc}(\gamma_i) = \begin{cases}\begin{bmatrix}top:t\\top:\text{top}(\gamma_r)\\bot:\text{bot}(\gamma_r)\end{bmatrix} & \text{if } \gamma_i = \gamma_r\\ \text{feats}(\gamma_i) & \text{otherwise}\end{cases} \tag{6}$$

$$\text{tr}_\text{lc}(\gamma_i) = (\text{nt}(\gamma_i), \text{feats}_\text{lc}(\gamma_i)) \tag{7}$$

Definition 9. The *left-corner transformed* feature-based RTG $G_\text{lc} = \langle S_S, N \cup N_S \cup N_A, \mathcal{F}_\text{lc}, \mathcal{D}, R_\text{lc}\rangle$ of a TAG $\langle \Sigma, N, I, A, S\rangle$ with feature structures in $\mathcal{D}$ has terminal alphabet $\mathcal{F}_\text{lc} = I \cup A \cup \{\varepsilon_A, \varepsilon_S\}$ with respective ranks $\text{rk}(\alpha) - 1$, $\text{rk}(\beta)$, 0, and 1, and set of rules

$$R_\text{lc} = \{X_S\left[top:t\right] \to \varepsilon_S(X\left[\begin{smallmatrix}top:t\\bot:t\end{smallmatrix}\right]) \mid X_S \in N_S\}$$
$$\cup\{(X, \text{feats}(\alpha_1)) \to$$
$$\alpha(\text{tr}_\text{lc}(\alpha_2), \ldots, \text{tr}_\text{lc}(\alpha_n))$$
$$\mid \alpha \in I, n = \text{rk}(\alpha), X = \text{lab}(\alpha_r)\}$$

$$\cup\{(X, \text{feats}_\text{lc}(\beta_1)) \to$$
$$\beta((X, \text{in}_\text{lc}(\beta)), \text{tr}_\text{lc}(\beta_2), \ldots, \text{tr}_\text{lc}(\beta_n))$$
$$\mid \beta \in A, n = \text{rk}(\beta), X = \text{lab}(\beta_r)\}$$

$$\cup\{(X_A, \text{in}(\beta)) \to$$
$$\beta(\text{tr}(\beta_1), \text{tr}_\text{lc}(\beta_2), \ldots, \text{tr}_\text{lc}(\beta_n))$$
$$\mid \beta \in A, n = \text{rk}(\beta), X = \text{lab}(\beta_r)\}$$
$$\cup\{X_A\left[\begin{smallmatrix}top:t\\bot:t\end{smallmatrix}\right] \to \varepsilon_A \mid X_A \in N_A\}$$

$$\square$$

Again, the translation can be computed in linear time, and results in a grammar with at worst twice the size of the original TAG.

5 Conclusion

We have introduced in this paper feature-based regular tree grammars as an adequate representation for the derivation language of large coverage TAG grammars. Unlike the restricted unification computations on the derivation tree considered before by Kallmeyer and Romero (2004), feature-based RTGs accurately translate the full range of unification mechanisms employed in TAGs. Moreover, left-corner transformed grammars make derivations more predictable, thus avoiding some backtracking in top-down generation.

Among the potential applications of our results, let us further mention more accurate reachability computations between elementary trees, needed for instance in order to check whether a TAG complies with the tree insertion grammar (Schabes and Waters, 1995, TIG) or regular form (Rogers, 1994, RFTAG) conditions. In fact, among the formal checks one might wish to perform on grammars, many rely on the availability of reachability relations.

Let us finally note that we could consider the string language of a TAG encoded as a feature-based RTG—in a parser for instance—, if we extended the model with topological information, in the line of Kuhlmann (2007).

References

Candito, Marie-Hélène and Sylvain Kahane. 1998. Can the TAG derivation tree represent a semantic graph? An answer in the light of Meaning-Text Theory. In *TAG+4*, pages 25–28.

Comon, Hubert, Max Dauchet, Rémi Gilleron, Christof Löding, Florent Jacquemard, Denis Lugiez, Sophie Tison, and Marc Tommasi. 2007. *Tree Automata Techniques and Applications*.

de Groote, Philippe. 2002. Tree-adjoining grammars as abstract categorial grammars. In Frank, Robert, editor, *TAG+6*, pages 145–150.

Engelfriet, Joost and Heiko Vogler. 1985. Macro tree transducers. *Journal of Computer and System Sciences*, 31(1):71–146.

Gardent, Claire and Laura Kallmeyer. 2003. Semantic construction in feature-based TAG. In *EACL'03*, pages 123–130. ACL Press.

Gardent, Claire. 2006. Intégration d'une dimension sémantique dans les grammaires d'arbres adjoints. In Mertens, Piet, Cédrick Fairon, Anne Dister, and Patrick Watrin, editors, *TALN'06*, pages 149–158. Presses universitaires de Louvain.

Hanus, Michael. 1994. The integration of functions into logic programming: From theory to practice. *Journal of Logic Programming*, 19–20:583–628.

Johnson, Mark. 1988. *Attribute-Value Logic and the Theory of Grammar*, volume 16 of *CSLI Lecture Notes Series*. University of Chicago Press.

Joshi, Aravind K. and Yves Schabes. 1997. Tree-adjoining grammars. In Rozenberg, Grzegorz and Arto Salomaa, editors, *Handbook of Formal Languages*, volume 3: Beyond Words, chapter 2, pages 69–124. Springer.

Kallmeyer, Laura and Maribel Romero. 2004. LTAG semantics with semantic unification. In Rambow, Owen and Matthew Stone, editors, *TAG+7*, pages 155–162.

Kanazawa, Makoto. 2007. Parsing and generation as Datalog queries. In *ACL'07*, pages 176–183. ACL Press.

Koller, Alexander and Matthew Stone. 2007. Sentence generation as a planning problem. In *ACL'07*, pages 336–343. ACL Press.

Koller, Alexander and Kristina Striegnitz. 2002. Generation as dependency parsing. In *ACL'02*, pages 17–24. ACL Press.

Kuhlmann, Marco. 2007. *Dependency Structures and Lexicalized Grammars*. Doctoral dissertation, Saarland University, Saarbrücken, Germany.

Pogodalla, Sylvain. 2004. Computing semantic representation: Towards ACG abstract terms as derivation trees. In Rambow, Owen and Matthew Stone, editors, *TAG+7*, pages 64–71.

Robinson, J. Alan. 1965. A machine-oriented logic based on the resolution principle. *Journal of the ACM*, 12(1):23–41.

Rogers, James. 1994. Capturing CFLs with tree adjoining grammars. In *ACL'94*, pages 155–162. ACL Press.

Rosenkrantz, Daniel J. and Philip M. Lewis II. 1970. Deterministic left corner parsing. In *11th Annual Symposium on Switching and Automata Theory*, pages 139–152. IEEE Computer Society.

Schabes, Yves and Richard C. Waters. 1995. Tree insertion grammar: a cubic-time parsable formalism that lexicalizes context-free grammar without changing the trees produced. *Computational Linguistics*, 21(4):479–513.

Shieber, Stuart M. 2006. Unifying synchronous tree-adjoining grammars and tree transducers via bimorphisms. In *EACL'06*. ACL Press.

Vijay-Shanker, K. 1992. Using descriptions of trees in a tree adjoining grammar. *Computational Linguistics*, 18(4):481–517.

XTAG Research Group. 2001. A lexicalized tree adjoining grammar for English. Technical Report IRCS-01-03, IRCS, University of Pennsylvania.

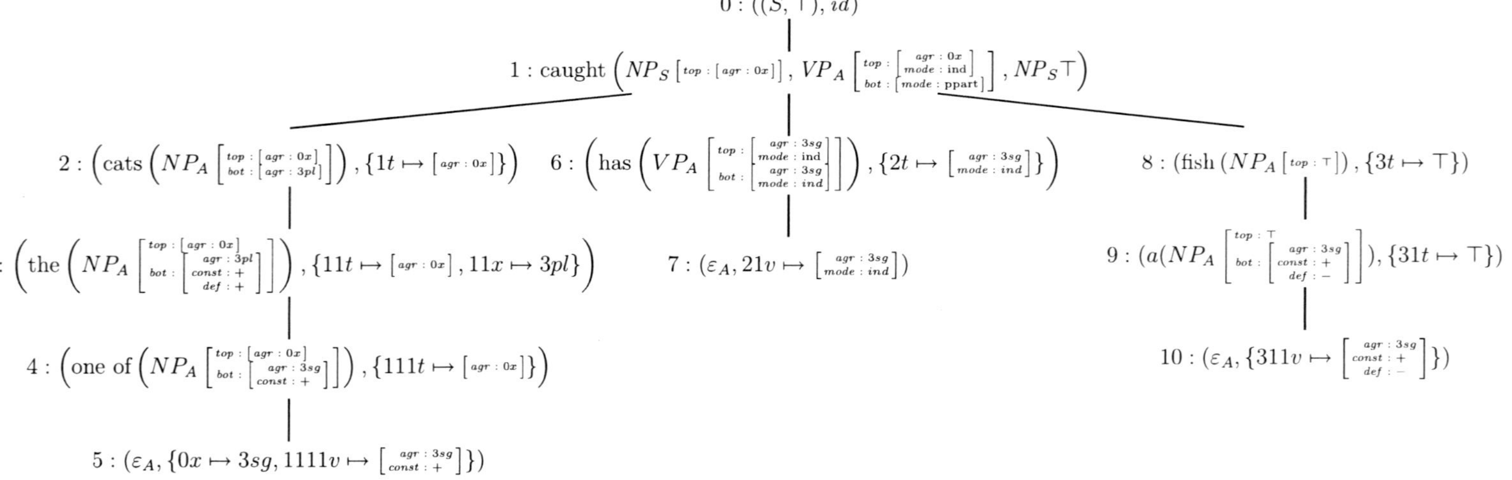

Figure 4: A rewrite sequence in the feature-based RTG for the sentence "One of the cats has caught a fish."

Reflexivity in English: an STAG analysis

Dennis R. Storoshenko
Department of Linguistics
Simon Fraser University
dstorosh@sfu.ca

Chung-hye Han
Department of Linguistics
Simon Fraser University
chunghye@sfu.ca

David Potter
Department of Linguistics
Simon Fraser University
dkp1@sfu.ca

Abstract

In this paper, we present an STAG analysis of English reflexives. In the spirit of Ryant and Scheffler (2006) and Kallmeyer and Romero (2007), reflexives are represented as a multi-component set in the syntax, with a degenerate auxiliary tree controlling the ϕ feature agreement between a reflexive and its antecedent. On the semantics side, the reflexive is a valence-reducing λ-expression, identifying two arguments of a single predicate. We then demonstrate that with minimal modifications, our analysis can be extended to capture raising and ECM cases. Finally, we argue that Condition A of Chomsky's binding theory can be derived as a consequence of our treatment of reflexives.

1 Introduction

Synchronous Tree Adjoining Grammar (STAG) provides an isomorphic mapping of derivations between a pair of TAG grammars. This mapping can be exploited to map a source syntactic derivation to an isomorphic semantic derivation, which derives a semantic representation for a sentence by combining semantic elementary trees (Shieber, 1994). As a result, STAG is a useful tool for analyzing natural language phenomena at the syntax/semantics interface (Han and Hedberg, 2006; Nesson and Shieber, 2006; Han, 2007; Nesson and Shieber, 2007). We extend that research by presenting an STAG analysis for reflexive pronouns in English, augmented with syntactic feature unification as defined in Vijay-Shanker and Joshi (1988). For the semantic elementary trees, we follow Han

(2007) in using unreduced λ-expressions. This allows λ-conversion to apply in the semantic derived tree, producing the final logical form. Our approach uses three different forms of the reflexive, T′-form, V′-form and TP-form, each represented as a multi-component set in syntax, following Ryant and Scheffler (2006) and Kallmeyer and Romero (2007), and as a reflexive function in semantics. With this, we capture all the core verbal argument cases of reflexive use. We further show how only one of the three forms is acceptable in a given sentence and how Condition A of Chomsky's (1981) binding theory can be derived as a consequence of our analysis.

While we adopt the same basic syntax as Ryant and Scheffler and Kallmeyer and Romero, semantically our approaches are quite different. The previous approaches employ semantic feature unification in the derivation structure (Kallmeyer and Romero, 2008), with composition taking place in a flat, conjunction-based semantics. Our approach uses λ-calculus on the semantic derived tree, which is constructed using the derivation structure on the semantics side that is isomorphic to the derivation structure on the syntax side. Through this, we are more readily able to capture the insights of Reinhart and Reuland (1993), representing our reflexive as a function upon predicates, rather than a relationship between two nominals, the reflexive and its antecedent. As a consequence of this, we make use of different forms of the reflexive depending upon where it appears in a predicate's argument structure. By choosing this approach in which the reflexive works upon a predicate, we are able to capture instances of reflexives occurring in both mono- and multi-clausal environments within the lexical entry of the reflexive itself.

In section 2, we present our analysis of reflexive binding in mono-clauses. We then extend our analysis to reflexive binding in raising sentences in section 3 and then to instances of exceptional case marking (ECM) sentences in section 4.

2 Mono-clausal Reflexives

In the simplest cases, a reflexive appears in the same clause as its antecedent.

(1) Jim_4 introduces $himself_4$ to $Bill_5$.

(2) Jim_4 introduces $Bill_5$ to $himself_5$.

(3) Jim_4 introduces $Bill_5$ to $himself_4$.

Elementary trees for (1) are in Figure 1. In (αintroduces), each DP argument substitution site is specified with an unvalued ϕ feature, which will unify with a ϕ feature from the substituted DP. We adopt the feature structures proposed in Vijay-Shanker and Joshi (1988) and the conception of feature unification defined therein. Each node has a Top feature (notated as t :), and a Bottom feature (notated as b :). At the end of a derivation, the Top and Bottom features at each node must unify; incompatible feature values will cause a derivation to crash. In (αintroduces), the ϕ features from the DP subject and the DP direct object are passed over as Top features on the sister bar-level node, and Bottom features on the next highest maximal projection. When adjoining takes place, the Top features of the adjoining site must unify with the Top features of the adjoining auxiliary tree's root node, and the Bottom features of the adjoining site unify with the auxiliary tree's foot node Bottom features. (αintroduces) is paired with a semantic elementary tree (α'introduces). In the semantic tree, F stands for formula, R for relation and T for term. We will assume that T can host reflexive functions as well as argument variables and constants. Boxed numerals indicate links between the syntactic and semantic elementary tree pairs; if an operation is carried out at one such node on the syntax side, a corresponding operation is carried out at the linked node(s) in the semantics. For simplicity, we only indicate links which are required in the derivation of the example sentences.

The reflexive employed for (1) is a T'-form, identified as $himself_{T'}$. In the syntactic multi-component set, (αhimself$_{T'}$) bears a ϕ feature

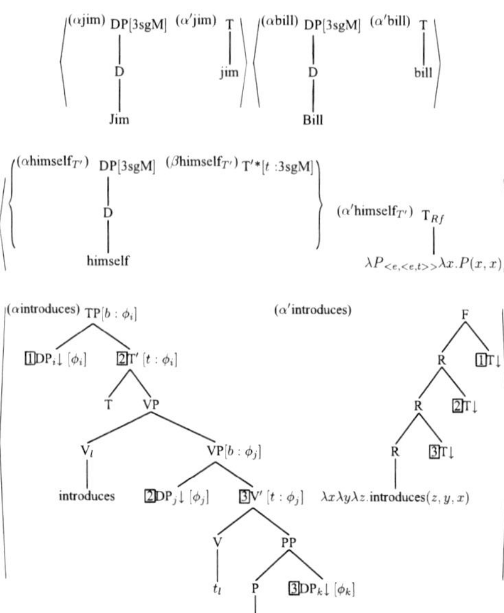

Figure 1: Elementary trees for Jim_4 *introduces* $himself_4$ *to* $Bill_5$

and will substitute into DP_j in (αintroduces), and (βhimself$_{T'}$) is a degenerate T' auxiliary tree, specified with a Top ϕ feature. As in Kallmeyer and Romero (2007), our (βhimself$_{T'}$) ensures the agreement between the reflexive and its antecedent, the subject DP in [Spec,TP], by adjoining at T' in (αintroduces). The Top ϕ feature of (βhimself$_{T'}$) must unify with the Top ϕ feature of T', which in turn must agree with the Bottom ϕ feature of TP and the ϕ feature of the subject DP in (αintroduces) through coindexation. Crucially, this is the only syntactic constraint at work. In the semantics, (α'himself$_{T'}$) introduces a function of type $<<e,<e,t>>, <e,t>>$. This function is labelled as T_{Rf} (Rf for reflexive), and substitutes into the T node labeled with link $\boxed{2}$ in (α'introduces). After λ-conversion, this function returns an $<e,t>$ type predicate where the argument variable corresponding to *himself* and an argument variable corresponding to the antecedent are identified. The isomorphic syntactic and semantic derivation structures are given in Figure 2, and the syntactic and semantic derived trees in Figure 3.

Virtually the same set of trees will derive (2). The only difference is that the form of the reflexive employed here is the V'-type, as defined in

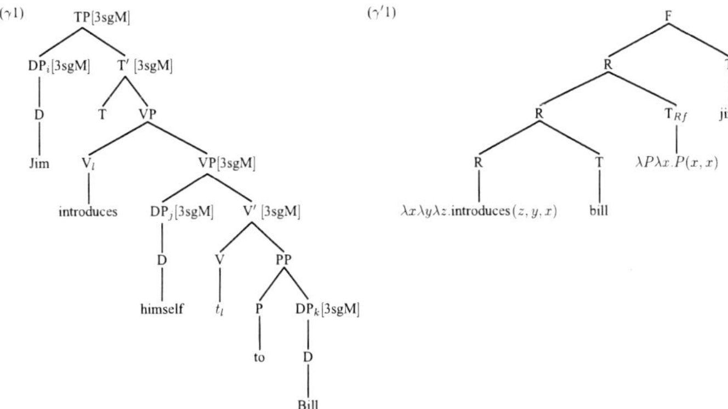

Figure 3: Derived trees for *Jim₄ introduces himself₄ to Bill₅*

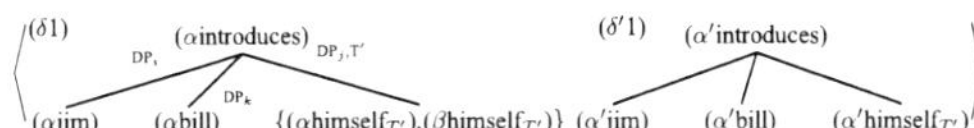

Figure 2: Derivation structures for *Jim₄ introduces himself₄ to Bill₅*

Figure 4. The $(\beta\text{himself}_{V'})$ adjoins at the V′ node in $(\alpha\text{introduces})$ in Figure 1, ensuring the agreement between the reflexive and its antecedent, the direct object DP in [Spec,VP]. On the semantics side, $(\alpha'\text{himself}_{V'})$ introduces a function of type $<<e,<e,<e,t>>>,<e,<e,t>>>$, performing essentially the same operation as $(\alpha'\text{himself}_{T'})$ in Figure 1. The derivation structures for (2) are given in Figure 5 and the derived trees in Figure 6. After λ-conversion has taken place on the semantic derived trees, the respective formulas for (1) and (2) are (4) and (5).

(4) introduces(jim, jim, bill)

(5) introduces(jim, bill, bill)

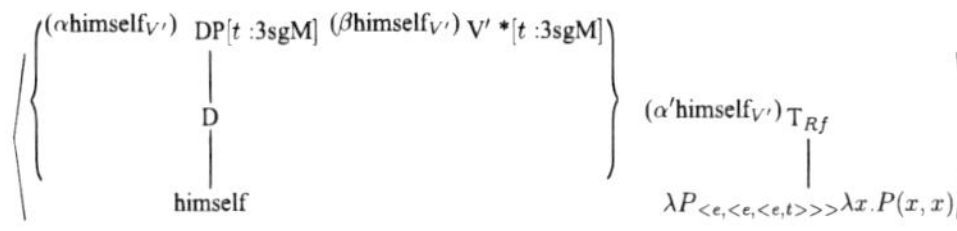

Figure 4: New elementary trees for *Jim₄ introduces Bill₅ to himself₅*

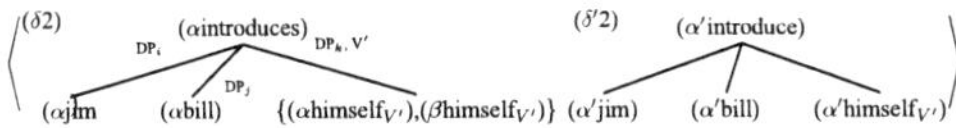

Figure 5: Derivation structures for *Jim₄ introduces Bill₅ to himself₅*

To derive (3), T′-type reflexive must be employed but with a different semantic elementary tree from the one in Figure 1. The new T′-type reflexive tree pair is given in Figure 7. $(\alpha'\text{himself}_{T'})$ in Figure 7 ensures that the variable corresponding to the indirect object *himself* and the variable corresponding to the subject antecedent are identified. The isomorphic syntactic and semantic derivation structures are given in Figure 8 and the syntactic and semantic derived trees in Figure 9. After λ-conversion has taken place on the semantic derived tree, the formula for (3) is (6).

(6) introduces(jim,bill,jim)

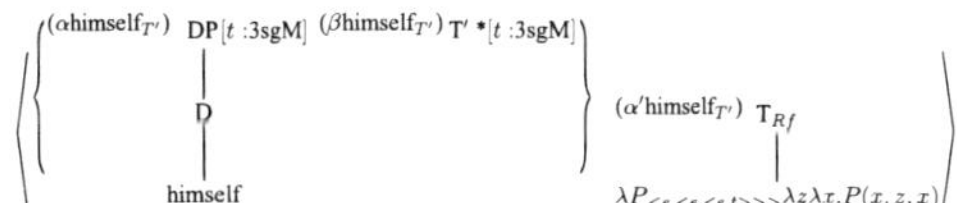

Figure 7: New elementary trees for *Jim₄ introduces Bill₅ to himself₄*

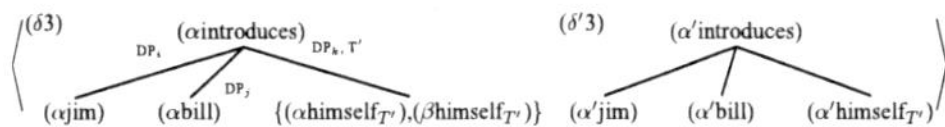

Figure 8: Derivation structures for *Jim₄ introduces Bill₅ to himself₄*

Syntactic constraints on derivation emerge when considering cases where there is no agreement between the reflexive and its antecedent, as in (7).

(7) * Jim₄ introduces herself₄ to Gillian₅.

Here, the reflexive would come with a degenerate T′ tree $(\beta\text{herself}_{T'})$ carrying a feature specifi-

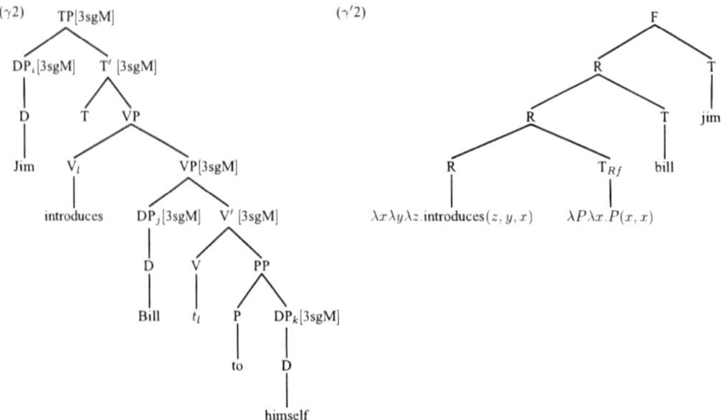

Figure 6: Derived trees for *Jim₄ introduces Bill₅ to himself₅*

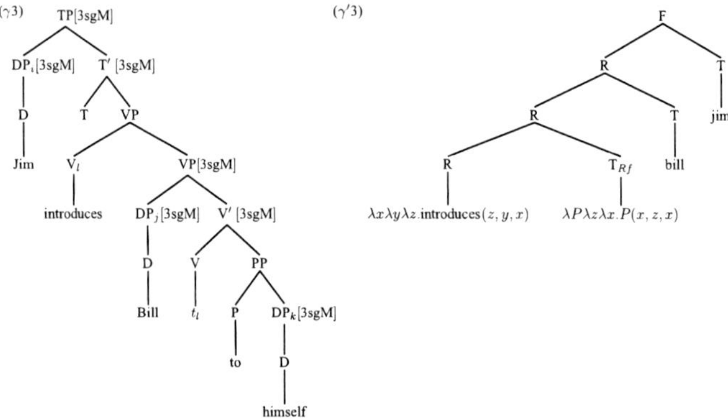

Figure 9: Derived trees for *Jim₄ introduces Bill₅ to himself₄*

cation of [3sgF]. However, substitution of (αJim) into (αintroduces) will transfer the value [3sgM] onto the T$'$ node of that tree. This would block the adjoining of (βherself$_{T'}$), as there would be a feature clash preventing unification.

Note also that (1) cannot be derived with the V$'$-type reflexive. While nothing in the syntax prevents the use of $\{(\alpha\text{himself}_{V'}), (\beta\text{himself}_{V'})\}$, following the links through to the semantics would result in an illegal derivation. (α'himself$_{V'}$), which takes an argument of type $<e<e<e,t>>>$ would be substituted at a node where its sister is of semantic type $<e<e,t>>$. The semantic derivation would crash at this point, as functional application cannot be applied.

Thus, both the syntax and semantics work in concert to obviate spurious derivations. What is worth considering here is that illegal derivations have been blocked without any recourse to a constraint such as Condition A. At its core, Condi-

tion A consists of two stipulations: a locality requirement, and a structural relationship between a reflexive and its antecedent. Under our approach, the locality requirement is provided by the formalism, in that the composition of the multi-component set must remain local to a single elementary tree. A binding domain is thus naturally defined. Similar to Kallmeyer and Romero (2007), the c-command relationship between the reflexive and its antecedent is also a consequence of our analysis. The difference is that our analysis accomplishes this without stipulating a dominance relationship between the two members of the reflexive set in the syntax. As shown above, the semantic type of the reflexive's tree governs the location where it can be substituted in semantics. Following the links from the semantics back to the syntax, this translates into a constraint upon the structural relationship between the α and β trees in the reflexive set. Only the derivation that produces a syntactic derived tree where the β tree of the reflexive set dominates the α tree can be mapped onto a fully composable semantic derived tree. As in the case of Kallmeyer and Romero, this necessary dominance easily translates into the c-command constraint embedded within Condition A, as the β tree of the reflexive must be adjoined at a sister node to a potential antecedent. As a result, both portions of Condition A are consequences of the present analysis and constraints upon semantic well-formedness.

3 Raising

Our analysis of English reflexives is extendable to instances of raising, as in (8) and (9).

(8) $Jake_4$ seems to $himself_4$ to be happy.

(9) $Julian_4$ seems to $Miles_5$ to love $himself_4$.

In the first raising case, (8), the reflexive is an argument of a different predicate than its antecedent. The elementary trees required for (8) are given in Figure 10. We use the *seems to* tree presented in Storoshenko (2006), extended with a matching semantic tree.[1] Following the derivation in Figure 11, in syntax, $(\beta himself_{T'})$ adjoins to the T' root of $(\beta seems\_to)$, unifying with its Top ϕ feature. This feature must then unify with the Top ϕ feature of T' in $(\alpha\ happy)$, the adjunction site for $(\beta seems\_to)$, and agree (through coindexation) with the Bottom ϕ feature of TP and the ϕ feature of the subject DP in $(\alpha happy)$. In semantics, $(\alpha himself_{T'})$ substitutes into $(\beta' seems\_to)$, which adjoins to $(\alpha' happy)$. Derived trees are shown in Figure 12. After λ conversion on $(\gamma' 8)$ is complete, the formula for (8) is (10).

(10)   seems_to(happy(jake), jake)

(11)   seems_to(love(julian, julian), miles)

In the second raising case, (9), both antecedent and reflexive are arguments of the same predicate, to which $(\beta seems\_to)$ adjoins with a sep-

arate experiencer. The new elementary trees required for (9) are in Figure 13. As shown in Figure 14, in syntax, $(\alpha Miles)$ is substituted into $(\beta seems\_to)$, which is then adjoined into (αto_love). Both components of the $himself_{T'}$ set then compose with (αto_love): $(\alpha himself_{T'})$ substitutes into DP_k, and $(\beta himself_{T'})$ adjoins onto T'. Here, we assume multiple adjunction, as defined in Schabes and Shieber (1994), so that $(\beta himself_{T'})$ and $(\beta seems\_to)$ adjoin to the same T' node in (αto_love). As $(\beta himself_{T'})$ is a degenerate auxiliary tree, the order of adjoining is unimportant, as either order results in the same derived tree. In semantics, $(\alpha' himself_{T'})$ substitutes into $(\alpha' to\_love)$ and $(\beta' seems\_to)$ adjoins to $(\alpha' to\_love)$. The derived trees are in Figure 15. $(\gamma' 9)$ yields the formula in (11) after λ-conversion.

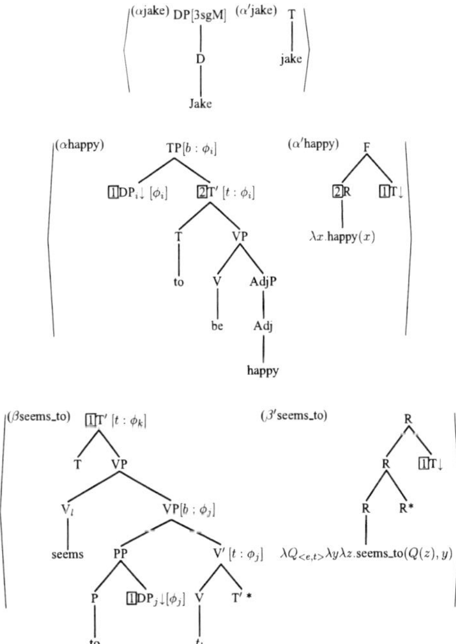

Figure 10: Elementary trees for *Jake$_4$ seems to himself$_4$ to be happy*

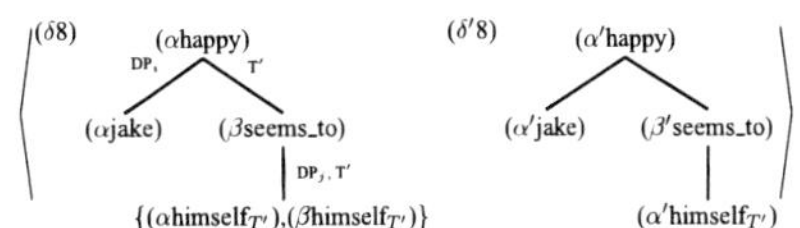

Figure 11: Derivation structures for *Jake$_4$ seems to himself$_4$ to be happy*

---

[1] A reviewer questions why the semantics of *seems to* presented here contains an argument slot for the subject of the embedded clause, when it is not present in the syntactic elementary tree of *seems to*. This is a function of the fact that the semantic elementary tree for *seems to* that we have defined adjoins to the predicate of type $<e,t>$ coming from the embedded clause. As this predicate takes an argument to return a proposition which is one of the arguments of *seems to*, an argument slot for the subject of the embedded clause is necessary in the λ-expression for *seems to*.

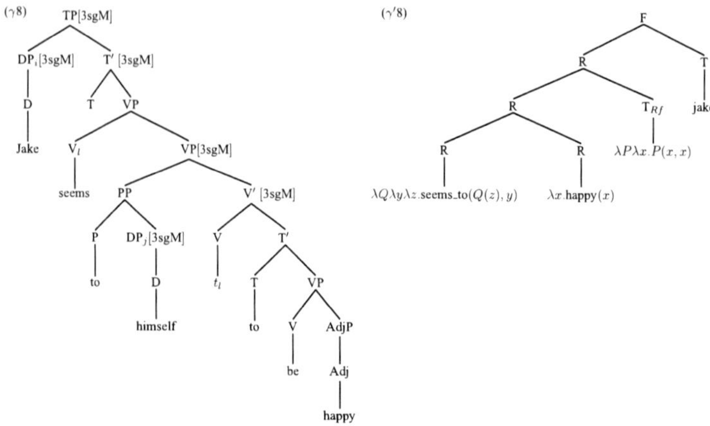

Figure 12: Derived trees for *Jake₄ seems to himself₄ to be happy*

Figure 15: Derived trees for *Julian₄ seems to Miles₅ to love himself₄*

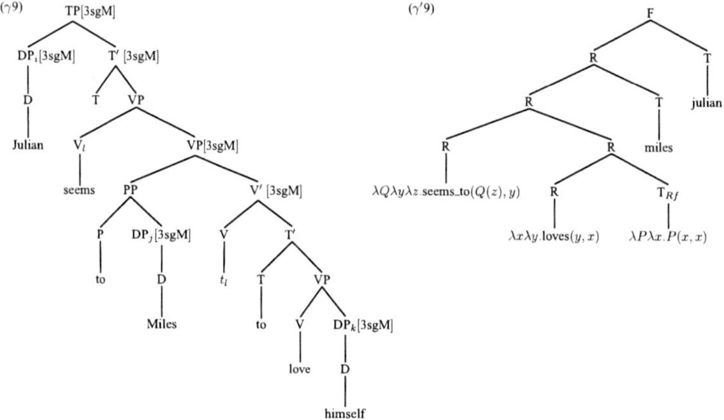

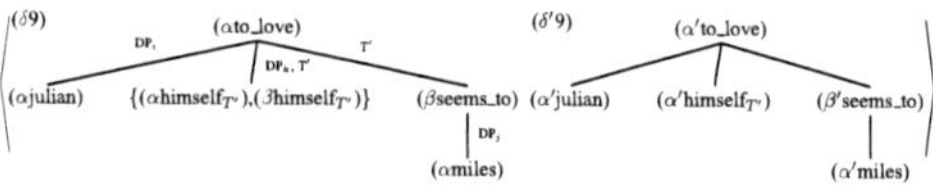

Figure 14: Derivation structures for *Julian₄ seems to Miles₅ to love himself₄*

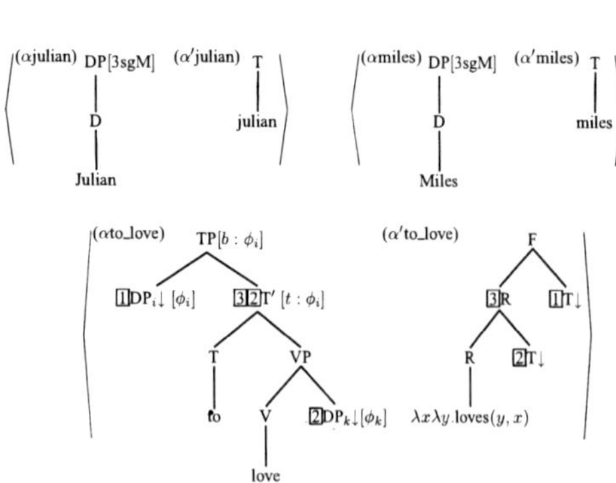

Figure 13: New elementary trees for *Julian₄ seems to Miles₅ to love himself₄*

4   ECM

Our analysis is also extendable to instances of ECM, as in (12).

(12)   Julian₄ believes himself₄ to be intelligent

The elementary trees required for (12) are shown in Figure 16. Here, we propose a third form of the reflexive, the TP-type, specified for subject positions. Because the reflexive is a subject, it is impossible for the antecedent to be found locally,

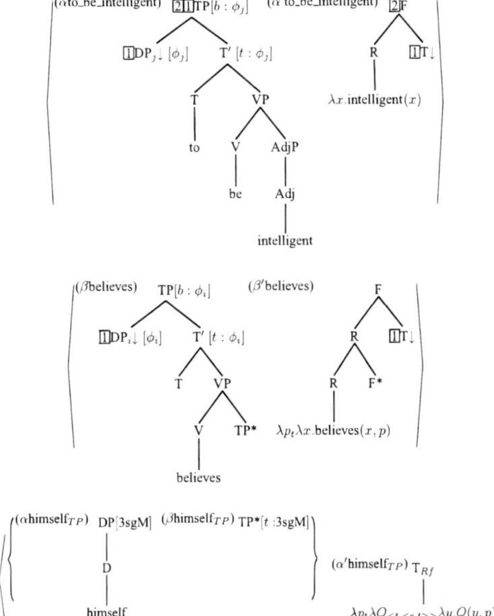

Figure 16: Elementary trees for *Julian₄ believes himself₄ to be intelligent*

motivating a distinct treatment bridging two separate predicates. (αhimself$_{TP}$) is unchanged from the previous forms, while (βhimself$_{TP}$), with its Top ϕ feature, is a TP-adjoining auxiliary tree. (α'himself$_{TP}$) introduces a function that ensures the identification of the subject argument of the embedded clause and the subject argument of the higher clause. Following the derivation in Figure 17, (βhimself$_{TP}$) and (βbelieves) multiply adjoin to the TP node of (αto_be_intelligent). The TP nodes of both (αto_be_intelligent) and (βbelieves) receive ϕ feature values from DP's substituted at their respective subject positions. Through adjoining (βhimself$_{TP}$) and (βbelieves) to the TP node of (αto_be_intelligent), the Top ϕ feature from (βhimself$_{TP}$) and the Bottom ϕ feature from the root TP in (βbelieves) must unify, as Top features present at an adjoining site must unify with the features of the root of an adjoining tree. This ensures the agreement between the reflexive which is the subject of the embedded clause and the antecedent which is the subject of the higher clause. Note that under Vijay-Shanker and Joshi's definition of feature unification, the Bottom ϕ features of the root TP node of (αto_be_intelligent) would not have to unify with the ϕ features of the root node of

(βbelieves); the reflexive's Top feature is responsible for carrying the agreement across clauses. The syntactic and semantic derived trees are in Figure 18. The final formula reduced from (γ'12) is (13).[2]

(13)   believes(julian, to_be_intelligent(julian))

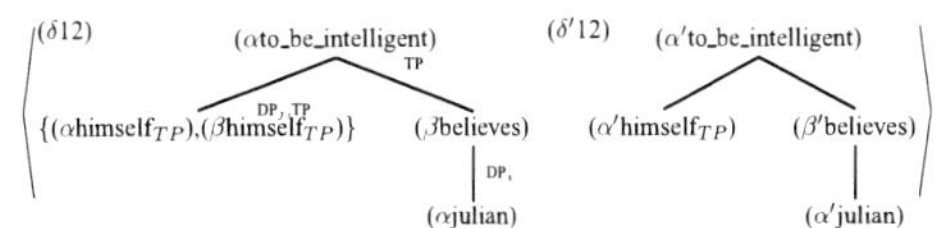

Figure 17: Derivation structures for *Julian₄ believes himself₄ to be intelligent*

In our analysis of ECM, we have required no ECM-specific featural specifications on the predicates, contrary to the ECM derivations in Kallmeyer and Romero (2007). There, the ECM predicate was endowed with special features to permit a variable representing the subject to be passed downward into the embedded clause; our approach limits the differences to the form of the reflexive itself.

5   Conclusion

Using STAG mechanisms including links and isomorphic syntactic and semantic derivations, we have shown that different binding possibilities for verbal argument reflexives are captured within the definition of the reflexive itself. Furthermore, we have shown that Condition A can be derived from constraints upon STAG derivation. We have not provided a treatment of 'picture' noun phrase cases here, preferring to see these as logophors (Pollard and Sag, 1992; Reinhart and Reuland, 1993), and we defer cases of non-argument reflexives, such as *Jim did it himself*, to future work.

Acknowledgment

We are extremely indebted to the three anonymous reviewers of TAG+9. Their insightful comments and criticisms were crucial in reshaping our paper. All remaining errors are ours. This work was supported by NSERC RGPIN/341442 to Han.

---

[2]Nothing in our analysis so far rules out (i).

(i)   * John believes that himself is intelligent.

An independent fact of the grammar that *himself* cannot receive accusative case from the subject position of a finite clause accounts for the ill-formedness of (i).

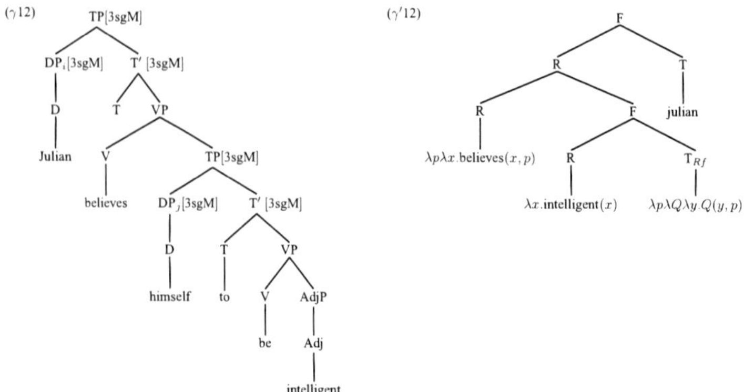

Figure 18: Derived trees for *Julian₄ believes himself₄ to be intelligent*

References

Chomsky, Noam. 1981. *Lectures on Government and Binding*. Dordrecht: Foris.

Han, Chung-hye and Nancy Hedberg. 2006. A Tree Adjoining Grammar Analysis of the Syntax and Semantics of *It*-clefts. In *Proceedings of the 8th International Workshop on Tree Adjoining Grammars and Related Formalisms (TAG+ 8)*, pages 33–40, COLING-ACL workshop, Sydney, Australia.

Han, Chung-hye. 2007. Pied-piping in relative clauses: Syntax and compositional semantics using Synchronous Tree Adjoining Grammar. *Research on Language and Computation*, 5(4):457–479.

Kallmeyer, Laura and Maribel Romero. 2007. Reflexive and reciprocals in LTAG. In Geertzen, Jeroen, Elias Thijsse, Harry Bunt, and Amanda Schiffrin, editors, *Proceedings of the Seventh International Workshop on Computational Semantics IWCS-7*, pages 271–282, Tilburg.

Kallmeyer, Laura and Maribel Romero. 2008. Scope and situation binding in LTAG using semantic unification. *Research on Language and Computation*, 6(1):3–52.

Nesson, Rebecca and Stuart M. Shieber. 2006. Simpler TAG Semantics through Synchronization. In *Proceedings of the 11th Conference on Formal Grammar*, Malaga, Spain. CSLI.

Nesson, Rebecca and Stuart Shieber. 2007. Extraction phenomena in Synchronous TAG syntax and semantics. In Wu, Dekai and David Chiang, editors, *Proceedings of the Workshop on Syntax and Structure in Statistical Translation*, Rochester, New York.

Pollard, Carl and Ivan Sag. 1992. Anaphors in English and the scope of binding theory. *Linguistic Inquiry*, 23(2):261–303.

Reinhart, Tanya and Eric Reuland. 1993. Reflexivity. *Linguistic Inquiry*, 24(4):657–720.

Ryant, Neville and Tatjana Scheffler. 2006. Binding of anaphors in LTAG. In *Proceedings of the 8th International Workshop on Tree Adjoining Grammars and Related Formalisms (TAG+ 8)*, pages 65–72, COLING-ACL workshop, Sydney, Australia.

Schabes, Yves and Stuart M. Shieber. 1994. An Alternative Conception of Tree-Adjoining Derivation. *Computational Linguistics*, pages 167–176.

Shieber, Stuart. 1994. Restricting the weak-generative capacity of Synchronous Tree-Adjoining Grammars. *Computational Intelligence*, 10(4).

Storoshenko, Dennis Ryan. 2006. Reconsidering raising and experiencers in English. In *Proceedings of the 8th International Workshop on Tree Adjoining Grammars and Related Formalisms (TAG+ 8)*, pages 159–166, COLING-ACL workshop, Sydney, Australia.

Vijay-Shanker, K. and Aravind Joshi. 1988. Feature structure based Tree Adjoining Grammars. In *Proceedings of COLING'88*, pages 714–719, Budapest.

A Layered Grammar Model: Using Tree-Adjoining Grammars to Build a Common Syntactic Kernel for Related Dialects

Pascal Vaillant
GRIMAAG
Université des Antilles et de la Guyane
B.P. 792
97337 Cayenne cedex
(Guyane Française)
`pascal.vaillant@guyane.univ-ag.fr`

Abstract

This article describes the design of a common syntactic description for the core grammar of a group of related dialects. The common description does not rely on an abstract sub-linguistic structure like a metagrammar: it consists in a single FS-LTAG where the actual specific language is included as one of the attributes in the set of attribute types defined for the features. When the `lan` attribute is instantiated, the selected subset of the grammar is equivalent to the grammar of one dialect. When it is not, we have a model of a hybrid multidialectal linguistic system. This principle is used for a group of creole languages of the West-Atlantic area, namely the French-based Creoles of Haiti, Guadeloupe, Martinique and French Guiana.

1 Introduction

Some of our present research aims at building formal linguistic descriptions for regional languages of the area of the Lesser Antilles and the Guianas, most of which are so-called "under-resourced languages". We have concentrated our efforts on a specific group of languages, the French-based (or French-lexified) Creole languages of the West-Atlantic area. We are concerned with providing users of those languages with electronic language resources, including formal grammars fit to be used for various Natural Language Processing (NLP) tasks, such as parsing or generation.

We are developing formal grammars in the TAG (Tree-Adjoining Grammars) framework, the tree-centered unification-based syntactic formalism which has proven successful in modelling other languages of different types. TAG grammars may be lexicalized, so they provide a lexicon-centered description of phrase constructions (Schabes et al., 1988); and have been equipped with the formal tool of double-plane feature structures, allowing the concept of feature structures unification to get adapted to the specific needs of adjunction (Vijay-Shanker and Joshi, 1988).

In the context we are working in, two practical reasons are leading to the search of solutions for factoring as much as possible of the grammars of those languages: first, the languages in this group are fairly close to one another, with respect to both lexicon and grammar; second, the resources dedicated to their description are scarce. The close relatedness makes it obvious for the linguist to try to leverage the efforts spent on describing the grammar of one of the languages, by factoring out all the common parts of the grammatical systems. This principle has been used by other research work (see below, Section 4).

The originality of our approach is that we delay the point at which a single language is actually chosen to the very last moment, namely at generation time (the same would apply to parsing time, but parsing has not been implemented yet). In the end, we propose a grammar which is not a grammar for one single dialect, but a grammar for a multidialectal complex, where language is one of the features selected in the grammar itself, like person, number, tense, or aspect.

Proceedings of The Ninth International Workshop on Tree Adjoining Grammars and Related Formalisms
Tübingen, Germany. June 6-8, 2008.

2   Coverage of the grammar

The portion of the grammar described so far represents only a small fragment of the grammar of the languages we are interested in. Until now, we have made attempts to describe: the determination of noun phrases; the system of personal pronouns and determiners; the core system of expression of tense, mood and aspect (TMA) of verbs — or, to put it more cautiously, of predicates —; the main auxiliary verbs used to express other aspectual nuances; the expression of epistemic and deontic modality; the combination of the negation with the above mentioned subsystems (tense, aspect, modality) in the predicative phrase.

The grammar and lexicon files are built upon an ad-hoc implementation of FS-TAGs in Prolog[1], which had originally been developed in another context and for another language, German (Vaillant, 1999), and later adapted to Martinican Creole (Vaillant, 2003).

The only function implemented at present is sentence generation; the starting point of the generation is a conceptual graph, expressed by a minimal set of spaning trees, which in turn select elementary trees in the grammar (initial trees for the first pass, auxiliary trees for the remaining parts). We are testing our grammar on a small sample tests of such conceptual graphs.

In the remainder of this article, we will focus the attention on two typical core subsystems of the grammar: determination in the noun phrase, and expression of tense and aspect in the predicate phrase[2].

3   Application to French-based Creoles

The family of dialects to which we apply the approach described is the family of French-based (sometimes called French-lexified) Creole languages of the West-Atlantic area. Those languages emerged during the peak period of the slave trade epoch (1650–1800) when France, like some other West-European nations, founded colonies in the New World and tried to develop intensive agricultural economic systems based on the exploitation of slave workforce massively imported from Africa. In the quickly developing new societies, at any given moment during that peak period, the number of people recently imported in any colony tended to be higher than the number of people actually born there — a typical situation for linguistic instability. Moreover, the slaves were brought from different regions of Africa and had no common language to communicate with, except the language of the European colons: so they were forced to use that target language, without having time to learn it fully before passing it on to the next generation of immigrants. This type of situation leads to a very specific drift of the language system, which begins to stabilize only when the society itself stabilizes. When observed in synchronicity at the present moment, those Creoles obviously appear as languages which share a very great portion of their vocabulary with French (more than 90 %), but have a very specific grammatical system, quite different from the French one.

The languages falling into the category comprise French Creole dialects born and developed in former French colonies of the Caribbean Arc and its two continental "pillars": from the present US State of Louisiana[3] to French Guiana (formerly the Cayenne colony), on the northern coast of the South-American mainland. Caribbean islands where a French Creole has developed include Hispaniola (in the western part of the island, the former French colony of Saint-Domingue, since 1804 the independant republic of Haiti), Guadeloupe, the island of Dominica, Martinique, Saint-Lucia, and Trinidad (the latter also nearly extinct). Among the languages listed, we leave apart, for lack of easily accessible sources and informants, the case of Louisiana, Dominica, Saint-Lucia and Trinidad, and concentrate on the four Creoles of Haiti, Guadeloupe, Martinique and French Guiana.

The question of how properly those languages qualify as a genetically related family has been discussed in the literature. A starting point would be

---

[1]Precisely: SWI-Prolog, developed and maintained by Jan Wielemaker, University of Amsterdam: http://www.swi-prolog.org.

[2]It may be inadequate to speak of *verb phrase* in the case of the Creole languages mentioned here, since any lexical unit (including nouns, but also some closed-class units like locative adverbs) may be inserted in the predicate slot of a sentence and bear tense or aspectual marks. So there probably are verbs, but possibly no "verb phrases" — see (Vaillant, 2003) for a discussion.

[3]A nearly extinct French Creole dialect — not to be confused with *Cajun* French — is still understood by some people in the parishes of Saint-Martin, Iberville and Pointe-Coupée.

the obvious statement that all of them have French as an ancestor[4], but this is not of much linguistic interest since, as we have seen, the relatedness with French lies principally in the vocabulary, whereas the Creole dialects have a great convergence in their grammatical systems, that they precisely do not owe to French. Some formerly proposed theories of monogenesis of *all* Creole languages are now largely out of fashion; however, if the question is restricted to monogenesis of a specific group of Creoles (e.g. French-based, or English-based) in a specific region of the world (e.g. the West-Atlantic area), monogenesis in this restricted acceptation remains a seriously discussed hypothesis. In any case, it has been established from historical sources that there was uninterrupted contact and interchange between the French colonies, from the first decades of colonization up to now, so that it is a safe bet to consider the different French Creole dialects as belonging to a dialect continuum. Pfänder (2000, p. 192–209), notably, proposes an analysis of the family in terms of dialectal area, opposing center (Antilles) and periphery (Louisiana and Guiana), and gives comparison tables for the systems of expression of tense and aspect.

For a more detailed presentation of those languages, of their history, and of the discussions they involve, the reader familiar with the French language may easily access (Hazaël-Massieux, 2002).

We will not enter into a detailed presentation of the grammatical systems of the Creoles. The most important thing to say here is that they are isolating languages, SVO ordered, with a strict positional syntax, and that tense and aspect are expressed by particles that are placed before the main predicate. As said above (Section 2), we will concentrate on the noun phrase and on the TMA core system within the predicate phrase. Tables 1 and 2 give an overview of those two systems. They have been compiled from different sources (most particularly (Pfänder, 2000) and (Damoiseau, 2007) for the comparative perspective, but also various other references for precise description points specific to some given language), and completed following our own observations on recent corpora.

3.1 Determination in the noun phrase

The four Creoles all possess four systematic degrees of determination of nouns: a generic, an indefinite, a specific, and a demonstrative. The generic is used when the concept is taken for its general features as a category; in English, the same meaning could sometimes be expressed with a singular, and sometimes with a plural (*zwazo gen de zel* (hait.): the bird has two wings / a bird has two wings / birds have two wings). For the sake of descriptive economy, in the formalization, we treat this generic degree as simply being one of the possible semantic values of the plural indefinite (which is also expressed by the bare noun, with no article)[5]. The indefinite degree, like in French or German, is expressed by a numeral (and its value is more specific, closer to the original semantics of the numeral, than it has become in French, for instance — where the indefinite article also is used to express the generic). The specific degree (roughly equivalent to English "the") is expressed by a postposed article, historically deriving from a French deictic adverb (*là*). Lastly, the demonstrative degree derives from the combination of a former demonstrative pronoun, now sometimes preposed (guia.) and sometimes postposed (other Creoles) to the noun, and to which the mark of the specific definite is added (with a case of fused form for Guadeloupean and Martinican).

The plural is expressed either by a preposed marker derived from a former plural demonstrative (mart., guad.), or by a postposed third-person plural personal pronoun (hait., guia.), which in the case of guianese got fused with the definite mark (*yé la* [historical form, described in 1872] > *ya* [contemporary form]).

In our formal model, we only keep three degrees of determination (indefinite, specific and demonstrative), which combine with two values for number (singular and plural). Also, since the indefinite mark does not combine with the others (when in contrast, there is a combination between the marks of demonstrative and specific, with demonstrative $\Rightarrow$ specific), we model the indefinite by an absence of determination feature; the specific is modeled by the feature $\langle spe = + \rangle$; and

---

[4]The atypical mode of language transmission has led some historical linguists (Thomason and Kaufman, 1988, p. 152) to refuse to apply the term of genetic transmission, but this point has been thoroughly criticized (DeGraff, 2005).

[5]This interpretation agrees with a number of linguistic facts, like anaphora *often* involving a plural pronoun (*zwazo gen de zel pou yo kapab vole*: bird[s] have two wing[s] for them [to be] able [to] fly).

		hait.	guad.	mart.	guia.	english
Generic		*moun*	*moun*	*moun*	*moun*	person (human)
Singular	indefinite	*yon moun*	*on moun*	*an moun*	*roun moun*	a/one person
Singular	specific	*moun nan*	*moun la*	*moun lan*	*moun an*	the person
Singular	specific	*tab la*	*tab la*	*tab la*	*tab a*	the table
Singular	specific	*chyen an*	*chyen la*	*chyen an*	*chyen an*	the dog
Singular	specific	*zwazo a*	*zozyo la*	*zwézo a*	*zozo a*	the bird
Singular	demonstrative	*moun sa a*	*moun lasa*	*moun tala*	*sa moun an*	that person
Singular	demonstrative	*tab sa a*	*tab lasa*	*tab tala*	*sa tab a*	that table
Plural	indefinite	*moun*	*moun*	*moun*	*moun*	people
Plural	specific	*moun yo*	*sé moun la*	*sé moun lan*	*moun yan*	the persons
Plural	specific	*tab yo*	*sé tab la*	*sé tab la*	*tab ya*	the tables
Plural	specific	*chyen yo*	*sé chyen la*	*sé chyen an*	*chyen yan*	the dogs
Plural	specific	*zwazo yo*	*sé zozyo la*	*sé zwézo a*	*zozo ya*	the birds
Plural	demonstrative	*moun sa yo*	*sé moun lasa*	*sé moun tala*	*sa moun yan*	those people
Plural	demonstrative	*tab sa yo*	*sé tab lasa*	*sé tab tala*	*sa tab ya*	those tables

Table 1: Determination in the noun phrase

the demonstrative by the combination of features $\langle \text{spe} = + \rangle$, $\langle \text{dem} = + \rangle$.

In some dialects, a phenomenon of nasal progressive assimilation changes the surface form of the postposed specific article (hait., mart., guia.); in others, in addition, the surface form of the article differs depending on whether the preceding word ends with a vowel or a consonant (hait., mart.). The four possible combinations are shown in table 1.

3.2 Tense and aspect in the predicative phrase

In Creole linguistics, a classical description given of the TMA (Tense-Mood-Aspect) system of the "Atlantic" Creole languages[6] mentions three optional components appearing in a very strict order: past tense mark; "mood" mark (able to take future or irrealis values, depending on contexts); imperfective aspect mark. A canonical version of this system has been given for French-based Creoles by Valdman (1978), who actually describes those three categories as one category of tense (*past*) and two categories of aspect (*prospective* and *continuative*). The "middle" mark (Valdman's "prospective") takes on an irrealis meaning when it is combined with the past tense.

So, there is a combinatory system: $(té / \varnothing) \times (ké / \varnothing) \times (ka / \varnothing)$ (if we call the three marks by the form they have in the three Creoles of Guadeloupe, Martinique and Guyane), which in theory generates eight possible combinations: $\varnothing$, *ka*, *ké*, *ké ka*, *té*, *té ka*, *té ké*, *té ké ka*. The eight combinations are attested to different degrees, with the semantic values given in table 2. In Haitian Creole, the corresponding forms are *te*, *va* and *ap*, and some combinations yield fused forms (va ap > vap; te ap > tap; te va > ta; te va ap > ta vap).

In fact, there are variations in this basic schema. For instance, the term "imperfective" covers a complex of diverse meanings (progressive, frequentative, or simply unaccomplished) which do not strictly overlap in the different dialects. For instance, if the mark *ka* may bear all the above-mentioned meanings in the Creoles of Guadeloupe or Martinique (up to some general temporal value roughly corresponding to the English simple present), it is not necessarily so in the Creole of Guiana, and it is quite false for the Creole of Haiti (where the unaccomplished is unmarked, and the only aspectual value of particle *ap* is the progressive, corresponding not to English simple present, but to English BE + -*ing* — and even able to take over the temporal value of a future). Table 2 shows these differences.

Lastly, it is important to notice that the combinations of the TMA marks are constrained by the semantics of the unit placed in the predicate position. For instance, a verb with a "non-processual" meaning (like *konèt*, to know), or an adjective referring to a state (like *malad*, ill), will hardly combine with an imperfective aspect marker like *ka*; if they do, however, it will necessarily produce a meaning effect that will shift the contextual meaning towards a less "stative" value. For example, an utterance like *mo ka malad* (I-IMP-ill) might be at-

---

[6]The schema also holds for English-based Creoles (Bickerton, 1981).

	hait.	**guad.**	**mart.**	**guia.**
Accomplished / Aoristic	*danse*	*dansé*	*dansé*	*dansé*
Unaccomplished / Present	*danse*	*ka dansé*	*ka dansé*	*(ka) dansé*
Frequentative	*danse*	*ka dansé*	*ka dansé*	*ka dansé*
Progressive	*ap danse*	*ka dansé*	*ka dansé*	*ka dansé*
Near Future	*pral danse*	*kay dansé*	*kay dansé*	*k'alé / kay dansé*
Future	*va danse*	*ké dansé*	*ké dansé*	*ké dansé*
Unaccomplished Future *(seldom)*	*vap danse*	*ké ka dansé*	*ké ka dansé*	*ké ka dansé*
Accomplished past (pluperfect)	*te danse*	*té dansé*	*té dansé*	*té dansé*
Unaccomplished past	*tap danse*	*té ka dansé*	*té ka dansé*	*té ka dansé*
Irrealis	*ta danse*	*té ké dansé*	*té ké dansé*	*té ké dansé*
Irrealis unaccomplished	*ta vap danse*	*té ké ka dansé*	*té ké ka dansé*	*té ké ka dansé*
Conditional / Optative	*ta danse*	*té ké dansé*	*sé dansé*	*té ké dansé*

Table 2: Core tense and aspect marking in the predicative phrase

tested; and it is to be interpreted, depending on the context, either as a frequentative (at every back to school time, I get flu), or as a progressive (I feel I am coming down to flu).

3.3 Some TAG model elements

In figures 1 and 2, we show the main components of the model for the noun phrase system presented in table 1, represented as elementary trees with a language parameter l[7].

It should be noted that the trees *Dem Det (gp,mq)* and *Plur (gp,mq)*, which concern only two dialects among the four (Guadeloupean and Martinican), are included in the common layer without risking to interfere with the construction of the demonstrative or plural in Haitian or Guianese (in fact, unification constraints forbid the adjunction of a GP/MQ demonstrative on a HT/GF demonstrative; likewise, they forbid the adjunction of a GP/MQ plural on a HT/GF plural).

The adjunction of the demonstrative in Haitian or Guianese is done above the level of the noun complements (attention to parameter *bar* in the trees *Dem (gf)* et *Dem (ht)*), but below the specific article; e.g. *moun Sentoma sa yo* (hait.): those people from Saint-Thomas; *sa moun Senloran an* (guia.): those people from Saint-Laurent.

The TMA system, on its side, is in a great part

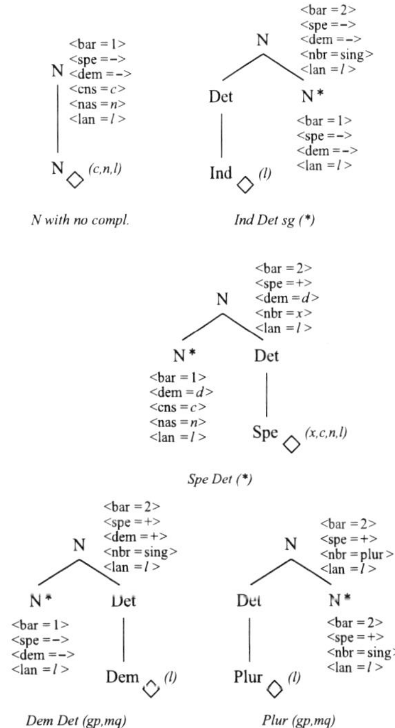

Figure 1: Common elements in the NP model.

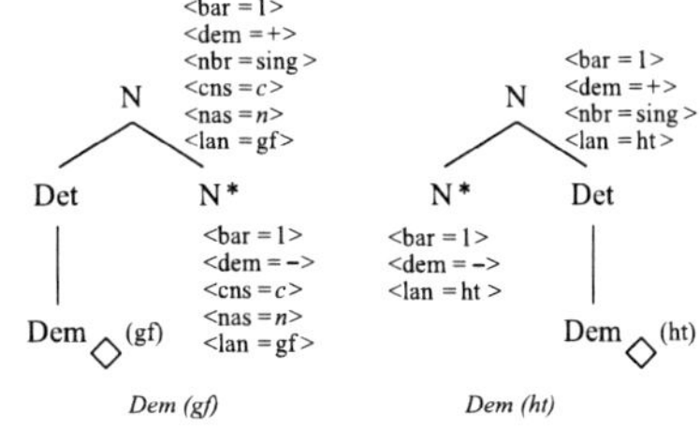

Figure 2: NP modelling elements specific to haitian and guianese

---

[7] The following abbreviations are used for the attributes: *bar* = bar level (1 = noun with complements, but no determination; 2 = noun phrase); *nbr* = number; *spe* = specific determiner; *dem* = demonstrative determiner; *cns* = the constituent ends with a consonant; *nas* = the constituent ends with a nasal syllable; *lan* = language. The values used to identify the four Creoles are based on the two-letter country codes defined in standard ISO-3166 for country names: HT for *Haiti*, GP for *Guadeloupe*, MQ for *Martinique*, and GF for *French Guiana* (going from North to South... and by decreasing population count.) Non-instantiated variables are in italics.

common to the four languages. Auxiliary trees modelling the adjunction of aspectual or temporal values hence are all common (fig. 3). The only nuance resides in the fact that the tree for adjoining an aspect particle to convey general values of imperfective (durative, frequentative) cannot unify when the `lan` parameter is set to Haitian. In the end, only the lexical (surface) values make the differences between the dialects[8].

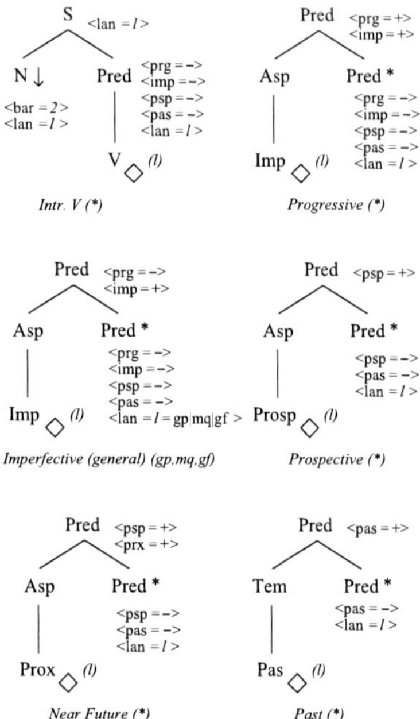

Figure 3: Common elements in the predicative phrase model

4   Related work

The idea of factoring some of the efforts of grammar modelling to exploit similar structures among different languages has already been tackled by some research works, among which we are particularly aware of those led at Jussieu within the FTAG project (Candito, 1998), the Lexorg project (Xia et al., 1998), the LinGO grammar Matrix (Bender et al., 2002; Bender and Flickinger,

2005)[9], the LORIA XMG project (Parmentier et al., 2006), and Bouillon et al.'s work (2006) on multilingual multipurpose grammars[10].

Works like Candito's (1998) (for French and Italian) or Xia and Palmer's (1998) (for English and Chinese), are based on the idea of using *meta-grammars*, that is higher-level descriptions of general properties of the language(s) described. The higher-level descriptions for different languages may be factored as long as the languages share typological features. In the end, an actual LTAG grammar is generated from the meta-grammar, tailored for one specific language. In this type of approaches, what is actually shared between the languages is a higher-level structure, not actual grammatical structures belonging to the LTAG description of the languages.

In the LinGO grammar matrix approach (Bender et al., 2002), underspecified HPSG structures (with a minimal recursion semantics) are used to share information between different languages. A system based on shell scripts is used to automatically generate grammar files for a specific language, when given a couple of general typological specific information (word order pattern, case marking strategy, etc.).

The approach which most resembles the one advocated in the present paper is Bouillon et al.'s (2006) way of devising quickly re-usable grammars for speech recognition programs, based on shared grammatical descriptions for related romance languages (French, Castilian Spanish, and Catalan). The authors include "macros" in their DCG-style upper-level description, and the macros allow to specify alternative points where the languages differ (like the position of clitics in specific verb forms, the optionality of determiners, the optional presence of prepositions for object complements, etc.). In a last stage, the DCG-style specification is compiled to ad hoc CFGs tailored for speech recognition engines, each for a specific language and task.

Our approach, in contrast, is not a meta-grammar approach; what is shared between the different languages are actual LTAG trees. The "language" parameter is embedded in the very fea-

---

[8]The following abbreviations are used for the attributes in fig. 3: Tense: *pas* = past; Aspects: *psp* = prospective; *prx* = proximal prospective ("imminent" aspect ̃ temporal value of a near future) ; *imp* = imperfective (general) ; *prg* = progressive (like in English "I am doing...").

[9]See   LinGO   grammar   matrix'   web   site:
`http://www.delph-in.net/matrix/`.

[10]Thanks to the reviewers of the preliminary version of this article for pointing to some useful references.

ture structures of tree nodes. So, our lexical-grammatical descriptions reside in one single level of description, but that level is "modularized": some descriptions are common to all the dialects described, some are shared by only part of them, and some are specific. In other works, even those which are not based on meta-grammars (like Bender's or Bouillon's), the goal is to generate a grammar for a single language in the end. In the present work we are aiming at giving a description of a multidialectal linguistic system.

5 Discussion

The above-mentioned modelling choice may seem counter-intuitive in the theoretical frame of structural linguistics. One might object that if the language itself is the whole object of description, then it is absurd to include it as a category in the description. This view is justified as long as one does not wish to take into account dialectal variation as an internal system variable. If this is the case, then every single dialect must be considered an isolate and be given a holistic, unitary description.

But in the context we are working in, several rationales lead us to think that it might be a good idea to include dialectal variation in the description.

We already have mentioned practical reasons (see above, in Introduction). The "time saving" and "resource sharing" rationales applies to our method as well as to others (like meta-grammars). A supplementary argument, which applies more specifically to our method, is the fact that in the cases we are studying, not only some syntactical properties of the languages are common, but also an important part of the vocabulary, until at the very surface level. This speaks for sharing bottom-level structures.

But there is another, less practical, type of argument: if we have a modular grammatical system model which "contains" more than one language in itself, we are able to model the linguistic competence in one of the languages, but also to model multilingual (in the present case, multidialectal) linguistic competence.

If our goal is to model monolingual competence, this is easily done by unifying the lan parameter with one of its possible values, and then erasing the (now redundant) parameter from the description.

However, in some cases, we might want to have a model of multidialectal variation. Considered from the E-language side, we then have a model of a dialectal continuum. Considered from the I-language side, we have a model of the linguistic competence of a multilingual speaker of related dialects. The interplay of grammatical structures of a multidialectal system, the possibilities of combination and unification given different levels of instantiation of the lan parameter, might provide us with a model for such linguistic phenomena as: specialized repertoires, code switching, code mixing, or *koinê* emergence. That work, at the present stage, is still to be done: it is a mere idea of future research directions to evaluate the potential of our modelling method. Yet it is an appealing idea, given that in some types of contexts, multilinguality among related dialects is a common situation[11], and that phenomena such as code switching or code mixing are more frequent than the opposite — the use of a single unitary language with a single norm[12]. It is also a matter of future research to evaluate the degree of parsing feasibility for mixed linguistic input.

References

Bender, Emily M. and Dan Flickinger. 2005. Rapid prototyping of scalable grammars: Towards modularity in extensions to a language-independent core. In *Proceedings of the 2nd International Joint Conference on Natural Language Processing IJCNLP-05 (Posters/Demos)*, Jeju Island, Korea.

Bender, Emily M., Dan Flickinger, and Stephan Oepen. 2002. The grammar matrix: an open-source starter-kit for the rapid development of cross-linguistically consistent broad-coverage precision grammars. In *COLING-02 Workshop on Grammar engineering and evaluation, Taipei (Taiwan), 1st September 2002*, pages 8–14.

---

[11] This is particularly the case in the regions where some of the languages we study are spoken: for example, in Guadeloupe and in French Guiana, there are communities of tens of thousands of people of Haitian descent, who tend to mix the Creole of Haiti with the Creole of the country. In the European mainland part of France, there also are large numbers of people from the French West Indies, who tend to form multidialectal speakers communities, where specific Creole differences between e.g. Guadeloupe and Martinique are vanishing.

[12] In another study, presented elsewhere (Lengrai et al., 2006), we have shown that within a corpus of several hours of recorded radio broadcastings in Creole of the Martinique, it is hard to find a single minute of speech where French and Creole are not mixed at the very intra-sentential level.

Bickerton, Derek. 1981. *Roots of language*. Karoma, Ann Arbor (MI, USA).

Bouillon, Pierrette, Manny Rayner, Bruna Novellas, Marianne Starlander, Marianne Santaholma, Yukie Nakao, and Nikos Chatzichrisafis. 2006. Une grammaire partagé multitâche pour le traitement de la parole : application aux langues romanes. *TAL (Traitement Automatique des Langues)*, 47(3):155–173.

Candito, Marie-Hélène. 1998. Building parallel LTAG for French and Italian. In *Proceedings of the 17th International Conference on Computational Linguistics (COLING 1998)*, pages 211–217, Montréal (Québec, Canada).

Damoiseau, Robert. 2007. Le créole guyanais dans la famille des créoles à base lexicale française de la zone américano-caraïbe. In Mam-Lam-Fouck, Serge, editor, *Comprendre la Guyane d'aujourd'hui*, pages 501–514, Matoury (Guyane Française). Ibis Rouge.

DeGraff, Michel. 2005. Linguists' most dangerous myth: the fallacy of Creole Exceptionalism. *Language in Society*, 34(4):533–591.

Hazaël-Massieux, Marie-Christine. 2002. Les créoles à base française : une introduction. *TIPA (Travaux Interdisciplinaires du laboratoire Parole et Langage d'Aix-en-Provence)*, 21:63–86. Available online at: http://aune.lpl.univ-aix.fr/lpl/tipa/21/tipa21-hazael.pdf.

Lengrai, Christelle, Juliette Moustin, and Pascal Vaillant. 2006. Interférences syntaxiques et lexicales du français dans le créole martiniquais des émissions radiophoniques. In *3. Freiburger Arbeitstagung zur Romanistischen Korpuslinguistik: Korpora und Pragmatik*, Freiburg in Breisgau (Deutschland), September. Proceedings to appear.

Parmentier, Yannick, Joseph Le Roux, and Benoît Crabbé. 2006. XMG – an expressive formalism for describing Tree-based Grammars. In *EACL*, pages 103–106, Trento (Italia).

Pfänder, Stefan. 2000. *Aspekt und Tempus im Frankokreol*. ScriptOralia. Günter Narr Verlag, Tübingen (Deutschland).

Schabes, Yves, Anne Abeillé, and Aravind Joshi. 1988. Parsing strategies with 'lexicalized' grammars: Application to Tree Adjoining Grammars. In *Proceedings of the 12th International Conference on Computational Linguistics (COLING 1988)*, pages 578–583, Budapest (Magyarország).

Thomason, Sarah and Terrence Kaufman. 1988. *Language Contact, Creolization, and Genetic Linguistics*. University of California Press, Berkeley (CA, USA).

Vaillant, Pascal. 1999. Learning to communicate in german through an iconic input interface: Presentation of the GLOTTAI project. Technical report, Humboldt Universität zu Berlin. Available online at: http://www.vaillant.nom.fr/pascal/glottai/presentation/.

Vaillant, Pascal. 2003. Une grammaire formelle du créole martiniquais pour la génération automatique. In *Actes de TALN 2003 (Traitement Automatique des Langues Naturelles)*, pages 255–264, Batz-sur-mer (France), June. ATALA.

Valdman, Albert. 1978. *Le créole : structure, statut et origine*. Klincksieck, Paris (France).

Vijay-Shanker, Krishnamurti and Aravind Joshi. 1988. Feature-structure based Tree Adjoining Grammars. In *Proceedings of the 12th International Conference on Computational Linguistics (COLING 1988)*, pages 714–719, Budapest (Magyarország).

Xia, Fei, Martha Palmer, Krishnamurti Vijay-Shanker, and Joseph Rosenzweig. 1998. Consistent grammar development using partial tree descriptions for lexicalized tree adjoining grammar. In *Proceedings of the 4th Workshop on Tree-Adjoining Grammars and Related Formalisms (TAG+4)*, pages 180–183, Philadelphia (PA, USA).

Towards Accurate Probabilistic Lexicons for Lexicalized Grammars

Naoki Yoshinaga
Institute of Industrial Science, University of Tokyo
6-1 Komaba 4-chome, Meguro-Ku, Tokyo 153-8505, JAPAN
`ynaga@tkl.iis.u-tokyo.ac.jp`

Abstract

This paper proposes a method of constructing an accurate probabilistic subcategorization (SCF) lexicon for a lexicalized grammar extracted from a treebank. We employ a latent variable model to smooth co-occurrence probabilities between verbs and SCF types in the extracted lexicalized grammar. We applied our method to a verb SCF lexicon of an HPSG grammar acquired from the Penn Treebank. Experimental results show that probabilistic SCF lexicons obtained by our model achieved a lower test-set perplexity against ones obtained by a naive smoothing model using twice as large training data.

1 Introduction

This paper proposes a smoothing model for probabilistic subcategorization (SCF) lexicons of lexicalized grammars acquired from corpora. Here, *an SCF lexicon* consists of pairs of words and *lexical (SCF) types* (*e.g, tree family*), from which individual lexical entry templates are derived by lexical rules (Jackendoff, 1975; Pollard and Sag, 1994) (*e.g.*, *metarules*: Becker (2000) and Prolo (2002)).[1] Recently, the corpus-oriented approaches have enabled us to acquire wide-coverage lexicalized grammars from large treebanks (Xia, 1999; Chen and Vijay-Shanker, 2000; Chiang, 2000; Hockenmaier and Steedman, 2002;

Cahill et al., 2002; Frank et al., 2003; Miyao et al., 2005). However, a great workload is required to develop such large treebanks for languages or domains where a base bracketed corpus (*e.g.*, the Penn Treebank: Marcus et al. (1993)) is not available. When the size of the source treebank is small, we encounter the serious problem of a lack of lexical entries (unseen word-template pairs).

Previous studies investigated unseen word-template pairs in lexicalized grammars acquired from the Penn Treebank (Xia, 1999; Chen and Vijay-Shanker, 2000; Hockenmaier and Steedman, 2002; Miyao et al., 2005); the words can be seen (sw) or unseen (uw), and similarly, the templates can be seen (st) or unseen (ut), so that there are four types of unseen pairs. All the studies reported that unseen (sw, st) pairs caused the major problem in lexical coverage.

This paper focuses on a verb SCF lexicon, and employs a latent variable model (Hofmann, 2001) to smooth co-occurrence probabilities between verbs and SCF types acquired from small-sized corpora. If we can obtain such an accurate probabilistic SCF lexicon, we can construct a wide-coverage SCF lexicon by setting the threshold of the probabilities (Yoshinaga, 2004). Alternatively we can directly use the acquired probabilistic lexicon in supertagging (Chen et al., 2006) and probabilistic parsing (Miyao et al., 2005; Ninomiya et al., 2005).

We applied our method to a verb SCF lexicon of an HPSG grammar acquired from the Penn Treebank (Miyao et al., 2005; Nakanishi et al., 2004). The acquired probabilistic SCF lexicons were more accurate than ones acquired by a naive smoothing model.

---

[1] In the linguistic literature, the term 'lexical rules' is used to define either syntactic transformations (*e.g.*, wh-movement), diathesis alternations (*e.g.*, dative shift) or both. In this paper, we use the term lexical rules to define syntactic transformations among lexical entry templates that belong to the same lexical type.

2   Related Work

In this section, we first describe previous approaches to the problem of unseen word-template pairs in the lexicalized grammars acquired from treebanks. We then address smoothing methods for SCF lexicons acquired from raw corpora.

2.1   Predicting unseen word-template pairs for lexicalized grammars

The problem of missing lexical entries has been recognized as one of the major problems in lexicalized grammars acquired from treebanks, and a number of researchers attempted to predict unseen lexical entries. In the following, we describe previous methods of predicting unseen (uw, st) and (sw, st) pairs, respectively.[2]

Chiang (2000), Hockenmaier and Steedman (2002) and Miyao et al. (2005) used a simple smoothing method to predict unseen (uw, st) pairs. They regarded infrequent words in the source treebank as unknown words, and assigned the lexical entry templates acquired for these words to unknown words. This treatment of unknown words substantially improved the lexical coverage, probably because infrequent words are likely to take only a few lexical entry templates (*e.g.*, those for transitive verbs).

There are two types of approaches to predict unseen (sw, st) pairs. The first type of approaches (Chen and Vijay-Shanker, 2000; Nakanishi et al., 2004; Chen et al., 2006) exploited an organization of lexical entry templates studied in the linguistic literature; namely, individual lexical entry templates are grouped in terms of higher-level lexical (SCF) types. When a word takes a lexical entry template that belongs to a certain lexical type t, it should take all the other lexical entry templates that belong to t. To identify a set of lexical entry templates that belong to the same lexical type, Chen and Vijay-Shanker (2000) associated the lexical entry templates with tree families in a manually-tailored LTAG (The XTAG Research Group, 1995), Chen

---

et al. (2006) converted the lexical entry templates into linguistically-motivated feature vectors, and Nakanishi et al. (2004) manually defined lexical rules. These methods, however, just translate the problem of unseen word-template pairs into the problem of unseen word-type pairs, and does not predict any unseen word-type pairs. We will hereafter refer to four types of unseen word-type pairs by (sw, sT), (sw, uT), (uw, sT), and (uw, uT) where sT/uT stand for seen/unseen lexical types.

Another type of the approaches has been taken by Hara et al. (2002) and Chen et al. (2006) to predict unseen (sw, st) pairs. Hara et al. (2002) conducted a hard clustering (Forgy, 1965) of words according to their lexical entry templates in order to find classes of words that take the same lexical entry templates. It will be difficult for the hard clustering method to appropriately classify polysemic verbs, which take several lexical types. Chen et al. (2006) performed a clustering of lexical entry templates according to words that take those templates in order to find lexical entry templates that belong to the same tree family. They reported that it was difficult to predict infrequent lexical entry templates by their method. These studies directly encode word-template pairs into vectors for clustering, which will suffer from the data sparseness problem.

In this study, we focus on probabilistic modeling of unseen word-type pairs in the lexicalized grammars, since we can associate lexical entry templates with lexical types by using the aforementioned methods (Chen and Vijay-Shanker, 2000; Nakanishi et al., 2004; Chen et al., 2006). This reduces the number of parameters in the probabilistic models drastically, which will make it easier to estimate an accurate probabilistic model from sparse data.

2.2   Predicting unseen word-SCF pairs for pre-defined SCF types

There are some studies on smoothing SCF lexicons acquired for pre-defined SCF types from raw corpora (Korhonen, 2002; Yoshinaga, 2004). These studies aimed at predicting unseen (sw, sT) pairs for the acquired SCF lexicons. Korhonen (2002) first semi-automatically determined verb semantic classes using Levin's verb classification (Levin, 1993) and WordNet (Fellbaum, 1998), and then employed SCF distributions for represen-

---

[2]Most of the previous studies attempted to avoid the problem of unseen (sw, ut) and (uw, ut) pairs by modifying the source treebank so as to generalize the resulting grammar; for example, Chen and Vijay-Shanker (2000) used a compact label set instead of one given in the original treebank. Nakanishi et al. (2004) predicted unseen (sw, ut) and (uw, ut) pairs for a given lexicalized grammar by newly creating unseen lexical entry templates using manually defined lexical rules.

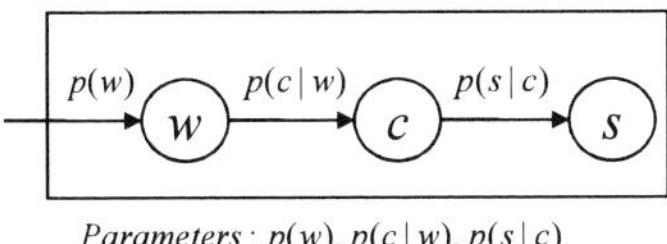

Parameters : $p(w), p(c \mid w), p(s \mid c)$

Figure 1: Probabilistic latent semantic analysis of a co-occurrence between words and SCFs

tative verbs in each obtained verb class to calculate accurate back-off estimates for the verbs in that class. Yoshinaga (2004) conducted clustering of verbs according to their SCF confidence vectors, and then used the resulting classes to predict possible SCFs. Both studies successfully predicted unseen word-type pairs for the pre-defined SCF types.

3   PLSA-based Probabilistic SCF Lexicon

This section first applies the probabilistic latent semantic analysis (PLSA: Hofmann (2001)) to co-occurrences between verbs and SCFs, and then describes a PLSA-based smoothing model to estimate the co-occurrence probabilities.

3.1   PLSA to model co-occurrences between verbs and SCF types

We employ the probabilistic latent semantic analysis to model co-occurrences between words and SCF types, where the latent variables are classes whose members have the same SCF distribution. Our modeling is inspired by the studies by Schulte im Walde and Brew (2002) and Korhonen et al. (2003), which demonstrated that a semantic classification of verbs can be obtained by clustering verbs according to their SCF distributions.[3] The PLSA is suitable for this task since it performs a kind of soft clustering, which can naturally handle highly polysemic nature of verbs.

We assume that a lexicon of a lexicalized grammar is acquired from a source treebank. Let the conditional probability that a word $w \in W$ appears as a member of a latent class $c \in C$ be $p(c|w)$, and each latent class $c \in C$ takes an SCF $s \in S$ with a conditional probability $p(s|c)$. Here, W and S are a set of words and lexical types seen in the source treebank. When we assume that a word w occurs with a probability $p(w)$, a co-occurrence probability between w and s, $p(w, s)$,

is given by:

$$p(w, s) = p(w) \sum_{c \in C} p(c|w)p(s|c).$$

Figure 1 shows our SCF modeling. This generative model has a smoothing effect since the number of free parameters becomes smaller than a simple tabulation model, which directly computes $p(w, s)$ from the observed frequency, by setting the number of the latent variables to a small value.

We then apply a variant of the Expectation Maximization (EM) algorithm (Dempster et al., 1997) called *tempered* EM (Hofmann, 2001) to estimate parameters of this model. In what follows, We first derive the update formulas for the parameters in our model by the EM algorithm, and then explain the tempered EM algorithm.

We assume that the set of parameters θ^t at the t-th iteration is updated to θ^{t+1} at the next iteration, and refer to the individual parameters at the t-th iteration by $p_{\theta^t}(\cdot)$. The update formulas for the individual parameters are derived by constrained optimization of $Q(\theta, \theta^t)$, which defined by

$$Q(\theta, \theta^t) = \sum_{w \in W} \sum_{s \in S} n(w, s) \sum_{c \in C} p_{\theta^t}(c|w, s)$$
$$\times \log[p_\theta(w) \sum_{c \in C} p_\theta(c|w)p_\theta(s|c)] \quad (1)$$

where

$$p_{\theta^t}(c|w, s) = \frac{p_{\theta^t}(c|w)p_{\theta^t}(s|c)}{\sum_{c \in C} p_{\theta^t}(c|w)p_{\theta^t}(s|c)}$$

and $n(w, s)$ is the observed frequency of a co-occurrence between w and s in the source treebank. Using the Lagrange multiplier method, we obtain the updated parameters $\theta = \theta_{t+1}$ which maximize the Q-function in Equation 1 as follows:

$$p_{\theta_{t+1}}(c|w) = \frac{\sum_{s \in S} n(w, s)p_{\theta^t}(c|w, s)}{n(w)},$$

$$p_{\theta_{t+1}}(s|c) = \frac{\sum_{w \in W} n(w, s)p_{\theta^t}(c|w, s)}{\sum_{w \in W} \sum_{s \in S} n(w, s)p_{\theta^t}(c|w, s)},$$

$$p_{\theta_{t+1}}(w) = \frac{n(w)}{\sum_{w \in W} n(w)}$$

where $n(w)$ is the observed frequency of a word w in the source treebank.

The tempered EM is closely related to deterministic annealing (Rose et al., 1990), and introduces *an inverse computational temperature β to the* EM

---

[3]Although a comparison between classes obtained by our method with those obtained by their methods must be interesting, we focus on the effect of smoothing in this paper.

algorithm to reduce the sensitivity to local optima and to avoid overfitting. The update formulas for the tempered EM are obtained by replacing p_{θ^t} in the original formulas by the following equation[4]:

$$p_{\theta^t}(c|w, s) = \frac{[p_{\theta^t}(c|w)p_{\theta^t}(s|c)]^\beta}{\sum_{c \in C}[p_{\theta^t}(c|w)p_{\theta^t}(s|c)]^\beta}.$$

We follow Hofmann's approach (Hofmann, 2001) to determine the optimal value of β. We initialize β to 1 and run the EM iterations with *early stopping* (as long as the performance on held-out data improves). We then rescale β by a factor η ($= 0.5$, in the following experiments) and again run the EM iterations with early stopping. We repeat this rescaling until it no longer improves the result.

3.2 Smoothing model for SCF lexicons

We then use the PLSA model described in the previous section to obtain accurate estimates for the co-occurrence probabilities between words and SCFs. In this study, we focus on smoothing co-occurrence probabilities of word-type pairs for seen SCF types, (sw, sT) and (uw, sT). Acquisition of unseen SCF types (and corresponding templates) is beyond the scope of this study.

In what follows, we first mention a smoothing model for co-occurrence probabilities of (uw, sT) pairs, and then describe a smoothing model for co-occurrence probabilities of (sw, sT) pairs.

3.2.1 Estimation of word-type co-occurrence probabilities for unknown words

Following the previous studies (Chiang, 2000; Hockenmaier and Steedman, 2002; Miyao et al., 2005) described in Section 2.1, we calculate a co-occurrence probability between an unseen word w' and a seen SCF type s as follows:

$$p_{unseen}^m(s|w') = \mu_1 p_{MLE}^m(s) + \mu_2 p_{MLE}(s) \quad (2)$$

where

$$p_{MLE}^m(s) = \frac{\sum_{w \in \{w|n(w) \le m\}} n(w, s)}{\sum_{w \in \{w|n(w) \le m\}} \sum_{s \in S} n(w, s)},$$

$$p_{MLE}(s) = \frac{\sum_{w \in W} n(w, s)}{\sum_{w \in W} \sum_{s \in S} n(w, s)}, \quad (3)$$

and μ_i is *a weight* of each probabilistic model, which satisfies the constraint $\sum_{i=1}^2 \mu_i = 1$. We estimate μ_i by the EM algorithm using held-out data.

In short, we regard infrequent words that appear less than or equal to m in the source treebank as unknown words, and use the observed frequency of SCFs for these words to calculate the co-occurrence probabilities. We assume $p_{unseen}^0(s|w') = p_{MLE}(s)$.

3.2.2 Estimation of word-type co-occurrence probabilities for known words

To estimate a co-occurrence probability between a seen word w and a seen SCF s, we interpolate the following three models. The first model provides the maximum likelihood estimation (MLE) of the co-occurrence probability, which is computed by:

$$p_{MLE}(s|w) = \frac{n(w, s)}{\sum_{s \in S} n(w, s)}.$$

The second model provides a smoothed probability based on the PLSA model, which is calculated by:

$$p_{PLSA}^n(s|w) = \sum_{c \in C} p(c|w)p(s|c)$$

where $p(c|w)$ and $p(s|c)$ are probabilities estimated under the PLSA model and n is the number of the latent classes. We should note that the above two models are computed using all the word-type pairs observed in the source treebank (including the word-type pairs for the infrequent words used in Equation 2).

The last model provides $p_{MLE}(s)$ in Equation 3, which is the maximum likelihood estimation of $p(s)$. We combine these three models by linear interpolation:

$$p_{seen}^n(s|w) = \lambda_1 p_{MLE}(s|w) + \lambda_2 p_{PLSA}^n(s|w) + \lambda_3 p_{MLE}(s)$$

where $\sum_{i=1}^3 \lambda_i = 1$.

In summary, when we regard words that appear less than or equal to m as unknown words, we obtain a co-occurrence probability of a word w and an SCF type s as follows:[5]

$$p^{m,n}(s|w) = \begin{cases} p_{seen}^n(s|w) & (n(w) > m) \\ p_{unseen}^m(s|w) & (n(w) \le m) \end{cases} \quad (4)$$

---

[4]The interested readers are referred to the cited literature (Hofmann, 2001) to see the technical details.

[5]We can use $p_{seen}^n(s|w)$ to estimate the co-occurrence probabilities for the infrequent words (*e.g.*, $0 < n(w) \le m$). However, preliminary experiments showed that it slightly deteriorates the accuracy of the resulting probabilistic lexicons.

Table 1: Specification of SCFs for HPSG acquired from WSJ Sections 02-21 and their subsets

| | SOURCE TREEBANK | | | | | | | | | | |
	02	02-03	02-05	02-07	02-09	02-11	02-13	02-15	02-17	02-19	02-21
# SCF types	78	93	135	151	164	175	197	209	215	235	253
# verbs	1,020	1,294	1,936	2,254	2,476	2,704	2,940	3,134	3,334	3,462	3,586
Ave. # SCFs/verb	1.46	1.53	1.61	1.68	1.69	1.72	1.75	1.78	1.80	1.82	1.85

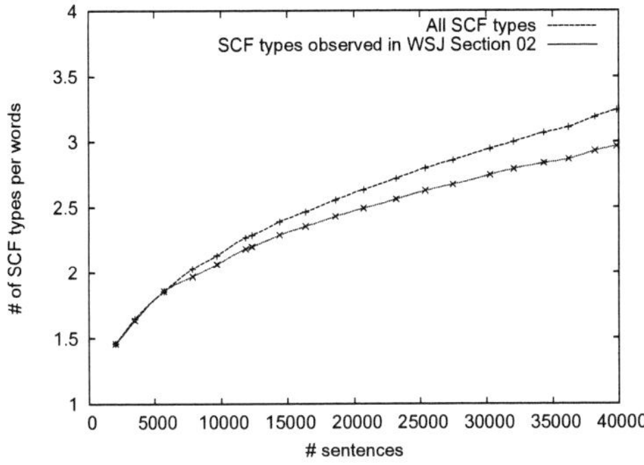

Figure 2: The average number of SCF types assigned to words in WSJ Section 02

In the following section, we compare the above smoothing model with a naive smoothing model, which estimates the co-occurrence probabilities only from $p_{\mathrm{MLE}}^m(s|w)$ and $p_{\mathrm{MLE}}(s)$ as follows:

$$p'^m(s|w) = \begin{cases} \lambda'_1 p_{\mathrm{MLE}}(s|w) + \lambda'_2 p_{\mathrm{MLE}}(s) \\ \qquad\qquad\qquad (n(w) > m) \\ p_{unseen}^m(s) \quad (n(w) \leq m) \end{cases} \quad (5)$$

where $\sum_{i=1}^2 \lambda'_i = 1$.

4 Experiments

We investigate the effect of our smoothing model on SCFs acquired for HPSG grammars.

4.1 Data and Settings

We start by extracting word-SCF pairs from Sections 02-21 of the Wall Street Journal (WSJ) portion of the Penn Treebank and their subset sections by use of the existing methods (Miyao et al., 2005; Nakanishi et al., 2004).

Table 1 shows the details of the acquired SCFs. The average number of SCF types acquired for each verb increases rather mildly with the size of the source treebank. However, when we focus on verbs that appeared in Section 2, the average number of SCF types for these verbs increases more

rapidly (Figure 2). This is because most of frequent verbs appeared in Section 2, and such verbs took the larger number of SCF types than other infrequent verbs. Figure 2 also confirms that most of the 'frequent' SCF types were seen in a small portion of the treebank (WSJ Section 2). Thus, predicting unseen word-type pairs for seen SCF types will have more impact on the grammar coverage.

We then applied our smoothing model to the acquired SCF lexicons. We constructed five PLSA models $p_{\mathrm{PLSA}}^n(s|w)$ for each acquired set of word-SCF pairs by ranging the number of latent variables n from 40 to 640, and then obtained the linear-interpolated models (Equations 4 and 5) with $m = 0, 1, 2$. The PLSA models and the weights of the linear interpolation are estimated by using WSJ Section 22 as held-out data. To estimate the PLSA models, we ran the tempered EM algorithm 100 times, and chose the model that obtained the largest likelihood on the held-out data, because the estimation of the PLSA models is likely to suffer from local optima due to the large number of free parameters. To estimate the weight μ_i of the models for unknown words $p_{unseen}^m(s)$ in Equation 2, we used word-type pairs (in the held-out data) for the infrequent words and words that did not appear in the source treebank, ($w \in \{w|n(w) \leq m\}$).

To evaluate the accuracy of the estimated co-occurrence probabilities, we employ *the test-set perplexity*, PP, which is defined by:

$$PP = 2^{-\frac{1}{N}\sum_{w \in W_t}\sum_{s \in S_t} n_t(w,s)\log p(w,s)}$$

where W_t and S_t are a set of words and lexical types seen in the test data, $N = \sum_{w \in W_t} n_t(w)$, and $n_t(w)$ and $n_t(w, s)$ are the observed frequency of a word w and a co-occurrence between w and s in the test data, respectively. This measure indicates the complexity of the task that determines an SCF type for a given verb $w \in W_t$ with a model $p(w, s)$.

Table 2: Test-set perplexity of $p(s|w)$ against the test SCFs acquired from WSJ Section 24 for the SCF types that are observed in WSJ Section 2

			SOURCE TREEBANK										
MODEL	m	n	02	02-03	02-05	02-07	02-09	02-11	02-13	02-15	02-17	02-19	02-21
unknown			10.809	10.779	10.769	10.750	10.747	10.754	10.759	10.751	10.746	10.748	10.739
naive	0		4.030	3.730	3.414	3.303	3.273	3.224	3.172	3.137	3.132	3.124	3.116
PLSA	0	40	**3.786**	3.532	3.253	3.192	3.157	3.118	3.056	3.039	3.048	3.026	3.025
	0	80	3.809	3.540	3.239	3.167	3.132	3.098	3.055	3.034	3.033	3.024	3.019
	0	160	3.843	3.500	3.241	3.153	3.126	3.081	3.051	3.038	3.023	3.023	3.027
	0	320	3.813	**3.498**	3.244	**3.139**	3.127	3.078	**3.037**	3.023	3.025	**3.008**	3.021
	0	640	3.804	3.524	**3.215**	3.142	**3.118**	**3.060**	3.039	**3.016**	**3.011**	3.015	**3.009**
naive	1		3.865	3.616	3.371	3.256	3.225	3.194	3.144	3.104	3.094	3.087	3.071
PLSA	1	40	**3.651**	3.432	3.217	3.147	3.110	3.090	3.031	3.006	3.010	2.990	2.982
	1	80	3.675	3.443	3.202	3.131	3.083	3.067	3.030	3.005	2.996	2.988	2.974
	1	160	3.704	**3.402**	3.210	3.106	3.078	3.058	3.025	3.006	2.993	2.988	2.983
	1	320	3.676	3.405	3.205	3.099	3.082	3.050	3.015	2.995	2.988	**2.975**	2.977
	1	640	3.671	3.425	**3.178**	**3.097**	**3.071**	**3.035**	**3.013**	**2.989**	**2.979**	2.979	**2.967**
naive	2		3.846	3.629	3.384	3.294	3.230	3.205	3.156	3.115	3.104	3.088	3.074
PLSA	2	40	**3.650**	3.460	3.232	3.185	3.125	3.102	3.040	3.014	3.017	2.991	2.985
	2	80	3.675	3.463	3.219	3.171	3.098	3.080	3.038	3.013	3.004	2.989	2.978
	2	160	3.694	**3.432**	3.225	3.147	3.089	3.071	3.033	3.014	3.001	2.989	2.986
	2	320	3.685	3.437	3.218	3.139	3.096	3.062	3.022	3.002	2.997	**2.976**	2.980
	2	640	3.676	3.449	**3.197**	**3.139**	**3.083**	**3.049**	**3.019**	2.996	**2.987**	2.980	**2.970**

4.2 Results

Table 2 shows the test-set perplexities against word-SCF pairs acquired from WSJ Section 24. In this result, we excluded SCF types unseen in WSJ Section 2 from the test set to compare models using different source treebanks. In Table 2, *unknown* refers to a model that uses only the observed frequency of SCFs, $p_{\mathrm{MLE}}(s)$, as shown in Equation 3. This model indicates the difficulty of this task. The models *naive* and PLSA refer to the interpolated models with and without the PLSA model which are defined in Equations 4 and 5, respectively. The treatment of unknown words reduced the test-set perplexity (cf. the models with $m = 0$ vs. their counterparts with $m = 1, 2$), and the PLSA-based models further reduced the test-set perplexity compared to the *naive* models, when they were estimated using the same size of corpora. It is also noteworthy that we can achieve a lower test-set perplexity by making the number of latent classes of the PLSA model larger. The optimal number of the latent classes would be between 320 and 640. The probabilistic SCF lexicons obtained with our PLSA-based models achieved a lower test-set perplexity against ones obtained with *naive* models with twice as much training data (cf. *naive* ($m = 1$) estimated with WSJ Section 02-21 vs. PLSA $((m, n) = (1, 640))$ estimated with WSJ Section 02-11), and even improved the

accuracy of the probabilistic SCF lexicon when we use the large source treebank (cf. *naive* and PLSA estimated with WSJ Section 02-21).

Table 3 shows a test-set perplexity against word-SCF pairs acquired from WSJ Section 24, when the test-set perplexity is calculated on all the SCF types observed in the source treebank. In this setting, only models in the same column can be fairly compared. For all the subsets of the treebank, our PLSA-based model achieved a lower test-set perplexity than the naive smoothing model.

5 Conclusion

We have presented a PLSA-based smoothing model for co-occurrence probabilities between verbs and SCFs to construct an accurate probabilistic SCF lexicon for a lexicalized grammar acquired from a small-sized corpus. We applied our smoothing model to SCFs for an HPSG grammar acquired from the Penn Treebank. The proposed smoothing model provided an accurate probabilistic SCF lexicon with a lower test-set perplexity against the one obtained with the naive interpolation model.

In future research, we plan to evaluate the acquired probabilistic SCF lexicon in terms of its contribution to the performance of supertagging (Chen et al., 2006) and probabilistic parsing (Miyao et al., 2005; Ninomiya et al., 2005). We will apply our smoothing model to SCFs for

Table 3: Test-set perplexity of $p(s|w)$ against the test SCFs acquired from WSJ Section 24

			SOURCE TREEBANK										
MODEL	m	n	02	02-03	02-05	02-07	02-09	02-11	02-13	02-15	02-17	02-19	02-21
unknown			10.809	10.837	11.134	11.162	11.214	11.213	11.349	11.355	11.344	11.338	11.354
naive	0		4.030	3.753	3.524	3.425	3.419	3.362	3.364	3.323	3.297	3.282	3.275
PLSA	0	40	**3.786**	3.552	3.348	3.299	3.280	3.236	3.213	3.197	3.193	3.165	3.169
	0	80	3.809	3.564	3.334	3.268	3.253	3.214	3.209	3.190	3.176	3.163	3.162
	0	160	3.843	3.520	3.337	3.254	3.250	3.197	3.207	3.194	3.168	3.162	3.172
	0	320	3.813	**3.520**	3.342	**3.241**	3.247	3.193	**3.193**	3.180	3.171	**3.148**	3.166
	0	640	3.804	3.543	**3.309**	3.244	**3.244**	**3.173**	3.195	**3.166**	**3.153**	3.156	**3.153**
naive	1		3.865	3.638	3.480	3.377	3.369	3.331	3.334	3.289	3.257	3.244	3.228
PLSA	1	40	**3.651**	3.452	3.311	3.253	3.232	3.207	3.188	3.163	3.154	3.127	3.124
	1	80	3.675	3.466	3.296	3.232	3.203	3.182	3.184	3.160	3.137	3.125	3.116
	1	160	3.704	**3.422**	3.305	3.206	3.201	3.174	3.179	3.160	3.136	3.126	3.126
	1	320	3.676	3.427	3.303	3.200	3.201	3.165	3.170	3.151	3.133	**3.114**	3.120
	1	640	3.671	3.444	**3.272**	**3.199**	**3.196**	**3.149**	**3.168**	**3.138**	**3.119**	3.118	**3.109**
naive	2		3.846	3.651	3.493	3.416	3.375	3.343	3.347	3.300	3.268	3.245	3.231
PLSA	2	40	**3.650**	3.480	3.326	3.293	3.247	3.221	3.197	3.172	3.162	3.128	3.127
	2	80	3.675	3.487	3.314	3.274	3.220	3.197	3.193	3.168	3.146	3.127	3.119
	2	160	3.694	**3.452**	3.320	3.248	3.213	3.187	3.188	3.168	3.145	3.127	3.129
	2	320	3.685	3.459	3.316	**3.242**	3.216	3.177	3.178	3.159	3.142	**3.115**	3.123
	2	640	3.676	3.468	**3.292**	3.242	**3.209**	**3.163**	**3.175**	**3.146**	**3.127**	3.119	**3.113**

LTAGs and other lexicalized grammars acquired from treebank, by using lexical rules (Prolo, 2002) to reduce lexical entries into lexical types. We will also investigate the correspondence between the verb classes obtained by our method and the semantic verb classes suggested by Levin (1993) and Korhonen and Briscoe (2004).

References

Becker, Tilman. 2000. Patterns in metarules for TAG. In Abeillé, Anne and Owen Rambow, editors, *Tree Adjoining Grammars: formalisms, linguistic analysis and processing*, pages 331–342. CSLI Publications.

Cahill, Aoife, Mairead McCarthy, Josef van Genabith, and Andy Way. 2002. Parsing with PCFGs and automatic f-structure annotation. In *Proceedings of the seventh International Lexical-Functional Grammar Conference*, pages 76–95, Athens, Greece.

Chen, John and Krishnamurti Vijay-Shanker. 2000. Automated extraction of TAGs from the Penn Treebank. In *Proceedings of the Sixth International Workshop on Parsing Technologies (IWPT 2000)*, pages 65–76, Trento, Italy.

Chen, John, Srinivas Bangalore, and Krishnamurti Vijay-Shanker. 2006. Automated extraction of Tree-Adjoining Grammars from treebanks. *Natural Language Engineering*, 12(3):251–299, September.

Chiang, David. 2000. Statistical parsing with an automatically-extracted Tree Adjoining Grammar. In *Proceedings of the 38th Annual Meeting of the Association for Computational Linguistics (ACL 2000)*, pages 456–463, Hong Kong, China.

Dempster, Arthur P., Nan M. Laird, and Donald B. Rubin. 1997. Maximum likelihood from incomplete data via the EM algorithm. *Journal of the Royal Statistical Society. Series B (Methodological)*, 39(1):1–38, January.

Fellbaum, Christiane, editor. 1998. *WordNet: An Electronic Lexical Database*. The MIT Press.

Forgy, Edward W. 1965. Cluster analysis of multivariate data: Efficiency vs. interpretability of classifications. *Biometrics*, 21(3):768–780, June.

Frank, Anette, Louisa Sadler, Josef van Genabith, and Andy Way. 2003. From treebank resources to LFG f-structures: Automatic f-structure annotation of treebank trees and CFGs extracted from treebanks. In Abeillé, Anne, editor, *Treebanks: Building and Using Syntactically Annotated Corpora*, pages 367–389. Kluwer Academic Publishers.

Hara, Tadayoshi, Yusuke Miyao, and Jun'ichi Tsujii. 2002. Clustering for obtaining syntactic classes of words from automatically extracted LTAG grammars. In *Proceedings of the sixth International Workshop on Tree Adjoining Grammars and Related Frameworks (TAG+6)*, pages 227–233, Venice, Italy.

Hockenmaier, Julia and Mark Steedman. 2002. Acquiring compact lexicalized grammars from a cleaner treebank. In *Proceedings of the third International Conference on Language Resources and Evaluation (LREC 2002)*, pages 1974–1981, Las Palmas, Spain.

Hofmann, Thomas. 2001. Unsupervised learning by probabilistic latent semantic analysis. *Machine Learning*, 42(1):177–196, January.

Jackendoff, Ray S. 1975. Morphological and semantic regularities in the lexicon. *Language*, 51(3):639–671, September.

Korhonen, Anna and Edward J. Briscoe. 2004. Extended lexical-semantic classification of English verbs. In *Proceedings of the Computational Lexical Semantics Workshop at Human Language Technology Conference and the fifth Annual Meeting of the North American Chapter of the Association for Computational Linguistics (HLT-NAACL 2004)*, pages 38–45, Boston, MA, USA.

Korhonen, Anna, Yuval Krymolowski, and Zvika Marx. 2003. Clustering polysemic subcategorization frame distributions semantically. In *Proceedings of the 41st Annual Meeting of the Association for Computational Linguistics (ACL 2003)*, pages 64–71, Sapporo, Japan.

Korhonen, Anna. 2002. *Subcategorization Acquisition*. Ph.D. thesis, Computer Laboratory, University of Cambridge, Cambridge, UK.

Levin, Beth. 1993. *English Verb Classes and Alternations: A Preliminary Investigation*. University of Chicago Press.

Marcus, Mitchell, Beatrice Santorini, and Mary A. Marcinkiewicz. 1993. Building a large annotated corpus of English: the Penn Treebank. *Computational Linguistics*, 19(2):313–330, June.

Miyao, Yusuke, Takashi Ninomiya, and Jun'ichi Tsujii. 2005. Corpus-oriented grammar development for acquiring a Head-driven Phrase Structure Grammar from the Penn Treebank. In Su, Keh-Yih, Jun'ichi Tsujii, Jong-Hyeok Lee, and Oi Yee Kwong, editors, *Natural Language Processing - IJCNLP 2004*, volume LNAI 3248, pages 684–693. Springer-Verlag.

Nakanishi, Hiroko, Yusuke Miyao, and Jun'ichi Tsujii. 2004. Using inverse lexical rules to acquire a wide-coverage lexicalized grammar. In *Proceedings of the Workshop on Beyond Shallow Analyses at the first International Joint Conference on Natural Language Processing (ijc-NLP 2004)*, Hainan Island, China.

Ninomiya, Takashi, Yoshimasa Tsuruoka, Yusuke Miyao, and Jun'ichi Tsujii. 2005. Efficacy of beam thresholding, unification filtering and hybrid parsing in probabilistic HPSG parsing. In *Proceedings of the ninth International Workshop on Parsing Technologies (IWPT 2005)*, pages 103–114, Vancouver, BC, Canada.

Pollard, Carl and Ivan A. Sag. 1994. *Head-Driven Phrase Structure Grammar*. University of Chicago Press and CSLI Publications.

Prolo, Carlos A. 2002. Generating the XTAG English grammar using metarules. In *Proceedings of the 19th International Conference on Computational Linguistics (COLING 2002)*, pages 814–820, Taipei, Taiwan.

Rose, Kenneth, Eitan Gurewwitz, and Geoffrey Fox. 1990. A deterministic annealing approach to clustering. *Pattern Recognition Letters*, 11(9):589–594, September.

Schulte im Walde, Sabine and Chris Brew. 2002. Inducing German semantic verb classes from purely syntactic subcategorisation information. In *Proceedings of the 41st Annual Meeting of the Association for Computational Linguistics (ACL 2003)*, pages 223–230, Sapporo, Japan.

The XTAG Research Group. 1995. A Lexicalized Tree Adjoining Grammar for English. Technical Report IRCS-95-03, IRCS, University of Pennsylvania.

Xia, Fei. 1999. Extracting Tree Adjoining Grammars from bracketed corpora. In *Proceedings of the fifth Natural Language Processing Pacific Rim Symposium (NLPRS 1999)*, pages 398–403, Beijing, China.

Yoshinaga, Naoki. 2004. Improving the accuracy of subcategorizations acquired from corpora. In *the Companion Volume to the Proceedings of the 42nd Annual Meeting of the Association for Computational Linguistics (ACL 2004)*, pages 43–48, Barcelona, Spain.

Association for Computational Linguistics
209 N. Eighth Street
Stroudsburg, Pennsylvania 18360

ISBN 978-1-5108-2680-9